INTERNATIONAL TRAVEL AND TOURISM

INTERNATIONAL TRAVEL AND TOURISM

DONALD E. LUNDBERG
CAROLYN B. LUNDBERG

John Wiley & Sons
New York   Chichester   Brisbane   Toronto   Singapore

Copyright © 1985, by John Wiley & Sons, Inc. Publishers

All rights reserved. Published simultaneously in Canada.

Reproduction or translation of any part of
this work beyond that permitted by Sections
107 and 108 of the 1976 United States Copyright
Act without permission of the copyright
owner is unlawful. Requests for permission
or further information should be addressed to
the Permissions Department, John Wiley & Sons.

Library of Congress Cataloging in Publication Data:

Lundberg, Donald E.

    International travel and tourism.

    Includes index.

    1. Tourist trade. 2. Travel. I. Title.

G155.A1L79 1985   380.1'459104   84-10433

ISBN 0-471-84228-1

Printed in the United States of America

10 9 8 7 6

CONTENTS

PREFACE

This book is for the addicted traveler, for those in the travel business, and for those who want to be in it. The perspective is American, why Americans go abroad, something about where they go, how they get there, and how they get around once they have arrived. Only the highlights of international travel are covered. A comprehensive world travel book would be overwhelming and probably boring to the average reader.

The travel statistics presented should not be taken as unequivocal fact. The methods of collecting the data, the definitions used, and the collectors vary. Keep in mind too that the travel world is one of rapid change. Today's fact is probably out of date tomorrow.

The amount of information presented about particular destinations varies according to their popularity for American travelers. Canada, Mexico, Western Europe, and the Caribbean receive much more attention than the less-visited regions such as Asia, Africa, and South America.

The book was written to meet the need for a textbook for a class in international travel, keeping in mind that a little humor and a light touch are often more effective than the beautifully organized heavy-handed textbook.

ACKNOWLEDGEMENTS

I am indebted to those public agencies here and abroad that collect and publish travel statistics and other travel information. Among these agencies are the U.S. Department of Commerce, the World Tourism Organization (WTO), the European Economic Community (OECD), the Pacific Area Travel Association, the International Air Transport Association, the U.S. Travel Data Center, the Tourism Research Association, the Caribbean Tourism Research and Development Center, the U.S. Immigration Service, the National Travel offices of numerous countries, the various state travel offices in this country, the World Bank, the international accounting firms of Laventhol and Horwath and Pannell Kerr Foster, the International Air Transport Association, the Air Transport Association, the Passport Office of the U.S. Department of State, the U.S. Travel and Tourism Administration, and the U.S. Census Bureau.

Compilation of much of this information is done each year by Somerset R. Waters and published by Child & Waters of New York City in the *Travel Industry World Yearbook, The Big Picture*. This publication is rightly called "The Big Picture" because it contains not only a formidable array of facts and figures but also a critical commentary of what is happening to travel and tourism around the world, a heroic task well done. I have drawn heavily on this information for current statistics. U.S. State Department publications, *Background Notes,* have been used freely.

Over the years my wife and I have traveled widely, and I have presented courses in travel and hotel management in such schools as Cornell University, Florida State University, The University of New Hampshire, California State University, Pomona, The University of Massachusetts, the University of Hawaii, The University of the West Indies, and Oregon State University. During summer vacations I have worked as a consultant for Intercontinental Hotels, Statler Hotels, AID in Jamaica, SAS in Scandanavia, and the U.S. Department of Commerce in Turkey. I express my gratitude to all those people who helped arrange for this travel, teaching, and consulting work.

Many managers of National Travel offices located in Los Angeles have generously given their time to lecture to my classes in travel management offered at California State Polytechnic University, Pomona. Thank you.

INTERNATIONAL TRAVEL AND TOURISM

INTRODUCTION

"Heavenly Father, look down on us your humble, obedient tourist servants, who are doomed to travel this earth, taking photographs, mailing postcards, buying souvenirs and walking around in drip-dry underwear."

Art Buchwald

The glamour girl of the tourist business is international travel. The traveler budgets, plans and anticipates the different scenery, the people, the food, and the customs. Travel is challenge: the new exciting experience of coping; the challenge of stepping into a new environment. Travel is fun. Travel is change. Travel can also be very frustrating and it is expensive. We in the U.S. spend about $20 billion in foreign travel including transportation costs. Worldwide the figure for international travel is about $100 billion.[1] While international travel is big business now it is almost certain to grow larger. Only about 4 percent of Americans go abroad by air each year. Even a rise of 8 percent would have worldwide repercussions.

International travel is relatively easy for the European. A short trip by car or train may take him across several borders. The West German hops in his car and is soon in Switzerland, Austria or France. The Briton crosses the English Channel and is in France. The Dane takes a ferry to Sweden. For most Americans international travel other than to Canada or Mexico is more complex. His first trip overseas is probably to Europe. If living in the Southwest, the first trip may be to Mexico. A five-and-a-half-hour jet trip from Los Angeles or San Francisco takes him to tropical Hawaii. A cruise takes him down the coast to the Mexican Riviera or north to Alaska. A fly/cruise Caribbean tour takes him to four or five Caribbean islands.

Costs and challenges go hand in hand. The affluent may take the *Concorde* to Paris and be chauffered around France. The young, budget traveler may choose the charter flight and then bike or hitchhike and hostel.

The traveler has a choice of lodgings from campground to chateaux. He may stay with a count, see the countryside in a hot-air balloon. Using a Eurail pass he can travel first-class over most of Europe plus Ireland for a fixed price over a specified period of time. In Ireland and the United Kingdom he can move in with a family for "bed and breakfast." In Spain he may experience a night in a former convent or a castle, one of the government owned and operated "paradors." The business traveler abroad often reserves at an American-owned or affiliated hotel, preferring the known to the less well-known, regardless of price.

A LIFE TRAVEL PROFILE

Business travel aside, a "life travel profile" for a middle-class American reflects discretionary time available, money, age, and desire for change. As children, people go where their parents go. As teenagers, middle- and upper-class Americans begin to strike out on their own—off to college, summer work in a far-away resort, perhaps a back-packing trip to Europe. Then comes marriage and the career that limits the travel urge. Middle age approaches and there are trips abroad. (Business travel peaks for the breadwinners.)

When the children leave home, the affluent parents see travel as a major pleasure, always a new place to go, probably traveling independently. Group travel is next in the travel profile. Lastly comes cruising, the easiest, least demanding, and safest means of travel with a bountiful table, almost continuous entertainment, a closed pleasure environment.

PLEASURE TRAVEL DESTINATIONS

The world is a supermarket of pleasure travel. Or is it? Subtract the oceans, the seas, and many of the lakes—70 percent of the total. That leaves 30 percent of the geography for travel if we delete cruising as a destination. Subtract the very cold regions, most of the Arctic and the Antarctic, another 10 percent at least. That leaves 20 percent of the globe as potential destination for pleasure travel. Subtract those inaccessible spots like the tops of the great mountain ranges such as the Andes, the Rockies, the Himalayas. Subtract another 5 percent. That leaves 15 percent.

Subtract those countries which bar tourists: Albania and Guinea. Subtract the places you would not want to go, like much of the Congo, the Amazon, the innards of Alaska, Northern Siberia, Mongolia and Tibet. That leaves less than 10 percent of the world up for grabs as a place to go, but 10 percent of a lot is still a lot.

Americans go "abroad" to Canada in the greatest numbers and spend the most. Mexico comes next. Then Western Europe, including Britain; then the Caribbean and so on. The addicted international traveler never runs out of destinations.

Pleasure travel thrives on convenience, low prices, destination interest, and safety for the traveler. To the novice traveler it may be a nearby city. To the veteran it is Katmandu, Nepal, the island nation of Mauritius or the Seychelle Islands. The exotic attracts the adventurer. The People's Republic of China is "in." The five-day trip on the Trans-Siberian railroad is an adventure. What next? Greenland, the North Pole, a free-balloon trip over Central France, the Amazon; a search for history, for archeological treasure, for fabled cultures, the bird of paradise, complete sex freedom, the perfect retirement place. Difficulty in reaching an exotic destination may only add to its allure. There is no place out of bounds for the travel adventurer.

International travel is as addictive as cocaine, and much healthier. It can be edifying, challenging, and unfortunately, debilitating or even lethal.

Basic information about the nations of the world is seen on pages 3-8, outdated even before publication because it changes so rapidly. It serves, however, to suggest the range of cultures, population figures, languages, religion and wealth. About a hundred of these countries did not even exist as nations before World War II. Some are not quite sovereign nations in the usual sense. Vatican City and San Marino are examples. Nevertheless each of these examples is an important travel destination.

GROUP TRAVEL INCREASING

International pleasure travel is more and more group travel including many FIT's (foreign independent travelers), the people who plan and travel independently. Nearly all sophisticated travelers use the services of a travel agent in securing tickets since there is no

FIGURE 1.1 *Basic information.* The nations of the world.[1]

Country	('000) Mid–1981 Population	Area (sq. km)	Principal Language(s)	Monetary Unit	Gross National Product $ per capita	Principal Religion(s)
Afghanistan	15,540	647,947	Pushtu, Dari	Afghani	200	Islam
Albania	2,797	28,748	Albanian	Lek	790	Islam
Algeria	20,388	2,381,741	Arabic, Berber, French	Dinar	1,420	Islam
Angola	6,761	1,246,700	Portuguese	Kwanza	442*	Animism, Roman Catholic
Argentina	27,411	2,776,889	Spanish	Peso	2,100	Roman Catholic
Australia	14,578	7,686,848	English	Australian Dollar	9,760	Christian
Austria	7,515	83,853	German, Slovene	Schilling	9,520	Roman Catholic
Bahamas	249	13,935	English	Bahamian Dollar	4,107*	Christian
Bahrain	421	622	Arabic, Persian	Bahrain Dinar	5,780*	Islam
Bangladesh	88,679	143,998	Bengali, Urou, English	Taka	115	Islam
Belgium	9,889	30,513	French, Dutch	Belgian Franc	11,170	Roman Catholic
Benin	3,664	112,622	French	Franc (CFA)†	310	Animism, Islam, Christian
Bhutan	1,324	47,000	Dzongkha, Nepali	Ngultrum	80*	Buddhism, Hinduism
Bolivia	6,069	1,098,581	Spanish	Peso	1,250	Roman Catholic
Botswana	786	660,372	Setswana, English	Pula	730*	Christian
Brazil	125,364	8,511,965	Portuguese	Cruzeiro	1,510	Roman Catholic
Brunei	2,390	5,765	Malay, English, Chinese	Brunei Dollar	8,580*	Buddhism, Islam, Confucianism
Bulgaria	8,919	110,912	Bulgarian, Turkish, Greek	Lev	3,370	Bulgarian, Orthodox
Burma	34,377	676,552	Burmese	Kyat	186	Buddhism
Burundi	4,630	27,834	French, Kirundi, Swahili	Burundi Franc	145	Animism, Roman Catholic
Cambodia (Kampuchea)	8,252	181,035	Khmer, French	Riel	115*	Buddhism
Cameroon	8,111	475,442	French, English	Franc (CFA)	670*	Animism, Christian
Canada	24,306	9,976,139	French, English	Canadian Dollar	10,110	Christian
Cape Verde Islands	331	4,033	Portuguese, Crioulo	Escudo	165*	Roman Catholic
Central African Empire	1,747	622,984	French, Sangho	Franc (CFA)	255*	Animism, Christian
Chad	4,611	1,284,000	French, Arabic	Franc (CFA)	145*	Animism, Islam, Christian
Chile	11,464	756,945	Spanish	Chilean Peso	1,880	Roman Catholic
China, People's Republic	995,323	9,561,000	Mandarin & dialects	Yuan	575	Confucianism, Buddhism, Taoism

[1]As of 1984 there were 169 sovereign nations, more than enough for the most addicted and adventuresome traveler to choose from as destinations. Capsule information about these places is seen in Figure 1.1: their populations, geographical size, languages, money, per capita income, and principal religions. The information is necessarily estimated for most countries; check with the local consulate for the most up-to-date information.

3

FIGURE 1.1 *Continued*

Country	('000) Mid–1981 Population	Area (sq. km)	Principal Language(s)	Monetary Unit	Gross National Product $ per capita	Principal Religion(s)
China, Taiwan	17,170	35,961	Mandarin, dialects, Japanese, English	New Taiwan Dollar	1,826	Buddhism, Confucianism, Taoism
Colombia	27,832	1,138,914	Spanish	Colombian Peso	1,100	Roman Catholic
Comoros	432	2,171	Arabic, French, Swahili	Franc	185*	Islam
Congo, People's Republic	1,563	342,000	French	Franc (CFA)	540*	Animism, Christian
Costa Rica	2,277	50,700	Spanish, English	Colones	2,065	Roman Catholic
Cuba	10,141	114,524	Spanish	Peso	1,407	Roman Catholic
Cyprus	657	9,251	Greek, Turkish	Cyprus Pound	3,350	Greek Orthodox, Islam
Czechoslovakia	15,473	127,881	Czech, Slovak, Hungarian	Koruna	5,540	Roman Catholic Other Christian
Denmark	5,155	43,075	Danish	Kroner	12,160	Danish Lutheran
Dominican Republic	5,587	48,734	Spanish	Peso	1,065	Roman Catholic
Ecuador	8,639	14,925	Spanish	Sucre	1,320	Roman Catholic
Egypt	42,434	1,001,449	Arabic, French, English	Egyptian Pound	575	Islam
El Salvador	4,592	21,041	Spanish	Colon	710	Roman Catholic
Equatorial Guinea	362	28,051	Spanish	Ekuwele	N.A.	Roman Catholic Other Christian
Ethiopia	31,989	1,221,900	Amharic, Arabic, English	Birr	125	Ethiopian, Coptic, Islam
Faeroe Islands	42	1,399	Faeroese, English	Faeroese Krona	N.A.	Lutheran
Fiji	646	18,274	English	Fiji Dollar	1,300*	Methodist, Hinduism
Finland	4,799	337,032	Finnish, Swedish	Markkaa	7,005	National Lutheran
France	53,924	547,026	French	French Franc	11,370	Roman Catholic
Gabon	554	267,667	French, Tribal	Franc (CFA)	4,185	Animism, Christian
Gambia	616	11,295	English, Tribal	Dalasi	280*	Islam, Christian
German Democratic Republic	16,720	108,177	German	DDR Mark	5,945	Protestant
Germany, Federal Republic	61,187	248,667	German	Deutsche Mark	12,470	Lutheran, Roman Catholic
Ghana	11,264	238,537	English	Cedi	500	Animism, Christian
Gibraltar	29	6	English	Gibraltar Pound	N.A.	Roman Catholic
Greece	9,653	131,944	Greek	Drachma	3,980	Greek Orthodox
Grenada	105	344	English	East Caribbean Dollar	660*	Christian

4

FIGURE 1.1 *Continued*

Country	('000) Mid–1981 Population	Area (sq. km)	Principal Language(s)	Monetary Unit	Gross National Product $ per capita	Principal Religion(s)
Guatemala	72,181	108,889	Spanish	Quetzal	1,065	Roman Catholic
Guinea	5,134	245,857	French, Tribal	Syli	N.A.	Animism, Islam
Guinea-Bissau	580	36,125	Portuguese	Escudo	N.A.	Animism, Islam
Guyana	848	214,969	English, Hindi, Portuguese	Guyana Dollar	660*	Christian, Hinduism, Islam
Haiti	5,087	27,750	French, Creole	Gourde	270*	Roman Catholic
Honduras	3,542	112,088	Spanish, English	Lempira	660	Roman Catholic
Hong Kong	4,906	1,045	English, Mandarin, Cantonese	Hong Kong Dollar	3,045	Confucianism, Buddhism, Islam
Hungary	10,814	93,036	Hungarian	Forint	3,665	Roman Catholic Other Christian
Iceland	231	103,000	Icelandic	Icelandic Kronur	9,405	Lutheran
India	681,454	3,287,590	Hindi, English	Indian Rupee	200	Hinduism, Islam
Indonesia	153,890	1,904,345	Bahasa, Indonesian	Rupiah	420	Islam
Iran	37,883	1,648,000	Farsi, Kurdish, Turki, Arabic	Iranian Rial	1,130	Islam
Iraq	12,596	434,924	Arabic, Kurdish	Iraqi Dinar	2,665	Islam
Ireland	3,710	70,283	English, Gaelic	Irish Pound	4,690	Roman Catholic
Israel	3,973	20,770	Hebrew, Arabic	Israeli Pound	3,425	Judaism, Islam
Italy	57,608	301,225	Italian	Lira	6,360	Roman Catholic
Ivory Coast	8,257	322,462	French	Franc (CFA)	930	Animism, Islam, Christian
Jamaica	2,197	10,991	English, Creole	Jamaican Dollar	1,095	Anglican, Baptist
Japan	118,614	372,313	Japanese	Yen	9,950	Shintoism, Buddhism
Jordan	3,054	97,740	Arabic	Jordanian Dinar	1,090	Islam
Kenya	16,487	582,646	Swahili, Kikuyu, English	Kenya Shilling	290	Animism, Christian
Korea, Democratic People's Republic	18,384	120,538	Korean	Won	825	Buddhism, Confucianism, Shamanism
Korea, Republic of	38,862	98,484	Korean	Won	1,390	Buddhism, Confucianism, Shamanism, Chondokyo
Kuwait	1,433	17,818	Arabic, English	Kuwaiti Dinar	19,200*	Islam
Laos	3,546	236,800	Laotian, French	Kip	86*	Buddhism
Lebanon	3,100	10,400	Arabic, French, Armenian	Lebanese Pound	975*	Islam, Christian
Lesotho	1,243	30,355	English, Lesotho	Rand	285*	Christian
Liberia	1,742	111,369	English, Tribal	Liberian Dollar	570	Islam, Christian, Animism

FIGURE 1.1 *Continued*

Country	('000) Mid–1981 Population	Area (sq. km)	Principal Language(s)	Monetary Unit	Gross National Product $ per capita	Principal Religion(s)
Libya	2,999	1,759,540	Arabic	Libyan Dinar	7,355	Islam
Liechtenstein	26	157	German	Franken	N.A.	Roman Catholic
Luxembourg	357	2,586	Luxembourgish, French, German	Luxembourg Franc	8,970	Roman Catholic
Madagascar	8,725	587,041	Malagasy, French	Franc	300*	Animism, Christian
Malawi	5,816	118,484	English, Chichewa	Kwacha	245	Christian, Islam
Malaysia	14,051	329,749	Malay, English, Chinese	Ringgit	1,665	Islam
Maldives	145	298	Divehi	Rupee	190*	Islam
Mali	6,627	1,240,000	French, Bambara	Mali Franc	N.A.	Islam
Malta	352	316	Maltese, English	Maltese Pound	2,805*	Roman Catholic
Mauritania	1,631	1,030,700	French, Arabic	Ouguiya	400	Islam
Mauritius	966	2,045	English, French, Creole	Mauritian Rupee	960	Roman Catholic, Hinduism, Islam
Mexico	74,365	1,972,547	Spanish	Mexican Peso	2,045	Roman Catholic
Monaco	25	1.5	Monegasque, French	Franc	N.A.	Roman Catholic
Mongolia	1,720	1,565,000	Mongolian	Togrog	780	Lamist, Buddhism,
Morocco	20,096	446,550	Arabic, Berber, French	Dirham	605	Islam
Mozambique	10,698	801,590	Portuguese	Mozambique	200	Islam, Animism, Christian
Namibia	961	824,292	Afrikaans, German, English	Rand	N.A.	Christian
Nauru	81	21	Nauruan, English	Australian Dollar	N.A.	Christian
Nepal	14,340	140,797	Nepali	Nepalese Rupee	140	Hinduism
Netherlands	14,334	40,844	Dutch	Guilder	10,590	Christian
Netherlands Antilles	252	961	Dutch	Guilder	N.A.	Roman Catholic
New Zealand	3,100	268,676	English, Maori	New Zealand Dollar	7,255	Christian
Nicaragua	2,657	130,000	Spanish, English	Cordoba	730	Roman Catholic
Niger	5,420	1,267,000	French, Hausa	Franc (CFA)	225*	Islam
Nigeria	79,453	923,768	English, Hausa	Naira	705	Islam, Christian
Norway	4,115	324,219	Norwegian	Norwegian Kroner	12,920	Lutheran
Oman	930	212,457	Arabic, Persian, Urdu	Rial	5,375	Islam
Pakistan	81,731	803,943	Urdu, English	Pakistani Rupee	310	Islam
Panama	1,930	75,650	Spanish, English	Balboa	1,670	Roman Catholic

FIGURE 1.1 *Continued*

Country	('000) Mid–1981 Population	Area (sq. km)	Principal Language(s)	Monetary Unit	Gross National Product $ per capita	Principal Religion(s)
Papua New Guinea	3,420	461,691	Pidgin, English	Kina	840	Pantheism, Christian
Paraguay	3,152	406,752	Spanish, Guarani	Guaranie	1,430	Roman Catholic
Peru	18,271	1,285,216	Spanish, Quechua	Sol	800	Roman Catholic
Philippines	50,894	300,000	Tagalog, Spanish, English	Philippine Peso	720	Roman Catholic
Poland	35,999	312,667	Polish	Zloty	3,515	Roman Catholic
Portugal	10,034	92,082	Portuguese	Portuguese Escudo	2,230	Roman Catholic
Puerto Rico	3,545	8,897	Spanish, English	U.S. Dollar	N.A.	Roman Catholic
Qatar	235	11,000	Arabic, Farsi	Qatar Riyal	31,840	Islam
Romania	22,472	237,500	Romanian, Hungarian	Leu	4,015	Orthodox
Rwanda	5,450	26,338	French, Kinyarwandu, Swahili	Rwanda Franc	230	Animism, Christian
San Marino	21	61	Italian	Lira	N.A.	Roman Catholic
Sao Tome & Principe	88	964	Portuguese	Dobra	N.A.	Christian
Saudi Arabia	10,179	2,149,690	Arabic	Saudi Riyal	14,075	Islam
Senegal	5,763	196,192	French, Tribal	Franc (CFA)	510*	Islam
Seychelles	66	308	English, Creole	Seychelles Rupee	N.A.	Roman Catholic
Sierra Leone	3,580	71,740	English, Krio, Tribal	Leone	300	Animism, Islam
Singapore	2,433	581	Chinese, Malay, English, Tamil	Singapore Dollar	4,490	Wide Variety
Somalia	3,922	637,657	Somali, Arabic, Italian, English	Somali Schilling	135*	Islam
South Africa	28,220	1,221,037	Afrikaans, English, Bantu	Rand	2,740	Christian
Spain	38,460	504,782	Spanish	Spanish Pesata	5,100	Roman Catholic
Sri Lanka	14,860	65,610	Sinhala, Tamil, English	Sri Lanka Rupee	255	Buddhism, Hinduism
Sudan	18,962	2,505,813	Arabic	Sudanese Pound	345	Islam
Surinam	441	163,265	Dutch, Creole, English	Surinam Guilder	2,375*	Christian, Hinduism, Islam
Swaziland	590	17,363	English, siSwati	Emalangeni	N.A.	Christian
Sweden	8,361	449,964	Swedish, Finnish	Swedish Kronor	15,460	Lutheran
Switzerland	6,297	41,293	French, Italian, German, Romansch	Franc	15,790	Christian
Syria	8,949	185,180	Arabic, French, Kurdish, Armenian	Syrian Pound	1,440	Islam

FIGURE 1.1 *Continued*

Country	('000) Mid–1981 Population	Area (sq. km)	Principal Language(s)	Monetary Unit	Gross National Product $ per capita	Principal Religion(s)
Tanzania	17,912	945,087	Swahili, English	Tanzanian Shilling	280	Christian, Islam, Traditional
Thailand	48,709	514,000	Thai, Chinese	Baht	690	Buddhism
Togo	2,602	56,785	French	Franc (CFA)	430	Animism, Christian
Tonga	92	699	Tongan, English	Pa'anga	N.A.	Methodism
Trinidad & Tobago	1,182	5,130	English, Hindi	Trinidad & Tobago Dollar	3,610	Christian, Hinduism
Tunisia	6,441	163,610	Arabic, French	Tunisian Dinar	1,035	Islam
Turkey	46,441	780,576	Turkish, Kurdish	Turkish Lira	1,100	Islam
Uganda	14,128	236,036	English, Swahili, Luganda	Uganda Shilling	255	Christian, Others
USSR	265,985	22,402,200	Russian	Ruble	4,820	Russian Orthodox, Islam
United Arab Emirates	836	83,000	Arabic, Persian, Hindi, Urdu	UAE Dirham	10,600	Islam
United Kingdom	55,950	244,103	English	Pound Sterling	9,495	Church of England, Other Christian
Upper Volta	6,900	274,200	French, Tribal	Franc (CFA)	165*	Animism, Islam
Uruguay	3,138	176,215	Spanish	New Uruguayan Peso	1,060	Roman Catholic
Vatican City	—	—	Italian	—	—	Roman Catholic
Venezuela	14,353	912,050	Spanish	Bolivar	4,350	Roman Catholic
Vietnam	51,552	332,559	Vietnamese	Dong	115	Buddhism, Taoism
Yemen Arab Republic	6,531	195,000	Arabic	Yemeni Rial	470	Islam
Yemen, People's Democratic Republic	1,969	332,968	Arabic	Yemeni Dinar	400*	Islam
Yugoslavia	22,533	255,804	Serbo-Croatian, Slovene, Macedonian	Yugoslav Dinar	3,230	Orthodox, Roman Catholic
Zaire	28,613	2,345,409	French, Tribal	Zaire	190	Christian, Animism
Zambia	6,014	752,614	English, Tribal	Zambian Kwacha	610	Traditional, Christian
Zimbabwe	7,646	390,580	English, Shona, Sindebele	Zimbabwe Dollar	510	Christian, Islam

Sources: The Statesman's Yearbook 1979–1980, The World Almanac 1980, Political Handbook of the World, The 1983 Multinational Executive Travel Companion

†Franc de la Communaute Financiere Africaine

*Year 1979

additional cost. More international travelers take advantage of travel packages because of the cost advantages offered. The traveler need not travel as a part of a group. The package may or may not include ground transportation, accommodations, meals, entertainment, and a variety of services. The big appeal is economy as compared to the purchase of similar things bought individually.

BUSINESS TRAVEL

International travel includes business travel, a component much prized by the airlines. It is prized because it constitutes so much of air travel, 60 percent or more on many airlines; and because the business traveler usually pays full fare. He cannot buy an APEX, an advanced purchase flight, because he has to go tomorrow. He usually eschews the "red-eye"

FIGURE 1.2 *First travel agent.* Thomas Cook, generally acknowledged as the first travel agent, started small by arranging tours within England. Later he "packaged" tours to the Middle East and Europe, built a railway up Mount Vesuvius near Naples, Italy, operated cruises on the Nile, and in 1872 conducted the first tour around the world. Thomas Cook and Sons developed into a large travel conglomerate, pioneering several aspects of the travel business.

night flight because he has to look decent and be alert during tomorrow's meeting. Top executives fly first-class, which can mean 50 percent or more revenue for a slightly larger seat and a little more food, drink, and service. Executives don't mind paying for first-class because it is the company that pays. Therefore the business traveler is wooed, given a "business-class" section with more leg room, free drinks, and a little status, gifts and awards for frequent flying with a particular airline.

Where does the business traveler go? Everywhere there is business opportunity and activity. The major capitals of the world see him most often. So too do the political capitals. The financial centers are like honey to the bee: New York City, London, and Paris are the obvious money markets. In the East it is Hong Kong and Tokyo—and more recently Singapore. Oil money flows through Bahrain, the little island-state off the Saudi Arabian coast. Very practical, the 350,000 people there welcome banks by placing few restrictions on them. The bankers like Bahrain because, unlike most other Arab states, alcohol flows freely there. It is close to Saudi Arabia, richest of all oil states, Kuwait and the United Arab Emirates. Because of its location and excellent communications facilities, money dealers can trade with Tokyo and Singapore in the morning and with London and New York after lunch.

Much of the appeal of some little nations, such as the Bahamas, the Grand Cayman islands and Panama, comes from their relaxed laws about banking and the secrecy imposed on money transfers. They are called tax havens by some; others call them money laundries, or refuges for hot money. Undoubtedly some of the travel to Switzerland and Liechtenstein has had a similar money-hiding motivation for a number of decades.

THE BIG INTERNATIONAL TRAVELERS

In terms of the numbers involved in international travel Western Europe is the all-out leader. Keeping in mind how easy it is to become an "international traveler" (crossing a national border) in Europe, West Germany provides the most international travelers of any country. With a population of about sixty-one million it saw about forty-one million classified as international travelers in 1979. The United States was second as a generator of international travelers with close to thirty million people so classified in 1979. In that year 68 percent of all international tourists came from but twelve countries. The number generated by each of those countries is seen here along with their resident populations:

	Number of international travelers, in millions	Resident population in millions
West Germany	41.3	61.2
USA	29.8	223.6
France	24.4	53.4
U.K.	17	55.9
Canada	13.7	23.7
Switzerland	13.4	6.5
Netherlands	12	14
Belgium	9.4	9.8
Austria	7.3	7.5
Japan	6.1	115.7
Italy	5.3	56.8
Sweden	3.5	8.3

Source: *Economic Review of World Tourism,* 1982 Edition, World Tourism Organization, Madrid.

Plainly, we Americans are pikers when it comes to per capita international travel. On a per capita basis the Swiss are the big travelers abroad. So too are the Austrians, the

Belgians, and the Dutch. In fact, only two of the big twelve country travelers do less international traveling than do we, Italy and Japan. Of course, as pointed out, traveling from Iowa to Switzerland is quite a different matter than crossing a Swiss border to France, Italy, Germany, or Austria.

This is not to say that tourist flows are easily explained in terms of distance—that is, shorter distances, more travel, greater distances, less travel. Other factors impinge on travel decisions. France and Germany are side by side but there is relatively little travel between the two. The same is true between Austria and Switzerland and between Italy and Austria. Austrians travel to Italy but not many Italians visit Austria. Germans pour over the border into Austria. The Dutch visit Britain in large numbers. Discretionary income of the traveler, personal security considerations, travel costs, historical ties, old enmities, exchange rates, language barriers and political relations, and a dozen other factors may play on a travel decision.

MAJOR AIRPORTS TRAFFIC FIGURES

Airport traffic statistics suggest the nodal points of travel, the air travel transit points, and where the travel action is taking place. Here are the passenger traffic figures for major gateway cities in the non-communist world for 1981:

O'Hare, Chicago, Ill.	37,992,151
Los Angeles, Ca.	32,722,534
Heathrow, London	27,512,945
Kennedy, N.Y.	25,533,929
Tokyo Haneda	21,235,185
Miami, Fla.	19,848,593
San Francisco, Ca.	19,848,491
Osaka, Japan	17,087,548
Orly, Paris, France	17,012,241
Frankfort, Germany	16,953,045
Toronto, Canada	14,512,400
Honolulu, Hawaii	14,344,225
Mexico Int'l	12,961,727
Fiumicino, Rome, Italy	10,923,564
Gatwick, London, Eng.	9,885,847
Schiphol, Amsterdam	9,668,976

The maps on pages 12 and 13 show the major airports of the world. They are both destinations and transit points. Studying these maps is a good way to familiarize oneself with the world's travel grids.

Whereas travel other than by air can take days, air travel is figured at something like five hundred miles per hour, once a plane leaves the airport. Looking at the air distances between major cities as seen on page 14, travel times between cities can be estimated. The distance between New York and London is seen as 3,473 miles. Dividing by five hundred gives a flight time of close to seven hours. Flight times going east are usually shorter than flying west. Airlines take advantage of the jet streams that flow west to east. Airliners flying west usually are slowed down by the jet streams.

TRAVEL SPENDING

The economic importance of international travel to particular countries is seen by the amount of money generated by visitors. The 1981 receipts by country in billions of dollars are shown in Figure 1.6.

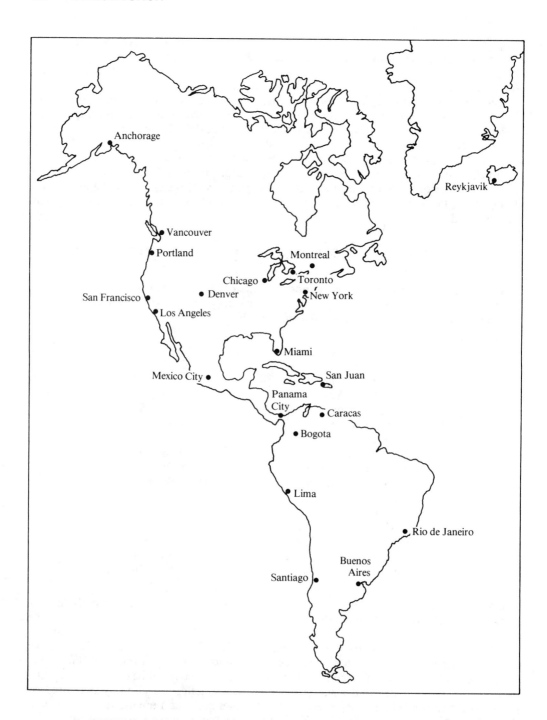

FIGURE 1.3 *Major air transit cities in the Western Hemisphere.*

Tourist spending varies greatly by country of origin. A Hawaiian visitor expenditure survey found that the average Japanese tourist spent $180 per day, Europeans visiting Hawaii, $74.92, Americans $71.24, and Canadians $65.30.

FIGURE 1.4 *Major air transit cities in Europe, Asia, and Australia.*

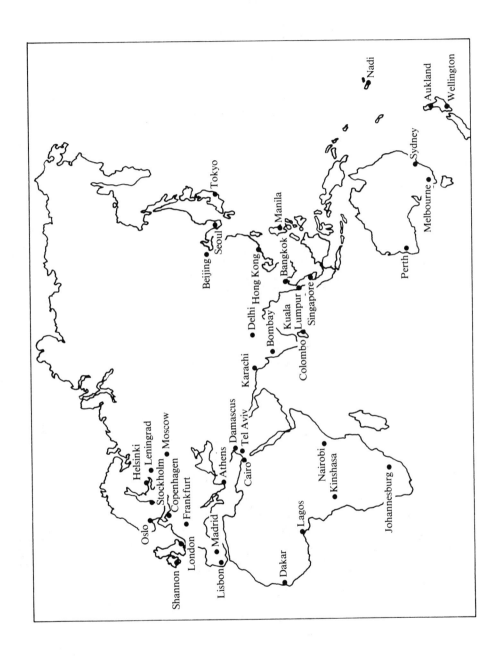

13

FIGURE 1.5 *Air distances between representative cities in the U.S. and the world (in statute miles).*

	Bangkok	Cairo	Caracas	Hong Kong	London	Madrid	Melbourne	Mexico City	Montreal	Moscow	Paris	Rome	Tokyo
New York City	8,669	5,598	2,124	8,061	3,473	3,596	10,352	2,086	333	4,680	3,638	4,805	6,757
Chicago	8,569	6,116	2,500	7,797	3,960	4,192	9,667	1,688	746	4,984	4,145	4,823	6,313
San Fran.	7,930	7,436	3,908	2,397	5,369	5,806	7,850	1,889	2,544	5,884	5,579	6,259	5,148
Honolulu	6,610	8,818	6,024	5,557	7,241	7,874	5,501	3,791	4,919	7,049	7,452	8,040	3,860
Houston	9,261	7,005	2,262	8,349	4,860	5,014	8,979	749	1,605	5,217	5,012	5,680	4,793
Seattle	7,455	6,809	4,096	6,481	4,799	5,303	8,176	2,340	2,289	5,217	5,012	5,680	4,793
St. Louis	8,763	6,370	2,414	7,949	4,215	4,426	9,476	1,425	978	5,248	4,398	5,073	6,407
Washington D.C.	8,807	5,800	2,051	8,157	3,676	3,794	10,174	1,883	490	4,873	3,841		

Source: USAF Aeronautical Chart

FIGURE 1.6   *International travel receipts.*

United States	$12.16
Italy	7.55
France	7.19
Spain	6.71
Germany	6.27
United Kingdom	5.93
Austria	5.71
Switzerland	3.03
Canada	2.54
Greece	1.88
Belgium-Luxembourg	1.58
Netherlands	1.57
Australia	1.24
Denmark	1.23
Portugal	1.02
Sweden	.96
Norway	.75
Japan	.73
Finland	.69
Ireland	.53
Turkey	.38
New Zealand	.25
Iceland	.22

Source: World Tourism Organization.

TRAVEL BARGAIN HUNTING

Price is a major factor in determining choice of pleasure travel destination. The travel sections of newspapers trumpet "bargain," "reduced fare" and "inexpensive." For the mass travel market, travel demand is elastic. In other words as the price comes down travel goes up. Each destination, however, has a limited luxury market segment. The airlines know this well and set aside a definite percentage of seats for first-class. For some destinations a B747 may have only ten first-class seats. For others the number may reach thirty or more.

Travel bargains vary with government policy concerning exchange rates and a variety of other factors. The strength of the American dollar as compared with other currencies is a major factor.

TRAVEL AND DISPOSABLE INCOME

If travel and tourism were merely a matter of people moving from one place to another, the large bulk of travel would take place in Asia. Leisure travel and most of business travel, however, depend upon disposable income, time available and the convenience of travel modes. A number of other factors also plays on travel or its absence. Among these factors are travel as a part of a culture, curiosity, the spirit of adventure and the freedom to travel. Travel-generating countries are the advanced industrialized nations. Australia and New Zealand are exceptions, both with high per capita travel. About fifteen million Americans hold passports, as a percentage of population relatively small compared to several European nations.

The number of hotel beds in an area provides another measure of the extent of tourism. The World Tourism Organization, based in Madrid, publishes information about tourism and includes these figures about the number of beds available regionally in hotels and similar establishments.[2]

Africa	250,000
Americas	6,545,000
East Asia & The Pacific	970,000
Europe	9,000,000
Middle East	135,000
South Asia	125,000

PINPOINTING THE INTERNATIONAL TRAVELER

Psychographic surveys provide information that helps pinpoint various travel markets. One such Canadian study distinguished between the "quiet lake" person and the "overseas traveler." The type of person who agreed with the statement: "A cabin by a quiet lake is a great place to spend a summer" might live next door to the person who says, "I would like to take a trip around the world." As might be guessed the self-concept and values of the two persons are widely different.

The "quiet lake" individual tended to agree with statements like:

"My children are the most important thing in my life."
"Part of every vacation should be educational."
"The father should be the boss in the house."
"A woman's place is in the home."
"The Army is a good career for young men."

The "overseas traveler" was quite naturally interested in new experiences, was active and aggressive, socially active, self-confident and interested in clothes. The "overseas traveler" tended to agree with statements such as:

"I like to be considered a leader."
"I like danger."
"I would do better than average in a fistfight."
"I like to shop for clothes."
"I expect my income to be a lot higher in the next five years."

About two-thirds of those surveyed preferred the quiet lake to the around-the-world vacation.[3]

A Canadian Government Travel Bureau study found that during vacation some people preferred to stay at home while others preferred to travel. These two groups were quite different in personality. Vacation-traveling Canadians were reflective, tended to constantly examine their own actions and those of others. This trait distinguished them the most from other Canadians who took no vacations at all. The traveling vacationers were also more active, more confident, more inquisitive, more outgoing and more sociable.

As might be expected world travelers are more apt to use credit cards.

Desire for change, says the head of Thompson's Travel, is the driving force for travel abroad. He should know because Thompson's Travel, an English concern, has some 800,000 clients and is probably the largest of the tour packagers. Some of Thompson's customers are so enamored of change that they buy tours to Siberia in mid-winter.

Plain, old-fashioned boredom is no doubt responsible for much international travel. For many people, travel has proved a healthful means of coping with tedium, a relatively fast, safe and usually educational way of changing perspective. Travel involves some planning, at least a little challenge, something to anticipate before a trip starts. Arrival at a destination is a change of environment; it can be like stepping through a door into a radically different culture. The jaded jetsetter may need to travel no less than the lonely widow to escape that bane of existence, boredom.

Once aroused, travel is an appetite which for many can be sated but seldom obliterated. The veteran traveler just returned from an exhausting trip swears never to leave home again. A few weeks later he is avidly reading the travel section of the Sunday paper, speculating on a choice of destinations.

Is the urge to travel genetically rooted, something that varies from person to person? J.R.L. Anderson calls it the Ulysses factor[4] after the Homeric hero who was driven to wander and explore for seven years. Perhaps the Ulysses factor is latent in everyone but in varying degree. The Australian aborigine is said to undergo a "walk-about" periodically, an inner clutch automatically engaged that compels him to move on.

Dr. Stanley C. Plog, a travel researcher, presents a theory that arrays people along a travel urge continuum from stay-at-homes to explorers. At one end of this spectrum are the outgoing, adventuresome types who constantly seek out the little known destination, who forego the familiar and the popular. These people he labels "allocentrics" (other oriented). As soon as a destination becomes easily accessible and subject to mass tourism the allocentrics go elsewhere. The great mass of vacation travelers, says Plog, are "midcentrics," who want a change but are not eager for much challenge or inconvenience. Allocentrics fly to their vacation spots. Once arrived, they rent a car and explore on their own. According to Plog, vacation destinations can be plotted on a psychographic chart which changes over time.

Allocentrics are the world travelers. Your died-in-the-wool psychocentric stays home. Cultural factors, personal age, affluence, convenience, and cost of travel must be fed into the psychographic profile. The elderly, affluent person with a travel urge may book a round-the-world cruise on the *QE* II. The impecunious student breaking out of the confines of the classroom may hitchhike in Europe and sleep in his tent. Both may be bona fide allocentrics, the spirit of Ulysses urging them on.

A major reason for engaging in foreign travel is "cultural," to observe different people and different ways of life. When surveyed, Europeans rank culture as a primary motivation for vacation travel. Their American counterparts place it number three. "People watching" in the broad sense is a large component of travel motivation, but not necessarily in places of high concentrations of people. The population as such of a country has little direct relation to its interest as a vacation destination.

The 4.7 billion people who live on this globe are not at all spread around logically or evenly; Asia with its 2.631 billion people has a disproportionately high concentration of people. Mainland China is the big winner in population, about one billion people. India comes next with close to 700 million, and growing.

All of North America has 377.4 million. South America has somewhat fewer people, 243 million. Middle America, which includes Mexico, Honduras, Belize, Nicaragua, El Salvador, Costa Rica and Panama, has a total of eighty-eight million. The total population of the Caribbean is thirty million. Oceania (Australia, New Zealand and nearby islands) has but twenty-three million. Europe has a total of 664.6 million.[5]

Here are the population figures by continent in millions of people:

North America	377.4
South America	243.1
Europe	664.6
Asia	2,631.6
Africa	482.4
Oceania	23

Population density is not necessarily related to poverty or interest in a destination. The Netherlands is one of the most densely populated nations in the world. Yet it is prosperous, healthy, and has a high quality of life. Japan is another heavily populated place, yet it has one of the highest per capita incomes. Slums and ghettos have other causes than large numbers of people in a small space.

It is often the countries who can least afford large populations that continue to grow out of control. Such countries usually generate relatively few travelers. China, and most of Africa and Latin America, attract relatively few visitors. Other factors such as political instability, political philosophy, and high prices also inhibit travel.

Many foreign "nations" are tiny places that most of us never heard of and have no desire to visit. Interestingly, thirty-seven nation states have populations smaller than most large American cities, less than about one million people.

Sovereign States With Populations of Less Than One Million

Bahamas	Djibouti	Guyana	Oman	St. Vincent
Bahrain	Equatorial Guinea	Iceland	Qatar	Surinam
Barbados	Fiji	Kiribati	Reunion	Swaziland
Botswana	Gabon	Luxembourg	Sao Tome &	Tuvalu
Brunei	Gambia	Maldives	Principe	United Arab
Cape Verde	Grenada	Mauritius	Seychelles	Emirates
Comoros	Guinea-Bissau	Nauru	Solomon Islands	Western Samoa
Cyprus				

WEATHER AS A TRAVEL DETERMINANT

In travel to an unfamiliar destination weather looms large in whether the place will be enjoyed. The traveler flip-flops the seasons when crossing the equator. He avoids extreme heat by traveling to the higher altitudes, even though they be in a tropical zone. On islands he stays on the leeward side to avoid excessive rain. Deserts can offer invigorating climates with low humidity during some months.

Ski in the summer? Go to Chile or New Zealand. Depending upon the presence of mountains, large bodies of water, warm ocean currents and prevailing winds, places of extreme latitude may have surprisingly mild climates. Examples include Juneau, Alaska; Bergen, Norway; Reykjavik, Iceland. Humidity greatly affects "sensible" temperatures, the way a temperature feels to a person. A temperature of eighty-five degrees plus in the Bahamas, with 90 percent humidity, can be enervating, especially if there is no breeze.

DESTINATIONS AND THE QUALITY OF LIFE

An assumption can be made that pleasure travelers will elect to visit those places that have the highest quality of life, an assumption that obviously does not apply to the hundreds of thousands who go to considerable expense, inconvenience and sometimes hardship to visit places of special interest to them. Travel statistics, however, bear out the fact that the average international traveler selects politically and physically safe places that offer an environment they judge to have a high quality of life.[7]

The editors of *International Living* have selected the ten factors (listed below) which together determine the quality of life. Each of the ten factors listed below have a possible weight of ten, a perfect score being 100.

1. COST OF LIVING. How much does it cost to live in a style reasonably familiar to the residents of the United States? Derived largely from the U.N. Employee Expenditure Index.
2. TAXES. What is the government's cut? In countries which do not have a tax system, i.e. the USSR and countries with largely subsistence economies, "taxes" mean the extent to which the individual may not keep and enjoy the fruits of his own efforts.
3. ECONOMIC HEALTH. How many goods are being produced per capita? Diversification of economic output. Distribution of income. Productivity, international debt. In short, is this nation financially robust or is it busted?
4. POLITICAL RISK. How great are the chances of revolution, change in

regime, war or other political upheaval?

5. CULTURE. How developed and thriving is the indigenous culture of this nation? How accessible is it to the foreigner? How much imported culture is available? What is there to eat, drink, see, hear, and read?

6. SERVICES/COMMUNICATIONS. Telephones, transportation, dry cleaning, etc. Can one live here comfortably and accomplish daily tasks—like making a telephone call—efficiently?

7. FREEDOM. Civil and human rights. Can you say what you want, move about freely, associate with whom you please? Or must you fit your actions to state policy?

8. RECREATION. The variety and quality of sports, gambling, amusements and other participatory diversions.

9. ENVIRONMENT. The variety of climate and terrain, as well as the physical character of the nation: rainfall, temperature, land use, pollution and the like.

10. HEALTH/SAFETY. Prevalence of disease. Personal safety. Standards of medical care and sanitation. Availability of doctors and medicines. Danger from political instability and crime.

For 1984, the Top Ten Countries in Quality of Life according to *International Living* editors are:

Switzerland	87
United States	86
Bermuda	85
Austria	81
Japan	81
Australia	80
Bahamas	80
Canada	80
France	79
West Germany	79

The Dirty Dozen Countries, Those With the Worst Quality of Life, are:

Chad	13
Vietnam	13
Angola	16
Ethiopia	16
Iran	16
Afghanistan	17
Guinea	17
Kampuchea (Cambodia)	17
Zaire	17
Central African Republic	18
Niger	18
Rwanda	19

Poor Chad is at the bottom of the bottom. Yet Libya is spending millions to gain control of the place. Notice that with the exception of Australia nearly all of the top-ranking countries are in North America and Western Europe. Most of the bottom-ranking countries are in Africa.

AVOIDANCE OF POOR COUNTRIES

Ironically some of the countries that desperately need visitor money get little because of their poverty. These include most of the Black African nations and most of Asia. Bangladesh's per capita income is $115 per year. That of Haiti is $270 a year. By comparison, in 1981 the per capita income of the U.S.A. (based on Gross National Product) was $12,730.

FIGURE 1.7 International Living's *Quality of Life Index.*

	Cost of living	Culture	Political stability	Political/civil freedom	Economic health	Tax burden	Recreation	Health/safety	Services/infrastructure	Environment	Total
Afghanistan	6	1	1	1	1	1	1	1	1	3	17
Albania	8	4	9	1	4	1	4	9	5	5	50
Algeria	5	5	4	2	5	5	5	5	4	4	44
Andorra	5	5	10	10	10	10	7	9	7	5	78
Angola	4	1	1	1	1	1	1	1	2	3	16
Argentina	9	7	3	6	2	6	7	7	5	10	62
Australia	3	9	9	10	7	4	10	9	9	10	80
Austria	6	9	10	10	9	4	8	9	8	8	81
Bahamas	3	8	10	8	10	10	9	7	7	8	80
Bahrain	3	3	9	4	8	10	3	4	5	3	52
Bangladesh	7	1	2	4	1	2	1	2	1	2	23
Barbados	3	5	9	10	10	2	8	8	6	8	69
Belgium	7	8	9	10	5	3	5	9	8	6	70
Belize	9	3	5	9	4	6	6	4	4	6	56
Benin	5	3	4	2	2	2	2	2	2	2	26
Bermuda	3	8	10	10	10	10	9	8	9	8	85
Bolivia	5	4	4	7	2	4	6	5	2	6	45
Botswana	7	3	6	7	5	3	3	3	3	3	43
Brazil	7	9	2	6	3	4	9	5	5	10	60
Bulgaria	5	4	9	1	4	1	4	9	4	5	46
Burma	8	2	8	2	4	3	4	3	1	6	41
Burundi	2	3	4	2	2	3	2	2	1	4	25
Canada	5	8	9	10	7	4	9	9	9	10	80
Cape Verde	8	2	5	2	2	2	2	4	2	2	31
Caymans	3	4	9	10	10	10	6	8	9	4	73
Central African Republic	2	1	2	3	1	2	2	1	3	1	18
Chad	2	1	1	2	1	1	1	2	1	1	13
Channels	5	5	10	10	10	7	4	9	8	6	74
Chile	4	4	3	3	2	7	6	7	4	8	48
China (PRC)	6	6	8	2	4	7	4	4	3	10	54
China (RO)	7	7	9	4	9	5	6	7	8	8	70
Colombia	3	4	6	7	3	4	5	5	4	6	47
Congo	3	2	3	2	4	2	2	3	3	1	25
Costa Rica	9	4	3	9	3	3	8	7	4	8	58
Cuba	5	2	8	2	2	1	6	5	3	4	38
Cyprus	8	5	9	9	4	3	7	8	6	8	67
Czechoslovakia	7	7	8	2	4	2	5	8	6	7	56
Denmark	6	9	10	10	7	2	8	9	9	5	75
Djibouti	2	3	5	3	6	3	3	5	4	1	35
Dominican Republic	6	3	6	9	4	6	8	5	4	9	60
Ecuador	9	4	6	8	5	6	6	5	3	8	60
Egypt	7	8	5	4	2	5	7	6	3	2	49
El Salvador	5	1	1	5	1	6	1	3	3	5	31
Equatorial Guinea	7	1	2	2	2	2	2	1	1	4	24
Ethiopia	4	1	2	1	1	1	2	1	1	2	16
Fiji	7	4	9	8	4	3	9	7	4	9	64
Finland	6	8	7	18	5	3	7	10	7	6	67
France	6	10	7	8	5	5	10	9	9	10	79
French Guiana	5	3	5	5	2	3	2	6	6	3	40
Gabon	4	4	6	2	6	3	3	3	3	2	36

20

FIGURE 1.7   *Continued*

	Cost of living	Culture	Political stability	Political/civil freedom	Economic health	Tax burden	Recreation	Health/safety	Services/infrastructure	Environment	Total
The Gambia	4	3	7	6	3	4	3	2	3	2	37
Germany (GDR–East)	8	6	8	1	5	2	3	9	6	7	55
Germany (FRG–West)	5	10	10	9	8	3	8	9	9	8	79
Ghana	1	1	1	3	1	1	2	3	2	5	20
Greece	8	8	6	9	2	4	7	9	5	8	66
Grenada	6	3	7	5	3	5	6	7	3	6	51
Guatemala	5	4	1	2	3	7	5	4	3	3	37
Guinea	1	2	2	1	1	2	2	2	1	3	17
Guinea-Bissau	4	2	5	2	2	2	2	1	2	2	24
Guyana	7	3	3	5	3	1	2	5	4	2	35
Haiti	6	2	3	2	1	5	3	2	2	8	34
Honduras	6	4	2	7	2	8	6	4	3	5	47
Hong Kong	2	9	9	9	9	7	5	8	10	5	73
Hungary	8	7	8	3	5	2	6	9	5	5	58
Iceland	10	4	7	10	2	2	5	10	7	3	60
India	10	9	4	7	2	1	5	2	2	10	52
Indonesia	3	4	4	4	6	4	7	3	2	5	42
Iran	5	1	1	1	1	1	1	1	1	3	16
Iraq	3	1	1	1	1	10	1	1	2	2	23
Ireland	6	7	8	10	5	2	17	9	6	8	68
Israel	5	8	2	8	2	3	6	8	7	3	52
Italy	6	10	6	9	5	4	8	9	7	9	73
Ivory Coast	7	6	6	4	4	6	5	2	3	4	47
Jamaica	3	4	5	7	2	2	8	6	4	7	48
Japan	3	9	10	10	10	5	6	10	10	8	81
Jordan	5	4	8	2	3	5	3	5	2	3	40
Kampuchea (Cambodia)	5	1	1	1	1	1	1	1	1	4	17
Kenya	8	5	5	4	4	2	6	3	3	7	47
Korea (North)	5	1	6	1	3	1	1	3	2	2	25
Korea, Republic of (South)	3	6	6	4	8	4	5	5	6	4	51
Kuwait	2	4	9	5	9	10	3	8	4	1	55
Lao People's Republic (Laos)	5	1	1	1	1	1	1	1	1	2	15
Lebanon	2	1	1	5	1	7	1	6	2	3	29
Lesotho	8	4	5	4	6	4	5	5	2	5	48
Liberia	3	4	4	2	2	4	3	3	2	1	28
Libyan Arab Jamahiriya	5	1	1	2	4	3	1	7	4	2	29
Liechtenstein	5	8	10	10	10	4	5	9	9	7	77
Luxembourg	5	8	10	10	10	3	5	9	9	5	74
Macau	8	6	6	8	5	8	4	3	4	3	55
Madagascar	5	2	7	4	1	3	3	3	2	8	38
Malawi	5	3	7	2	2	3	1	2	2	4	31
Malaysia	3	6	8	5	6	4	6	7	4	7	56
The Maldives	6	4	8	4	5	5	3	3	1	5	44
Mali	3	2	2	2	2	2	3	2	2	2	22
Malta	8	5	10	7	5	2	4	9	6	4	60
Mauritania	5	2	4	2	2	2	2	2	2	2	25
Mauritius	7	4	7	8	2	1	7	5	3	5	49
Mexico	9	9	2	5	3	4	9	5	4	7	57
Monaco	2	9	10	10	10	6	4	10	10	6	77
Montserrat	5	3	9	9	4	9	7	5	5	7	63

FIGURE 1.7 *Continued.*

	Cost of living	Culture	Political stability	Political/civil freedom	Economic health	Tax burden	Recreation	Health/safety	Services/infrastructure	Environment	Total
Morocco	9	5	6	5	4	3	5	5	3	4	49
Mozambique	7	2	2	1	2	1	1	2	2	3	23
Namibia	5	2	3	5	2	4	1	4	4	2	32
Nauru	3	3	7	8	5	10	2	8	8	2	56
Nepal	7	3	8	5	4	8	6	3	2	7	53
The Netherlands	4	9	10	10	7	7	5	9	8	6	75
New Zealand	6	6	10	10	5	2	10	9	8	10	76
Nicaragua	5	1	1	1	1	6	1	5	2	3	26
Niger	3	2	2	2	1	2	2	1	2	1	18
Nigeria	2	6	3	7	3	5	4	2	3	2	37
Norway	4	8	10	10	8	4	8	10	8	5	75
Oman	2	3	7	2	8	10	2	3	3	1	41
Pakistan	6	2	2	2	1	4	2	2	2	4	27
Panama	5	4	6	4	7	7	6	6	4	3	52
Papua New Guinea	6	2	6	8	2	4	3	4	2	6	43
Paraguay	7	4	7	4	7	7	6	6	4	4	56
Peru	5	4	4	7	2	3	6	5	3	8	47
The Philippines	7	4	1	3	2	6	4	4	3	5	39
Poland	9	7	5	2	2	1	5	9	4	7	51
Portugal	10	4	1	6	5	2	7	7	4	6	62
Qatar	5	6	10	7	2	10	2	6	5	2	47
Romania	6	3	1	8	4	2	6	8	4	5	53
Rwanda	2	2	2	2	1	2	2	1	2	3	19
San Marino	7	5	10	10	3	7	3	9	4	3	61
Saudi Arabia	1	4	8	2	9	10	4	5	4	2	49
Senegal	6	5	7	5	3	4	4	2	3	5	44
Seychelles	7	2	7	2	5	4	7	7	4	6	51
Sierra Leone	8	5	7	4	1	4	4	2	2	5	42
Singapore	3	6	9	5	9	6	5	8	8	3	62
Somalia	2	2	2	1	2	2	2	2	2	3	20
South Africa	7	8	2	3	4	4	10	5	5	9	57
Spain	8	9	8	9	4	6	8	8	7	7	74
Sri Lanka	6	4	2	7	2	2	8	4	2	8	45
Sudan	8	3	7	4	1	3	3	3	2	3	37
Suriname	5	4	9	3	2	5	5	6	5	3	47
Swaziland	7	2	5	4	5	3	2	5	3	6	42
Sweden	6	8	10	10	6	1	8	10	9	6	74
Switzerland	5	9	10	10	10	6	9	10	10	8	87
Syrian Arab Republic	4	2	5	3	3	2	2	5	4	2	32
Thailand	3	9	6	5	4	3	5	5	7	5	52
Togo	6	3	3	2	2	3	2	2	2	3	28
Trinidad & Tobago	2	3	5	9	5	2	6	7	4	6	49
Tunisia	8	5	8	4	7	5	6	5	4	2	49
Turkey	8	5	7	5	3	3	4	5	4	5	49
Uganda	6	1	1	4	1	1	1	1	1	4	21
Union of Soviet Socialist Republics	5	7	10	2	4	1	6	8	4	10	57
United Arab Emirates	3	3	8	4	7	10	2	4	6	2	49
United Kingdom	5	10	10	10	5	3	7	9	7	9	75
United Republic of Cameroon	6	4	8	2	5	3	3	3	3	4	41
United Republic of Tanzania	4	3	1	2	2	1	2	3	2	4	24

FIGURE 1.7   *Continued*

	Cost of living	Culture	Political stability	Political/civil freedom	Economic health	Tax burden	Recreation	Health/safety	Services/infrastructure	Environment	Total
United States of America	5	10	10	10	8	4	10	9	10	10	86
Upper Volta	3	2	2	3	2	2	2	1	2	1	20
Uruguay	9	4	5	5	3	8	6	7	4	5	56
Venezuela	5	7	4	9	4	8	6	8	5	6	62
Vietnam	4	1	1	1	1	1	1	1	1	1	13
Western Samoa	6	3	9	5	4	3	7	6	3	6	52
Yemen Arab Republic (North)	3	2	8	3	4	3	2	2	2	1	30
Democratic Yemen (South)	3	2	6	2	1	2	2	3	2	1	24
Yugoslavia	8	7	9	3	5	2	8	8	5	7	62
Zaire	1	1	2	2	1	2	1	3	1	3	17
Zambia	6	3	5	3	3	1	1	3	3	4	32
Zimbabwe	7	2	2	5	2	3	1	3	3	6	34

Source: International Living, Vol. 3, Number 9, Jan. 1984.

Per capita income can be misleading in that income may be unevenly distributed. Mexico, for example, has a per capita income exceeding $2,000, with a relatively few rich and the vast majority of people desperately poor. The president of Cameroon rides around in a gold-plated limousine. Some of the rich in India are very rich.

Those who enjoy visiting countries where almost no one is poor should visit most of Western Europe but especially the Scandinavian countries (Norway, Sweden, and Denmark), West Germany, and Switzerland.

Of course travel is related to its root word, "travail." The act of traveling in itself can be highly stressful. Assorted diseases and parasites are out there, especially in the less developed countries, waiting to make life miserable if allowed into the body. Visitors are fair prey in a number of countries.

Entrance requirements can be draconian. Before arriving at the United Arab Emirates, travelers should drink any and all liquor they may be carrying. Visitors are subject to arrest if they attempt to import any alcoholic beverages.

As for illegal drugs, do not take any to Malaysia. The dealth penalty is mandatory if one is convicted of drug trafficking. By definition conviction follows if the quantity meets the minimum amount set by the government.[8]

During the past sixty years air travel has become one of the phenomena of our time. The *Concorde* travels at mach 2, twice the speed of sound. Traveling and distance has been compressed into hours; journeys that took weeks, even months, can be undertaken over a weekend. Millions of people can visit their families on another continent. Business travelers can schedule trans-Atlantic meetings without a second thought. Pleasure travelers can "explore" the Amazon or the Arctic. What of the future?

Even today only one in six hundred persons flies. What if that figure reaches two in six hundred or one hundred in six hundred? Will air travel become just another hassle in getting from point A to point B? In some places that has already occurred. Will it become very nice just to stay at home?

How will the air vehicle itself change? Ballistic travel (passenger rockets shot to follow a parabolic path into the upper atmosphere and then return, following a path, for example, from San Francisco to Sydney, Australia) is technically feasible. Planes carrying one thousand passengers are not far off, and others can be built to carry even more passengers.

Will international travel spread disease as well as cultures? The spread of the anopheles mosquito by air from Africa to Brazil has already occurred. Rapid transmittal of disease is a distinct danger.

Will world peace be furthered by international travel? There is no strong evidence that this has happened. The way an international traveler affects host people seems to be influenced by a number of factors, such as political and cultural differences, differences in affluence, educational level, the personalities of the individual travelers and of the individuals in the host nation.

International travel results in an array of benefits to some groups. To other groups international travel is a liability, accompanied by noise and overcrowding. The new Narita Airport forty miles outside of Tokyo, for example, maintains a security force of eighteen hundred men to safeguard the airport from the farmers and others of the region who see it as a menace to their way of life.

The effects the instant information revolution will have on international travel are a matter of speculation. When the home TV operates as a telephone, and a video disc player can be hooked into massive information and entertainment libraries, the urge to travel may be dampened or stimulated. Visualize a four- by six-foot screen in every living room linked to a vast entertainment and education system. Operating from a panel removed from a computer-controlled console, the operator will be able to call most places in the civilized world and speak to a person or group seen on the screen. Views of vacation destinations can be called up, the actual scene of say Champs d'Elysses in Paris or of Waikiki Beach.

Any one of hundreds of education programs can be called up from central video libraries. Stock travel marketing tapes can be displayed at will. Undoubtedly a catalog of films on various countries and vacation destinations will be available. Current travel costs, best air routing and flight schedules will be instantly displayed.

The individual will have a choice of actual travel or being an armchair adventurer. Will this kind of ready access to films and cassettes work to make for a more knowledgeable traveler, one who can more appreciate the destination? Will it stimulate travel or inhibit it?

The right to travel fits well with Thomas Jefferson's rights to "life, liberty and the pursuit of happiness." The "pursuit of happiness" is a universal good unfortunately denied the majority of world citizens today. As that right becomes available to millions because of greater affluence and political freedom the numbers involved in pleasure travel could be astounding. One thing is certain: international travel will continue to be one of this century's most amazing forces for change.

ENDNOTES

1. *Travel Industry World Yearbook*–1983, Somerset Waters, Child and Waters, N.Y.C. 1983.
2. The figures are for 1979 and appear in the *Economic Review of World Tourism*, World Tourism Organization, 1982 Edition, Madrid.
3. Reported in Chapter 4, *The Psychology of Leisure Travel*, Mayo and Jarvis, CBI Publishing Co., Boston, 1981.
4. J.R.L. Anderson, *The Ulysses Factor* (New York: Harcourt Brace Jovanovich, 1970).
5. *World Almanac*, Rand McNally, 1982.
6. *Ibid.*
7. This material used courtesy of the editors of *International Living*, Baltimore, Md.
8. A World Status Map covering danger areas; advisories from the U.S. Department of State; current passport, visa, and vaccination requirements; and Center for Disease Control reports is published monthly by E.M. Electronics Co., Box 2533, Fairfax, VA 22031.

2

CANADA AND ALASKA

CANADA

"America borders on the magnificent" reads a Canadian tourism ad. The ad is in part right. The Canadian outdoors is magnificent, "A land larger than any one person can hope to comprehend." There are also fine cities and a culture rich in history and diversity. Canada's twenty-four million people occupy the world's second largest country in land area. It shares a fifty-three-hundred-mile border with the United States, much of it along the 49th parallel in latitude. It has thousands of lakes, rivers, streams, and swamps. The Canadian Rockies are even more grand than those Rockies in the United States. Canada is a storehouse of vast quantities of energy and minerals.

A striking difference between the U.S. and Canada is that in Canada a third of the population speaks French. Many of them do not understand English and the English-speaking Canadians are not too keen on being taken as Americans. They are Canadians. As someone put it, "A Canadian is someone who has turned down a chance to go and live in the United States."

Canadians have been called "the quiet Americans," more reserved than their friends in the U.S., more mannered and, in many parts of Canada, more class conscious. Private clubs are taken quite seriously; rank and status are respected. Regional attitudes are strong. It is largely a middle-class society, hard-working, materialistic, conservative—and cheerful.

Culturally, Canada has the strong heritages of Britain and France. Quebec is predominantly French and insists on maintaining its "Frenchness" even to the point of wanting separation from the rest of Canada. Other Europeans have brought their ethnicity to Canada making some cities, especially Toronto, the largest city, multi-racial and multi-cultural. Some sixty thousand Indians still live on reservations, the Pacific Coast Indians with quite different cultures than those living near Hudson's Bay.

Not surprisingly, the greatest "international travel" by United States residents and by Canadians is between the two countries. The travel statistics are impressive: sixty-eight million total crossings—thirty-eight million from the United States into Canada and thirty-two million the other direction. (Mexico is a very distant second in the border-crossing

FIGURE 2.1 Canada.

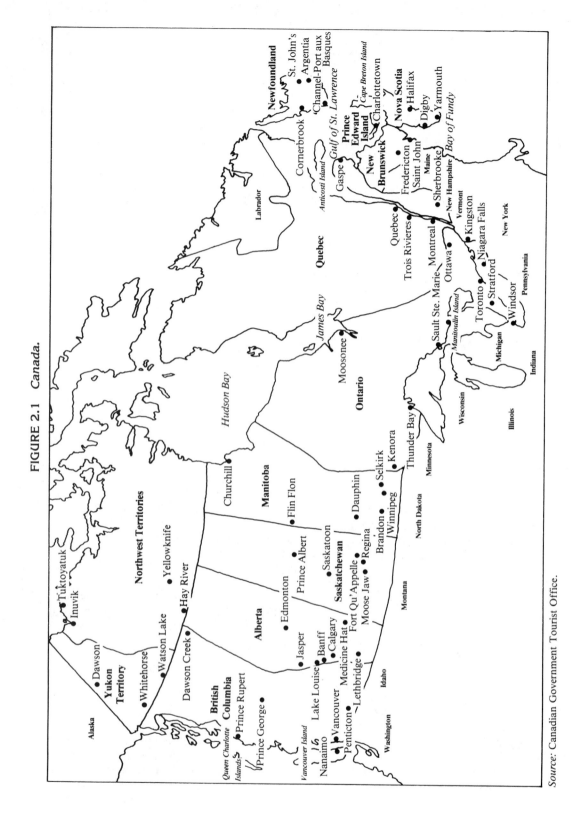

Source: Canadian Government Tourist Office.

26

sweepstakes.) Most visitors between Canada and the United States stay close to the border where life is hardly distinguishable from home. Except in French-speaking Quebec, Canada's language is English.

Eleven million U.S. visitors in Canada remained for one or more nights in 1981. They left $1.85 billion. Other visitors spent $815 million in 1981. Two-thirds of U.S. visitors to Canada go to Ontario. Quebec receives the second largest number. British Columbia is next, then Alberta, Saskatchewan and New Brunswick.

Geographically, Canada can be divided into five different regions. Beginning in the East are the Atlantic or Maritime provinces, settled for the most part along the coasts (in New Brunswick along the rivers); then the nation's population core: Quebec and Ontario; the Prairies; the Mountain West; and the North. The natural division between the Mountain West and the Prairies is the most dramatic. The Great Divide in the Canadian Rockies marks the place where rainfall flows either east or west, a line of demarcation between the provinces of Alberta and British Columbia. The West has the great national parks of Waterton Lakes, part of the International Peace Park shared with the U.S., Banff, Yoho, Jasper, Kootenay and others. These parks vie in grandeur with their neighbors to the south: Glacier National Park and Yellowstone National Park.

Good roads make access in and around the parks easy. Campers are no less inspired than those who want deluxe hotel accommodations in such hotels as Banff Springs, Chateau Lake Louise or Jasper Lodge, places with views that rival anything found in Switzerland. Chateau Lake Louise sits on one end of a milky-white lake fed at the other end by a glacier. The far north is for the adventurer, the hunter, the canoeist, the explorer.

In the abbreviated summer, fishermen can fly into lakes of the Northwest Territory and catch fish that only dreamers and fishing tale liars have seen. On one 250-mile-long lake only eight fishermen made up the entire fishermen population during one week in July. Eight-pound trout are caught, the kind it takes two hands to hold up while photographing the catch for posterity.

To escape the long winters, many Canadians travel to the Bahamas and the Caribbean on vacation. San Diego is a major winter destination for Western Canadians, and Britain, the ethnic home for 45 percent of Canadians, is a summer destination. Upstate New York and New England are also summer destinations. As with most affluent nations, Canadians spend more when traveling abroad than is taken in from visitors. The result is a "travel deficit." The cause is understandable. People with money travel more, and to more places than people with less money.

The Canadian Government Office of Tourism is concerned that the average U.S. resident perceives Canada only as rustic and rural whereas the majority of Canadians live in metropolitan centers with cultural amenities and visitor attractions that equal or excel those in U.S. urban centers. Actually only a little more than 4 percent of the whole country is under cultivation and it is estimated that only 7 percent ever can be.

Rural living, mountain climbing, fly-n'fishing are in Saskatchewan, Alberta, British Columbia, and few places can equal the tractless distances found in the Yukon and Northwest Territories. The great concentration of people, however, is within a hundred-mile range of the U.S. border. The cities of Vancouver, Toronto and Montreal are world-class metropolises. Rough it if you like or enjoy urban luxury. Take a farm vacation or shop for "haute couture" in underground Montreal, the city under a city, with literally miles of suburban shops, boutiques, restaurants, bars and clubs. There are more than a thousand such stores, as well as art galleries and movie theaters, linked by climate-controlled passageways and the Metro, Montreal's subway system.

Travel to Canada from the continental United States is quick and easy. Dozens of major border crossing points are provided from the United States and no visa is required. Millions of United States and Canadian residents cross the border to work, shop, vacation and do business. Travel by auto across Canada is expedited by the Trans-Canada Highway, just under five thousand miles (the world's longest paved road), stretching from Victoria, British Columbia, on the west coast, all the way to St. John's, Newfoundland, on the east. Ferries connect the highway with its extensions on Prince Edward Island and Newfoundland. Whitehorse, in the Yukon Territory, to Montreal is 3,627 miles. Distances between major Canadian cities are seen in the chart below. The other notable highway is the 1,524 mile Alaska Highway—two-thirds of it is in Canada.

Driving the Alaska Highway is something of an accomplishment. It stretches from Dawson Creek in the south, then north through Ft. St. John and Fort Nelson, up to Alaska. In Canada mile 0 is Dawson Creek. Mile 1520 is Fairbanks, Alaska. The British Columbia/Yukon portion of the highway has an improved seal-coat surface and is paved through the major towns along the route. During rainless periods the road can be extremely dusty and driving is done with the headlights on at all times. During the spring break up it can get soggy in spots. The Alaska portion of the road is paved. Two good spare tires and a jumper cable are recommended.

Since a large portion of travel into and around Canada is by auto some pointers are in order. U.S. citizens can enter Canada without a passport or visa but should have proof of U.S. citizenship such as a driver's license or social security card. There is no national speed limit as in the U.S.A. Speed limits vary and are posted.

U.S. car insurance offered by most companies is valid in Canada.

For best money exchange rates use the local banks. Duty exemption from U.S. customs is $400 but you must have been in Canada for at least forty-eight hours. If the stay is less, the exemption per person reduces to $25. The $400 exemption is available only once every thirty days. Use Canadian stamps if mailing anything in Canada.

Figure 2.1 gives some idea of Canada's immensity and the fact that nearly all of the cities are within a hundred miles or so of the northern border of the U.S. The Canadian North is so sparsely settled that it has been likened to the Sahara Desert. The Northwest and Yukon Territories, which make up the bulk of the Canadian North, occupy one-and-a-half million square miles, roughly 40 percent of Canada. The population totals less than 100,000.

Canada has excellent air, rail and road systems. Major gateway air terminals are at Vancouver, Calgary, Montreal and Toronto. Toronto experiences the most international air traffic.

Canada, coast to coast, can be enjoyed via the Trans-Canada Highway or by taking VIA Rail. Halifax, Nova Scotia, to Vancouver, B.C., is about three thousand miles. Flying time is seven hours and fifty-five minutes (including one change). Via rail the trip lasts four days and about eighteen hours and covers 3,895 miles. VIA Rail was created in 1977 as a corporation to operate all intercity and transcontinental passenger service previously operated by the Canadian National and Canadian Pacific Railways. It is similar in concept to Amtrak, the semi-public corporation that operates most U.S. train passenger service. The two computer reservation systems are interconnected so that reservations for one can be made by the other. As the transcontinental train rolls across the country the dining car menu reflects the Canadian cuisine. In the East it is solid British entrees like steak-and-kidney pie, plum pudding and tarts. Maritime seafoods—lobster, shrimp and cod—are included. In Quebec there are croissants. Around the Great Lakes there are whitefish and farther west, trout and beef.

Ask U.S. citizens to name their favorite city and San Francisco often pops up. Ask Canadians the same question and the answer is likely to be Toronto. Toronto is Canada's leading city in population and in other ways as well. Per capita income is 21 percent higher than in the rest of Canada. Its stock exchange is second only to the New York Stock Exchange and handles 81 percent of Canada's stock transactions. It is a city known for its casual style, cleanliness and safety. It has a good subway system as well as being a place for pedestrians, a place with up-scale shops and numerous ethnic restaurants.

After Paris, Montreal, in Quebec province, is the largest French-speaking city worldwide. A metropolis of three million, it is a series of twenty-eight small cities around central Montreal on a river island twenty-five miles long. Each has its own mayor and fire department. Montreal is food conscious, a place, it is said, where restaurants and food come second only to language and politics as a topic of conversation. There are three thousand restaurants. Montreal's subway ranks with those of Mexico City and Moscow in being colorful and pleasurable to use. Churches are plentiful and in the French tradition of church architecture.

FIGURE 2.2   Canadian mileage chart.

	Atlanta	Boston	Buffalo	Calgary	Chicago	Cleveland	Dallas	Detroit	Edmonton	Halifax	Los Angeles	Minneapolis	Montreal	New York	Ottawa	Philadelphia	Quebec City	San Francisco	Seattle	Toronto	Vancouver
Boston	1108																				
Buffalo	907	465																			
Calgary	2367	2636	2148																		
Chicago	708	1004	539	1608																	
Cleveland	728	657	191	1964	348																
Dallas	822	1753	1364	1935	921	1189															
Detroit	732	799	361	1901	275	172	1156														
Edmonton	2399	2611	2212	183	1691	2039	2118	1966													
Halifax	1777	715	1180	3175	1714	1372	2468	1439	3112												
Los Angeles	2191	3017	2584	1692	2048	2382	1399	2288	1879	3732											
Minneapolis	1121	1390	949	1244	410	758	949	685	1269	2105	1857										
Montreal	1199	310	399	2332	847	583	1770	572	2301	828	3081	1182									
New York	854	208	371	2427	809	471	1559	649	2500	923	2794	1217	382								
Ottawa	1280	437	353	2236	763	544	1733	488	2173	951	2993	1043	127	430							
Philadelphia	748	315	360	2405	785	428	1443	609	2476	1030	2703	1195	469	106	536						
Quebec City	1381	409	563	2441	1010	747	1922	735	2449	668	3018	1346	160	566	283	633					
San Francisco	2483	3128	2667	1355	2173	2483	1752	2399	1529	3843	387	1979	2959	2930	2936	2902	3122				
Seattle	2625	3016	2576	730	2052	2391	2131	2327	910	3731	1134	1653	2883	2841	2795	2816	3069	810			
Toronto	1101	609	105	2170	515	296	1435	240	2107	1199	2744	906	344	516	248	465	463	2627	2564		
Vancouver	2756	3155	2703	652	2176	2493	2234	2418	766	3842	1278	1733	3014	2943	2886	2898	3123	954	144	2820	
Washington	618	448	405	2485	709	360	1307	516	2499	1163	2646	1090	607	237	666	131	771	2843	2721	753	3180
Winnipeg	1575	1790	1405	844	862	1214	1308	1114	813	2316	1996	456	1488	1660	1364	1614	1597	1951	1463	1296	1526

Winnipeg – Washington: 1526

Source: *Travel Times* in cooperation with the Canadian Government Office of Tourism.

29

FIGURE 2.3 Distances between major Canadian cities.
(kilometres and miles)

	St. John's		Halifax		Montreal		Ottawa		Toronto		Winnipeg		Regina		Edmonton		Calgary		Vancouver		Victoria	
	km	mi	km	mi	km	mi	km	mi	km	mi	km	mi	km	mi	km	mi	km	mi	km	mi	km	mi
Halifax	1503	932																				
Montreal	2602	1613	1249	774																		
Ottawa	2792	1731	1439	892	190	118																
Toronto	3141	1947	1788	1109	539	334	399	247														
Winnipeg	5010	3106	3656	2267	2408	1493	2218	1375	2099	1301												
Regina	5581	3460	4228	2621	2979	1847	2789	1729	2670	1655	571	354										
Edmonton	6367	3947	5013	3108	3764	2334	3574	2216	3455	2142	1357	841	785	487								
Calgary	6334	3927	4973	3083	3743	2321	3553	2203	3434	2129	1336	828	764	474	299	185						
Vancouver	7403	4590	6050	3751	4801	2977	4611	2859	4492	2785	2232	1384	1822	1130	1244	771	1057	655				
Victoria	7775	4821	6154	3815	4905	3041	4715	2923	4596	2850	2337	1449	1926	1194	1349	836	1162	720	105	65		
Whitehorse	8452	5240	7099	4401	5850	3627	5660	3509	5528	3427	3524	2185	2871	1780	2086	1293	2385	1479	2697	1672	2802	1737

Quebec City is the most European city on the North American continent, with one of the famous old hotels dating back to 1892—Le Chateau Frontenac.

Quebec City is one of American's best-kept historical centers with old walls, cobblestone streets, old battlefields. The city's citizens, the "Quebecois," are fiercely independent and continue to demand independence from Canada. "Quebec Libre!" appears on walls. The provincial flag, white fleur-de-lis placed in each quarter of royal blue, flies everywhere. Quebec is Catholic; most of the rest of Canada is Protestant.

Quebec, the province, has a population of six million; five million speak only French. Canadian money is printed in French and English. All labels and directions for product use are printed in both languages. The province of Quebec, bent on retaining its French character, rates its hotels and other hostelries by a system of fleurs-de-lis, the French heraldic device resembling three petals of an iris. Instead of the one to five stars often used in rating, the Quebec tourism department awards one to five fleurs-de-lis. Hostelry dining rooms get one to four forks, depending on quality of cuisine.

Politically the country is divided into ten provinces and two territories. In the east are the Atlantic provinces: Nova Scotia (the Nova Scotia Peninsula and the island of Cape Breton), Prince Edward Island, Newfoundland and New Brunswick. Area—208,000 square miles. Population—2.2 million.

Of the four Maritime provinces of Canada, Nova Scotia has the most developed tourist industry. Halifax, the capital, is joined to Dartmouth by two suspension bridges. Together they form the largest metropolitan area east of Montreal. Being an island, no part of Nova Scotia is more than thirty-five miles from the sea.

New Brunswick has vast, virgin forests and glistening white seashores. The Bay of Fundy tides are the highest in the world. After rising forty feet they rush back to the open sea leaving miles of tidal flats. Fundy National Park features camping, hiking, boating, horseback riding and nature trails.

Unlike the other Atlantic provinces tiny Prince Edward Island is given over to gently rolling hills where the visitor is never more than twenty miles from the sea. Two ferry services bring visitors from neighboring Nova Scotia and from New Brunswick. Potato farming, fishing, and lobstering are principal occupations on the island. One of the best ways to enjoy the lobsters is to dine with the residents at the lobster dinners sponsored by the churches and local communities. Attractions include the Anne of Green Gables Festival, as well as lobster, strawberry and potato blossom festivals and craft fairs. Prince Edward Island, or P.E.I., is the smallest Canadian province.

Newfoundland, Canada's newest province, offers camping, hunting, fishing, and sightseeing. Its capital, St. John's, is the oldest city in North America north of Mexico and is a good base for exploring eastern Newfoundland's scenic and historic Avalon Peninsula. St. John's is built on hills and the people speak with an Irish accent.

The bed and breakfast package is widespread in Canada but particularly within the Maritime provinces. The government assures the visitor of their being of acceptable standard and publishes guides. How could anyone resist this description of The Ash Tree home in Nova Scotia:

"...There is a wildlife park only ten minutes from our home. We are within walking distance of the beach. Churches are nearby....We have a color TV with cable in our sitting room which we would be more than happy to share with you; also a quiet, relaxing backyard and a black tom cat called Fred. Bedtime snack is on us. A chance to get acquainted."

With so much space and relatively few people it is hard not to think of Canada as a nature-lover's dream—at least during the summer months. Parks it has aplenty. Saskatchewan alone has more than 1.2 million acres of provincial parks, two national parks and ninety-nine regional parks.

The Canadian Rockies are even more rugged than their American counterpart. The Prairie provinces' population centers—Winnipeg, Edmonton, Saskatoon, Regina and Calgary—are much like our Great Plains towns. In the Rockies everyone's favorites for scenic beauty are Banff and Lake Louise, located on the eastern slopes of the Rockies in southwest Alberta province.

FIGURE 2.4 *Niagara Falls.* Shared by the U.S. and Canada, Niagara Falls is one of the world's great natural tourist attractions.

Source: Canadian Government Office of Tourism.

With the discovery of vast quantities of oil and gas the Province of Alberta has also taken on aspects of the world of big money and big business. Calgary, once a ranching and agricultural center, has become the prairie provinces' banking center.

The welcome that can be expected in rural Canada is suggested by Manitoba's VIP Program, a Volunteer Visitor Information Program. Volunteers display a sign in the back window of their cars.

FIGURE 2.5 *Volunteer Visitor Information Person.* Manitoba's VIP program welcomes tourists.

The volunteers are ready with directions and information on the province's museums, sights and special events.

The province of British Columbia is a favored vacation destination. Vancouver, Canada's third largest city, after Toronto and Montreal, is tucked away in the extreme southwest corner of British Columbia. More than 1.5 million people live in metropolitan Vancouver. The city overlooks the Strait of Georgia, which separates the mainland from Vancouver Island, home of Victoria, the provincial capital of British Columbia. The city of Vancouver has a beautiful land-locked, ice-free harbor. To the north are wooded mountains four thousand feet tall and snowcapped much of the year. Chinatown in Vancouver has an international reputation for good restaurants and is second in size only to that of San Francisco. For a spectacular view of the city take the gondola up the side of Grouse mountain. The climate resembles Seattle's, with few extremes of heat or cold. Temperatures rarely reach 80 degrees in summer, and winters have relatively few days below freezing. About sixty inches of rain falls annually in Vancouver but there is little snow.

British Columbia has a varied geography. The coast is said to be similar to that of Norway. The sagebrush-filled plateau land of the northeast looks like Texas. The green valleys resemble those of western Oregon. The coast has mild winters and cool summers. The inland areas have greater temperature extremes and much less rainfall than the coastal areas.

Vancouver Island, a mecca for Northwest U.S. and British Columbian residents, is almost three hundred miles long. Its moderate year-round climate has attracted 300,000 permanent residents and many more yearly visitors. Visitors seem uniformly impressed with the sedate Empress Hotel on Vancouver Island and the Englishness of the place, including the "teas" and the food in general. Buchart Garden, built in an abandoned stone quarry, has an international reputation.

The Vancouver-Victoria coastal region is one of the sunniest with warm, relatively dry summers. Sorry, it is cool and wet the rest of the year. Twelve hundred miles north of Los Angeles, many Western Canada residents vacation in Southern California during the winter.

Totem poles have become a tourist trademark for the British Columbian coast. Along with a number of primitive cultures the Indians of the region carved these handsome poles to represent their totem, a mystical, or even real, relationship to some animal, plant, bird or inanimate object. People of the same totem were prohibited from marrying with the totem kin and might be prohibited from killing or eating whatever the totem represented.

It is customary to close these discussions with a quick commentary on the country's cuisine, an impossibility in the case of Canada because of its ethnic and geographical diversity. Suffice to say that visitors to the Maritime provinces expect and get a rich array of seafood with lobster the centerpiece. The same is true for British Columbia except that the centerpiece is salmon. Nothing can compare with the planked salmon cooked over an open fire with the Pacific Ocean pounding in a few yards away. Quite naturally Quebec lays out the French couvert with all of its subtleties and nuances. Canadian cheese, fruits and berries are notable and those Canadians of English heritage have lost none of their affection for good roast beef. The visitor to Canada will not go hungry, in fact, will find good food a large part of the travel experience.

ALASKA

Tourism is a major Alaska industry, one that the State Division of Tourism officials feel will flourish and fill in the economic gap left as the supply of oil diminishes. Alaska's natural beauty will remain even though its salmon and haddock come and go and the price of timber rises and falls. In 1981, 660,000 visitors came to Alaska mostly to revel in its natural beauty and to experience America's last frontiers. They left something like $434 million while cruising, traveling the few Alaskan highways, fishing, hunting, and viewing scenery as spectacular or more so than any in the world. They arrived mostly by ship or air —necessarily because there is only one highway into the state, that from the neighboring Yukon Territory, the Alaska Highway, the engineering marvel of World War II.

Alaska is sold on selling Alaska to more people. The current governor is the state's largest hotel owner and operator. The Division of Tourism's budget for 1983 is $6.25 million and it will spend two million of it on national TV advertising the wonders of Alaska. All told, depending on how a hotel is defined, there are ten thousand to twelve thousand guest rooms in Alaska. In 1983 a statewide lodging association was formed.

Visitors tend to fall into one of three groups: those who arrive by ship—generally retired, older and fairly affluent; adventurous families who come via the Alaska Highway from the "lower states" and Canada; and those who come by air, who represent a middle-age and middle-income group.

Travel costs range widely. The backpacker may take a state-operated ferry from Seattle; the Belgian doctor pays out $6,000 for a week and gets the head of a mountain goat to hang in his den back home. Accommodations range from a cabin rented from the U.S. Forest Service for $10 a day to a room at the Hilton, Cook, or Sheraton hotels in Anchorage for $100 a night. The cabin comes equipped with a supply of firewood and sometimes a boat. The Sheraton sports an Alaskan jade staircase. The bed and breakfast phenomenon is spreading to Alaska just as it has within the continental U.S. in the last few years. Overall costs of living are about 20 percent higher than in Seattle, Washington.

For most people the immensity of this forty-ninth state is difficult to comprehend: one-fifth the size of the "lower forty-eight," it makes Texans tongue-tied when it comes to the word "biggest." Two-and-a-half times as big as Texas, it covers four time zones. The coastline is greater than that in all of the continental U.S. Climate varies widely largely because of the warming influence of the Japanese current that sweeps north and east from the mid-Pacific.

Anchorage is strategically located on the polar route between Europe, the U.S., and Japan and is a major international airport city. About halfway, or seven-and-a-half hours flight time, between Europe and Asia, the Anchorage International Airport is a refueling point. New York City is 3,374 air miles; Tokyo—3,449 air miles; London—4,487 miles. The map shows Anchorage as a logical break point in intercontinental travel. Some 1.5 million passengers disembark briefly at the airport. The Alaska tourist people are consid-

FIGURE 2.6 *Only way to go.* Ferry liners cruise the Inland Passage of Alaska's southeastern waters. Owned and operated by the state of Alaska, they are the principal means of travel to the several towns that share no road access.

ering ways of making the stopover a longer event, one that could easily double income from tourism.

The Alaska Highway is one of the adventure roads of the world. Driving the 1,490 miles from Dawson Creek, British Columbia, to Fairbanks, Alaska, takes about seven days. The Canadian segment of the highway is mostly gravel, with paved sections near larger towns. Once Alaska is reached it is all paved. Seasoned north country residents prefer to drive the highway in winter, when it is less crowded and the road surface is smooth and frozen, free from dust and flying gravel. An interesting statistic: during the month of July Germans and Swiss were second in numbers using the highway, after Californians.

THE ALASKA MARINE HIGHWAY

Unique to Alaska is the long-route ferry service provided by the state, the Alaska Marine Highway. Residents of the little towns served by the "Highway" see nothing strange about its name. To them it is the only surface transportation out of their communities. The $30 million deficit experienced by the "Highway" each year is looked upon by those served as an expense to be borne by the state the same as paid for road construction and maintenance. A fleet of nine large ferryliners, each costing about $50 million, transports passengers and vehicles within Southeast Alaska and within certain portions of Central and Southwest Alaska. The system also connects Southeast Alaska with Prince Rupert, British Columbia, and with Seattle, Washington. Ferry terminals are interconnected by computer.

Almost 300,000 passengers and 70,000 vehicles travel the highways along twenty-seven hundred miles of coastline each year. Most of the ferries are huge, carrying about five hundred passengers and 110 cars. Staterooms, lounges, solaria, and cafeterias make them like a cruise ship minus the hoopla and continuous entertainment. The food served is solid fare, the menus put together by the head cook on duty. Food prices are high by lower-forty-eight standards. Ferry fares are reasonable and are reduced by 25 percent between October 1 and May 15. Persons over sixty-five, Alaskan or not, can ride free during this off season. Of all visitors to Alaska 10 to 12 percent come by ferry. Attesting to the popularity of the system is the fact that reservations for the summer season must be received before January.

A jet foil is scheduled for appearance in the Inland Passage, the area used by the ferries. The jet foil, traveling at fifty knots, will be on trial and can reduce the eighteen-hour travel time between Ketchikan and Juneau by two-thirds.

Move away from the coast into Central Alaska and winter temperatures drop into the minus forty-degree range.

With half of Alaska's population, Anchorage is Alaska's only real city. In this relatively sophisticated metropolis, a diner can find two truffled chocolates for $3 on the menu in at least one elegant restaurant. On Cook Inlet, the Japanese current spares it the severe winter weather of the interior. Anchorage has eighteen hotels/motels and 118 restaurants. Juneau, the state capital, is a town of nineteen thousand. Fairbanks, the trade and transportation center of the interior, has twenty-six thousand. Ketchikan and Sitka both have about eight thousand residents.

Of the several villages and towns served by the Alaska Marine Highway Sitka stands out. Picture-postcard beautiful, it is protected from the open sea behind a series of islands. Sitka presents a new face. During the past three decades fires have leveled much of the downtown area so that most of the buildings are new. This includes the simple little Russian Orthodox church, an architecturally balanced beauty. Sitka also has one of the more attractive climates in Alaska even though it receives ninety-four inches of rain a year. The most historically interesting of Alaskan towns, it was there that Russia had its capital of its American territory. On a hill in Sitka one of the greatest real estate coups in history took place when the U.S. purchased what is now Alaska for two cents an acre. Vestiges of Russian influence can be seen in the church, the bishop's palace, and in the sprightly Russian dances performed for tourists.

The graphics of Alaskan tourism center on the totem pole, that expression of the woodcarver unique to the natives of the northwestern U.S., British Columbia and Alaska. Paris has its Eiffel Tower, London its Big Ben clock. Alaska has its totem poles. The totem pole takes on a character almost as pervasive in today's tourist Alaska as was true in the native villages of the last century. They blazon tourist literature, enliven hotel lobbies and brochures and are prominently displayed in almost every museum.

The original totem poles were commissioned by families or chiefs to commemorate an event, to make a statement, and sometimes to deride another family who failed an obligation, such as nonpayment of a debt. The old photographs showed numbers of totem poles standing before waterside villages facing toward the sea, the first thing seen by a visitor. Clan symbols like the raven, the eagle, and the frog stare out from the poles. Some poles told a story. Bold in color and striking in design, the totem pole message is read from the top down. Today the totem pole is a kind of logo for Alaska.

Totem poles, some as tall as thirty feet, can be seen near Ketchikan at Totem Bight State Historical Park and at Saxman Village, next to Ketchikan. In Ketchikan itself the city finances a Totem Heritage Center where totem poles and other examples of totemic art have been collected from village sites where the damp climate was causing rapid decay. Sitka, too, has a National Historic Park and an Indian Culture Center. The Alaska State Museum in Juneau also displays totemic art.

Alaskans look upon themselves as a special group, frontierspeople separated from the "lower forty-eight." When they go south it is "going outside." Only five-and-one-half hours north of Hawaii, many Alaskans vacation in Hawaii, especially on Maui. Long-time

FIGURE 2.7 *Alaskan logo.* Totem poles are the informal Alaskan logo, vestiges of a unique native culture that thrived up until the turn of the century. The boldly carved images tell a story, commemorate an event or send a message.

residents take pride in being Alaskans and do not look kindly on transients who come to Alaska only for high wages.

Alaska has one popular ski area, Mt. Alyeska Resort. It is on 4000-foot Mt. Alyeska, forty miles south of Anchorage. Since the area gets only a few hours of daylight in mid-winter, several of the slopes are lighted. The resort is owned by Seibu Alaska, an Alaskan subsidiary of a Japanese conglomerate.

One of the great rail trips can be taken between Anchorage and Fairbanks via the Alaska Railroad. The train passes through Denali National Park and Preserve, Alaska's best known wilderness recreation area. Traveling the Park road almost assures the visitor of seeing grizzly bears, moose, fox, caribou or sheep. Mount McKinley dominates the area and well it should. From base to summit it is the tallest mountain in the world (the Himalayas start at higher elevations).

From Anchorage to Fairbanks, trains run daily from mid-May through mid-September. Once-a-week service is available during the winter months. Tourists usually break up the trip by stopping at Denali Park for a day or two.

3

MEXICO

Aficionados of Mexico proclaim it to be the destination to end all destinations: a land of contrasts and wonder, offering beaches, mountains and fascinating Indian ruins—inexpensive, colorful—the land of friendly people, exciting food and drink. The detractors reply: Yes, the food is exciting, especially when loaded with E.coli germs that cause uninterrupted diarrhea and vomiting. Some people are not very friendly, certainly not the police on the take, where justice seems more related to influence than reason. It is the land of the "mordida," the payoff, where bribery is a way of life. A land of contrast between the very rich who care very little for the masses of the very poor. All of this is true.

As of 1983 the Mexican peso had fallen drastically and the American dollar made Mexico a travel bargain. Public transportation, including air, bus and rail within the country, was ridiculously cheap. Travel expenses within Mexico vary widely from time to time. Every few years the government devalues the currency and for a while Mexico becomes a real travel bargain. Inflation then again appears, pushing up the prices.

After Canada, Mexico is the most visited foreign country by North Americans. Some sixty-five million Americans pour across the border to taste a different culture, to shop and to sin. About four million North Americans visit Mexico each year for longer stays and leave about $2 billion. Tourists favor the Mexican Riviera, the warm-weather beach cities stretching from Mazatlan in the north to Acapulco in the south. Americans also visit what may be the world's largest city, Mexico City, called simply "Mexico" by the Mexicans. Sitting out in the Gulf of Mexico on the Yucatan Peninsula is Cancun, newest of the beach resorts, another favorite.

Mexico, the third largest in size of the Latin American nations (after Brazil and Argentina), is second largest in population, about seventy-two million, and growing rapidly. Though it has vast oil reserves Mexico has tremendous debts, about $80 billion in 1983. Paradoxically the discovery of these large oil and gas reserves only hastened Mexico's descent into debt. International bankers relied on the petroleum reserves as collateral as the Mexican government built huge public works and created a monstrous bureaucracy. Little of oil income ever reaches the masses. Corruption is rife. Politicians routinely syphon off

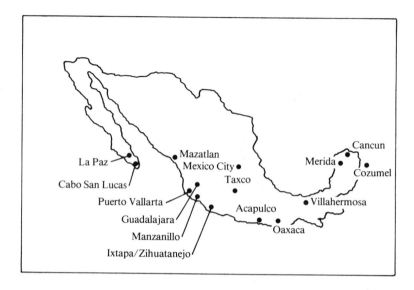

FIGURE 3.1   *Map of Mexico with major cities noted.*

fortunes while in office, unmindful that most people are desperately poor and large numbers malnourished. About half the working population are either unemployed or underemployed. In 1950 two-thirds of the population was rural; today two-thirds is urban.

On weekends day-trippers form lines several blocks long going into and coming from Tijuana and other border towns. As recently as 1920 Tijuana was a small town, and during prohibition in this country Tijuana was a place for border residents to get a drink. Then it was simply called El Rancho de Tia Juana (Aunt Jane's Ranch). Today, thanks to tourism and proximity to San Diego its population is close to one million. The city offers bullfights, dog races and a radical change in culture. The same is true of Juarez, across the border from San Antonio, Texas, and to a lesser degree, the smaller American/Mexican border towns.

A number of U.S. residents take the highway from Tijuana south to Ensenada. A smaller number continue south through Loreto and into La Paz on the narrow highway that extends to the southern tip of Baja California. These are the adventuresome and fishermen. At the tip of Baja California is Cabo San Lucas, with a few first-class hotels that mostly attract the addicted fishermen.

Mexico City is the primary city of Mexico, headquarters for government, industry and banking. It attracts some three million North Americans each year; business travel to Mexico City grows each year. At about eight thousand feet, the city is never hot. The burgeoning population is believed to exceed fifteen million people, which the city is ill-equipped to handle.

Major attractions are the Anthropological Museum, Chapaultepec Castle, built by Emperor Maximillian during his brief reign in the 1860s, and the stupendous pyramids, San Juan de Tehauntepec, thirty-five miles north of the city. One guidebook comments "to miss them would be like visiting Egypt and not seeing the pyramids there." The word "massive" is often loosely used, but not in connection with these pyramids. The Pyramid of the Sun, the larger of the two main pyramids, sits on a base 750 feet square and rises 215 feet. It was built between 400 and 800 A.D. as a city. It is believed the builders, the Toltecs, migrated to Yucatan and merged with the Mayas there. A light and sound program is offered in the evening during the dry season.

The National Museum of Anthropology, beautifully designed, is fascinating to even the non-museum-goer. To many people it is the finest in the world. A series of chambers circling a patio, the museum portrays the various civilizations of Mexico, including the Toltecs, the Olmecs, the Mayans and the Aztecs. The second floor is set up to exhibit life-size replicas of rural village life.

For evening entertainment most visitors to Mexico City head for the Zona Rosa (the pink zone), the swinging section of Mexico, with eighteen hotels, some two hundred restaurants, and four hundred shops. Each Mexican town has a Zocolo, the town plaza. The one in Mexico City is second in size only to Red Square in the Soviet Union.

During the busy part of the day Mexico City is a nightmare as regards traffic. Even the side streets are clogged. For lack of parking space car owners park their cars on the sidewalks. The Paseo de la Reforma is the most impressive of the city's boulevards.

Church lovers will want to visit the Guadeloupe Shrine, holiest of the Catholic churches in Mexico.

The bullfights are a major part of the Mexican entertainment scene, part sport, part ritual, a place to vent primitive passions. For some the bullfight is an art-form; for others it serves a function similar to professional football. (Other principal towns and cities have their own corridos, bullfighting stadiums, where toreadors become national heroes, or die trying.)

Jai-alai games provide an outlet for gambling. For more placid enjoyment there are the Floating Gardens of Xochimilco, a reminder of the days when Mexico City, under the Aztecs, was a series of islands in a lake.

Mexico City's climate is notably affected by the mountains that control rainfall and temperature. Rains come in the summer. The rest of the year the place ranks with Los Angeles and Tokyo as smog capitals of the world.

The Valley of Mexico (or Anahuac), the great basin in which Mexico City lies, is about 96×46 kilometers, bounded by mountains on three sides. The snowcapped peaks of Popocateptl (5,414 m) and Iztaccihuatl (5,286 m) can be seen in the distance. (Pronounce their names correctly and you win a free bicycle trip to Mexico.) Much of the area is an old lake bed without underlying bedrock. The unstable subsoil and the volcanic nature of the region accounts for the earthquakes experienced there and for the fact that Mexico City continues to sink.

Number one destination for sun lovers in Mexico is Acapulco. After Mexico City it is the number two Mexican destination for North Americans. For several centuries Acapulco was a sleepy little port town connected by a poor road to Mexico City. When Miguel Aleman became Mexican president, Acapulco sprang to life. A heavy investor in Acapulco real estate, Aleman funneled government money to that city for roads and other infrastructure. The highway is called Costera Miguel Aleman after the former president. He was the most prominent personage connected with tourism in Mexico.

In the 1960s and early 1970s Acapulco flourished. Then it began to die as tens of thousands of Mexico's poor came to live on the sides of the hills that look down on Acapulco Bay. The Bay itself became polluted with the city's garbage and sewage. Visitors lying on the beach were besieged by hundreds of souvenir sellers.

Again the government stepped in. The squatters, tens of thousands of them, were moved to the other side of the hills, while in their place a magnificent visitors and convention center was built, perhaps the most attractive of any convention center in the world. Continuous entertainment, restaurants, and craft shops are part of the center. The main streets were widened, beach pollution stopped, and Acapulco is alive again. The spectacular Princess Hotel, built like a pyramid, is a complete lodging and entertainment complex with air-conditioned tennis courts, restaurants and enormous swimming pools. It is located on the road to the airport. (Don't try the beach; it is dangerous.) Las Brisas, now under Westin Hotels management, is another memorable hotel with dozens of individual rooms spaced on the sides of a hill. All overlook Acapulco Bay; most have their own swimming pools, albeit small ones.

A glance at the climate chart shows that the best time of year to visit Acapulco is from December through April when the place is warm, but not hot, and dry. May through October brings heavy rainfall and high temperatures. Even the ocean temperature is too warm to be pleasant for many people until November.

With Acapulco as the southern base, other coastal towns turned to tourism—Ixtapa/Zihuatanejo, Manzanilla, Puerto Vallarta and Mazatlan. Together they form the Mexican Riviera, warm the year-round. After Acapulco, Puerto Vallarta (P.V.) is the most popular. These coastal cities vibrate with visitors during the winter. Over Christmas and Easter, Mexicans come from Mexico City to take their vacations. The weather is warm and humid. During the summer the weather becomes hot, the humidity oppressive.

Las Hadas (the fairies), near Manzanillo, is an oddity in hoteldom, a hotel of Moorish design, built by a rich Bolivian, sitting on a Mexican bay. It is described as "an elegant preserve for the privileged enjoying their privileges." Included are a two-hundred-room hotel, a large condominium development, golf courses, and a yacht club cum marina.

Club Mediterranee has two "villages" on the Mexican Riviera, both substantial and attractive: one near Ixtapa, 130 miles north of Acapulco; the other near Manzanillo.

Visitors from all parts of the U.S. and Canada make up most of Mexico's tourists and they have been going to Mexico's west coast since the 1960s. Much closer for those from the Eastern Seaboard, the Midwest and the South is Cancun, sitting on the tip of the Yucatan Peninsula, as it reaches into the Gulf of Mexico. Cancun is the first of the "computer planned" resorts developed by Fonatur (The National Fund for Tourist Development) and financed by that agency. This luxury spa is a series of widely separated hotels on an island connected by causeway to Yucatan. Unlike Acapulco, which is pressed by a huge population nearby, Cancun has its own Cancun City, located on the mainland, where the personnel operating the Cancun hotels and resorts reside. Cancun has received uniform praise for its location and beauty. The palm-lined beach—twelve miles long—is close enough to Mayan ruins to give the resort goer intellectual stimulation as well as the chance to swim and dive in the pellucid waters of the Gulf of Mexico. Antiquarians can spend weeks examining the ruins of MesoAmerican civilization constructed across the Yucatan Peninsula and in Guatemala, Honduras, El Salvador, and Belize. Excavation is continuing to unearth magnificent towns and cities all built, it is believed, before 900 A.D. According to scholars these ruins were the centerpieces of large, highly structured communities, some with a population of 100,000 persons, cities that carried on trade with each other as well as being agricultural and religious centers.

Merida, capital of the Yucatan, is the usual base for viewing the Mexican Mayan ruins. Chichen Itza and Uxmal are the best known and the most visited because they are relatively close to Merida and Cancun. If the visitor has time for only one Mayan ruin, Chichen Itza, seventy-five miles east of Merida, near the tip of the Yucatan Peninsula, should be the choice. From Cancun, Chichen Itza is forty-five minutes by plane. This archeological site encompasses hundreds of buildings and covers three square miles. The city represents the peak of Mayan/Toltec civilization. So strong was the belief in the hereafter among those who built the great stone temples at Chichen Itza that the prize of the captain of the winning team was to have his head cut off.

Uxmal, forty-eight miles south of Merida, is considered second only to Chichen Itza and has the most impressive Mayan structure in existence, the colossal "Palace of the Governor." Tulum, the only Mayan ruin on the coast, is close enough to Cancun for a day-trip of viewing.

Palenque, in the Mexican state of Chiapas, is said to be the most beautiful of the Mayan ruins. Palenque is 399 miles from Merida over a new paved road, or the visitor can fly to Villahermosa, ninety miles northwest of Palenque. Similar archeological sites are found in northern Guatemala (Tikal is most grand). Copan is in Honduras.

About twenty miles south of Cancun is the island of Cozumel ("Island of Swallows" in the Mayan language), where a sleepy style of tourism has developed. Cozumel has an international airport. Several flights a day connect the two islands as does a service by hydrofoil. Cozumel is mostly tangled jungle, flat, nine by twenty-nine miles. The visitor can scoot around the island's one highway on a rented moped and snorkel or scuba dive among the coral reefs just offshore.

Guadalajara is Mexico's second largest city, population one and three-quarters million. Again because of its altitude, 1,567 meters, it has a pleasant climate, warmer than Mexico City, with the same dry winters and wet summers.

South of Mexico City, still in the mountains, are Cuernavaca, Taxco and Oaxaca. From Mexico City Cuernavaca takes about an hour-and-a-half. Cuernavaca (kwehr-nah-VAH-cah), capital of the State of Morelos, is a summer capital for vacationers from Mexico City. Winters are dry while summer brings rain. Taxco is ninety minutes farther south from Cuernavaca and known for its silver-working craftsmen. Few know that it was a young American writer who was largely responsible for getting the silver craft started back in 1929. Declared a national monument, the town will retain its colonial character because modern structures are prohibited.

Oaxaca (pronounced wah-ha-cah), the farthest south most North Americans go in Mexico, has been called a "Mexican Classic," an Indian city, with another massive ruin, Monte Alban. The ruins, once a community center for perhaps fifty thousand people, overlook Oaxaca.

San Miguel de Allende, another tourist town, is an art center in the mountains east of Mexico City on the road to Guanajuato, the old silver-mining center.

Fonatur, the government tourism development agency, is developing another resort area south of Acapulco, Escondido. As yet there are no good roads or airport in the area. In Baja California, Loreto, on the Gulf of Cortez, has one El Presidente Hotel, one of the twenty-five-unit chain of hotels operated by the Mexican government. Loreto is about halfway down Baja, and is served by Aeromexico, the government-owned airline. Loreto is scheduled for further development by Fonatur.

Air transport to and within Mexico is well developed. Major airports are at Acapulco, Mexico City, Puerto Vallarta and Guadalajara in the Central region; La Paz, Mazatlan, and Tijuana in the North Pacific; Monterrey in the North; and Merida in the Gulf Coast region. Most are spacious and attractive, many with marble flooring. In all, the government owns two hundred airfields. Mexico has two international air carriers, Aeromexico, government owned, and Mexicana, privately owned. Mexicana is by far the more efficiently operated. Both airlines schedule numerous flights within Mexico and some to United States cities. A number of United States air carriers have flights into Mexico, especially to the resort communities on the Pacific, to Mexico City and to Cancun.

Mexico's railroads do not amount to much, even by Amtrak standards. First-class means you get to sit down; second-class probably means a space in an aisle unless the traveler arrives first via a window. Second-class means that animals, such as chickens and goats, are on an equal basis with people when it comes to space. "Rapido" does not mean "rapid," as intended. The run from Nogales to Mazatlan on the "Rapido" takes twenty-two hours. The American students using the train during spring holidays think of it as a great lark. And so it is! Because of the peso devaluation the cost of the trip in 1983 was only $22. If all first-class seats are sold out, the middle-class Mexican accepts the necessity of bribing the conductor to acquire a seat.

The rail system is an integrated network of six different lines, five of which are government owned. The railroad connects with the United States at the north region cities of Ciudad Juarez, Laredo, Piedras Negras, Reynosa, and Matamoros. Central American connections are via Guatemala.

Trolleys still operate in Mexico City, Veracruz and some other cities.

TRAVEL BY ROAD

Mexico has several top-notch highways, especially those around and radiating from Mexico City. Altogether Mexico has a network of 125,000 miles of paved roads. A central super-highway runs straight up and down the center of Mexico. Except for these well maintained and much traveled roads, the visitor is urged to avoid nighttime auto travel. Cattle find the paved roads warm and comfortable for bedding down for the night. As a rule the roads are not as well marked as in the U.S. Signing for turns may consist only of city or town names.

A narrow highway runs the length of Baja California, a road not to be undertaken lightly because of the long distances without services and the possiblity of breakdown. It is for the fisherman, hunter and adventuresome. Winding down the eight-hundred-mile peninsula, the road covers eleven hundred miles. For long stretches it is only 19½ feet wide, often without shoulders. Trucks and bus drivers sometimes barrel down the road. Let the car driver beware! "Green Angels," government vehicles painted green, cruise the road twice a day, between 9 a.m. and 9 p.m., servicing travelers with car problems at no charge. MEX. I, the major route down the Baja peninsula, can be covered in as few as three days. The traveler passes a few small towns going south, Santa Rosalia, Mulege, Loreto, then La Paz. At the southern tip of Baja is Cabo San Lucas, a luxury resort destination.

Five other main highways enter Mexico from U.S. border towns: MEX 2, Nogales–Mexico City; MEX 45, the Pan-American Highway, El Paso–Mexico City; Eagle Pass–Mexico City; MEX 85, Laredo or Brownsville–Mexico City and Brownsville–Mazatlan.

In reaching Mexico City from the U.S. the motorist climbs to altitudes over two thousand meters. The Nogales–Mexico City road reaches 3,060 meters.

Special auto insurance is a must. Without it the traveler may find himself in jail if involved in an accident, guilty or not. Even with the insurance the writer's experience in dealing with one Mexican travel insurance company was anything but satisfactory. In Mexico anyone involved in an accident is deemed guilty until proven otherwise. Comprehensive insurance coverage by a Mexican insurance company may mean repairs must be made within Mexico or reimbursement for repair costs done in the U.S. is based on what the repairs would have cost in Mexico.

Bizarre tales are told about shakedowns experienced by auto travelers in Mexico. On an icy road a car slips off the road and is impounded by the police. They refuse to release it until the owner pays a $500 fine for "damaging the highway." A child runs onto a road and is hit by a car despite the driver's efforts to avoid the child. The car driver is held until nearly all of his possessions are paid over to the police and to lawyers. A car stopped at an intersection is hit by another car coming from the opposite direction. The police arrive and instruct the innocent victim to follow the police car to the police station. The police roar off amidst a city's congested area leaving the victim to speed after or be lost. This victim and his family were detained in the police station for four hours. Traffic violations are fined at a flexible rate depending on what the violator is believed to be able to pay.

Truck drivers sometimes enjoy playing the game of "chicken" with auto drivers. The game involves scaring the wits out of the other driver by forcing him off the road, not permitting him to pass, and worse.

Again, it is not wise to drive anywhere in Mexico after dark. An American who has been involved in an accident, guilty or not, can be detained for days. Part of the detainment is a ploy to shake down the visitor for money.

As in the U.S. there are plenty of ambulance-chasing lawyers who, when an accident occurs, are on hand to extract the maximum amount possible from the tourist. Some old Mexican hands, persons who have lived in Mexico for some time, declare, "If involved in an accident, don't stop, and drive like hell." An extensive bus system also provides services throughout the country and to and from the United States. The buses are usually so crowded that not many North Americans take them.

In many small villages, some still not reachable by road, the natives speak only their Indian tongues. About one million of the sixty-eight million population are of pure Spanish descent. About half the rest are pure Indian, the remainder a mixture of Indian and Spanish.

Politically, Mexico comprises thirty-one states plus the federal district. Population is about seventy million and growing fast. (Only forty years ago the population was about thirty-five million.)

Geographically Mexico is part of North America even though the Mexicans refer to U.S. residents as "Norte Americanos." Its extensive coastline borders the Pacific on the

FIGURE 3.2 *Map of Mexico.*

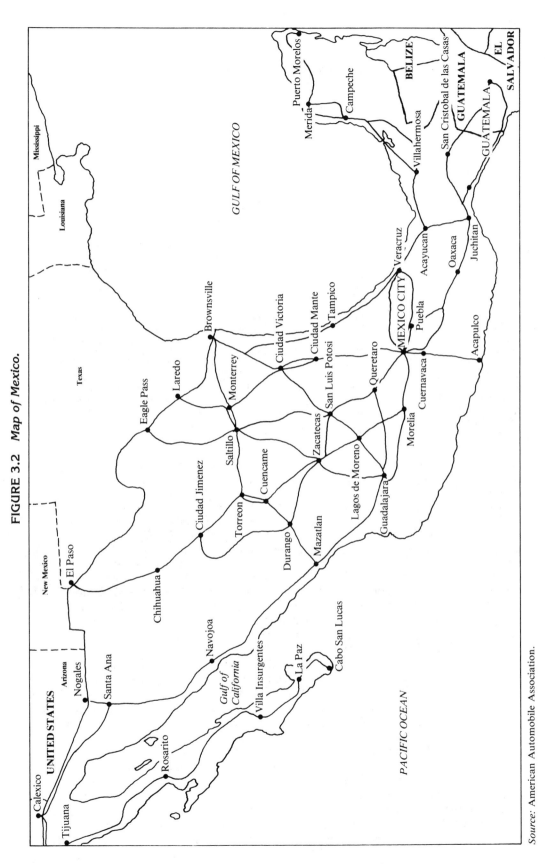

Source: American Automobile Association.

FIGURE 3.3   *Some information about Mexican states.*

State	Abbreviations	Area (square kms.)	Population	Capital
Aguascalientes	Ags.	5,471	504,300	Aguascalientes
Baja California Nte.	B.C.	69,921	1,320,000	Mexicali
Baja California Sur	B.C.S	73,475	188,000	La Paz
Campeche	Camp.	50,812	349,000	Campeche
Chiapas	Chis.	74,211	1,984,000	Tuxtla Gutierrez
Chihuahua	Chih.	244,938	2,062,000	Chihuahua
Coahuila	Coah.	149,982	1,364,000	Saltilo
Colima	Col.	5,191	332,000	Colima
Distrito Federal	D.F.	1,479	9,377,300	Mexico City
Durango	Dgo.	123,181	1,149,000	Durango
Guanajuato	Gto.	30,941	2,896,000	Guanajuato
Guerrero	Gro.	64,281	2,075,000	Chilpancingo
Hidalgo	Hgo.	20,813	1,435,000	Pachuca
Jalisco	Jal.	80,836	4,294,000	Guadalajara
Mexico	Mex.	21,355	6,684,000	Toluca
Michoacan	Mich.	59,928	2,873,000	Morelia
Morelos	Mor.	4,950	906,000	Cuernavaca
Nayarit	Nay.	26,979	725,000	Tepic
Nuevo Leon	N.L.	64,924	2,457,000	Monterrey
Oaxaca	Oax.	93,952	2,378,000	Oaxaca
Puebla	Pue.	33,902	3,133,000	Puebla
Queretaro	Qro.	11,449	639,000	Queretaro
Quintana Roo	Q.R.	50,212	139,000	Chetumal
San Luis Potosi	S.L.P.	63,068	1,561,000	San Luis Potosi
Sinaloa	Sin.	58,328	1,787,000	Culiacan
Sonora	Son.	182,052	1,468,000	Hermosillo
Tabasco	Tab.	25,267	1,101,000	Villahermosa
Tamaulipas	Tamps.	79,384	1,969,000	Ciudad Victoria
Tlaxcala	Tlax.	4,016	512,000	Tlaxcala
Veracruz	Ver.	71,699	5,091,000	Jalapa
Yucatan	Yuc.	38,402	926,000	Merida
Zacatecas	Zac.	73,252	1,115,000	Zacatecas

Source: Mexican Government Bureau of Statistics, 1980 census.

west and the Gulf of Mexico and the Caribbean on the east. The Sierra Madre mountains dominate the topography. In the southern state of Oaxaca the Sierra Madre divides and runs northward. The Sierra Madre Oriental mountains form the eastern edge, the Sierra Madre Occidental mountains the western edge of the high central plateau region, where most of the population, government, and industry takes place. Hundreds of volcanic peaks punctuate the landscape while deep valleys and canyons support luxurious vegetation. In the south Mexico borders Guatemala and Belize (formerly British Honduras).

The river system is relatively insignificant for such a large country. The Rio Grande moves down from Texas. Other rivers are the Coalzacoalcos, in the isthmus region; the Grijalva, which moves out of Guatemala; and the Balsas, which rises in the state of Tlaxcala. None of the rivers is navigable for any length.

Mexico has only two lakes of any size, Lake Chapala, the largest, and Lake Patzcuaro. Near Chapala a sizable number of North Americans have retired. Lake Patzcuaro has several Tarascan villages on its shores, accessible only by water.

During summer and winter both coasts are subject to hurricanes. The most common hurricane path circles clockwise across the Caribbean Sea allowing storms to batter the Mexican coast and then continue, with diminished fury, to Texas coastal cities.

Characteristic plants of Mexico include cacti, one type of which is used for making the well-known alcoholic beverage, tequila. The town of Tequila gives the beverage its name. The cactus' inclusion on the Mexican coat of arms testifies to its importance.

The turkey buzzard, a useful scavenger, is Mexico's most familiar large bird; the small Mexican eagle is the country's national symbol. Parrots, parakeets, and macaws are plentiful in the southern tropical lowlands.

Much of Mexico's scenery is stark and barren because of the near desert-like conditions. Only about 10 percent of the country gets adequate rainfall throughout the year. Even so, during the rainy season in the summer, rain can deluge the roads and countryside. "Sunny Mexico" does not apply during the rainy season. In winter months it is quite possible to slip off a mountain road in the State of Chihuahua because of icy conditions.

Baja California is one of the world's most important sanctuaries for marine animals. Elephant seals make their home at Guadalupe Island in the Pacific Ocean, and gray whales mate and nurse only in the Gulf of California.

Mexico offers striking contrasts in climate and topography. Beautiful coastlines, steaming jungles, towering mountains and high plateaus are all there.

The country's sixteen-hundred-mile boundary with the United States meanders along the Rio Grande River from the Gulf of Mexico west to El Paso, Texas, continuing along the state lines of New Mexico, Arizona and California to the Pacific.

Mexico is a land of few cities and a multitude of villages. Typically the villages have a central plaza, a town hall, a parish church, a bandstand, a well, and one or two stores. The large cities have a large "zocolo," town square.

Most Mexicans live in the highlands because the high elevation offers a good climate. Since pre-Columbian times, the population of tropical Mexico has been concentrated at elevations above three-thousand feet. The northern half of Mexico lies outside the tropics, the southern half within. The climate varies as much with altitude as with degree of latitude, however. In Mexico City the temperature averages about sixty degrees the year-round and there is light but adequate rainfall. Only ten degrees separate the temperatures in the warmest month from those of the coldest. Throughout the year the daytime temperatures remain pleasant while evenings and nights are cool.

The climate chart of Mexico in Figure 3.4 shows average temperatures (given in Celsius) and rainfall (given in centimeters) for each month. The conversion table for changing Censius into Fahrenheit is pictured in Figure 3.5.

THE SOCIAL SYSTEM

Knowing a little about Mexico's social system makes the people more understandable. Mexico has a highly stratified class system: the Indian peasant at the bottom; a relatively small middle class of professional people, military officers, middle class bureaucrats; and at the top, a small number of rich, an oligarchy of politicians, industrialists and large landowners who control the country. The president of Mexico has vast powers for a period of six years. Similarly the state governors have power undreamed of by their counterparts in the U.S. The extended family is the group to which the individual owes first loyalty. Since there is no social security system as part of government, the family takes care of its own, and as a result is more important to the individual.

Bribery and corruption are denounced but are more or less accepted as part of life. The average Mexican is poor, possibly malnourished and stoical. Bureaucrats feel underpaid and in return work as little as possible. The upper class Mexican tends to be shrewd, proud and self-seeking.

Upper class Mexicans, like most of Latin America's upper class, are much aware of their Spanish heritage. They are lavish hosts and if their visitor is really accepted are loyal friends. In business relations, North Americans are urged to get all agreements in writing and, if possible, payment in advance or guaranteed by a bank. "Influence" based on friendship or deals is very important in getting things done. "Manana," putting things off until tomorrow, is commonplace. The old Latin hand accepts the fact that running things by the clock is not esteemed the way it is in the industrialized world. Appointments and other engagements are not really expected to occur at the scheduled time. Social relations

FIGURE 3.4 Climate chart of Mexico.

	January		February		March		April		May		June		July		August		September		October		November		December	
	Temp.	Rainfall	Temp.	Rainfall	Temp.	Rainfall	Temp.	Rainfall	Temp.	Rainfall	Temp.	Rainfall	Temp.	Rainfall	Temp.	Rainfall	Temp.	Rainfall	Temp.	Rainfall	Temp.	Rainfall	Temp.	Rainfall
Acapulco, Gro.	26	1	26	—	26	—	27	—	29	30	29	44	29	22	29	25	28	36	28	17	27	3	26	1
Ciudad Juarez, Chic.	6	—	9	1	12	1	18	1	21	2	26	1	27	3	26	3	22	3	17	3	10	1	6	1
Cuernavaca, Mor.	18	—	20	—	21	—	22	1	24	5	21	20	20	22	20	22	20	25	20	8	20	1	19	—
Chihuahua, Chih.	10	—	11	—	15	1	18	1	24	1	26	3	25	8	24	9	22	9	18	4	13	1	10	2
Ensenada, B.C.	12	8	13	7	15	3	15	3	17	1	18	—	20	—	21	—	20	—	17	2	16	2	14	7
Guadalajara, Jal.	15	2	16	—	18	—	21	—	22	2	22	19	21	25	20	20	20	18	18	5	16	2	15	2
Guanajuato, Gto.	14	1	16	1	18	—	20	—	22	3	20	14	19	18	19	14	18	15	17	5	16	2	15	2
Guaymas, Son.	18	1	19	—	21	—	23	—	26	—	29	—	31	5	31	8	30	5	27	1	22	1	18	3
Manzanillo, Col.	24	2	24	1	24	—	25	—	26	—	27	10	29	14	27	19	27	39	26	6	26	1	25	5
Mazatlan, Sin.	20	1	20	1	20	—	21	—	24	—	26	3	27	17	27	24	27	27	26	10	24	1	21	4
Merida, Yuc.	23	3	24	2	26	2	27	3	28	8	27	15	27	14	27	13	27	15	26	3	24	3	24	3
Mexico, D.F.	12	1	13	1	16	1	17	1	18	—	17	11	16	12	16	10	16	12	15	3	13	2	12	1
Monterrey, N.L.	15	2	17	2	20	2	24	3	26	4	27	8	27	7	28	6	26	21	22	11	17	3	14	2
Oaxaca, Oax.	17	—	19	—	21	1	22	3	23	6	22	12	21	9	21	10	21	17	20	4	18	3	18	1
Tampico, Tamps.	18	5	20	2	22	1	25	1	27	5	28	20	28	15	28	15	27	34	26	18	22	6	20	4
Veracruz, Ver.	21	2	22	2	23	1	25	2	26	5	27	27	27	35	27	30	27	35	26	15	24	9	22	2

Temperatures are expressed in degrees Celsius, rainfall in centimeters. Figures represent official monthly average means over a 5-year period.

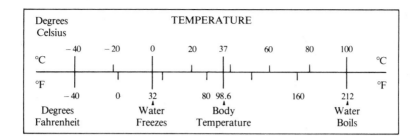

FIGURE 3.5   *Conversion table from Celsius into Fahrenheit.*

often override business relations in business discussions. "Machismo," an overemphasis on manliness, may lead to what people from other cultures think is ridiculous or bizarre behavior. The matador, the cult hero, is "muy macho," very brave. A man's sense of masculinity, his sense of "dignidad," ranks high in the person's sense of worth, and is something to be protected at all costs. Among men who can afford it the practice of keeping a mistress is part of the person's need to show his masculinity.

MEXICAN FOOD

Mexican food has been a part of the cookery of the American Southwest since all of that area, including California, was settled by Spanish-Mexicans long before the "Anglos" arrived. Restaurant chains featuring Mexican food with its comparatively low prices and zesty flavor have accelerated its popularity. If the trend continues, the taco and burrito could become as well-known as the hamburger, French fries and milkshakes. Connoisseurs of food are aware that Mexico's food offers a wide range of items, based on rice, beans, corn, chilies and lard, with which meat is used sparingly.

When the conquistador Cortez marched into Mexico he found the native Indians living around a corn, bean, and cocoa food economy. Chocolate, peanuts, and vanilla were new to Spaniards. A protein-poor cuisine, it was supplemented occasionally by eating dogs and one's enemies.

Today's gastronomical map of Mexico shows a widely varied and elaborate cookery incorporating fish, seafood, pork, chicken, cheese, goat, and beef. Just about every Mexican dish begins with a tortilla, originally made from cornmeal pounded out on a metate (flat stone) and shaped by hand. Today's tortilla is factory made, whether from flour or cornmeal. Eaten like bread, it is also used like a pancake or crepe as a base for a variety of items.

Deep-fried and U-shaped it becomes a taco, filled with combinations of hamburger, rice, beans, cheese, lettuce, or cheese. A smaller taco is a taquito.

Deep-fried flat and piled high with such items as beans, cheese, meat, mounds of shredded lettuce, diced tomato, avocado slices, and olives, it becomes a tostada.

Enchiladas are tortillas filled with meat or cheese, rolled up and deep-fried.

The burrito is usually a soft tortilla (not fried) filled with beans, meat, or cheese or combinations of the three.

Mexican meal service varies considerably from that north of the border. Mexicans start work early and take time out for the main meal of the day around 2:00 p.m. The ambitious middle-class Mexican is back, hard at work again, in the evening, probably until 8:00 p.m. The evening meal is not served until around 8:00 or 9:00 p.m., sometimes later.

Frothy hot chocolate, chocolate Mexicano, is a beverage not to be overlooked. Steaks are popular with visitors, but are most likely to be tough, even stringy, because the cattle from which they come are likely grass fed.

The quesadilla is a soft taco with cheese and green chili, usually served with rice and beans.

A tamale is corndough (masa) wrapped around mildly spiced bits of meat and chili sauce, then cooked by steam.

Nachos are tortilla chips which can be spread with melted cheese or other items such as tomato bits, onions, and peppers.

"Real" Mexican food is cooked in lard and often seasoned with cilantro (seeds of cilantro are coriander). For maximum flavor, most Mexican food must be served hot, on a hot plate.

Some Mexican dishes are not popular with tourists: "menudo," tripe soup, is an example.

In the typical Mexican restaurant, the hacienda-style building with colorful tiled fountains and bars, lots of reds and browns produce a gala atmosphere. Mariachi music livens the place.

Ironically the leading restaurants in Mexico City are likely to feature French menu items.

Tequila, made from one variety of the cactus plant, was once considered a peasant drink. Now it is one of the most popular of strong spirits in the U.S. and is the number one drink in Mexican restaurants. Mescal, also made from the cactus plant, is drunk mainly by the country people, the "campesinos." Beer is the other widely popular alcoholic beverage, and is favored by many tourists as a way to avoid drinking contaminated water.

To help avoid contracting diarrhea and other food and beverage-born diseases, visitors to Mexico and most less developed nations can take these precautions:

1. Eat only food which has been thoroughly cooked and, hopefully, not contaminated by food handlers prior to service. Avoid any uncooked food, such as pork, which may harbor the trichinosis worm, which gets into the blood stream and fastens onto the muscle tissue. Meat, not completely cooked, may harbor a tape worm whose larvae can migrate through the blood stream and lodge in the brain. When this happens there is no known cure.
2. For beverages, drink only water which has been boiled for at least fifteen minutes or which has been purified by a halogen tablet according to instructions. Drink only pasteurized milk and/or well-accepted bottled drinks such as Coca-Cola. Drink beer or wine, which are self-purifying because of acidity or alcohol present.
3. If the water supply is unsafe, so too are the ice cubes made from the water.
4. Don't forget that the water condensation on the outside of cans or bottles can be contaminated by the ice in which it has been packed. Dry them before opening and pouring.
5. To purify suspect water, use ten drops of 1 percent bleach per quart of water if the water looks clear, and twenty drops if it is cloudy. Let it stand for thirty minutes. If you don't detect a slight chlorine odor, repeat the process. Iodine can be used for water purification. Five drops of iodine or 2 percent iodine per quart of clear water, ten drops per cloudy.
6. Eat no fruit or vegetables which have been contaminated on their surfaces when growing, or that have been contaminated by water used in cleaning. To be safe, eat only fruits which can be peeled. Avoid salads.
7. Avoid those foods in which bacteria can thrive—foods such as milk products, eggs, or any protein food which is not in an acid condition.
8. Frequently and thoroughly wash your own hands. A study in Mexico revealed that 15 percent of coins and paper money had diarrhea-causing micro-organisms on them. It makes little sense to insist on peeling your own oranges if your hands are contaminated.

Unfortunately, Mexican food, with all the variety and flavor, is also the source of most of the "tourista," the intestinal upsets, that half or more North Americans experience while in Mexico or soon after returning home. Many of the food-borne diseases are passed from the food handler to the consumer simply because the food handlers, cooks and servers have failed to wash their hands after using the toilet. Food poisoning is only one of the several diseases spread for lack of elementary food protection.

Mexico has numerous first-class hotels, most of the best of which are part of the Camino Real chain. The chain is a co-venture of a leading Mexican bank and Westin Hotels (headquartered in Seattle). A number of Holiday Inns in Mexico are privately owned and franchised.

Mexico's largest hotel chain, El Presidente, is government-owned and -operated. Presidente's president reports to a board headed by the Minister of Tourism. In 1982 El Presidente owned or managed twenty-six hotels. A principal purpose of the chain is to develop tourism in less developed destinations, such places as Oaxaca, Ixtapa and Loreto, and to maintain employment by keeping failing hotels open. Defunct hotels are taken over by El Presidente and, in areas where the government wishes to develop tourism, new El Presidente hotels are funded and their operation subsidized.

Like similar government-operated hotels in Jamaica, the Bahamas, Puerto Rico, and Venezuela, the Presidente chain loses large sums of money each year. A large reason for the losses comes when that dreaded disease, bureaucratitis, sets in. When government bureaucracies take over, efficiency departs. Trying to reach some of El Presidente officials is like placing a call to the moon. "Gone to lunch." "In conference." "Left early." "Back next week."

In the past the two carriers of Mexico, Aeromexico and Mexicana, presented a comparison of government versus private ownership. Aeromexico, the government-owned line, never failed to show a large operating deficit. Mexicana Airlines was privately owned and profitable. As things happen in Mexico, the government forced Mexicana into an excessively costly labor contract, and when the airline lost money, took it over.

4

UNITED KINGDOM

OFFICIAL NAME: UNITED KINGDOM OF GREAT BRITAIN AND NORTHERN IRELAND

The North American's first trip overseas is most likely to be to Britain and Europe. Landing in London the traveler has the largest museum city in the world to explore. Two airports serve the international traveler, Heathrow and Gatwick. Both have links into the heart of London. Gatwick to Victoria Station is a thirty-eight minute train ride. Heathrow to Piccadilly Station is forty minutes by Underground (subway). Heathrow is one of the top five busiest airports in the world.

Most Americans who fly to the United Kingdom arrive and depart from the London, Glasgow or Belfast airports. They seldom travel by air within Britain.

Seeing Britain by rental car or by rail are the preferred means of transport. Even so, Britain has twenty-nine international airports. Few of them are served by direct flights from the U.S.

RAIL TRAVEL IN BRITAIN

While Amtrak is a shadowy ghost of the once proud rail system in the United States, British Rail is still the prime mover of people in the United Kingdom. The trains are frequent and usually on time. The average speed of Amtrak is less than forty mph; that of BritRail is seventy-eight mph. A few crack trains, the Intercity 125's, run between Edinburgh, Glasgow, and London. The five-hundred-mile run between Edinburgh (pronounced Edinboro) can be done in under five hours, with the trains reaching speeds of 125 mph. On the negative side, most of the cars other than on the name trains are old and tired. By continental train standards some British trains are filthy. BritRail, however, is developing better trains. An electrified advanced passenger train designed to reach 155 mph is scheduled for 1984.

Advertising by BritRail suggests that the rail traveler in Britain can enjoy a first-class meal on trains, served in style and lavishly prepared. Don't believe it. Most trains include a buffet car, a stand-up snack bar with little or no hot food. Passengers with first-class Brit-Rail passes are surprised to find that many trains have no first-class coaches and no food service. This is true in most of Highland Scotland. Particularly exasperating is the experience of boarding a train only to find all seats occupied and being forced to stand.

Like food service, baggage service also has largely vanished. In BritRail's favor the larger stations do provide carts for luggage at no charge. "Left-luggage" rooms mean a sizable charge and often a wait in line both to check in and to check out bags. A few stations have coin-operated luggage lockers.

The days of traveling with a number of bags are over on BritRail unless the traveler is a weightlifter and agile enough to move the bags on and off trains fast. Stopping times at stations are limited to a few minutes or even seconds.

In Scotland the train "guards," the conductors, are extremely polite, even solicitous. A guard in the Edinburgh-London run closes each announcement with "And God Bless You." They stand ready to advise you on the better buys in accommodations and which hotels to avoid as "too pricey."

London is the hub of BritRail; the spokes are trains arriving and departing for all of England, Wales, and Scotland. The uninformed traveler assumes that direct connections can be made between trains. Not so. Trains arrive at different stations. Connections by subway or cab are necessary.

Fortunately for the train traveler most stations for the larger trains have tourist information centers where accommodations can be reserved. Most charge a nominal fee for reservations. Some offices, however, are several blocks away from the station.

Literally hundreds of trains have been cut from the schedule and it is impossible to reach some of the more picturesque areas of Britain by train. The Scottish Highlands around Inveraray has no train service and most of the Cotswolds is reachable only by car or by infrequent buses.

For visitors who enjoy rail travel there is the BritRail Pass, purchasable for various periods of time at large savings over taking individual rail trips. The BritRail pass is good all over Britain. Persons over sixty can buy the economy pass and choose first-class rail cars at no extra charge. Scotland has a Scottish Highland and Islands Travel pass, another travel bargain.

BritRail can be booked by travel agents who are subscribers to the computer services, PARS (the TWA computer service) or APOLLO (the United Airlines computer service). Travel agents can also book BritRail by writing it up on a British Airline ticket. The "rail ticket" can be converted into a rail pass at any one of fifty railway stations in London.

ARRIVAL BY SEA

A surprisingly large number of ports serve the sea traveler in Britain and Ireland. Southhampton was once the predominant port for the great Atlantic steamers. Portsmouth is a well-known naval base. The Dover to Calais route is well-known to travelers between London and France. Jet foil service is offered between Dover and Ostende, Belgium. Hovercraft service is available between Calais and Dover and between Dover and Boulogne.

GEOGRAPHY AND ATTRACTIONS

The British Isles, divorced from continental Europe by the English Channel, the Strait of Dover and the North Seas, comprise three contiguous nations—England, Scotland, and Wales. Add Northern Ireland, separated from the other three countries by the North Channel and the Irish Sea, and we have the United Kingdom. The southern part of what was the whole of Ireland has since 1949 been the independent Republic of Ireland. The total population of Britain is about fifty-seven million.

In total area, Great Britain and Northern Ireland are surprisingly small, about the size of Oregon. Together, England, Scotland, and Wales stretch about six hundred miles from northernmost Scotland to southernmost England. At its widest part the country spreads 250 miles from the west coast of Wales to the east coast of England. The Irish Republic and Northern Ireland share an island about three hundred miles north to south and two hundred miles east to west.

London is the epicenter of England and once was of the British Empire. London is the money market, the political center, the city where legitimate plays rise or fall, the shipping and trade center of the British Isles. Few capitals dominate their respective nations as London does England.

The easiest way to see London is by the public double-decker buses or the Underground, the London subway system. A go-as-you-please seven-day pass permits travel around London via London Transport.

Day-long excursions are fun using BritRail Britain-Shrinker tours. BritRail provides a choice of fourteen thousand trains a day, including the 125 mile express trains.

A day-tripper can head west to the elegant town of Bath. Or visit England's second largest city, Birmingham. Or south to Winchester at the edge of New Forest. Or toward the English Channel to Canterbury. Cambridge and Oxford are within easy compass.

FIGURE 4.1 *Royal residences dot Europe.* Best known to North Americans is Buckingham Palace, London residence of Britain's royal family.

Source: British Tourist Authority.

After London, one of the major metropolitan areas of the world (about eight million people), come the other large cities: Manchester (about one million), Liverpool (three-fourths of a million), Sheffield (6½ million), all north of London.

England is divided into counties. Those nearest London are called the home counties. The Midlands refer to the central counties. The Cotswolds, part of the Midlands, are a tourist attraction, hilly with honey-colored stone used in many of the villages. Broadway is one of the better known of these garden villages dotted with pubs and small hotels. Chipping Camden lies on the northern edge of the Cotswolds. Cirencester is in its center. Gloucester and Oxford are border towns of the area, each with its own historical and architectural interest.

A road map of England shows London to be the centerpiece of the country. Eight of the major motorways, the M system, converge on London from around the country. The 1 (M) starts with London and heads north into Scotland. The M 5 starts south at Plymouth and joins the M 6, then heads north to Scotland. The M 4 stretches east and west, from Cardiff, Wales, on the west to London on the east.

Time was when Britain ruled the British Empire, which covered a large part of the world's land mass. "The sun never set on the British Empire," and on the more than 372 million people who were in it. Granted most of the people were in poverty-ridden India and Africa. Nevertheless the grandeur of The Empire reached a zenith. Uniforms, parades and plenty of pomposity were the order of the day. Young Englishmen administered vast stretches of land and people while Scots, Welch and Irish troops made sure English orders were carried out. The Empire is now shadow, but its panoply and pageantry remain. No one, not even Hollywood, rivals the British in pageantry. A sense of history pervades the place. The Guard regiments are on duty in downtown London providing an unmatched

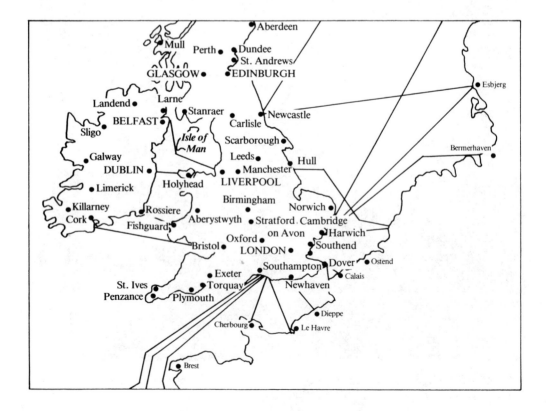

FIGURE 4.2 *Ferry connections between Britain and Europe.*

tourist attraction. The changing of the Guard, the Trooping of the Colors, and the Opening of Parliament are events that warm the cockles of the hearts of the British Tourist Authority. Cinderella's Castle in Disneyland, Versailles palace, and Ludwig's Bavarian Castle pale beside a real live royal family living in the splendor of Buckingham and Windsor Castles.

Britain itself is remarkably compact—less than six hundred miles from Dernnet Head, northern tip of mainland Scotland, south to England's southernmost point, Land's End.

London has been described as a collection of villages run together. London also has two cities, the city of London and the city of Westminster. You know you are in the city of London when nearly every male is wearing a bowler hat, carrying an umbrella, and maybe a briefcase. It is the financial city of Europe and home of the Bank of England and the Stock Exchange.

Two miles up the river Thames is the city of Westminster, with Buckingham Palace, Westminster Abbey and the Houses of Parliament. Big Ben, London's landmark clock, looks down from the Houses of Parliament on the Thames River.

The West End is like New York City's Fifth Avenue on Central Park. It's where the monied people live and includes Mayfair and St. James.

London is large, larger than New York City, Paris, Rome or Berlin, about thirty miles in diameter. To get around London most people take the Underground. It is the easiest and least expensive way. Compared to the New York subway it is more attractive, more pleasant to use and much safer. It too is noisy and boring. (Moscow's subway outdoes them all.)

The taxis of London are mostly diesel and roomy. The cab drivers are a race apart from New York City's cabbies, mostly restrained, quiet and polite.

London's legitimate theater is generally considered the best in the world and costs about half that of New York City's. There are more than forty live theaters. Exhibitions,

FIGURE 4.3 *Guidelines for driving in Britain.*

Driving licenses

A visitor can drive in Britain on current International Driving Permit or on his or her current domestic driving license (which should be carried), subject to a maximum of 12 months from his or her last date of entry into Britain. Otherwise a British driving license must be obtained.

Speed limits

Unless signs indicate otherwise—
70 miles per hour (113 kph) on motorways and dual carriageways.
60 miles per hour (97 kph) on single carriageways.

Seat belts

Although strongly recommended, it is not compulsory to wear a seat belt in the United Kingdom.

Parking

In the centers of many towns, parking on the street is allowed only at meters, on payment. Where a single continuous yellow line is painted parallel to the curb, parking is prohibited during the hours shown on the nearby time-plates. A double yellow line, or zig-zag marking near pedestrian crossings, prohibit parking at all times. Most towns have off street car parks; a charge is usually made.

Petrol (Gas)

Petrol is graded by a star system: 2 star (90 octane), 3 star (94 octane), and 4 star (97 octane). At the time of going to press, the approximate cost of a gallon of petrol was £1.40. Prices are very liable to change and vary from garage to garage and region to region. One Imperial gallon of petrol equals 1.2 North American gallons, or 4.5 liters.

Disabled

Disabled drivers are usually given dispensation to park in otherwise restricted areas, but they should have a word with a policeman or traffic warden before leaving their vehicle. They will usually find a sympathetic response.

---

galleries, and concerts abound. Several of the great museums are in London. The British Museum, the grandfather of museums, is best known and very crowded. The best examples of Greek art are there, purloined away from Greece by Lord Elgin. The Rosetta Stone, key to the ancient Egyptian hieroglyphics, is also there.

London is known for its parks, most of them a legacy from the royalty and the nobility. What are now Hyde Park, Regents Park, and Kensington Gardens were once owned by the Dukes of Devonshire, Bedford and Westminster. Westminster is still a large London landlord. Hunting grounds and open spaces around noble grounds now make for the best and most extensive parks in the world. History abounds. Marble Arch stands on one side of Hyde Park, where once stood a gallows. The nobility always got the best. If a lord was to be hung, he was entitled to a silken rope.

Undoubtedly London's biggest tourist attraction is the royal family: their palaces, their guards and their antics. Buckingham Palace is real and the Queen does live there—part of the time. The government supports the royal family to the tune of about $40 million a year, an investment in tourism as well as tradition.

Britain's number one place to visit is The Tower of London, sitting close by the Thames River. Grisly reminder of bygone royal power, The Tower can be a little frightening. Traitor's Gate was not the place to pass through for a pleasant walk. Those who entered The Tower through this gate knew it would be for the last time. The Crown Jewels of England are on display in The Tower—there are no samples. Westminster Abbey is where the great and powerful of the British Empire are buried. The steady progression of visitors over the stone floors are wearing them down. Nearly every tourist thrills to the chiming of Big Ben. Parliament buildings and Big Ben have become London's trademark, much as the Eiffel Tower is to Paris. London has palaces aplenty both in and around the city, but principally there is Buckingham Palace and, outside of London, Windsor Castle, seats of the royal family.

FIGURE 4.4 *The Tower of London*

Several of London's leading hotels have been social centers for more than seventy years: the Connaught, the Savoy, Claridges's, the Dorchester, the Ritz, and Grosvenour House. The newer class hotels, the Intercontinental, the Inn on the Park, the Hilton, the Berkeley, Carlton Tower, are all highly priced to be used by the right people. The hotel staff can be a European melange: French chefs, Spanish chambermaids, West Indian dishwashers, and Americans sitting in the bars paying prices the English think outrageous (and are).

The British do many things with style. Where else will the hospitality officer of the Grosvenour House meet you at the airport. If arriving by ship in Southhampton, "The Man with the Red Carnation" will take you through customs and send you along to Waterloo Station (the Underground), where you will be picked up by another Grosvenour House employee.

B & B, the bed and breakfast experience, is available in London homes where middle-aged ladies, sometimes helped by retired husbands, provide a room with a bath down the hall, or up a flight, or elsewhere. The breakfasts are almost uniformly good. In fact, they are much better than some of the continental breakfasts that come with the room at some of the pricey hotels. These hotel breakfasts, set up the evening before, may include a croissant. Come morning it is in a state of mortification. The B & B's are often much more interesting places to stay than the hotels, the guests more representative of the English than in a name hotel. (Many B & B guests are British.)

For a price the traveler can move in with an aristocrat and in the past could dine with a duke. Everyone can visit Blenheim Palace, home of the Duke of Marlborough, near Oxford. Apsley House, in the heart of London, is home for the Duke of Wellington and much of the palace is open to the public. Farther north is Chatsworth, home of the Duke of Devonshire. The Marquess of Bath has a fine estate plus a vintage automobile collection open to the public for a fee. Woburn Abbey, not far from London, is the seat of the Duke of Bedford, the latest of whom unabashedly developed the estate as a tourist attraction. His son, the Marquis of Tavistock, now operates the place.

Pub crawling can be undertaken by the accomplished American drinker. Some seven thousand pubs (public houses) await the intrepid. Many are loaded with history, some with Dickensian characters. Some offer the ploughman's lunch, usually consisting of bread and butter, moist cheddar cheese, tomato, lettuce, pickled onion or chutney. Some offer cold meat pies. Anglophiles on a budget swear by them. The London residents become affixed and affiliated with a favorite pub and seldom venture abroad. It has been said that if home is the Englishman's castle, the pub is his Vatican.

The pub often sports an outgoing lady of ample proportions who "jollies" the customers and keeps them interested for hours on end. These barmaids will have nothing to do with diets and usually are of an age that none of the customers think of them as daughters.

London has its gaming clubs where the greedy can maneuver for an advantage against the house, the drunk can quickly run out of cash and run up a debt, the curious can have an excellent meal at reasonable cost and hopefully rub elbows with a celebrity or his "betters." Membership is required at these clubs. Easy to come by, but a would-be gambler must be a member for at least forty-eight hours or be a guest of a member before being permitted to gamble.

London casino owners love Arabs, especially those who arrive by private jet carrying wads of 100-pound notes and intent on recycling petrodollars. London has nineteen casinos, the most highly regulated in the world. The "clubs" open at 2:00 p.m. and close at 4:00 a.m., except on Sunday morning, when 2:00 a.m. is the time to gloat or despair over lady luck's treatment. London provides no Las Vegas or Atlantic City razzle dazzle. Only two slot machines are allowed to a club, and some have a minimum blackjack bet of $150. No alcoholic beverages are served at the tables. Business is heaviest during summer, when even the Arabs find the heat at home too much.

London is for shoppers. Harrods receives the imprimatur of the Queen and of the well-heeled visitor. It stocks everything from prams (baby buggies) to potted partridge. Compared to the large American shopping malls, Harrods seems small scale. Fortnum &

Mason on Piccadilly is another name store, specializing in fine groceries. Saville Row gets the nod for gentlemen's bespoken tailors (who do the made-to-order kind). The best buys in Britain, or so the British testify, are found in Marks and Spencer, the clothing store chain found in most British cities. Two are in Oxford Street, London. Christies and Sotheby's are well-known art and furniture auction houses where the bids may run into the millions.

Hampton Court Palace, on the outskirts of London, is a major tourist attraction. It also attracted Henry VIII, who appropriated it from Cardinal Wolsey, who had built it for himself. It can be reached by road or by boat on the Thames River. That river leads northward to Oxford and beyond, a great river for boating with plenty of pretty riverside towns.

Do not expect to spend a quiet day exploring the stacks in London's libraries. The libraries are jammed and the wait to get a book can stretch into hours.

Windsor Castle, an excursion out of London, is awesome in dimension. The public school of Eton is nearby, best known of all private schools. The place is suitably medieval and the boys appear in costume.

The number two attraction in Britain? You guessed it, Stratford Upon Avon, Shakespeare's home. As the name implies, the village sits upon the little Avon River, northwest of Oxford. Don't overlook Ann Hathaway's cottage and the beautiful church on the edge of town.

The Southwest is England's favorite playground. Appropriately, the tip of England, in Cornwall, is called Land's End. East of Cornwall is Devon, with coasts on both the English Channel and Bristol Channel. Torquay is one of the better known beach towns on the English Channel. Devon is home to the famous Devon Teas, a baking powder biscuit plus jam and heavy clotted cream. (If clotted cream is unavailable, use heavy whipped cream.)

East of London is Bath, popular since its founding by the Romans for its curative hot springs and since the eighteenth century for its Georgian style of architecture.

Oxford and Cambridge, north of London and dating back to the eighteenth century, are England's renowned university towns. Architecturally, Cambridge is the more interesting of the two because of its variety of building styles ranging from Norman to modern. Not far from Oxford is Bleinheim Palace, home of the first Duke of Marlborough and his heirs. Impressive in its own right, the Palace gained further fame as the birthplace of Winston Churchill.

To the southeast of London is the County of Kent, the garden county. Going east from London on the M 2 is Canterbury, famous for its cathedral. This has been a shrine for centuries. Nearly every high school English class includes some reading of Geoffrey Chaucer's *Canterbury Tales,* the fictionalized story of a group of pilgrims on their trip to Canterbury from London about 1390.

The south coast of England has several well-known resort towns—Bournemouth, Cowes, Portsmouth, and Eastbourne. Largest and best known is Brighton on the M 23 south of London and also served by fast rail from London. Brighton reflects eighteenth century England when the Prince Regent built Brighton Pavilion as a palace and made Brighton the "in" place. The Pavilion is still a major tourist attraction open to the public.

The Lake District, in northwest England, has been celebrated in verse and prose. It is the mountainous area occupied by lakes in Cumberland, Westmoreland and Lancashire, close to Scotland. Windermere and Bowness sit at the foot of Orrest Head Lake, largest in England. The poet Wordsworth was much taken with the place, as are present-day visitors who water ski, fish, hike or pony-trek the Lake District.

The British pay homage to history by preserving its remains. Castles and mansions, even whole villages have been taken over by the government or by the conservation societies, the National Trust or the Scottish Trust. The London-based National Trust owns or protects nearly two hundred historic buildings, 416 miles of unspoiled coastline and more than a half million acres of land. It has thirty complete villages and hamlets, castles and abbeys, and lakes and hills. It owns lengths of inland waterways, bird sanctuaries, nature reserves, wind and water mills, and working farms. It has coastal waterways, conservation camps, gardens, gift shops, and restaurants. It even owns a section of Hadrian's Wall. Many of its properties can be rented by visitors for a few days or weeks.

Britain is famous for its stately homes. Something like one thousand are open to the public. Death duties have broken up the huge landed estates. Most of the owners cannot afford to maintain them, let alone replace the wood-rotted roofs. By giving them to the government or to the National Trust, many owners have elected to continue to live in sections of these mansions, the bulk of the estates being made public property. The stately homes constitute a taste of history and have become unique tourist sites attracting millions of national as well as foreign visitors.

Garden and flower lovers adore England. The damp, mild climate makes the country ideal for roses, rhododendrons and azaleas. No matter how small the house, it seems each has a little flower garden in front of it. Mansion owners feel obligated to keep large gardens, formal clipped gardens, gardens with ponds, gardens with "follies," buildings with no special purpose other than to embellish the grounds, gardens with gazeboes, puzzle gardens with mazes designed to lose the stroller, French gardens, Italian gardens, miniature and massive gardens. Garden shows are not only for horticulturists, they are high social occasions.

Kew Gardens in London is the biggest and best known. The Rothschild forest garden, about one hundred miles southeast of London in St. Exbury, is said to be the finest forest garden in the world. Best time to visit it and its thousands of rhododendrons and azaleas is between March and June. Sixty thousand garden lovers stroll the twenty-six-hundred-acre estate each year. Many stately homes include an orangerie and extensive greenhouse for growing plants, fruits and vegetables year-round.

Every history buff will thrill to walking Hadrian's Wall. The wall, 73½ miles over hills and plains, from the North Sea to the Irish Sea, was built by the Emperor Hadrian's legionnaires starting in 122 A.D. It marked the boundary between Roman domination of what is now England and the north, left to the wild Picts and Scots. The methodical Romans built a fort every five Roman miles and at every Roman mile, a milecastle, a small fort with barracks for a garrison of eight to thirty-two men. Turret watchtowers were built between the milecastles. Legionnaires built the wall, provincials manned it. Their enlistment period was twenty-five years.

What is left of the wall—and many stretches of it are intact—runs from Bowness-on-Solway on Solway Firth to Wallsend in the east. The Cheviot Hills and the Scottish border are farther north. The Lake Country is just south. Newcastle-upon-Tyne, near the eastern end of the wall, is the nearest large town. To reach the wall requires a car.

The British are the most class-conscious of peoples. Everyone is placed in a social pecking order from the dustman to duke. Birth and breeding count. Breeding relates to education. The "best" is provided by the public schools, really expensive private schools. Accent, dress, and manner tend to place everyone on the social scale. The English hardly know where to place Americans except that they respond well enough to those traveling first class and stopping at expensive hotels.

Bona fide English food is not known for its gourmet appeal. Some of the food combinations startle the American visitor: eggs over spaghetti or over French fries, baked bean sandwiches. On the other hand, some local dishes are memorable: the fresh fish, lobster and crab from Cornwall or Devon, for example. The fish and chips are addictive. Roast beef and Yorkshire pudding fit the American palate. The clotted cream on fresh fruit makes one a believer. The English specialize in candy and biscuits (cookies), hence the large number of false teeth. On a cold day it is Shepherd's pie or steak and kidney pie.

Beer lovers love the English pub, a social institution as well as a bar. Emigrants from England have been known to return simply over nostalgia for the genuine pub, more than sixty-six thousand strong throughout Britain. Each pub has its own following, and most have colorful names. White Horse, Punch and Judy, Black Friar, and Ye Olde Cheshire Cheese are samples. More than one thousand brands of beer are sold; a few pubs brew their own beers.

Britain's beer vocabulary is much more extensive than ours just as the French food lexicon is incomparably richer in subtleties. Basic beer is made from malted barley (grain allowed to germinate), hops for flavor, yeast and water. During seven days of fermentation the yeast turns the sugars into alcohol and carbon dioxide. The "pint" ordered in a pub is called ale in America. In Britain it is bitter beer. Indeed some of it is much too bitter for the American taste. Porter, stout and extra stout are the most bitter varieties. Ireland's famous bitter ale, Guiness, takes a few years of dedicated drinking to really enjoy.

Barley wine (old ale) is a rich fruity beer, occasionally matured for up to eighteen months and drunk in small glasses. Real ale has not been pasteurized and comes in barrels in which fermentation is still taking place.

Lagers are the light beers to which Americans are accustomed. Lager and lime is a popular drink, lager with a splash of Rose's Lime Juice added.

The visitor should not expect the beers heavily laden with alcohol as in days past. Brewers are taxed on the amount of alcohol contained in their beer. The bitters contain about 4 percent. Stout and strong ale contain around 5.5 percent and barley wine up to 8 percent.

Traditionalists deplore the good old days when pub food was premise-prepared. Today the sausages, pork pies, sausage rolls, and cornish pastries are mass produced.

Some think the English "tea time" an inspired custom, designed to lower the blood pressure, hasten tooth decay and assure equanimity. "Teas" are served in all manner of places, from truly homestyle places to the elite hotel sitting rooms. The teapot often appears wrapped in a cozy towel, accompanied by a pot of boiling water for second and third helpings from the same tea leaves. A pitcher of warm milk, scones, crumpets, or biscuits may also show up. Clotted cream and scones are the trademark of the Devonshire teas.

WALES

Wales, on the west of Britain, extends out into the Irish Sea. Like Scotland it is a nation within a nation. Tourism is big business. Most of the Welsh even welcome the English. In 1982 an estimated twelve million visitors left eight hundred million dollars and created eighty thousand vital jobs. A geography pedant's paradise, some of the place names are almost incomprehensible to an outsider. Try this one on your tongue: Llanfairpwllgwyngllogerychwyrndrobwelllanlysiliogogogoch. The Germans do it too, compound their words, but this little Welsh town has to be a winner in the longest name contest. The residents wisely abbreviate the name to Llanfair P.G.

There is also a Betws-y-Coed, no relation to the popular song of a few decades ago that goes "Betty Coed Has Eyes of Blue," etc. The capital city, Cardiff, is easy enough to pronounce.

Wales is small, about eight thousand square miles, with a total population of about 2.8 million. Most of the people and industry are in the south. Anglesey Island is connected to the mainland by bridge in the north. The north is also known for the Snowdonia Mountains where hiking, pony-trekking and mountain climbing are popular. The mountains are small but grand and were used by the conquerors of Mt. Everest as a training ground. The Welch seacoast has numerous sandy bays and quiet towns. Freshwater fishing is the most popular of outdoor sports. Some of the riverside hotels own fishing rights along the banks on which they sit.

In Wales all road signs appear in both English and Welsh. The Welsh have a long memory. About 20 percent of them can speak Welsh, a language full of gutturals that bears almost no resemblance to English. The last Welsh prince, Llywelyn, was killed in 1282, and in 1536 Wales was merged into the English state. Even so, a sizable number of Welsh think of themselves as Welsh first, members of the United Kingdom second. A separate TV channel operating twenty-two hours a day is presented in the Welsh language.

Wales has relatively good roads. Train service is also good, except on Sundays when nearly everything closes down. All Wales is castle country, most of them built by the

English to keep the Welsh under control. Most of them are in ruins. Northwest Wales has the most. Of the more than two hundred castles, some one hundred are open to visitors. Cardiff Castle is really a pseudo castle since it was built in the Victorian period.

In August Cardiff Castle sports a resounding military tattoo, Britain's first and largest military marching performance. From London Cardiff is a two-hour trip by high speed train.

Caernarvon Castle in the north is the most restored and best known. It houses the Regimental Museum of the Royal Welsh Fusilliers. It is also the scene of the investiture of the Prince of Wales. The walled town of Conway, farther north, has its walls flanked by twenty-one towers and pierced by three gateways. Its castle was built in the late thirteenth century. Tourists to Wales usually visit Snowdonia National Park. A pony-trek aboard the little Welsh ponies, called cobs, is a favored Welsh experience.

SCOTLAND

Scotland the Brave, Scotland the Romantic. Scotland the home of the Loch Ness Monster, and mother to Scots around the world who, wherever they are, harbor a mystical warmth for the mother country. Climatically the place is pretty miserable. The weather seldom climbs above seventy degrees. The skies are overcast much of the year. There is more than enough rain. Yet the place reflects romance.

Part of the reason are the hills and dales, the lakes and valleys, the surrounding oceans. The place is small enough that at one time the Duke of Sutherland could travel across its northern section all the way on his own land. That possibly also says something about Scottish history and social struggles, the nurturing of heroes and martyrs.

Only as little as one-fourth of the land is suitable for the usual agriculture. But oats do grow and have constituted a staple food for which the Scots are well-known, oatmeal. (Samuel Johnson defined oats as something eaten by horses and Scots.)

The North Sea bounds Scotland on the east, the Atlantic does so on the west. Traditionally Scotland is divided into the Lowlands, in the center of the country, and the Highlands, the northern half. The Uplands are in the south. The Highlands are sparsely populated and have been since "The Clearances," back in the eighteenth century when the huge landowners, the Chiefs and nobility, decided it was more profitable to raise sheep and cattle than to allow the small farmers, the crofters, to remain eking out a marginal life on relatively small plots of land. (The Clearances was one of the reasons there are more Scots living abroad than in Scotland itself.) The landowners hastened the crofters' departure by burning their homes, neglecting sometimes to check whether anyone was still inside. Even today 80 percent of the land is owned by 7 percent of the people. Aristocrats and the wealthy keep an ample supply of lovely lochs, mountains and moors for fishing and boating.

Considered some of the most romantic of mountains, the Highlands are not really high at all as mountains go. Inverness is the northernmost town of any size in the Highlands.

The ballad which includes the line, "You take the high road and I'll take the low road and I'll be there a fore you," tells much about the Scottish love of country. The singer who was about to be hanged on an English gallows was referring to going back to his home around Loch Lomond, traveling via the "low road," the spirit world.

The Lowlands, grassy hills and dales, has the two major cities, Glasgow and Edinburgh, and the Lowlands holds two-thirds of the population and nearly all of the industry. In Scotland the bays are called firths and the lakes, lochs. Just about everyone has heard of Loch Lomond, longest of the Scottish lakes, and about an hour's drive from Glasgow.

Loch Ness is home to Nessie, the Loch Ness Monster, which has appeared from time to time, apparitionally or otherwise, since the seventh century. The lake is deep and dark, just right for a monster that may or may not exist.

On the west coast, the Solway Firth (remember a firth is a bay) is shared by both Scotland and England. Merging with the Firth of Clyde, it leads inland to Glasgow (about 900,000 people), and the major manufacturing city. Robert Burns country is not far south of Glasgow.

On the east coast, the Firth of Forth finds Edinburgh Castle, official residence of the reigning British monarch when in Scotland. This is a major attraction. Edinburgh is a city of marked architectural style, beautifully landscaped gardens and squares.

Below Glasgow are the Southern Uplands, where fishermen gather along the banks of the rivers Tweed, Fay, Dee, and Spey to angle for salmon. Do not expect to march up to a stream and fish. Acres along the rivers are owned or leased.

Perth (pronounced pearth by the Scots) is a base for Highlands exploration. Aberdeen, on the northeast coast, is a base for the North Seas oil drilling. It is a city of granite in that most of the public buildings, schools and many homes are made of granite. Balmoral Castle, summer retreat for the royal family, is nearby.

Off the jagged coast of western Scotland are some six hundred islands called the Inner Hebrides and the Outer Hebrides. Some are still completely owned by a noble family with all residents paying rent. Skye is the largest and most popular and is a short ferry ride from Kyle of Lochalsh. The Inner Hebrides include the islands of Islay, Jura and Mull. Part of Jura has its own micro-climate that has permitted the development of subtropical gardens.

Farther south lies the island of Arran in the Firth of Clyde with its Brodick Castle, ancestral home of the Dukes of Hamilton. As with many castles, this one too is now owned and maintained by the National Trust of Scotland. Arran, also reached by ferry, is alive with summer visitors.

North and west, out in the Atlantic, are the Outer Hebrides. To the northeast are the Shetlands, home of the Shetland pony. It was bred to be no higher than forty-two inches at the shoulder so that it could work in the mines. They are now most popular as pets. Of the more than one hundred Shetland islands only twenty-four are inhabited. It is easy to see why less than twelve thousand people live there. Short summers and constant wind prevent most farming. Sheep, however, thrive and provide the wool for the Shetland woolen goods. Tourists enjoy the Viking celebration of Up-Helly-Aa. A festival with that name has to be good!

Off the northeast coast of Scotland are the Orkney Islands. Of the sixty-seven outcroppings that can be accurately called islands, twenty-six are occupied. The island, Mainland, boasts two towns, Stromness and Kirkwall. Fly from London, Edinburgh or Aberdeen if you like, or take a P & O steamer for six miles from Scrabster, Scotland.

The islands, warmed by the Gulf Stream, seldom see snow, but there are more than enough gale force winds, usually from mid-September until May. Winds and ocean salt spray are blamed for an almost treeless environment similar to that of Iceland. Londoners are more likely to know Miami than their own Orkney Islands. It is cheaper to fly on a package for two to Miami than to travel to the Orkneys. The islands still share traces of Viking invasion and habitation. Even a few Norse words creep into an islander's conversation.

A favorite auto tour of Scotland heads north from Prestwick Airport, Scotland's major International Gateway, to Fort William, loops around the Highlands to Inverness and south, ending up at Edinburgh, Scotland's capital.

The BritRail pass, or a special Scottish rail pass, gets you around much of Scotland. Some interesting places like the Dukes of Argyll's home and the village of Argyll are reachable only by village road.

In Scotland there are more brooding castles with romantic names—Inveraray, Cawdor, Elair, Glamis, Edinburgh and Sterling. The Highlands of Scotland call Scotchmen from around the world. They provide natural beauty aplenty; bountiful Scottish breakfasts; fishing, hiking, shopping and touring of stately homes; and accommodations ranging from private homes (bed and breakfast) to Gleneagles Hotel, one of the best. Gleneagles and St. Andrews are the most famous of Scotland's numerous golf courses. Several castles and mansion owners take in guests on a discreet, pre-arranged basis, with payment made to a London tourist office. Some farmers also take in guests and it is well worth the time to reserve them in the local tourist offices. Most fishing and hunting must be prearranged with the landowner or the person owning the fishing rights along the streams. Some of this can be very expensive.

Scotland has several unique tourist attractions, one being the Scotch Whiskey Trail in northeast Scotland, centered around the rivers Spey, Avon and Livet. The distilleries themselves are not too different from one another. But then neither are the wineries on the wine tour of the Napa Valley of California, or the pubs one is supposed to "crawl" between in places like London. It is the spirit of the thing, especially since at many of the distilleries the guest is treated to something completely un-Scotsmanlike, a free dram of whiskey. The official Whiskey Trail is seventy miles long, with signposts along the way. Visitors should allow at least an hour for each of the five malt distilleries on the trail. Incidentally, because of high taxes Scotch whiskey costs more in Scotland than the same bottle in the United States.

Scottish food is hearty and straightforward. Elegant dining tends to favor French dishes, understandably, because of Scotland's long association with France before becoming a permanent part of Britain. Haggis, a mixture of meat, oatmeal, and spices, cooked in a sheep's stomach, is really not as bad as it sounds. The fresh fish and other seafood and "short" (meaning plenty of shortening is used) biscuits are memorable.

TRAVEL CAPSULE

GEOGRAPHY

The United Kingdom of Great Britain and Northern Ireland lies off the northwest coast of the European Continent, separated from it by the English Channel, the Strait of Dover, and the North Sea. At the closest point, England is only 35 kilometers (22 mi.) from France. Its capital and largest city is London, with a population in 1979 of about 6.9 million.

Scotland is north of England. Its Lowlands, about 97 kilometers (60 mi.) wide, divide the farming region of the southern Uplands from the granite Highlands of the north. Edinburgh (pop. 470,000) is Scotland's capital. Glasgow (881,000), one of the United Kingdom's great industrial centers, is Scotland's largest city.

Wales borders England to the west and is almost entirely hilly and mountainous. Its largest city is Cardiff (284,000).

Northern Ireland occupies the northeast corner of Ireland across the North Channel from Scotland and is primarily industrial. Its capital and largest city, Belfast, has an estimated population of 368,000.

Because of prevailing southwesterly winds, the climate of the United Kingdom is temperate and equable. Temperatures range from a mean of about 5 °C (40 °F) in winter to about 16 °C (60 °F) in summer. Average annual rainfall is 80-102 centimeters (35-40 in.), distributed relatively evenly throughout the year.

AREA: 243,977 sq. km. (94,200 sq. mi.); slightly smaller than Oregon.

CITIES: *Capital*—London (pop. about 6.9 million in 1979). *Other cities*—Birmingham, Glasgow, Leeds, Sheffield, Liverpool, Manchester, Edinburgh, Belfast.

TERRAIN: 30% arable, 50% meadow and pasture, 12% waste or urban, 7% forested, 1% inland water.

CLIMATE: Generally mild and temperate; weather is subject to frequent changes but to few extremes of temperature.

PEOPLE

The population of the United Kingdom was estimated at 55.9 million in 1979, about 3.4 million more than in 1961 and a sevenfold increase since 1700. Its population is the fourth largest in Europe (after the USSR, the Federal Republic of Germany, and Italy), and its population density is one of the highest in the world. Almost one-third of the total population lives in England's prosperous and fertile southeastern corner, with population declining in the more rugged areas to the north and west. The population of the United Kingdom is predominantly urban and suburban.

The contemporary Briton is descended mainly from the varied ethnic stocks which settled there before the end of the 11th century. A group of islands close to the European Continent, Great Britain has been subject to many invasions and migrations, especially from Scandinavia and the Continent, including Roman occupation for several centuries. Under the Normans—Scandinavian Vikings who settled in northern France—the pre-Celtic, Celtic, Roman, Anglo-Saxon, and Norse influences were blended into the Briton of today.

Although the Celtic languages persist to a small degree in Northern Ireland, Wales, and Scotland, the predominant language has long been English, a blend of Anglo-Saxon and Norman-French.

The high literacy rate in the United Kingdom (99%) is attributable to the introduction of public primary education in 1870 and secondary in 1900. In 1981, nearly 11 million students attended educational institutions, most of which are publicly financed in whole or in part. Education is mandatory from ages 5 through 16.

The Church of England (Episcopal), with 27 million baptized members, is the largest church.

ANNUAL GROWTH RATE: Negligible.

ETHNIC GROUPS: Briton, West Indian, Indian, Pakistani.

RELIGIONS: Church of England, Roman Catholic, Presbyterian.

LANGUAGES: English, Welsh, Gaelic.

EDUCATION: *Years compulsory*—12. *Attendance*—nearly 100%. *Literacy*—99%.

HEALTH: *Infant mortality rate*—13.3/1,000. *Life expectancy*—males 69 yrs., females 76 yrs.

WORK FORCE: (about 26.4 million in 1979), *Agriculture*—11.5%. *Industry and commerce*—54.4%. *Services*—29.9%. *Government*—6.6%. *Self-employed*—7.6%.

TRAVEL NOTES

CLOTHING: Fall and winter clothing is needed from about September through April; spring and summer clothing is useful the rest of the year.

HEALTH: Good medical facilities are available. Living conditions are generally excellent, and no unusual health hazards exist.

TELECOMMUNICATIONS: London and nearly all UK localities have an automatic dial-through telephone system. Cities in the U.S. and Western Europe can also be reached by direct dialing. Internal and international services are efficient. London is five time zones ahead of US e.s.t.

TRANSPORTATION: Great Britain is a crossroads for international air and shipping routes and is also accessible by highway and train from points throughout Europe. Rail, air, and bus transportation in the UK is excellent, and travel between all points is quick and easy. Rental cars are available. Traffic moves on the left.

5

WESTERN EUROPE

Travel between North America and Europe has taken on astounding proportions and promises to grow even larger. It has all been made possible by the jet plane, rising incomes and rising expectations. While travel to Europe was once the province of the rich or the scholar, today some four million Americans make the trans-Atlantic flight each year and leave as much as $4 billion before returning home. As many as 370 commercial jets carrying eighty-three thousand people are in the air over the Atlantic on a given day, half or more of them pleasure travelers.

More than any other place Europe is a treasure trove of ethnic memories, a collection of cultures and artifacts, political and social systems. We know more about Europe than the other continents. Many of our forebears originated there. The U.S. fought two world wars on its soil. It contains an abundance of the world's great cathedrals, palaces and gardens. Some 482 million people offer a range of lifestyles. Cross a national border and you may change language, religion, and political system.

Technically Europe is "a continent in the Western part of Eurasia, separated from Asia by the Ural Mountains on the East and the Caucasus Mountains and the Black and Caspian seas on the Southeast."

Is England a part of Europe? In British usage, Continental Europe is sometimes contrasted with Britain. An arm of the Atlantic Ocean, the English Channel, separates Northern France and Southern England. (At one time swimming the English Channel, about twenty miles wide at the most narrow point, was a great achievement. Later an American did it both ways nonstop.)

To get the labels right, since 1707 the term "Great Britain" has referred to England, Scotland and Wales. Include Northern Ireland and we get the "United Kingdom." The British Commonwealth of Nations in something else again, a large group of nations and dependent territories spread around the world, united by a common allegiance to the British crown.

The Soviet Union is a federal union of fifteen constituent republics, partly in Eastern Europe and in Northern and Western Asia, occupying nearly one-sixth of the world's land surface.

France is the largest of the West European countries in space. West Germany has the most people.

To keep the European countries in perspective think of all of Sweden as having about the same population as New York City, all of Scandinavia about the same number of people as California.

Europe also has its micro-states, the smallest being the Vatican with one thousand people living within that enclave. Andorra, sitting between France and Spain in the Pyrenees Mountains, has thirty-four thousand. Liechtenstein, between Austria and Switzerland, has twenty-six thousand. San Marino, the village atop a small Italian mountain, has twenty-one thousand.

Counting the mini-countries Europe includes thirty-one countries. The island republic of Malta, in the Mediterranean, and Iceland, in the Atlantic, are also sometimes considered part of the European region.

Much of the continent is mountainous, especially Eastern and Southern France, Switzerland, Southern Germany, Austria, Northern Spain and Northern Italy. The Alps are the best known of the mountain ranges. There are also the Pyrenees, the Sudeten, the Erz, the Urals, and the Caucasus. The Balkan Mountains extend from Western Bulgaria to the Black Sea.

European weather varies widely depending upon latitude, altitude, and the presence of large bodies of water. Of particular importance to Western Europe is the Atlantic Drift (the diffusion of the Gulf Stream) that moderates the climate and is responsible for much of Europe's rain.

FIGURE 5.1   *Some facts on the countries of Europe.*

Region and Country	Population (Millions)	Area (Square Miles)	Capital
The British Isles			
Great Britain	56.0	94,226	London
Ireland	3.4	27,136	Dublin
France	53.9	211,207	Paris
Scandinavia			
Denmark	5.1	16,629	Copenhagen
Finland	4.8	130,119	Helsinki
Norway	4.0	125,181	Oslo
Sweden	8.3	173,731	Stockholm
Portugal	9.8	35,553	Lisbon
Spain	37.7	194,896	Madrid
Austria	7.5	32,374	Vienna
Belgium	9.8	11,779	Brussels
East Germany	16.8	41,768	Berlin
West Germany	61.8	95,976	Bonn
Netherlands	14.3	15,770	Amsterdam
Switzerland	6.3	15,941	Berne
Greece	9.4	50,944	Athens
Italy	57.1	116,303	Rome
Eastern Europe			
Albania	2.6	11,100	Tirana
Bulgaria	8.8	42,823	Sofia
Czechoslovakia	15.3	49,370	Prague
Hungary	10.7	35,919	Budapest
Poland	35.9	120,699	Warsaw
Romania	22.4	91,699	Bucharest
The USSR	267.7	8,649,489	Moscow

FIGURE 5.2 *Temperatures in the major cities of some European countries.* Temperature averages—maximum/minimum. Temperatures are in Celsius.

City/Country	January		July	
	High	Low	High	Low
Vienna, Austria	1	−4	24	15
Paris, France	0	6	24	13
Berlin, Germany	0	−3	23	12
London, England	6	2	22	13
Athens, Greece	12	6	35	23
Reykjavik, Iceland	−1	−1	14	14
Rome, Italy	11	4	30	19
Amsterdam, Netherlands	6	−1	21	12
Madrid, Spain	9	1	30	17
Geneva, Switzerland	−1	−15	21	15
Moscow, USSR	−10	−15	21	12

The Gulf Stream affects Iceland's climate greatly. Reykjavik, the capital and home to most of the country's people, never gets very warm but seldom drops below freezing even in winter. The same is true of Ireland and Scotland. Greece, on the other hand, experiences temperatures of ninety-five degrees in July and August. Because of its altitude, Switzerland has a pleasant average July and August temperature of about seventy degrees. Stockholm, much farther north, gets warmer in the summer and colder in the winter but its climate is not severe because it is a city of connected islands. Madrid has pleasant summer temperature because it sits on a two-thousand-foot plateau surrounded by mountains. Moscow experiences the widest range of temperatures of the European capitals, bitingly cold in winter, fairly warm in summer. The Mediterranean is subtropical; the northern part of Norway is the Arctic. Also accounting for these climate differences are distances involved between Northern and Southern Europe.

The Mediterranean is Europe's Caribbean, ringed by vacation spots and dotted with islands that elicit the Ulysses in millions, be they butcher, baker, or candlestick maker.

Until seventy million years ago the Mediterranean was open to the Atlantic. Then the rocks of Africa and Iberia closed in and the Mediterranean basin became a desert. The natural dam later broke and the Atlantic rushed in. Today deep waters from the Mediterranean flow out into the Atlantic through the eight-mile gap between Gibralter and Morocco. (King Hussein of Morocco would have a bridge span the Straits of Gibralter, making it easy for millions of Europeans to visit his country.) Indeed a bridge does join Asia and Europe, spanning the Bosphorus, the passage between the Mediterranean and the Black Sea.

Europeans travel widely. The largest number, about 5.5 million, or 42.5 percent, come to the Americas. Another 3.37 million, or 26.1 percent, go to Africa. East Asia and the Pacific attract 2.48 million (19.2 percent) of the total. South Asia and the Middle East each attract seventy-nine million or together 12.2 percent of the total.[1]

About three-quarters of all international border crossings take place within Europe; only 15 percent take place within North America. Interregional travel is something else. The United States accounts for a substantial portion of the total. Over half of U.S. travelers abroad head for Western Europe.

What does the average American tourist want to do and see? What is important to the middle-class traveler from New York, Chicago, or Los Angeles? Temple Fielding, whose travel guides to Europe have been coming out since 1948, says, "The fact is that most travelers don't give a damn for the sights except for the very famous ones. They pay lip service to museums, tombs, battlefields, but they care the most about their hotel—and if they're comfortable they generally like the city. Their second concern is restaurants and shopping. Sightseeing comes a bit down the list." Apparently a lot of Americans agree with Fielding since more than three million of his guidebooks have been sold.

Judging from the number of music festivals held in Britain, Europe, and elsewhere, the music festival is an excellent way of attracting visitors. Some thirty countries offer festivals featuring music each summer. Edinburgh, Scotland, holds one of the biggest of the festivals. Some are elitist concerts attracting the affluent. The Salzburg Festival, held each year, attracts thousands and for several weeks insures full occupancy of all the hostelries in and around Salzburg, Austria. Tickets go for as high as $100 for each performance.

Because it is mostly rimmed by mountains the winter climate is mild and the Mediterranean coasts have been attracting vacationers since Roman times. Wealthy Europeans have been visiting Italy for several centuries. The British, the first "tourists" of modern times, took to the Cote d'Azur in the late 1800s. If they were around today, they might be more than amused by the millions of people crowding most of the coasts of Spain, France, Italy, and the Greek Islands. They enjoy mild winters and the nearly rainless summers that characterize the Mediterranean climate (found also in Southern California, Chile and South Australia). The some 230 million permanent residents who live around the Mediterranean welcome the money brought by the millions of Northern Europeans and others. As for welcoming the tourists themselves, well?

As a region Europe attracts more Americans than any other, a total of almost four million a year. As for all regions the numbers fluctuate annually reflecting economic, political, and social conditions in those particular countries and in the U.S. The United Kingdom attracts by far the most Americans. West Germany has been the number two choice primarily because of the large number of U.S. military personnel traveling there. France is number three followed by Italy, The Netherlands, and Spain. As for European cities, London ranks first in tourist popularity, followed by Paris, Rome, and Amsterdam. The totals in thousands for each European country are seen in Figure 5.3.

Air travel to Europe is made easier by numerous airlines and frequent flight schedules. Every country of any importance has at least one airline that connects with the continent. Many nations that have no economic justification for underwriting a national airline do so anyway because of national pride. Nearly all fly to one or more of the national capitals of Europe.

Heaviest air traffic to and from Europe takes place on the trans-Atlantic routes. Direct flights from a number of United States cities take place daily or weekly. New York City to London routes carry the most passengers but numerous direct flights are scheduled from as far away as Los Angeles. They go not only to London but to Paris, Lisbon, Amsterdam, Glasgow, and Copenhagen.

Most of the major airports in Europe serve the European capitals. Principal airports used by North Americans in Europe are Heathrow and Gatwick outside of London; Orly and DeGaulle airports that serve Paris; the Frankfort airport in Germany; the airports that

FIGURE 5.3   *A tourist popularity poll of countries in Europe.*

United Kingdom	1,281
France	863
Italy	726
Switzerland	502
Germany	834
Austria	306
Denmark	208
Sweden	173
Norway	167
Netherlands	330
Belgium-Luxembourg	252
Spain	397
Portugal	138
Ireland	167
Greece	350

FIGURE 5.4   *European cities and airline codes.*

AMS	Amsterdam, Netherlands
ATH	Athens, Greece
BCN	Barcelona, Spain
BER	Berlin, Germany
BEY	Beirut, Lebanon
BRU	Brussels, Belgium
BUD	Budapest, Hungary
CMN	Casablanca, Morocco
CPH	Copenhagen, Denmark
DUB	Dublin, Ireland
FRA	Frankfort, Germany
GLA	Glascow, Scotland, U.K.
HEL	Helsinki, Finland
IST	Istanbul, Turkey
LIS	Lisbon, Portugal
LON	London, U.K.
MAD	Madrid, Spain
MIL	Milan, Italy
MOW	Moscow, USSR
MUC	Munich, Germany
NCE	Nice, France
OSL	Oslo, Norway
PAR	Paris, France
PRG	Prague, Czechoslovakia
ROM	Rome, Italy
STO	Stockholm, Sweden
THR	Tehran, Iran
TLV	Tel Aviv, Israel
WAW	Warsaw, Poland
ZRH	Zurich, Switzerland

serve Copenhagen, Denmark, and Lisbon, Portugal. All are terminals for nonstop flights from various North American cities. (See Figure 1.4, page 13.)

A problem with intra-European air travel is its cost. European airlines in the past have set fares that are much higher than for comparable flights outside of Europe. Travel packages that include intra-European flights usually offer less expensive air travel.

Figure 5.4 shows the airline codes for the major cities of Europe. Airline codes are used in the identifying circles.

Rail travel within Europe can be fast, efficient and a travel bargain. Frequent schedules and spotless trains are the norm in several European countries. The best trains are part of the Trans-European Express network. The TEE network ranges from Barcelona in the south to Hamburg in the north. London is connected by rail and ferry to Rotterdam to join the network. Le Mistral, a famed TEE between Paris and Nice, is equipped with a boutique, hairdresser, secretarial service, and a top restaurant. Some of the other European trains are dirty and depressing.

A great many Americans see Europe via the Eurail system. The system incorporates the best rail service in sixteen European countries and its trains crisscross Europe from northern Lapland to the southern tip of Italy, and from the shores of Brittany in France through Europe's mountains and along much of its shores. Altogether the Eurail system covers more than 100,000 miles of rail lines. The Eurail pass is good for periods from two weeks to three months and must be purchased in the U.S.

Veteran travelers state that it may be cheaper to travel without the Eurail pass and that if you really want to get to know the people, go second-class. In parts of Europe second-class is not bad. In Morocco it provides a reclining seat in a spotless air conditioned car with white-jacketed steward service. When traveling without a pass it must be remembered that everything must be purchased separately. A reserved seat is a good idea. The modern express trains make a surcharge. Additional tickets are needed for sleepers. The best buy on

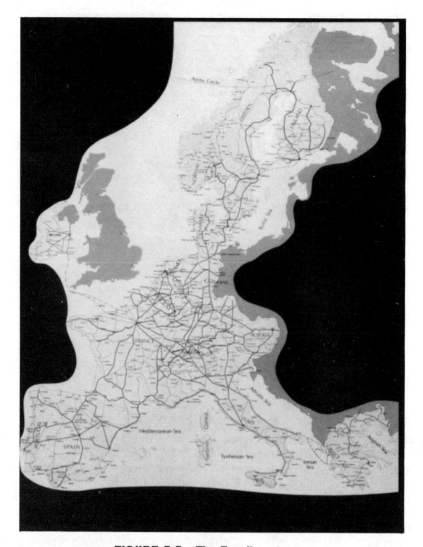

FIGURE 5.5 *The Eurail system.*

European trains is a couchette—a simple berth with a fixed charge regardless of class or distance traveled. The fee includes a blanket and a pillow, but on some trains, no sheets, washing facility or privacy.

Many European trains provide the equivalent of our pullman cars, called Wagon-lits. On English trains, compartments similar to Wagon-lits are known as sleepers. A pullman in Britain gets a seat similar to those in our parlor cars.

Many travelers take food with them on the train, especially if traveling second-class. Travel light in order to get off and on the trains easily. Some women take a sturdy metal cart with telescoping handles. If traveling second-class take along a supply of paper tissues and packets of pre-moistened towels. If the restroom nearest the traveler's seat is unappealing, perhaps the others are better. Nonsmokers can get seats in nonsmoking compartments. When boarding a train be sure you are in the right section. Different cars may go to different destinations.

The International Union of Railroads lists major trains serving nineteen European countries from Scandinavia down through Greece and Turkey. Copies can be had free from the French National Railroads, 610 Fifth Avenue, New York 10020. Cooks Continental Timetable can be had from Thos. Cook & Sons, 45 Berkeley St., London, WIA IEB.

Traveling second-class in Britain is much cheaper than first-class but does not usually entitle the rider to use the dining car and may entitle him to a little snobbery on the part of the conductors. Drinking water is not available on European trains. Take your own in a canteen. Wine and soda water are available, but not the greatest for brushing the teeth.

The InterRail card is another travel bargain, this one for persons under twenty-six, good for second-class travel in twenty-one European countries. The Youthpass is less expensive than the Eurail pass, good only for sixteen countries. For persons sixty-five or older there is the Senior rail card with a sizable reduction, good in seventeen European countries. Britain has its own reduced fare ticket, BritRail, which offers unlimited economy or first-class rail travel in England, Scotland, and Wales, as well as a number of daily intercity trains. Sweden, Switzerland, and other European countries offer special reduced fares for senior citizens. A Benelux Tourrail is good for rail travel in Belgium, Holland, and Luxembourg. A Scandinavian Rail Pass is valid in Denmark, Finland, Norway, and Sweden. Australia offers the Austrailpass; India the Indrail Pass; Finland a Finnrailpass.

The first-class trains of Europe are far superior in equipment, scheduling, and service to America's Amtrak. One reason is that millions of people use the European trains. Both the European and American trains are heavily subsidized by national governments. An advantage in using European trains is that they arrive and depart from the very heart of the cities, where accommodations and other services are readily available. Also, because of the distances involved and the inconvenience of airports, train travel within Europe is often quicker than plane travel.

Study of the Eurail map (Figure 5.5) provides a bonus in visualizing Europe. Look at the vast length of Norway. Its length if folded southward would extend down to Italy. Notice how Ireland sits off by itself in the Atlantic; Spain, Italy, Greece append themselves to the body of Europe. The smaller countries, Luxembourg, Liechtenstein, Monaco, Andorra, and San Marino, are not marked on this map.

It can be seen that the rail system of Ireland joins up by water with that of Europe at Cherbourg and Le Havre, France. BritRail, the British Rail System, is joined by boat at Calais, France. Denmark's rail system is moved by ship from Frederikshavn to Goteburg, Sweden.

Other than in Norway, Sweden, and Finland, distances within Europe are relatively short. A day's trip by rail or car can mean crossing the borders of several countries. Representative distances and travel time by rail are seen in Figure 5.6.

Notice the time 8:14 hours between Copenhagen and Stockholm. The reason is that a lengthy ferry trip between Denmark and Sweden is involved. Slow trains and poor connections account for the 8:20 hours required between Barcelona and Madrid.

FIGURE 5.6 *Rail distances and travel times.*

From	To	Distance (miles)	Travel Time
Amsterdam	Cologne	159	1:53 hrs.
Barcelona	Madrid	430	8:20 hrs.
Brussels	Paris	193	2:25 hrs.
Cologne	Mainz	116	1:42 hrs.
Copenhagen	Stockholm	404	8:14 hrs.
Frankfurt	Munich	263	3:49 hrs.
Geneva	Bern	298	1:39 hrs.
Luxembourg	Basel	227	3:26 hrs.
Paris	Bordeaux	363	3:50 hrs.
Rome	Florence	198	2:40 hrs.
Salzburg	Vienna	198	3:14 hrs.

The French have now taken first place in the world rail sweepstakes with their super-trains.

The streamlined pride of the French railroad system, *Tres Grande Vitesse* (very high speed), operates between Paris and Lyon. It hits speeds of 175 mph with a ride for passengers so smooth that a glass of water sitting on an armrest is not disturbed.

The system is scheduled to be extended on to Marseille, linking Paris with the next two largest cities in France. One problem: it takes three minutes to brake going at 160 mph. This really is not a problem, however, in that the system runs on its own rail corridor with no rail crossings.

Look for resemblances between the food service on the *Tres Grande Vitesse* and that provided on the commercial airline.

Probably the fanciest, certainly the most glamorous, train in history, the Orient Express, has been revived. The original Orient Express ran from Paris to Istanbul and was a favorite of royalty and the haut monde.

At a cost of $20 million the old cars have been carefully refurbished by the Sea Container Corporation. A train runs between London and the east coast of England. The passengers cross the English Channel and are picked up by a second train, which travels overnight to Venice.

Meals, service, and entertainment are in the atmosphere that served as a setting for Agatha Christie's thrillers, a memorable train ride.

There are really three Orient Expresses, the Nostalgic Orient Express that runs occasionally between Paris and Istanbul as did the original Orient Express; the Venice Simplon Orient Express that runs between Boulogne and Venice twice a week and from Paris to Venice three times a week; the English end of the Venice Simplon Orient Express that runs from London to Folkestone. Passengers cross the English Channel by ferry and then board the Venice Simplon Orient Express proper.

A popular way to see Europe is by rental car, often included as part of a travel package. The road planning map is usually courtesy of Auto Europe, a large rental car company.

The motorways of Britain have London as the focal point. Paris is the centerpoint of France's superhighways. In Germany the autobahns have no real speed limit and more highspeed driving than in any other country. Once the motorist gets off the superhighways, driving times can be very long because of narrow winding roads and the necessity of passing through innumerable towns and villages.

Much of continental Europe is served by multi-laned, divided highways. Many segments of these highway systems are toll roads. A complex of superhighways serves the Benelux countries (Belgium, The Netherlands, and Luxembourg).

Several toll roads radiate from Paris. A major one leads south to Dijon, Lyon, and Marseille. A branch goes all the way into Spain, then down the coast of Spain to Valencia.

Italy has a principal toll road (autostrada) running from Milan that branches off to reach Rome and Salerno (where the Americans landed in World War II). A separate branch skirts the Adriatic coast and moves to the heel of Italy at Taranto.

From Frankfort, a major international airport in Germany, a traveler can rent a car and drive by superhighway down through Stuttgart and Munich in Bavaria, then on to Salzburg, Austria, and across to Vienna. Or the traveler can head directly south from Frankfort, past Heidelburg and Freiburg and into Switzerland.

The person wanting to see the Cote d'Azur, the French Riviera, can get on a toll road north of Marseille and go east through Nice and Monte Carlo. The same road goes into the French Riviera at San Remo, through Geneva and to La Spezia.

Of the Communist Bloc countries, East Germany has the best divided highways.

Driving customs and regulations vary somewhat from country to country. Spain requires an international driver's license. West Germany, Italy, and Austria require home-state licenses to be translated. (An International Driving Permit carries nine languages: English, French, Spanish, Italian, German, Arabic, Greek, Japanese, and Swedish.)

In France the minimum age for renting a car is twenty-five; in Britain it is twenty-three; in most other European countries the minimum is twenty-one. In Britain and Ireland some car agencies will not rent to people over sixty-five.

Left-hand driving in Britain takes some getting used to. Better get an automatic shift, especially when starting off in a large city. (Other countries with left-hand driving are Ireland, Jamaica, the Bahamas, Japan, Kenya, New Zealand, Australia, South Africa, Zimbabwe, and the U.S. Virgin Islands.)

When driving in the left lane and approaching a traffic circle (called round-abouts in Britain), drivers must yield to motorists already in the circle.

In Scandinavia the practice is to drive with headlights on. This is law in Sweden and Finland. The practice is believed to reduce accidents. In Italy and Germany the custom when passing a car is to blink the headlights in addition to using the left-hand directional signal.

FIGURE 5.7 *Tiny Luxembourg has a number of medieval castles, this one is Vianden.*
The entire population numbers about 360,000. Icelandic Airlines and two Caribbean based airlines use Luxembourg as their European base.

Source: Luxembourg National Tourist Office.

Visitors to Europe should consider buying one of the standard guidebooks that give travel information, village by village, road by road and which also list museums, restaurants, and hotels. Karl Baedeker was the granddaddy of these guidebooks and some are considered classics. The books are very thorough, very detailed and humorless; more recent guidebooks are lighter, witty, and more selective.

Baedeker published twenty-five guidebooks covering Europe and North America. Louis Nagel, operating out of Geneva, Switzerland, is more comprehensive in countries covered in his forty-three books. When Richard Nixon was about to make his historic fence-mending trip to China, he and his entourage needed quick knowledge of the country. The White House called Nagel and received fifty volumes of his thick, red-jacketed guidelines on China. The books came via SwissAir along with a bill for $3,250.

Nagel tells more than many travelers want to know, including information about art, industry, agriculture, history, political science, and economics. Asked about the needs of readers who were interested in pure pleasure, Nagel retorted, "They are not our clients."

Americans traveling in Europe are probably best acquainted with the "Michelin Guides," Red and Green. The "Green Guides" include detailed city and town maps. The "Red Guides" are best known. They are the ones that rank hotels and restaurants. An establishment owner is highly pleased to receive a one-star rating. Two stars can mean a small fortune. Three stars, fortune and fame as well. Restaurant owners who lose a star have been known to commit suicide. The Michelin Guides are highly recommended for France and Germany. The "Blue Guides" are recommended for Greece, Russia, Spain, Ireland, and Britain.

THOSE IMPORTANT FOREIGN PHRASES

A travel book should probably include information about how to get into and around various countries. It would be valuable to include foreign language translations of much-used phrases like:

> In Greek: "George, your donkey has just eaten my passport."
> In Italian: "Please get your hand out of my pocket."
> In Chinese: "Sorry sir, you just stuck your chopstick in my eye."
> Most important is the question in all languages: "Where is the nearest toilet?"

It is reported that in Japan a European or American woman in the jam-packed trains is likely to be fondled or pinched. A possibly apocryphal story goes that one such lady grasped the offender's hand, lofted it into the air and called out, "Whose hand is this?"

An old guidebook issued to GI's in Europe during World War II is supposed to have translated this statement, "I am a lonely, wounded soldier looking for a friend." It probably worked.

Phrase books in the language of the country visited are also useful. Contrary to what is often heard, "Everyone speaks English," there are many parts of Europe where almost no one speaks English.

FRANCE

La Belle France. For many France is food, France is wine, France is an assorted bouquet of palaces and places.

After England, France is second in popularity for American tourists traveling to Europe. About 900,000 visit there each year. Some thirty million visitors each year leave more than $7 billion. The French spend close to $6 billion a year in foreign travel.

Like London, Paris has two principal airports, De Gaulle and Orly. Be sure you know which one you are leaving from. They are miles apart. The traffic in and out of these airports makes Paris the second busiest air center in Europe after London.

August is the best time to visit because the Parisians have departed in droves on vacation, and just as well. Paris is known for its high prices and some say that Paris would be a nice place if it were not for the Parisians. Don't expect the French police to be courteous. They won't disappoint you. Make fun of them and you land in jail.

The French are not your smiling, friendly hosts. The British visit France more than any other foreign country yet in one survey only two percent of the British respondents said they were fond of the French. Being fluent in French makes the visitor much more acceptable.

"Why shouldn't the visitor," asks the Frenchman, "learn French, the most civilized language in the world?"

More Germans visit France than any other national group and it is little wonder that they are not particulary loved by the French. World War I and II memories are not easy to erase.

There are a variety of reasons why France is so popular with visitors. It has long been known for art, architecture, literature, and love. The music is effervescent; so too is the champagne. Each region has something different to offer. To many, Paris is the center not only of France, but of the universe. For centuries French was the language of most European courts. Wine lovers have a choice of regions to explore, beginning with Bordeaux, moving on to Burgundy, on to the Champagne region and to a dozen other areas, each producing its own special wine. So, too, are there the regional cuisines to linger over.

The French Riviera has its own ambiance, sunshine, gambling and gamboling for all seasons. Normandy and Brittany represent other worlds.

Normandy and Brittany, once joined with England under one king, occupy the western coasts of France. Normandy, closest to England, was the scene of the Allied landings in World War II. Its sandy beaches and resorts are especially popular with French vacationers in the summer.

Normandy has the incomparable Mont St. Michel, the island monastery. It can be reached by land only when the tide is out. Then there are the Loire Valley and the French Alps, and so on.

France is easy to get around in. It has a few superhighways and some of the fastest trains. There are pleasure trips via barge-and-canal and for something different, balloon rides and lunch with a countess.

Wine lovers feel they must visit the chateaux wineries of Bordeaux, which extend south from the city of Bordeaux and along the Dordogne river. Burgundy is in Central France with Beaune as its wine capital.

The Rhone Valley, southeast from Lyon and south of Marseille on the Mediterranean, has numerous Roman ruins. The southern provinces of Languedoc and Provence are popular vacation areas with the French.

Many Americans travel to Reims, capital of the champagne country in northeastern France. Farther east is Strasbourg, an important industrial center best known to gourmets as the home of pate de foie gras, the fat goose liver pate.

It comes as a surprise that Paris is a good deal farther north than Quebec. Even so the Gulf Stream and the Mediterranean produce a temperate climate where in most of France it usually rains when you think it is about to snow.

American visitors go first to Paris to savor its architecture, museums, haute couture, and especially its food. They take the cityrama bus tour, cruise the Seine, visit the racetrack at Longchamps, ride the elevator up the Eiffel Tower, stroll what is perhaps the world's most famous avenue, the Champs d'Elysses, and are properly awed when visiting Les Invalides.

Next they are likely to radiate out from Paris into the Ile de France, of which Paris is the center. The Ile de France is described as "being within five miles of Paris in any direction." Chateaux and cathedrals abound in the area. Versailles, the most impressive of all palaces, is nearby. So too is the little Rueil-Malmaison palace, home of Josephine, Napoleon's first wife. Fountainbleau Palace is thirty-five minutes from Paris by train. The Chateau Chantilly, built by the Princes of Condi, is there, the place where the maitre d'hotel of the reigning prince committed suicide because the fish did not arrive in time to be served to Louis XIV, who was expected for lunch. The forests were once the scene of royal hunts, pre-hunt feasts, sounds of horns and hounds and stags brought to bay.

The Eiffel Tower is the universal symbol of Paris, France's number one tourist attraction. Unlike its counterpart London attraction, The Tower of London, the Eiffel Tower has always been a fun place. Constructed by Gustave Eiffel in 1889 for the Paris World Exhibition, it was built by a public company. It was once the world's loftiest piece of construction, 1,050 feet tall. Now it is 60 percent owned by the City of Paris.

Platforms at various levels within the Tower dispense long-distance views, food at various prices and ambiance, a small movie theater, and at the very top the best view of Paris around. The summit is open until 11 p.m. and has four remote control elevators to serve it. The first-floor restaurant, La Belle France, offers a fixed price lunch and dinner and such a la carte main dishes as veal with roquefort sauce, salmon fillet, and sirloin steak. On the same floor is the Salle Gustave Eiffel, a multipurpose room for rent to conference groups and others. Snack bars serve croissants, quiches and pate sandwiches. And for the postcard-sending tourist there is a post office which affirms that the visitor has indeed been to the Eiffel Tower by stamping outgoing mail with an Eiffel Tower seal.

The Louvre in Paris is probably the best known art museum in the world. It occupies what was an enormous palace. It is really six separate museums which for the museum-lover will take weeks of study. Notre Dame Cathedral sits in the very core of Paris, the Ile de la Cite, awesome in its majesty. The Arc de Triomphe is another Parisian landmark, located at the top of one of the world's great avenues, the Champs d'Elysses (the Elysian Fields). Largest of its kind, the arch was built in tribute to Napoleon, who despite his eventual defeat remains one of France's great heroes. The Invalides, tomb of Napoleon and the Sacre-Coeur Basilica are "musts."

Paris offers a unique tour into and along the sewer system of Paris. A trip on the Seine carries the visitor past Notre Dame and through much of old Paris. Then most visitors enjoy sitting with an aperitif or wine in a sidewalk cafe.

The Loire Valley, the "Garden of France," about two hours by car or train from Paris, is perhaps the next stop. More than 120 chateaux with names like Amboise, Chambord and Richelieu grace the Valley. Tours is the principal town. Loire wines such as Vouvray and Chinon served with the local fish, cheese, and desserts are rewards unto themselves.

Each chateau tells a story of love or power or greed or conspicuous consumption. At Mainey the Chateau Vaux-Le-Vicomte is a story of greed and covetousness; greed on the part of Financial Secretary Fouquet who built the chateau with tax money; covetousness by young King Louis XIV, who on August 17, 1661, arrived for a sumptuous feast. The palace was more beautiful and impressive than any held by Louis. Soon afterwards Fouquet was arrested and the chateau changed hands. Today the gardens, waters, grottos, and park are considered the most beautiful in France after those at Versailles.

Sixty miles southwest of Paris is Chartres Cathedral, one of the best known and loveliest of the world of cathedrals. It is less than an hour by train from Paris' Montparnasse station. It is said to be the only great Gothic cathedral to have survived wars, reformations and revolutions comparatively unscathed. Chartres rests on seven hundred years of history and has three thousand square feet of stained glass illustrating aspects of life and faith during the Middle Ages. It displays so much fine sculpture that Rodin, the famous French sculptor, called it "the French Acropolis."

The beach tourist area for France is the French Riviera, or as the French call it, The Cote d'Azur, the blue coast. It extends from Marseille in Southeast France all the way across Southern France and into the Italian Riviera, ending at La Spezia in Northwest Italy. The sun shines year-round on places like Cannes, Juan-les-Pins, Nice and Monte Carlo.

Thanks to Lord Brougham, at the time Lord Chancellor of Britain, Cannes was started on its way to being one of the first winter resorts of modern times. It was 1834 and he was on his way to Nice when turned back by a cholera epidemic. Stopping at the little port (it derives its name from the canes growing in a nearby marsh), he liked the place so well he built a house. Friends followed and by 1890 as many as sixty members of Europe's royalty were spending their winters there—more than enough to give the place a cachet.

The French Riviera has been a winter retreat for the British, a playground for the playboys, and more recently for the middle-class visitor from hither and yon. It's nice to be in Nice, the center of the Rivera where many streets have English names, thanks to the British who began their sojourning in the middle of the nineteenth century. The Cote d'Azur has a series of art museums and fine restaurants. The term "Nicoise" applied to a dish means fresh vegetables, tuna and anchovies, named for the people of Nice. Bouillabaisse, the spicy fish stew, originated here, and farther west in Marseille, Provencal cookery emphasizes onions, garlic, tomatoes, and olive oil.

Fruits, vegetables and herbs can be had in colorful open markets. Shops generally close for two hours at midday, reopening for several hours until early evening. Cannes is known for its annual film festival. Men enjoy ogling the topless bathing beauties while the ladies pour over four blocks of chic beachfront shops. In Nice the Hotel de Paris and the Negresco rank among the world's best.

The villas of the 1920s have given way to condominiums and cheek-by-jowl hotels. Compared to the great sandy beaches of Maui or even California, the rocky little beaches of the glamorous Riviera are small potatoes. True, hotels like the Negresco and the Hotel du Cap ($300 a day) recall the days of ostentatious affluence. The high season of yesteryear has changed from winter to summer, peaking in July and August. The shoulder periods of May, June, and September are less expensive.

The rail trip beginning at Marseille and skirting the Mediterranean coast into Italy is not as well-known by Americans as other scenic rail trips. Some people who take the trip say they became so enthralled by the scenery that they spent much of the time standing between carriages so as not to miss any of the splendid views. The Corniche roads along the French Riviera are also spectacular, as witness the numerous chase scenes filmed on them for spy-thriller movies.

True wine devotees must make the pilgrimage to the Bordeaux and Burgundy wine regions, Bordeaux running north and south in western France, Burgundy in the east.

France has had the island of Corsica since 1769. Ethnically Italian, it had been in the hands of Genoa and Pisa for at least three hundred years. It is called "The Scented Island" because of the aroma that rises from the maquis, a dense undergrowth of plants, shrubs, wildflowers, aromatic herbs, ferns, arbutus, myrtle, lavender, and bay. Tourist attractions are few other than the birthplace of Napoleon Bonaparte in Ajaccio, the capital. Population is 200,000; its dimensions are fifty by one hundred miles.

France has a well-developed road system, about 420,000 miles of it, with superhighways, toll roads, between Paris–Lille; Paris–Lyons; Paris–Normandy; Lyons–Marseille; Esterel–Cote d'Azur; and Orange–Narbonne. Driving is on the right-hand side of the road. Yellow head lamps are compulsory on French cars. There is no overall speed limit in France, but on most roads the speed limit is 110 kilometers per hour (sixty-six miles per hour).

The TGV is in the same tradition for the French as the *Concorde*—lots of speed. In fact, TGV trains are the fastest in the world. There are eighteen round-trips a day between the Gare de Lyon in Paris and Lyon, France's second city in population. The trip takes two hours and ten minutes to cover the 266 miles. Geneva, Switzerland, takes three hours and a half; Paris to Lausanne, three hours and thirty-six minutes.

The TGV ride is similar to that in an airplane. In first-class, one row of single seats and one of twin seats made of molded plastic. Second-class cars hold four seats across with less padding. Attendants bring drinks and food via a trolley and food service is by tray. Cold platters are available in second-class and a stand-up bar that separates first- and second-class cars has sandwiches and croque-monsieurs. Rail buffs deplore the lack of mystique and the absence of dining cars.

The name Paris hotels, The Ritz, Crillon, Georges V, Bristol, Plaza Athene, and the like, are expensive. In 1984 a room cost between $100 and $200, and not so strangely 30 to 50 percent of their clientele are Americans. Staff outnumber rooms about two to one. Of these grand hotels only the Crillon is French-owned, owned by the Taittinger champagne family. Smaller hotels in the same general vicinity, in the heart of Paris, are reasonably priced, and many believe have more character. Individually owned, each has its own personality and is often managed by the proprietors. Many are within walking distance of Notre Dame Cathedral.

France's forty thousand tourist hotels are graded by the government according to the one to four-star system; four-star L and four-star are deluxe and first-class. The one-star hotels are "simple but comfortable."

The grading system applies to "hotels de tourisme" only. Others are not officially graded and their rates and conditions are not controlled.

Many hotels offer "pension" and "demi-pension" rates. "Pension" is equivalent to American Plan with three meals included in the rate. "Demi-pension" is similar to the Modified American Plan, MAP, which includes breakfast and lunch or breakfast and dinner.

"Les Auberges de Vacances" are inexpensive country inns. The "Relais de Campagne and Chateaux-Hotels" is an association of castles, abbeys and manor houses offering elegant accommodations and meals. The meals are expensive in some cases, more so than the cost of the rooms. Not all of the owners are your friendly host type; some are more concerned with their seignorial lineage than with service to their guests.

French hotel rooms are likely to come equipped with a bidet, not for washing your clothes, feet, or hair. They are for hygenic washing of the "private parts," straddling the bidet while the water flushes up. Bathtubs often come with a hand-held shower spray, and in the smaller hotels and pensions bring your own soap.

A good many tourists select France merely to dine well. Judged by most food authorities, France is pre-eminent in cooking and restaurants. A restaurant ranked three-star by Michelin's Guide has an accolade that insures the restaurant owner's fortune and constant concern in maintaining the rating. The French gave the world such delicacies as pate de foie gras (pate of goose liver), escargots (snails), onion soup, frog legs, duck in orange sauce, and beef burgundy. Much of their culinary lexicon and many of their food preparation methods are now part of English and other languages.

The French repertoire of foods ranges from songbirds to snails. It is said that the French eat anything that moves. Cole Porter, the song writer, remarked that "Americans keep horses as pets, the British ride them, but the French eat them."

French cuisine has something for everyone, peasant, bourgeoisie, and aristocrat. The peasant perfected the "pot-au-feu," the pot-on-the-fire, for a very practical reason. He could simmer a pot full of bouillon, cheap cuts of beef and whatever vegetables were available on a slow fire for hours while he and his wife worked in the field. Now it is served in fine restaurants and called by a food writer, "French poetry in a pot." A good red wine as accompaniment no doubt is mandatory to achieve the poetry.

Do not ask for ketchup in a French restaurant. The French take great pains in making their sauces. Coffee is drunk only after the meal, with dessert. During the meal, it is wine or mineral water. Ice water with the meal is only for heathens.

French restaurants run the gamut from hole-in-the-wall to gastronomic shrine; from small places called Bistros with checkered tablecloths and paper placemats, to cafes and bars; from "libre-service" (self-service) cafeteria style to the attentive service including a maitre d'hotel, captain, chef de rang and commis found in three-star, very expensive restaurants with worldwide reputations.

"Restorontes" are snackbar restaurants attached to service stations along the highways. "Brasseries" are a cross between a restaurant and a bar. Most restaurants post a menu outside. The "prix-fixe" (fixed-price) is usually cheaper than ordering a la carte (item by item). Many restaurants post a "menu touristque" which usually includes an appetizer, a main dish chosen from the day's a la carte menu, and cheese or dessert.

Probably no people except the starving take food as seriously as the French. The French notion of eating is a linear progression from the spicy appetizer through fish, flesh, salad, cheese, fruit, sweet, and coffee.

Word-of-mouth is usually the best advertising for travel destinations, accommodations, attractions and restaurants. Next best for Europe, according to many people, are *The Michelin Guides* for France, Britain and Ireland, Spain and Portugal, Western Germany, and the Benelux countries. The gastronomic gospel according to the Michelin committee in Paris is laid out according to a star system. Three stars go to restaurants that are culinary paragons.

France has recently had only eighteen to twenty-one such restaurants. About ninety French restaurants receive two stars. Some 530 restaurants get the one-star accolade. In Michelin parlance a three-star rating means "exceptional cuisine, worth a special journey." Two stars denotes "excellent cooking, worth a detour." A one-star restaurant apparently is not worth going out of the way but "very good cooking in its class."

The Michelin inspectors think very few three-star restaurants exist outside of France. No other country gets more than one or a few such ratings. The Michelin books have the virtue of experience; the first were published in 1900. They also contain maps, information on hotels, repair services and other travel information.

WEST GERMANY

West Germans spend more on international travel than people from any other country, including the U.S. Income from foreign visitors for 1981 was $6.3 billion; outgo was $17.8 billion, leaving a travel deficit of $11.6 billion, by all odds the largest in the world.

Germans average more than twenty-seven days a year vacation time and they work only 31.6 hours a week compared to thirty-five for Americans and thirty-nine for the average Japanese. Where do the Germans travel? Everywhere. Look out from a cliff on the island of Madeira. A solitary swimmer is out 500 yards, pumping away as if in a race. Chances are he's a German. Who is hunting the stag in Scotland? Probably a German. Climb the Matterhorn and there you find the Germans ahead of you.

Most of Germany's visitors are from neighboring countries: the Netherlands, Austria, France, Switzerland, and Denmark.

Frankfort is the major gateway and West Europe's busiest airport.

The Frankfort terminal has train service leaving from below the airport. Fifteen minutes later the passenger is in the city's central train station. Germany's railroads are efficient and clean. Germany—the size of Oregon—has fifteen thousand miles of track over which twenty thousand trains serve forty-seven cities daily. Forty express trains run between Frankfort and Cologne.

Lufthansa, the national air carrier of Germany, has arranged for a novel "Lufthansa Airport Express" to serve air travelers flying from the Frankfort Airport. Three Speedtrains ET 403 of the German Bundesbahn travel four times daily from the Dusseldorf Railroad Station. Passing through Cologne and Bonn, the nation's capital, they connect with continental and intercontinental flights at the Frankfort Airport. The Rheingold, a trans-European express train, is put together especially for tourists. It is the only train in Germany with a bar car. In winter, the Rheingold connects Amsterdam and Basel, Switzerland. In summer, three cars are detached at Mannheim and take the scenic route to Munich. A stewardess pours Rhine wine and serves a five-course lunch.

Germany was a pioneer in building the superhighway. The first autobahn was built under Hitler during the 1930s. Theoretically the speed limit is eighty mph, but Germans let out their macho by roaring along at speeds well over one hundred mph. Woe to the driver who gets into the passing lane at a normal speed. Accidents are frequent. Secondary roads

FIGURE 5.8 *Map of West Germany.*

wind up and down and around. One of the most beautiful is that which follows the Moselle River Valley. Here are the vine-laden slopes which produce the flower-scented Moselle wine. Picturesque villages with lovely small hotels line the river. At its southern end the Moselle forms a winding boundary between Germany and Luxembourg. Flowing north, the river joins the Rhine.

One of the most pleasant ways to see much of romantic Germany is to boat down the Rhine River. Luxury boats stop along the way for passengers to walk about the towns and villages. Meals are taken aboard. The boats are spotlessly clean.

Berlin, as can be seen on the map, is deep inside another, unfriendly, country, the German Democratic Republic, popularly called East Germany. A major autobahn (super-highway) runs from Hanover, West Germany, all the way across East Germany, passing close to Berlin. Most North American tourists fly into Berlin. The well-known wall dividing Berlin from East Berlin is not a real barrier to tourists, most of whom visit East Berlin as day-trippers. Potsdam, the old Prussian capital, is interesting for its royal architecture. East Germany's poulation is about seventeen million compared to West Germany's sixty-two million. East Germany has the highest living standard of the Communist bloc. The Bach Festival in Leipzig, the Handel Festival in Halle and the Schumann Competition in Zwickau are international attractions in East Germany.

Bavaria is a tourist center for Germany, with good reason. The people are ''gemutlich,'' more congenial, the mountains more pleasant, the forest more agreeable and then there are those fairy tale palaces that inspired Disney and his Cinderella Castles. King Ludwig II, who built these best known of the Bavarian palaces, may have been mad but he was also an architectural genius.

Munich, Bavaria's capital, is said to be every German's favorite city. Its Oktoberfest is when the million and half "Muenchners" invite the rest of us to join them drinking beer for three weeks in the fall.

Munich's main railway station, Hauptbahnhof, is quickly reached by airport bus. Like most of Germany, Munich has excellent public transportation, including streetcars, buses, a subway system, and the S-Bahn, a rapid-transit system.

Besides the beer, which Bavarians drink copiously, there is "weisswurst," a fresh sausage traditionally eaten before ten in the morning. It's made the night before of finely ground veal, parsley, grated lemon peel, white pepper and a choice of spices selected by the sausagemaker. It is served piping hot from a pot or grill with tart-sweet mustard and a crisp roll or coarse peasant bread.

Shopping centers with pedestrian walks are around the Marienplatz. On the city's outskirts is Schloss Nymphenburg, formerly the palace of Bavarian royalty.

Wurzburg, a Franconian wine town, has been called a jewel box of the rococo. About an hour-and-a-half by train from Frankfort, it is also a great place to start on Germany's Romantic Road. The Road runs from the Main River to the Bavarian Alps, through wooded hills, past vineyards, ruins, castles and museum towns. Rothenburg Ob der Tauber preserves a number of Renaissance buildings and squares.

Like Salzburg, below Bavaria, Wurzburg's buildings were created by noble archbishops. The bishops' Residenz is an anomaly, a palace fit for a king; the Hofkirche is said to be the most dazzling of all German rococo churches.

Overlooking Wurzburg is the fortress of Marienberg, the residence for the bishops before the Palace was built. The town itself is replete with pastry shops, tearooms and taverns. Wurzburg is known for its vineyards and the white wines produced. The local beer and sausage have also acquired a reputation.

Germany provides a range of accommodation from youth hostel to hotel, farmhouse to "fremdenheimes" (rooms for rent in homes), campgrounds to castles. Look for the sign "Zimmer frei." The youth hostels, primarily for young people under twenty, are probably the most efficient, up-to-date in the world. They total some six hundred with sixty-five thousand beds. Bikers and hikers love them. The tourist can also pitch a tent at more than twenty-one hundred camp sites.

The deluxe hotels are really deluxe; even the water in the bath is tested by a large thermometer to make it the exact temperature desired.

Germany has some 250 health resorts, of which Baden Baden is the best known. Here the visitor seeking rejuvenation takes the baths and drinks the waters. Gambling and "being seen" are part of the appeal.

As it is with Australians beer is a way of life for Germans. The Germans think of it as very much a part of the "gemutlich" life, the agreeable life, also a principal nutrient. Bavarians, particularly, have a reputation for being more easygoing and fun-loving than northern Germans—partly, no doubt, because the average Bavarian drinks more than 220 quarts of beer a year (compared with one hundred quarts for the average American). Thirty percent of the daily nutritional intake of the average Bavarian is from German beer.

By law German beer must be made from malt, hops, and water. The ingredients may be basically the same but Germany's thirteen hundred brewers have come up with six thousand different beer brands. Munich can be called the beer capital of the world since it is also the capital of Bavaria, where nine hundred brewers are busy brewing away. As yet "thin is not in" in Germany.

The German culinary tradition emphasizes pork and veal, potatoes, cabbage, dumplings, and beer. German wines are among the best but are not produced in the quantities found in Italy, France, and Algeria. Lard is the common fat used in cooking. A typical German meal includes sausage, bread, potatoes, and beer. In some places beer is less expensive than milk.

The three favorite foods of Germany, says one report, are yellow pea soup with bock-wurst (a chubby frankfurter), bacon along with eisbein (pig hock) and sauerkraut. Roast goose with dumplings is also a favorite.

Germans like dozens of sausage varieties. Blutwurst, blood sausage, is one of their favorites. The French like their variety "boudin noir" even more. Blood pudding, as the English call it, is not quite de rigueur. Blutwurst, say the Germans, is best served with plenty of beer or added to choucroute, fresh sauerkraut combined with meat. Or the blutwurst may be lightly smoked, dried, and sliced for snacking. The best known sausage of German origin, of course, is the frankfurter.

THE NETHERLANDS

Officially Holland is called The Netherlands. Holland was the largest Dutch Province and incorporated the country's three largest and most prosperous cities: Amsterdam, The Hague and Rotterdam. The original Province is now divided into Noord-Holland and Suid-Holland. About the size of Maryland, The Netherlands is low and flat, which makes for great bicycling. The North Sea gives the country a mild, damp climate. The North Sea has also given Holland much of its land. Rather, the Dutch have taken the land away from the North Sea by enclosing sections of the sea with dikes, pumping the water into the sea, thereby adding land. A fifth of Holland's acreage is still under water. A Dutch motto goes: "God made the world with the exception of Holland, which was made by the Dutch."

Originally the water was pumped out by windmill, which became a tourist trademark. A century ago about eleven thousand windmills were at work; now the figure is close to nine hundred fifty, of which three hundred are still used for a variety of agricultural and commerical purposes. Each windmill has two doors—for a reason. The vanes are constructed to be rotated 360 degrees to catch the wind from any direction. A person entering the mill took the door that was safe from the rotating vanes. Today some of the old windmills have been turned into cozy, round homes.

Coming into Holland by air the visitor usually lands at Amsterdam's international airport, Schiphol. Amsterdam, like Stockholm, is a city of islands—ninety islands, forty canals and four hundred bridges. It is an interesting city to explore. The canals, not streets, set the pattern. They carry visitors and residents on a variety of watercraft. Narrated tours, including a dinner cruise, travel over a large part of the city. Efficient trolleys are another travel choice, moving along the major avenues, crossing canals and connecting main squares. Amsterdam is the constitutional capital of the country; The Hague is its de facto capital.

The Hague, home of the Queen, and the Binnerhof, the complex of medieval buildings where Parliament meets, is thirty-four minutes away from the airport by trains that depart every half hour. The Hague is a music-loving city with weekend concerts, numerous jazz cafes and theaters that offer ballet, opera, and chamber music.

Trains also run every half hour between The Hague and Amsterdam, fifty-five minutes apart. A brief bus or train ride from The Hague is Scheveningen (skay-vuh-ningen), Holland's version of Atlantic City. On the North Sea, Scheveningen had been a popular seaside resort town, then began to deteriorate. In 1973 the Hague Town Council began a ten-year redevelopment plan. The Kurhaus (cure house), the landmark hotel, was rebuilt into a luxury hotel that includes a casino.

No swimming in the North Sea unless you are interested in joining the Polar Bear Club. The water is frigid and polluted. Even so, in the summer the beaches are crammed with cabanas. The air is bracing. A week of continuous sunshine is a novelty. Dutch sun worshipers ship out to the south of France and to Spain. Summer temperatures seldom exceed seventy-five degrees. The winters are long and damp. The weather in The Netherlands, as in England, is a major topic of conversation.

The Dutch are very much interested in food. Heavy breakfasts of bread, meat, eggs, fruit are similar to those in Denmark. Holland is known for its dairy products and because

FIGURE 5.9 *National symbol.* Think of Holland and you think of waterways, dikes, and wind-mills.

Source: Netherlands National Tourist Office.

of its long association with Indonesia (formerly the Dutch East Indies) includes the traditional rice table, the rijsttafel, and curried dishes.

The Dutch have a reputation for cleanliness, so much so that a cleanser powder, Old Dutch Cleanser, was named after them. They are also known to be very tolerant. For several years counter-culture groups parked themselves in one of Amsterdam's squares, openly took drugs and carried on in ways few other cities would have tolerated. After a time even the Dutch had enough and moved them out. Tolerance for German visitors is also strained because of memories of the occupation of The Netherlands by the Germans during World Wars I and II.

Literacy, learning and languages are prized in the Dutch culture. Nearly every Dutch person speaks English. Many are familiar with other languages as well as their Dutch language. The Dutch are music lovers; The Amsterdam Concertgebouw orchestra and the resident philharmonic orchestras in The Hague and in Rotterdam are often featured in fine recordings. Their public gardens also rank among the best in the world.

SPAIN

Spain, a country of 37.5 million people, sees forty million visitors, mostly other Europeans, each year who contribute $6.5 billion to the Spanish economy. There is more than enough to see and do in Spain. There are castles in Spain, a multitude of churches, shopping, a unique cuisine, bullfights, a long coast on the Mediterranean plus islands off the Mediterranean coast and off the northwest coast of Africa. Nowhere is there a wider and more interesting range of lodging offered than in Spain. At the deluxe end of the scale are the Ritz and Palace hotels in Madrid. Each of the government-owned paradors is different, many an experience. The converted castles and palaces are particularly interesting and usually house the best restaurants in their areas. (What with their large staffs, overly long menus and reasonable prices, the paradors cannot be profitable. Coordination in marketing and operation also is lacking.)

Hanging down from Europe, Spain is part of the Iberian Peninsula, with Portugal to the west making up the rest of the peninsula. Spain is the third largest country in Europe after Russia and France. To the east in the Mediterranean Sea are the Balearic Islands—Ibiza, Mallorca, Minorca and Formentera. Majorca (the Spanish is Majorca, English is Mallorca) has a low mountain range along its northeastern coast. Ibiza is hilly, Minorca mostly flat. Also a part of political Spain are the Canary Islands, sixty-five miles off the northwest coast of Africa. Mountains characterize Spain proper with Mulhacen, the highest peak, at 11,411 feet. The Pyrenees help define Spain by barracading it from the European continent to the north. In some places they are actually higher than the Alps, the best known of the European mountains. Mountains also skirt much of the East Coast that makes up seven-eighths of the Spanish border. By blocking the moist sea winds, most of Spain experiences a pleasantly dry climate (also a shortage of water in many places). The upper mountain slopes have snow most of the winter and there are a few ski resorts. Summers are hot and dry. Short, heavy rainstorms are common in the winter. The river Tagus flows west through Central Spain and Portugal to empty into the Atlantic Ocean.

Madrid is to Spain what Mexico City is to Mexico, the capital city and the center of most activity—business and political. Its population of about 3.3 million makes it by far Spain's largest city. It sits on a plateau surrounded by mountains.

Principal tourist attractions in and near Madrid are the Prado Museum, with one of the great art collections of the world, featuring a Goya collection, several Rubens and Van Dykes, the Royal Palaces in Madrid, one at Aranjuez and another, El Escorial, a great somber pile, twenty-seven miles northwest of the city.

The museum towns of Toledo and Avila, looking much as they did five hundred years ago should not be missed. If at all possible stay at the Parador that overlooks Toledo and buy yourself a replica of the sword used by El Cid in his battles against the Moors (Toledo is known for its finely crafted swords).

Barcelona, Spain's second largest city (about 1.8 million people), is Spain's leading seaport and greatest industrial center.

Valencia, the third largest city, has a population of about 700,000. It is a sunny garden city surrounded by orange groves, a port city on the Mediterranean.

Seville, with about 600,000 population, ranks as a tourist center because of its historical buildings and cultural heritage. Seville has Spain's largest cathedral which also is the largest Gothic building in the world.

Spain is regionalized, each region somewhat different in topography and custom. The people of Astoria in northwest Spain are blue-eyed. The northeast is Basque, the people with strong, prominent noses and a great desire for their own government. Castile sits in central Spain; the people have narrow faces and sallow skins. The inhabitants of Andalusia in the south have olive skin with dark brown or black hair. Andalusia is a meld of Spanish and the legacy of the Moors is seen in the coloring of the people and architecture of Seville, Cordoba, and Granada.

There are indeed castles in Spain, castles the like of which are not seen in the rest of Europe. The best known, the most intricately built, the loveliest of castles is not strictly Spanish. It is the last stronghold and palace of the Moors, who after eight hundred years relinquished their power in southern Spain to Columbus's patrons, Ferdinand and Isabella. That was in the fifteenth century. Today the Alhambra with its sister palace/garden, the Generalife, is the number one tourist attraction in Spain.

The Alhambra, on the outskirts of Granada, is seventy-seven miles from Malaga, one of the international gateways to Spain. It also has direct flights from Madrid. The Alhambra suggests the Arab's idea of heaven, complete with flowers, tinkling waters and beautiful houris. It is a palace with twenty-five or more interiors and courtyards. The Court of the Lions is the Alhambra's "piece de resistance." In the center of the courtyard is a fountain supported by twelve amiable lions, each spewing water from its mouth. Each side of the court is backed by a room, artistic in its own right. The visitor can imagine the robed courtiers, the veiled beauties of the harem, muted voices and the intrigue.

The Parador San Francisco has replaced a convent which in turn replaced a Moorish palace on the Alhambra grounds. There are only twenty-six double rooms. Like all paradors, it is rated four-stars, one star less than the five-star luxury hotels. At least take a meal in the Parador. Two other four-star hostelries are in Granada nearby.

In Cordoba a major cathedral has been built within a mosque, a rare accommodation made by one religion to another.

Much of Spain's tourist activity lines up on the Mediterranean Coast, especially along the Costa del Sol, south of Malaga. Only a few years ago the "sun coast" was a sleepy series of villages. Now it is solid hotels, restaurants, villas, and condominiums. The town of Marbella is at its center. Malaga is a departure point for Morocco via ferry or hydrofoil.

The Costa Brava (the brave or wild coast) centering on Barcelona is to the north. It is difficult to get to by road, less crowded and unspoiled. Cadaques is the recommended town. Avoid it though during August, when the Spanish, like the French, take their vacations.

The image of all-season swimming on the Mediterranean beaches of Spain is misleading since winter is sunny but definitely not warm enough for swimming.

The Balearic Islands—Mallorca, Minorca and Ibiza—in the Mediterranean are sizable tourist centers. Englishmen found them less expensive for spending the winter than remaining at home. Cheap charter flights and tours bring hundreds of thousands of Germans and other Northern Europeans south to the islands and to the Costa del Sol.

For those who really want to live dangerously there is Pamplona, where a tourist may manage to join in the crowd of Navarre youths who risk life and limb in the running of the bulls. Fortified with enough wine, those participating climb over the barriers into the street where a herd of bulls are coursed. It is part of the Fiesta de San Fermin, between July 6 and 20.

Spain's Canary Islands, sixty-five miles of Africa's northwest coast, are two-and-a-half hours by jet from Madrid and are popular with Northern Europeans because of the benign climate and low cost. They have not really been discovered by Americans. The Canaries' most populous island, The Gran Canaria, has a population of 520,000 and boasts a year-round swimming climate. Scenery varies from lush tropical jungle to stark and arid deserts. The islands have over nine hundred varieties of flowering plants and two hundred twenty species of birds, including the native canary. Las Palmas has more than one hundred hotels and twice as many restaurants. Las Palmas on Gran Canaria is the hub for Canary Island tourism.

Spain is mystery, Spain is exotic, much of Spain is a little eerie. Its most awesome attraction is the "El Valle de los Caidos," the Valley of the Fallen, hammered out of solid rock at the direction of General Franco, by thousands of prisoners from the Spanish Civil War. The place is a sepulcher equipped with an organ. The bones of hundreds of soldiers who died in the Civil War are interred there. So, too, is General Franco.

About an hour's drive from Madrid, the setting, high in the mountains, is awesome with clouds as a close backdrop. It is a huge cavern with a supernatural feeling. The National Tourist office does not promote the place. Perhaps it evokes overmuch of the Spanish past when brother fought brother, no quarter given, none asked.

Catholic Spain. Few countries are more homogeneous in religion. In the past it was Catholicism gone amuck. Religion was a convenient rationalization for enslaving millions of Indians in Mexico and South America. The Inquisition was an act of faith for rooting out and preferably disposing of any who believed other than the "true" faith. Church and state were almost one entity.

Today the church is more tolerant, church and state less compatible. Rituals are still very important. Nearly every Spaniard passes the milestone rituals of life—baptism, first communion, marriage and a funeral mass—in the church.

Bullfighting is another widely observed ritual. Leading toreadors are national heroes.

Like the Oriental, the Spaniard is much concerned with appearances and sometimes behaves illogically to save face. The Latins' concern with "dignidad" comes quite naturally from Spain. Carried to an extreme it becomes "machismo," the absurd concern for "manliness."

Tourism in Spain showed spectacular growth in the 1960s under dictator Franco. By artificially controlling labor costs and prices, the Franco Government made Spain a major tourist destination, vying with France and Italy in attracting hundreds of thousands of visitors yearly. Room and meal prices are specified according to a rigid set of criteria. Hotels are classified according to room size and furnishings, luxury of appointments and extent of the menu and service. Hotel construction was fostered with low interest loans and tax advantages. The Spanish police, The Guardia Civil, kept an iron hand on crime. No foreigner had cause for complaint of purse snatching or being bothered in any way. Since Franco's demise inflation blew most of the bargain prices away. Now there are nineteen gambling casinos. Today, in Spain and Italy, ladies are often robbed of their purses and satchels by men sailing by on motor scooters. One drives, the other snatches. To foil them ladies are advised not to carry over-the-shoulder bags or to wear them on the side opposite the street.

In Spain, eat when the Spaniards do. This means late suppers, beginning about 9:00 p.m. For nondieters there are topa bars to frequent before dinner. Topas, Spanish hors d'oeuvres, range from stuffed mushrooms to baby eels. Patrons are expected to buy wine or sherry.

Stay up all night and the in thing is to show up at a churria after 4:30 a.m. for churro or porra. Both are similar to deep-fried doughnuts. Dipped in thick, sweet Spanish-style hot chocolate, they are part of the all-night-out ritual.

The culinary experience in Spain centers around the many seafood dishes and an array of wines. Sherry is Spain's claim to wine fame. In fact, the name sherry comes from the way the English perceived the name Jerez, the town that is the sherry capital of the world. A tour of the wine storehouses, the "bodegas," is informative, and the sherry sampling a pleasure. Jerez de la Frontera is in the south of Spain; Northern Spain produces a number of table wines, some excellent.

Roast suckling pig, "cochinillo," is a favorite food in Spain. For groups the piglet is served spread-eagle, head and all, on a sizzling platter. Roasted so that the glazed skin is crackling crisp, the meat beneath a layer of fat is well done, tender and garlicky. Other dishes, exotic to the American palate, include baby squid in their own ink, with rice; lima beans with pork ears and feet; garlic soup. This soup as it cooks loses most of the characteristic garlic flavor and takes on a personality of its own. Of course, if a visitor is to pick the one Spanish dish to remember, it is paella, the medley of seafood and boiled rice. Restaurants usually require orders in advance to prepare it.

PORTUGAL

Sharing the Iberian Peninsula with Spain, the little country of Portugal has a growing number of visitors. Lisbon, the gateway city, has a number of direct flights from New York City. A good road system and few automobiles make for interesting tours by rental car, especially for the culturally and historically oriented visitor. Royalty and aristocracy have been officially displaced. Their castles and palaces constitute built-in tourist attractions and a few are available as hotels.

Lisbon is a beautifully laid out city thanks to the Marquis de Pombal. Following a great earthquake and resultant tidal wave that leveled most of the city, he decreed that much of what was left be razed and a new city built along broad avenues. Lisbon also has the advantage of overlooking the Tagus River, which runs 566 miles through Spain and Portugal and empties into the Atlantic Ocean.

The old section of Lisbon is medieval with windings streets and a walled castle. Not far away on the Atlantic coast is Estoril, a favorite residence for nobility and for kings and queens who are no longer wanted in their home countries.

Up the coast is Oporto, from whence Port, fortified wine, is shipped to England and other overseas countries.

Visitors to Portugal increase as word spreads of the range of its attractions, from metropolitan Lisbon to the wine country of Oporto north to the Algarve resort region along the southern coast. Hotels are graded by the government, five-star being the top. In a class by itself is the Hotel Ritz in Lisbon, built at the request (read command) of the last dictator.

FIGURE 5.10 *"Campo Pequeno."* On a sunny Sunday afternoon this scene in front of Lisbon's Moorish bullring changes into a mass of activity—tourists and aficionados pour into the "Campo Pequeno" for a few hours of color, high excitement, and comedy. Best of all, no one gets hurt, not even the bull, for it is against the law to kill the bull in Portugal.

Source: Portuguese National Tourist Office.

Also the Reid Hotel on the Island of Madeira, a part of Portugal, is in a class by itself. Built by a sergeant who had served his time in the British army in India before returning to England, it is stepped on the side of a cliff. At the turn of the century when the Reid Hotel was built, Madeira was a coaling stop for ships and its principal export was Madeira wine. Reid Hotel gives a glimpse of the grand hotel style of the 1920s. The service is impeccable. Also there is a grand view of the Atlantic.

To live like a marquis try the Hotel Palacio de Setais, near Sintra, about an hour out of Lisbon. A true palace, it was built by a Dutchman who had cornered the Brazilian diamond market. Later a Portuguese marquis made it his residence. Not far away is a fairy

FIGURE 5.11 *Funchal, Madeira.* Funchal rises like an amphitheater behind the crescent bay.

Source: Portuguese National Tourist Office.

tale royal palace, the summer home of the last Portuguese royalty. (The last king abdicated in 1910.)

To feel the ambiance of another time try one of the twenty-five government-owned "pousadas," several of them modernized castles, palaces and monasteries, most of them beautifully sited, and furnished to reflect the cultural tradition of the area.

To partially experience life in medieval times, dine and stop overnight in the pousada in the walled town of Ubidos. It stretches the imagination to see people living in the exact same rooms that have been inhabited for centuries.

For the devout Catholic there is the shrine of Fatima, built on the spot where it is believed the mother of Christ appeared six times to three of the local children. Hundreds of thousands visit the shrine for renewal of faith and in the hope of miraculous cures.

A five-and-a-half hour drive over two-lane highways or a thirty-minute flight from Lisbon takes the visitor to the Algarve. The word Algarve is Arabic for Al-Gharb, "the West." The Algarve, a Moorish kingdom before becoming Portuguese, forms the base of Portugal and boasts five five-star hotels, intervaled along the coast. The beaches are magnificent. White stone buildings, filigreed mineret-like chimneys, twisting alleys and grillwork balconies suggest North Africa. The whitewashed buildings reflect the intense summer sun. In January and February there is a spectacular show of almond blossoms. Late spring and early fall are the really comfortable periods in which to visit. Winters are mild, a kind of microclimate set aside from the rest of Portugal, but not mild enough for swimming.

Sagres sits at the western end of the Algarve, eighty-five miles from the Spanish border on the east. Roads here are narrow and winding. Albufeira is called the St. Tropez of the Algarve, partly because numerous hippies are in evidence selling beads and bracelets.

The town of Lagos has the dubious distinction of being the site of Europe's first slave market.

The Spanish border at the eastern end of the Algarve is marked by the Guadiana River. Rinky-dink ferries run frequently between Vila Real de San Antonio on the Portuguese side to Ayamonte, Spain.

Portuguese food is a close cousin to that served in Spain. The two countries were for a long time under the same rule. The Portuguese chowder "coldeirada" is especially good, with onions, tomatoes, and fish. Coastal villages and towns feature seafood. Grilled sardines, seven inches long, are a specialty, sprinkled with coarse salt and served with lettuce and tomato. Sole, "linguado"; sea bass, "robalo"; swordfish, "peixe espada" are served grilled or steamed with boiled potatoes. For something different there are squid, "lula"; baby octopus, "polvo"; and couger eel, "safio." "Arroz do mariscos" is the Portuguese version of Spain's paella. The dessert menu is limited. Creme caramel, a boiled custard similar to Mexican flan, is usually on hand. Portuguese wine, especially Port, and "vinho verde," green wine, slightly bubbly and pleasantly acidic, are outstanding.

ITALY

Italy, according to ENIT, the Italian National Tourist Board, ranks as one of the top two or three tourist destinations of the world. About fifteen million foreign visitors arrive each year. Germans are the most numerous. The French are the second largest group of visitors. Visitors from the United States rank third. The province of Venetia with its crown jewel, Venice, attracts the most visitors. The ancient cities of Verona and Padua are part of the province. Rome and the province of Latium are number two. Then comes Tuscany, which boasts Florence, Pisa, and Siena. Figure 5.12 shows Venice sitting on the Adriatic Sea in Northeast Italy. Rome, where "all roads lead to," is seen in Central Italy. Florence is almost directly north of Rome.

The Romans built the super-highways of the ancient world. Roads followed the conquering legions and formed a network that laced together the Roman Empire. Slaves, convicts and legionnaires cut roadbeds and laid stone to form roads which by decree were built

FIGURE 5.12   *Map of Italy.*

to last forever. Some are still being used today. The most famous is the Appian Way, running south from Rome and then across Italy to the Adriatic Sea and eventually to Brindisi.

Huge volcanic paving blocks topped the road, fitted together without mortar. Where possible the road runs straight as an arrow. Started in 312 B.C. it begins near the Colosseum in Rome and runs 360 miles. It took ten to fifteen days to travel, but the emperors were transported by carriers working in relays in six days.

Which side of the road did Romans use, the right or the left? Looking at the ruts left by the iron-rimmed wheels, the ancient Romans did the same as modern-day Romans—they used the middle.

Americans usually reach Italy by flying first to Rome or arriving from Switzerland or France by train or road.

Autostradas (superhighways) traverse Italy and all are toll roads. Four of the European superhighways terminate in Italy: the E 2 runs from London to Brindisi; the E 6 from Oslo to Rome; the E 7 from Warsaw to Rome; the E 14 from Prague to Trieste.

Rome's Fiumicino Airport is twenty-five miles outside the city. Blue airport buses run every fifteen minutes to the central Termini station, a trip taking about forty-five minutes.

Italy has been a leading tourist destination since the days of The Grand Tour, an adventure in antiques and human volatility. Englishmen of means were sent abroad to round off their education. Accompanied by an older person, they usually first toured the principalities of Northern Europe, then ended up in Italy, where they viewed the art collections, met with the resident Englishmen and sowed some wild oats. Back home they built Palladian-style mansions based on the neoclassical style of Palladio, architect of palaces in Northern Italy.

It is doubtful if any destination in the world has had more descriptive superlatives used in its behalf than Venice. "See Venice and die," "The Doges Palace is surely one of the most beautiful and surprising buildings in the world," "As the sun strikes the golden, onion-shaped domes of the Cathedral and all the spires and belfries blaze like wings of Golconda, my heart leaps for the glory spread before me." Bonaparte called the Piazza "the most beautiful drawing room in the world." Even the ubiquitous pigeons in the square must tend to their matters of toilet elsewhere.

The place smells of history. (Some of the canals just smell.) A city-state no more than three miles long and scarcely two miles wide, a world power for several hundred years—no small accomplishment. At one point, forty-five ships were built each day in its famous Arsenal. Venetian "cristallo," the prized clear-thin glass, could not be duplicated elsewhere. The monopoly was secured by sending assassins to find and kill any glassblower foolish enough to leave Venice.

Venice is a maze of 118 islets ringed by canals, some three thousand bridges, squares, and alleyways. And you find Venice's trademark, the gondola. There were eleven thousand of them in Venice in the sixteenth century.

The city is literally built on tree trunks. Over a million stilts were hammered into the mud to support the Church of the Salute. Venice floats—but is gradually sinking into the mud.

Generated by wind, the Adriatic is frequently driven up the Venetian Lagoon to flood the streets and squares of Venice. In 1979 merchants along St. Mark's Square, a low part of the city, were forced to close their shops two hundred times. A siren warning is given and ground-floor apartment dwellers roll up their rugs and block up their furniture. Tourists teeter along on raised planks across St. Mark's Square, unable to give much attention to the famed Doges Palace. Of course, the Italians would like Americans to send money to save the city from sinking further.

Venice, the city without roads, has some of the most modern garages to be found anywhere. Motorists can enter Venice on a two-mile bridge crossing the Venetian Lagoon. The first buildings seen are the garages, seven-story blocks of steel, concrete and glass. Only two of Venice's 118 islands can be reached by auto. For the other 116 you walk, take a water-bus, or a gondola (very expensive).

Do not expect to lie back in peace and quiet listening to the laments of a gondolier. It's against union rules. If you want music you hire a singer and instrumentalist. The canals are busy, complete with traffic lights and once in a while traffic jams. The Grand Canal is two-and-a-half miles long and eighty yards wide. Most of the rest of the 150 canals are narrow and often smelly.

In summer, some days bring 100,000 visitors to Venice, the majority of whom board a vaporetto, so-called because they were once steam driven. These 150-seat boats carry passengers up and down the Grand Canal to the Piazza San Marco and to and around the Arsenal and the architectural wonders of Venice. Some boats head toward the Adriatic Sea with stops at the beaches of the Lido.

Florence, first among Italian renaissance cities, dominated and ornamented by the Medici family, is the art lover's Mecca, exemplar of what was best in Renaissance art. Florence is the number one choice of Americans interested in the painting, sculpture and architecture of the fourteenth and fifteenth centuries.

FIGURE 5.13 *One of the world's best known tourist gathering spots is San Marcos Square in Venice, Italy.*

Source: Italian Government Travel Office.

   Visitors to Florence find the place jammed in the summer, the prices and temperatures high. They have great difficulty in finding a table in the town's most famous square, Piazza della Signoria. It was here in 1497 that the fiery Dominican priest, Savonarola, touched the Florentines' sense of guilt from too much good living, and set the torch to books, paintings and musical instruments. Unfortunately for Savonarola, the guilt feelings were fleeting. The next year in the same square the torch was set to Savonarola.
   The merchant families of Florence had prospered during the period of the Crusades from trade in wool. The fine gold stamped with a lily, the florin, became an international currency. By the 1420s the Medici clan had emerged as Florence's leading family and in 1434 Cosimo Medici became Florence's ruler. Other Medicis followed in power. Cosimo, and especially Lorenzo the Magnificent, collected art and built palaces. Cosimo provided the first public library in Europe. Lorenzo, his grandson, by the time he died in 1492, had amassed an unsurpassed art collection. The Medici family ruled until 1737. Their palace is still the government headquarters of Florence. Their villa at Castillo nearby houses a scholarly academy. Their offices, the Uffizi, are crammed with art treasures. Their family motto, "In the name of God and good luck," put into action by a shrewd and energetic family, has meant a lot of good luck for the city of Florence and for the millions of visitors who have come to experience a living Renaissance city.
   Jewelry shoppers will probably visit the Ponte Vecchio Bridge over the Arno River where the shops of jewelers and goldsmiths have been located since the fifteenth century. They will probably not know that the bridge was first occupied by the town's butchers who located there so they could toss their by-products into the Arno River. They built their

homes on top of their shops. The odors got so vile that the ruler had them replaced by the jewelers and goldsmiths.

If the average American were asked to name the five most important cities in the world, Rome would probably be one of them. A major reason is that Rome surrounds Vatican City, a separate entity governed by the Pope and his cardinals. One of the ironies of travel is that the tiniest of all states attracts more visitors than most nations. Vatican City, 108.7 acres in size with a population of one thousand, attracts as many as eight million of the faithful and the curious. The USSR, the biggest country, attracts a relatively small number other than from neighboring communist bloc countries. Religion may be the opiate of the people but it also stimulates great numbers of believers into taking long journeys—not only Christians to Rome, but Muslims by the millions to Mecca. To carry comparisons even further, Disney World attracts at least 50 percent more visitors than Vatican City.

Vatican City is entertainment as well as art and architecture. The very serious Swiss Guards wear striped red, yellow, and blue uniforms with leg-of-mutton sleeves. St. Peter's Basilica overpowers the viewer, esthetically and in sheer size, the largest and most awesome church in the world. It has standing room for 100,000 people and contains a library of one million volumes. The Vatican Woods and Gardens has trees, flowers, footpaths, fountains of all shapes and, of course, marble angels. There is the seventeenth century Galleon complete with water cannons and a marble boy at the prow blowing a spray through his horn. Vatican Radio is one of the world's most powerful, broadcasting programs in thirty languages. The Teutonic Cemetery goes back to the year 799 A.D. and some of its soil was brought from the hillside in Jerusalem where Christ died on the cross. A three hundred-bed "hotel" operated by nuns caters to pilgrims. On the west side of St. Peter's Square is the Vatican Tourism Information Office.

Rome is the principal gateway city by air to Italy via the Leonardo da Vinci Airport. As the old saying goes, "All roads lead to Rome." Roads radiate from Rome like spokes in a wheel. A circular road, the Grand Raccardo Anulare, twelve kilometers from the city center, allows motorists to bypass the central city or enter it from the most convenient direction. The Stazione Termini, the main railroad station, is one of Europe's largest.

Rome is the sightseer's city. Nearly every American has heard of the Colosseum, the Forum, and the Pantheon.

Rome is also for the romantic. Who has not heard of the Trevi Fountain that inspired the song "Three Coins in a Fountain"? One coin tossed over the shoulder assured the visitor of returning to Rome, two guaranteed happiness. What the tourist does not notice are the rather sinister young men watching the performance who have little of the romantic in them. They guard the coins, amounting to several hundred dollars daily, as they are dropped into the fountain. At night this mafia group take turns in sweeping up the money. The Italian police, cynics to the core, do not bother the collectors. Their answer: "If we do not let them take the coins, they will steal them from the tourist." So much for "three coins in a fountain."

When in Rome do as the Romans do; well not quite. Rome needs no more noisy scooters rattling the windows of houses on narrow streets at midnight. Rome needs no more rip-off artists who are glad to relieve visitors of their money. Rome needs no more auto drivers who think they are charioteers whirling through the Pincio Gate and around the dozens of monuments from ancient Rome.

Driving a rental car in Italian cities is only for the brave or the oblivious. Who needs traffic lights when driving can be a game of dodge-em or chicken. Street signs are not a part of the culture and streets change names without notice. One-way streets are not necessarily one-way. Double parking on Italian streets is quite normal. It's not your everyday variety of *dolce vita*.

The weather in Rome is usually fairly pleasant. But every once in a while Rome is struck by a sirocco, the hot, sand-laden wind from out of the Libyan desert, south across the Mediterranean. The wind usually lasts three days and is more frequent in late summer and fall. The Romans, said to be quite sensitive to weather changes, are reputed to experience a sirocco syndrome. According to one observer the people get dejected or quarrelsome;

office workers, sales assistants and waiters are listless and scowl; the suicide rate and the incidence of traffic accidents rise. If domestic violence occurs during a sirocco, a court may later consider the weather an extenuating circumstance. Pity the poor Romans in a real sandstorm.

Romantic Verona sits at the base of the Italian Alps, surrounded by hills and fed by the Adige River. Fortunately it avoids the crush of tourists found in Venice, an hour away, or of Florence, farther south. Lake Garda is less than an hour through rolling hills. Shakespeare was Verona's best publicist, writing Romeo and Juliet. Juliet's tomb is there and the little church where she and Romeo were married is next door.

The largest extant Roman amphitheater, seating twenty-five thousand, is an open-air opera in Verona during the summers. A Shakespeare festival, ballets and concerts also fill the amphitheater.

The Due Torri (Two Towers) hotel is the place to stay. Originally the official guest house of the ruling Scaligeri family, it was rebuilt in 1958. Each floor has its own parlor-library, each of the one hundred rooms and suites its eighteenth and nineteenth century antiques. Verona itself is almost a museum town; remnants of ancient Roman architecture dot the city. Ten bridges cross the Adige River. One, the Ponte Pietra, dates from the end of the Roman Republic.

Summertime in Verona, like that of most Italian cities, finds the citizens and visitors alike ensconced in the alfresco cafes sipping cappucino, the concentrated coffee pick-me-up, or enjoying a local tart (a sweet, that is), or roll. Ices, similar to sherbets, are also popular, and in many places a needed antidote to the heat. In Verona it is the Piazza Erbe (Square of Herbs) that is the gathering point. It once was the local Roman forum around which chariot races were held.

East of Verona is Vicenza with its more than one hundred mansions, many of which were designed by Palladio, whose name is associated with the Palladian style of architecture. The city is a kind of land-based Venice. Venice itself is less than an hour beyond.

Naples, once considered an architectural paragon and premier place to visit, is not recommended today. The city has lost its charm due to traffic jams, pollution, huge unemployment, and a high crime rate.

Herculaneum, near Naples, has been likened to a time capsule buried beneath more than sixty feet of ash when Mount Vesuvius erupted in 79 A.D. Four thousand people had lived there on the seaside with a view of the Bay of Naples. Now it sits in a pit surrounded by the modern town of Ercolano, a suburb of Naples, and a series of greenhouses. Herculaneum, like Pompeii, not far away, is like a peepshow into the past.

The Isle of Capri has captured the imagination of Roman emperors and modern day tourists. It is reached by steamer or hydrofoil from Naples. The steamer takes one-and-a-half hours, the hydrofoil about forty minutes. The island offers a variety of landscapes, grottos, sea caverns, and the remains of the Emperor Tiberius' lavish villa on top of Monte Tiberio.

Capri is a major tourist attraction because of its rugged topography, several secluded coves suitable for year-round sunning and swimming and its Blue Grotto. The Grotto encloses a small body of water with an opening so small that it must be entered by rowboat. Inside, the water is a luminous blue. Needless to say, Capri is jammed during the summer high season. Two small towns, Capri, and above it, Anacapri, occupy the island.

Besides Rome the other major Italian cities are Milan (1.7 million); Naples (1.3 million), sitting above the toe of the boot; and Turin (1.15 million) in the industrial north, capital of Piedmont region (the Fiat auto originates there).

The Italians are one of the most expressive of people, with gestures, eyes and body language. All this gives talking about even things like the weather dramatic quality. Another means of expression is the strike. Strikes come frequently and unpredictably. Air travel employees like to strike. At one point Alitalia pilots were ready to strike because they were not given transport to the airport, separate from the other cabin crew. Buildings and public performances are closed without prior notice. Even the Sistine Chapel closes at 1:00 p.m. Museums are closed for no apparent reasons. Advice to the visitor when he sees a "chiuso" (closed) sign—repair to the nearest restaurant and order a cup of cappucino, that is, if the restaurant has not closed.

Italians take a lot of kidding from other nationalities. A Russian satirist writes: "All the Italians ever do is just sing and draw. I mean, an Italian will stand and sing and next to him another will be drawing the one who's singing. And nearby will be a third Italian singing about the one who is drawing. It's a sight to make a man sad. But they can't understand that."[2]

Young girls traipsing about Italy are almost certain to be pursued, and vigorously, by young Italian men—sometimes to the point of distraction. The introductions may be crude: "Come on Bebe, let's make a babe." The tourist season is seen by some of the natives as the opening of the hunting season. A true incident: a visitor to Naples grasped the wrist of a pickpocket as he was making his heist. The visitor yelled for a policeman, who eventually arrived. To the astonishment of the visitor the cop was on the side of the pickpocket and berated the tourist, demanding he release the pickpocket with the simple logic: "That's his only way of making a living."

Purse-snatching is an old Italian custom. One story has it that in 1932 excavators of ancient Herculaneum found two perfectly preserved bodies. One, apparently a patrician, lay on his face. Next to him lay a second body, his hand in the patrician's money bag. The report says, "Death caught the thief in the act." Modern day thieves don't stop with purses. They grab luggage in airports and rail stations. Visitors are urged not to leave valuables in hotel rooms or even in locked autos. And check the change received when making a purchase.

Italy's place on the world map is a surprise to most of us. It is a long, thin country covering eleven degrees of latitude. The north is on a level with Quebec, its southern tip with North Carolina. Parts of Italy may experience three months of snow while Sicily is subtropical.

Florence, Rome, and Venice are endeared to art lovers. The Italian Riviera is a geographical continuation of the French Riviera. The better Italian beaches are mostly privately owned, called lidos, with admission fees. Mediterranean pollution is widespread. One expert says that 70 percent of all Italian beaches present a health hazard. At times smog is as bad in Rome, Turin and Milan as in Tokyo, Los Angeles, or Mexico City.

Sardinia, second largest island in the Mediterranean after Sicily, has mostly clean water touching its many miles of beaches. Sardinia presents a range of tourist accommodations, from inexpensive to deluxe, a summer resort for the European jet set, most of it the work of the Aga Khan and friends. Their resorts are served by their own air service from mainland Italy.

Northern Italy shares the Alps with Switzerland. Lake Como is not far from Milan, and Milan can be reached directly by plane from New York City. The Trans-European express train from Paris takes eight-and-a-half hours. At Cernobbio the Villa d'Este Hotel floats its own pool in Como Lake—no pollution that way. Usually, more than half the guests at the hotel are American.

The Tlahan lake country boasts of clean air and in the winter is a favorite ski area. In addition to Lake Como, two other lakes, Lake Gorda and Lake Maggiore, are popular resort spots. Lake Gorda, the largest, is two miles wide and forty miles long. Lake Maggiore is shared by Italy and Switzerland.

Visitors to Italy are almost always taken with the abundance of cafes, pastry shops, and restaurants, many with alfresco seating. Italian cookery is justly famous. It was the fourteen-year-old Caterina de Medici, princess of Florence, who in the sixteenth century married the French Dauphine, and triggered the French concentration on food preparation. She brought with her to France three chefs and Italian recipes. At that time, tomatoes, which originated in the new world, had not gained favor. Today Italian cuisine is built around pasta and tomato paste, polenta, olive oil, and veal. The pasta comes in dozens of forms, each with its own name. There are cappelletti (little caps), conchiglie (conch-shaped shells), farfalle (tiny bow ties), pater nostri (elbow macaroni), tagliatelli, lasagna, and ravioli, to name a few. Add spinach and you have "verde," green pasta.

Think of Italian cooking and think of onions, shallots and garlic, anchovies and black olives. The usual Italian cheeses are the grating cheeses but there are also the blue cheese, Gorganzola, the mild Bel Paese, and a number of lesser known varieties.

Italian cooking is regionalized. Pasta and tomato sauce characterize Southern Italy. Spicing is used throughout Italy: parsley, sweet basil, marjoram, rosemary, sage, bay leaves, oregano. Thyme, mint, fennel, juniper berries are also a part of the culinary scene. Food from Bologna in the north is rich with butter and cream, subtle and more complex than in the south.

Polenta (corn meal) is popular in Northern Italy. Rice (risotto) is used widely, as is sausage, especially mortadella.

Bologna is known for its mortadella, its special thick pork sausage, as well as for its twenty-two miles of covered porticoes in mid-city. It is known for its "pasticcerias" (pastry shops), as well as for its two twelfth-century towers, one of which, the Garisenda, leans more than its more famous cousin, the Leaning Tower of Pisa.

Veal is more popular than beef and "osso buco" appears on most complete Italian menus. The dish is composed from the simmered shinbone of veal with added butter, olive oil, celery, onion, rosemary, and sage. A typical Italian dessert, "Zuppa Inglese" resembles the English trifle, layered sponge cake, with fruit preserves, vanilla custard, and whipped cream.

Italian ice cream, gelato, is given more care and variety than that produced by either Howard Johnsons or Baskin Robbins. Who has tasted artichoke, mango, whiskey or rhubarb ice cream? Italian gelato is not as deeply frozen as American ice cream and it usually contains fresh eggs and cream. The Italian variety is spared the several stablizers used in American ice cream. When traveling in Italy save several thousand lire to visit the local gelato haven, as one writer puts it, a place of cold comfort.

Italy's most popular drink is espresso, the concentrated black coffee, expressly brewed for immediate consumption. Espresso bars dot Rome, Naples and the larger cities, stand-up bars where the patron gets a jump-start in the morning, recoups his energy once or twice during the day. An espresso completes the evening meal at home or in a restaurant.

The espresso machine creates steam that passes through freshly deep-roasted and ground coffee. A quantity of concentrated brewed coffee pours into a small cup, capped with a thin wreath of brown foam. With milk it becomes cappuchino. Brandy can be added.

Like beer, the character of espresso comes from the water used. The pantheon section of Rome has the reputation of being one of the best places for the caffeine fix. The water in the area flows through a fourteen-mile aqueduct functioning since 19 B.C.

Espresso bars also offer soft drinks, beer, hard liquor, sandwiches, hamburgers, or other fast food. The places themselves almost always gleam with chromium and marble. Neon lighting adds a garish note.

The espresso bar is no place to linger. Patrons get in and out fast. Five to ten minutes to pay for the coffee, leaving a few cents tip and then join the locals who feel they deserve a break, are bored, feel low or want to come elbow-to-elbow with other people.

Italian hotels are government ranked, deluxe at the top, first-class and down to third-class. Italy's hotel classification system is such that the second-class hotel ranks in quality with most of America's first-class hotels, but is lower in price. The Campagnia Italiana Grande Alberght (CIGA) chain is the best known of the more expensive Italian hotels. Service charges of 15 percent are usually added to the room rate. Other taxes may also be added so that the basic room rate may be increased by one-third.

SWITZERLAND

As someone once said, "Money alone does not bring happiness; one must also have it in Switzerland." Switzerland has been called "the playground of Europe," a country with incomparable natural beauty, a vigorous proud people who do not mind at all serving visitors as long as it is profitable.

Tourism brings Switzerland about $3 billion a year income and a worldwide reputation as superior innkeepers. Something like a half million Americans enjoy the country each year. The Swiss are also big travelers. On a per capita basis, they are the biggest of all international travelers, even though that may mean only going a few miles to cross a national border.

Switzerland attracts the athletic, mountain climbers, skiers, tobogganers, and hikers. It is one of the cleanest countries in the world: a mixture of mountains, lakes, and valleys found nowhere else. The British are credited with initiating world tourism to Switzerland

FIGURE 5.14 *Typical scene.* Think of Switzerland and we think of mountains, lakes, and skiing. One of the best known mountains in the world, the Matterhorn, is seen here in the background of Zermat.

Source: Swiss National Tourist Office.

in the 1860s. Mountain climbing in Switzerland has long been a favorite visitor experience. The tradition of the Swiss guide goes back for more than a hundred years, services that should be employed in making any of the more hazardous ascents. The visitors can cross glaciers, hike to most of the climbing huts and even climb the 11,500 foot peaks without using ropes. The Alps are the greatest of the several wonders of Switzerland, mountains that are sharply defined rock and snow. These features are highlighted by a valley of hay-fields, alpine flowers, chalets, and cows.

The Alps mountain chain runs approximately east and west through the southern part of the country and constitutes about 60 percent of Switzerland's total area. The Jura Mountains, a spur of the Alps, stretch from the southwest to the northwest and occupy about 10 percent of the land area. The remaining 30 percent is a plateau between the two ranges where large cities and industrial activity are concentrated.

The Swiss Alpine Club, founded in 1863, teaches mountaineering courses to those who want to learn climbing, both beginning and advanced. The major mountain ranges include the Pennine Alps in the southcentral canton of Valais and the central range of the Bernese Oberland, the easterly ranges of the Engadine and Bergell that abuts the Italian border.

The Matterhorn shares with Mt. Fuji in Japan the accolade, "The most photographed mountain in the world." Jungfrau, 13,640 feet, is one of the most beautiful mountains anywhere. Just below it is a restaurant and cafeteria above-the-clouds.

Anyone suffering from heart trouble, weak lungs, or high blood pressure should consult his doctor before taking any of the mountain trips.

Switzerland is home for the International Red Cross and is highly sophisticated in mountain rescue. Even so, helicopters have not completely replaced the Saint Bernard in mountain rescues.

Think of an "in" place to ski and Switzerland leaps to mind: mountain villages, lively inns and unexcelled ski facilities. Today the cognoscenti of skiing, that is the more affluent ones, choose the Swiss Alps not only for the skiing but the civilized pleasures that go with a Swiss vacation. Alpine grandeur is complemented by the Disneyland style of Swiss village life. Where else can downhill skiers experience runs up to fourteen miles long? Starting in Zermatt, for example, you can ski to Italy for lunch, then ski back to Zermatt in time for supper. St. Moritz and Gstad are internationally known ski centers. Celebrities also choose Gstad and several own chalets there. Elizabeth Taylor, for one, likes Gstad so much that she has brought all eight husbands there (one at a time).

Switzerland is a little more than half the size of Maine and nothing is very far from the main roads and railroads. Cog railroads and cable cars go to the middle heights and well defined paths to the feet of the climbs. Comfortable huts are spotted throughout the mountains.

Little Switzerland manages to have three international gateway airports: Zurich, Geneva and Basel. Travel is quick and highly scenic by car or train throughout the country. The electrified rail system covers three thousand miles.

With a 400,000 population Zurich is the nation's largest city and its leading banking and financial center. Geneva enjoys an international reputation for culture and sophistication and is home to the World Trade Center and the United Nations. Basel, second-largest of Swiss cities, sits on the Rhine River and like Zurich is a business and corporate head-quarters city. Switzerland's capital is Bern.

Geneva is headquarters for more than 140 international organizations whose bureaucrats knew what they were doing when they selected Geneva for a home. The Rhine River rises in the heart of Geneva as it leaves the Lake of Geneva. The city also sits astride the winding river called the L'Arve and, as a backdrop, has the Alps, with Mt. Blanc at 15,771 feet the highest peak in Europe.

Since Geneva is a city of conferences and business meetings that take place mostly at times other than the summer, July and August are good months for a choice of accommodations. The Geneva Tourist office offers the free use of a sightseeing map and of a tape keyed to a two-hour walk through the historic section of the city. The tapes come in five languages.

The Swiss climate is invigorating and varies with the altitude. Ticino is Switzerland's Italian corner, where in the shadow of the Alps palm trees grow. Zermatt lies below one of the best known of mountains, the Matterhorn. More people live in the zone with the moderate climate than in all of the rest of Switzerland.

Schaffhausen-on-the-Rhine is just about where you would think it would be—on the Rhine—but not in Germany as might be suspected by the name, but in Switzerland. The residents do speak German just as inevitably as French is the mother tongue of Geneva and Italian is what is heard around Lake Lugano in the southernmost province of Switzerland. The Rhine Falls are just above Schaffhausen in Switzerland, close by where the Rhine emerges from Lake Constance (the Germans call it Bodensee). The Falls is the mightiest in Europe. Two million Europeans visit the place each year. It has not yet been "discovered" by many Americans.

A sign outside a restaurant in the Canton of Valais, "Ici raclette," makes many a mouth water. For inside, a half wheel of cheese made from whole milk is being toasted before a fire. As the sliced part of the cheese melts it is scraped off, served with boiled potatoes in their skins along with a white wine. These cheese scrapings, with their smoky flavor, eaten between bites of a boiled potato are beginning to acquire followers as enthusiastic as are cheese fondue lovers. For a do-it-yourself raclette, buy "fromage a raclette."

It is difficult to put a label on Swiss cookery because it blends with the cuisines of its neighbors, Germany, France, Italy, and Austria. Suffice to say that dairy products and the local wines are featured. Swiss chocolate has an international reputation. The Swiss, a very practical people, do not live for the table as do the French. Neither do they favor sausage as much as the Germans, nor pasta as do the Italians.

AUSTRIA

OFFICIAL NAME: REPUBLIC OF AUSTRIA

Austria is a precious little country where a good share of the farmers turn innkeeper for the summer. Almost $6 billion a year is derived from tourism. The sign "zimmer frei" (rooms for rent) is seen on homes in all of the scenic areas, and most of Austria is highly scenic—scenic in summer as a place to auto, hike, and sightsee; scenic in winter as a ski center. It is also a cultural bonanza, especially Innsbruck, Salzburg, and Vienna. Give Austrians high marks for cleanliness, punctuality and hard work. Give all those Austrian housewives who take in guests a round of applause for the ubiquitous flower boxes full of blooming geraniums.

Three-fourths of Austria is mountainous, much of it kept as Alpine meadows. Agriculture is possible at much higher elevations than normal because of the warm, dry wind from the south called the foehn. Average temperature for January is twenty-seven degrees; for June it is about sixty-seven degrees. Scenic finger lakes lie to the north and east of Salzburg. Lake Constance is shared with Switzerland.

The Germans are well aware of Austria's attractions and pour south over the German border by the thousands. They should! The food is close to being German—with beer, sausages, wiener schnitzel, potatoes. The wine, too, is close to the light whites of Germany. A night in Grindzig, on the outskirts of Vienna, with wine in mugs, rotisseried chicken, and violin and accordian music, is a night to remember. Each year about 400,000 Americans make the journey to Austria.

Vienna moves in three-quarter time. The violins tell of the beautiful blue Danube, unfortunately not blue any more. Nevertheless, the inner city is one of the really interesting living museums of our day. In the very center is St. Stephens Cathedral, sitting as the hub of a wheel, with the principal streets radiating out. The Hofburg Palace was the center of the Austro-Hungarian Empire. Until 1918 it was the administrative center for the fifty million people who made up the empire. Today its twenty-six hundred rooms are much alive as offices for national Austria, reduced to some seven million.

Tourists line up to see the crown jewels. Another line forms to see the beautiful Lippizaner horses of the Spanish Riding School, the most impressive such academy in the world.

Three imperial palaces left over from the days of empire grace Vienna. In addition to the Hofburg in the center of the city, there is Schonnbrunn, "the purest realization of the melody of Austrian baroque." About half the size of Hofburg, it has only 1,441 rooms, and sits on the outskirts of Vienna. Empress Maria Theresa, who built the palace, had sixteen children and each had to have his or her own princely suite and own small court. The Belvedere Palace, originally built for Prince Eugene of Savoy, military hero in battles against the Turks, is the third royal palace—later a residence of the Archduke Franz Joseph.

The Wienerwald, the Vienna Woods, is a resplendent green area of trees and hills around Vienna, stretching from the southwest to the north of the Danube. It is a greenbelt similar to London's greenbelt. Half-day tours, originating at the State Opera House, take you outside Vienna to the old Roman town of Baden and the Hinterbruhl, also to an old abbey, then to Mayerling where the son of the last emperor shot his mistress, then himself. (The hunting lodge where the suicide took place has been razed.)

Fifty miles from the Opera House is the Seagrotte, the old gypsum mine, so deep and large that during World War II it was used as a subterranean airplane factory by the Germans. Today it is a tourist attraction where at 180 feet below the surface is Europe's largest underground lake, 6,200 square feet in area, thirty-five feet at its deepest. Here the visitor can take a boat ride. The warmest part of the mine is fifty-five degrees.

Vienna is a city of streetcar travel; excellent streetcars cover the city. Visitors to Vienna should know that the streetcars often run in the opposite direction to automobile traffic in streets with one-way signs prominently displayed. Look both to right and left before crossing. Several tourists have been killed by not being aware of this. A visit to yesterday can be taken via antique streetcar on Sunday mornings, a trip that ends up at The Prater, one of the first large amusement parks in Europe.

Travel through Austria is easy via excellent roads or rail. No one should miss Salzburg (salt town) sitting on the Salz River. Its early importance came from its proximity to salt mines and to the river down which the salt was carried.

Its importance today comes largely from its baroque old town and annual music festival. The fact that Mozart was born and worked there gives added interest.

The entire old town of Salzburg is a living museum and just outside is a pleasure palace that appeals to all ages. Built by one of the archbishops of Salzburg, the place is replete with "water tricks," deer whose horns spout water at unsuspecting passers-by, chairs that soak the sitter when a hidden valve is turned, grottos that shower the viewer. There is even a water-driven organ and a miniature village of wooden figures, all activated by water power.

The range of accommodation is wide, from farmhouse to castle and, in common with Germans and Swiss, cleanliness is a compulsion. What with the natural attractions, its history, its architecture, the music and the attractive people, Austria is a place that urges return visits. The affluent traveler can stop with a count in a bona fide palace (for a price).

A scenic way of entering Austria is to fly to Zurich, Switzerland, then take a train into Austria. Briefly, on the way, the train passes through tiny Liechtenstein. Mountainous Austria was made for cross-country and downhill skiers. More than four hundred tracks are laid out covering some 3300 miles in Carinthia, Salzburg, Styria, Vorarlberg, and Lower and Upper Austria. Innsbruck is one of the well-known downhill ski centers. Grog and Linz are other major cities in Austria; neither is a tourist center.

The mountains are also for climbing, but use a guide. Some seven hundred are available for hire, four hundred in Tyrol alone. Wind currents in the mountains are superior for gliding. Innsbruck and Kufstein are good for "foehn gliding," gliding in the warm, dry "foehn," the south wind coming over the Alps.

Austrians like soup, particularly leberknoedelsuppe, meat broth with liver dumplings. Gulyassuppe, goulash soup, was borrowed from the Hungarians. Wiener schnitzel, breaded

FIGURE 5.15 *Mozart and music.* Salzburg, Austria, with its Hofburg Castle overlooking the old town, has become a major museum town partly because of the Mozart music festival held there each summer.

Source: Austrian National Tourist Office.

deep-fried veal steak, is popular. Holsteiner schnitzel means the same, plus a fried egg and an anchovy garnish. Cordon Bleu means schnitzel stuffed with ham and cheese, then deep-fried. Roast pork with dumplings, sausages, red cabbage and bread are particularly good. But best of all is the Austrian strudel, loaded with butter and apples. "Palatschinken" is the Austrian answer to the French crepe. Salzburger Norcherl, a souffle of eggs, sugar, butter, and flour, is a Salzburg special, made to order only. Coffee and a torte is an Austrian experience. And don't forget to try the sausages and beer.

The visitor to Vienna should not overlook the Latin origin of the name Vienna, which is Vin do Bona—or "good wine." Only about 10 percent of the region's wine is bottled—the rest is drunk locally, much of it in the suburb of Grinzing where it is downed to the accompaniment of the violin, accordion, and spitted chicken. The Vienna coffee house is more than a place for dispensing coffee. A travel writer describes it: "The Viennese coffee house is a singular institution, a club, a rendezvous, an office, a cultural society, the right place to be alone when you require company of others to do so; even a philosophy."[3] Unlike the California coffee shop where sociability gets short shrift and the emphasis is on quick seat turnover, the Vienna coffee house courts its patrons. One coffee buys you a seat for as long as you like plus access to an array of newspapers and periodicals. The institution goes back to 1683 when Vienna was besieged by the Turks. One Franz Georg Kolschitzky became something of a hero when he slipped behind the Turkish lines and reported back that the Turks were weaker than believed.

When the Turks left they also left the brown beans that have helped the Viennese through the day and bad times as well. Georg was awarded the beans and the right to brew and serve them. Thus the Viennese coffee house. If you want it black, ask for schwarzer or mocca. Kopuziner is more interesting: coffee with a dollop of cream, strewn with cocoa or chocolate flakes. Coffee goes well with Viennese pastry.

Demel's, one of the pastry houses, produces fifty-five different cakes and 250 kinds of cookies. Apple strudel topped "mit schlag," heavy cream, can be had all over Austria. (Get it early in the day. A few hours on the shelf and it becomes soggy.) In Austria gluttony is not a sin and the ladies are fashionably robust.

SCANDINAVIA

The name Scandinavia evokes images of Vikings, the midnight sun, blue water, and red-cheeked maidens. The five nations of Northern Europe—Sweden, Norway, Denmark, Finland and Iceland—collectively call themselves Scandinavia. Tourist-wise they market themselves as a group. Norway, Sweden, and Denmark together own and operate Scandinavian Airlines and parcel out management positions among the three countries, careful to avoid enmities, for the three have a history of rivalry and war. Norway was once a part of Denmark and its royal family was originally Danish. Iceland has its own Icelandic Air; Finland has Finnair. For North Americans Copenhagen is the major gateway.

FIGURE 5.16 *Finland's lake district.* An aerial view of spa city, Savonlinna, in the heart of Finland's Eastern lake district, shows the contrast between the city's modern architecture and medieval Olavinlinna Castle (see in the foreground) on an island of its own. Each summer, grand opera is presented during two weeks in the courtyard of the fifteenth century castle, which seats three thousand music lovers at each performance.

Source: Finland National Tourist Office.

To keep Scandinavia in perspective remember that the entire population of Sweden, the largest in population, is about the same as that of New York City. Denmark, the smallest, most southerly, lowest lying and most fragmented of the Scandinavian countries, is also one of the most interesting, especially for those who like sailing, biking, and eating. It has the most visitors. Without a doubt Copenhagen is the most interesting of the Scandinavian cities. Like Norway, Denmark has lakes that were once fjords but that are now closed to the sea by beaches. Other fjords form natural harbors, the solace of sailors. Denmark has a five-thousand-mile coastline.

DENMARK

OFFICIAL NAME: KINGDOM OF DENMARK

Denmark, located at the mouth of the Baltic Sea, consists of Jutland, a peninsula, and about five hundred islands, one hundred of them inhabited. Jutland occupies about 70 percent of the country. The straits between the islands connect the Baltic and the North Seas.

Denmark proper and the Faeroe Islands together are slightly smaller than Vermont and New Hampshire combined. Greenland, largest island in the world (857,159 sq. mi.), is part of Denmark under the constitution of June 5, 1953.

Jutland is the only part of Denmark not an island. The name Jutland is appropriate: the peninsula juts out from West Germany, a place of farms. Raincoats and umbrellas are important in Denmark travel. Arhus, the unofficial capital of Jutland, is highly recommended as a place to use as a base when visiting the peninsula of Jutland. Located in the center of Jutland, all points in Jutland are within three hours driving time.

Thanks to the Gulf Stream and the Atlantic Drift, Denmark's climate is surprisingly mild even though it is far north. The same is true of Southern Norway. Temperatures in Denmark seldom drop below freezing. Hours of daylight in all of Scandinavia vary greatly. In mid-June darkness falls for only a few hours in the twenty-four-hour day. In mid-December sunlight appears from only about 10:00 a.m. to 3:00 p.m.

Denmark has numerous castles and mansions open to visitors. Southern Sweden is known as chateaux country. Iceland has none. Finland has a few castles for public viewing. A number of Danish mansions take in guests as do some two hundred farm families. Farms are carefully inspected by the national tourist office and a farm must raise some livestock, mostly cattle and pigs, to be recommended. The Danish Farm Vacation is aimed at the family who wants a one- to three-week farm experience. Meals are eaten with the farmers. Country inns, known locally as "Kros," are a place to meet and mingle with the Danes.

The "Danmenu" program, sponsored by the government, offers inexpensive and typical Danish menus in more than five hundred restaurants. Member restaurants are categorized from inexpensively priced to moderately priced and characterized as "hearty and served in quantity." Danish food is not highly spiced. Onions, parsley, chives, horseradish, and pickled beets are used to add flavor. The most popular fruit pudding is "Rodgrog mid Flode," raspberry and currant juice plus heavy cream. As in Germany, pork is much more popular than beef.

All visitors, and especially if traveling in a group, should try a smorgasbord. A typical one might include five kinds of herring, fish pate, fish fillets, smoked halibut, shrimp, salmon, ham, fish stew, salads, cheeses, and fresh fruit. Hot meat entrees could include beef stroganoff, rib roast, or roast beef carved at the table.

Frikadeller, ground veal and pork patties, often served with pickled beets and boiled potatoes, vies as a national dish with the "smorrebread" (smear bread), the open-faced sandwiches spread with butter to prevent soakage.

Copenhagen, the capital and principal tourist center of Denmark, sits on an island, well away from the North Sea. It is an attractive, clean city with a sizable ocean front. Its climate, like all of Denmark, is "temperate marine," moderated by the surrounding waters, not too cold in winter, never hot in summer. Average rainfall is twenty-six inches annually. July and August are the wettest, the spring months the driest.

Shoppers in Copenhagen stroll the mile-long pedestrian street called Stroget. Furs, porcelain, woolen sweaters, crystal, figurines and, of course, Danish furniture are favorites.

Copenhagen, like all of Denmark, is the biker's paradise (except for the rainy days). Denmark is flat, making biking easy, and a number of bike tours are available. Of the 1.5 million people who live in and around Copenhagen, at least 300,000 are addicted pedalers. Excellent bike paths border most city streets and thread parks, plazas and public grounds. Phalanxes of bikes, even on main streets, seem to take precedence over autos. Tivoli Gardens are known worldwide even though tiny compared with entertainment complexes like Disneyland or Disney World.

Little Denmark has a tourist promotion budget of $8 million a year, larger than that for our U.S. Travel Office. Yet the country has only five million population.

FIGURE 5.17 *A familiar symbol.* The Little Mermaid sits pensively at the entrance of the harbor to Copenhagen, like the Statue of Liberty in New York City harbor, symbols of their respective cities.

Source: Danish National Tourist Office.

Denmark levies a 22 percent sales tax on accommodations, probably the highest any-where. A service charge is also included in the price of hotels, motels, inns and other guest accommodations.

The ancestors of Danes were Germanic tribes, Anglos, Saxons, and Danes. Today the typical Dane has the Nordic qualities of being tall, blond, blue-eyed and fair. Scandina-vians better meet the Nordic ideal, as proposed by Hitler, than does the typical German.

Danes are almost all Lutherans; 96 percent belong to the Evangelical church. The women's rights movement had a head start in Denmark, which may be good or bad for the ladies, depending upon one's viewpoint. Unmarrieds living together is common. So, too, are pregnant brides. Divorce is also common. About one in four marriages ends in divorce. In industry, it is equal rights with equal pay.

The Danes are socially advanced. They believe strongly in the welfare state and, like others who are fond of big government, resent the high taxes necessary to pay for it.

What are the Danes like as people? They are described as modest, nonfrivolous, hard working and proud. They are optimists, nature lovers, and as was amply demonstrated when the Germans took over during World War II, more than capable of standing up for decency even at great danger to themselves.

They seem to get along with each other better than in most places. One reason is the homogeneity of the people. The phone book is loaded with Andersens, Christiansens, Knudsens, and Jensens.

Copenhagen and Sweden are close neighbors, separated only a few miles by the Ore-sund, the narrow link between the North and Baltic Seas. A one-day trip from Copenhagen gives the visitor a taste of both countries. Trains leave Copenhagen every half hour for Helsingor, one hour to the north, along the "Danish Riviera." Helsingor is the site of the castle in Shakespeare's *Hamlet*. A short car-ferry ride lands one across the chan-nel in Helsengburg, Sweden. A ninety-minute train ride south, past the university town of Lund and rolling farmland, and the visitor is at Malmo. A hydrofoil run of forty minutes carries the visitor back to Copenhagen.

SWEDEN

OFFICIAL NAME: KINGDOM OF SWEDEN

Blue is the omnipresent color of Sweden. Blue waters, blue skies: in the sunlight, spark-ling blues; ominous blues when the skies are overcast. Even the Swedish flag is a yellow cross set in a field of blue.

Stockholm is the blue city, mainly because it is a series of fourteen islands, the "Venice of the North." The blueness sets off what is probably the most imaginative sculpture garden in the world. Millesgarden, the sculpture garden setting along the water, was given to Stockholm by Carl Milles. His sculptures seem to leap into the blue of the sky. Of the two great Scandinavian sculptors, Vigelund in Oslo and Milles in Stockholm, Milles is in the Greek tradition; man is beautifully proportioned. Milles' figures fly into space, images of Gods. Oslo's Vigelund Sculpture Park shows men and women as heavy, blocky figures, struggling upward. Vigelund's view is evolutionary, many straining upward from the soil, suffering, heavy and barely overcoming.

As cities go, Stockholm is low-rise, no skyscrapers blocking the sun. Compared to Paris, London or Vienna, Stockholm as a whole is architecturally commonplace. The City Hall, The Royal Palace, The Opera House, The House of the Swedish Nobility, "Reddarhuset," are noteworthy. The Royal Palace is massive enough, 250 rooms, but a block structure with minimal grace.

Outside of Stockholm is Drottingholm Palace, a small Versailles, with French park, straight-lines walkways, fountains, reflecting pools and heroic sculpture. It also has a court theater where summer operas are performed.

About an hour north is the museum village of Sigtuna, first capital of Sweden, a pleasant, lake-sited place with the preserved homes and stores of the past. Not far away is the university town of Uppsala, with a cathedral notable for its clean lines and bright mien, far cry from the oppressively dark cathedrals of Southern Europe.

Sweden is the most prosperous and the largest of the Scandinavian countries. Stockholm is the major gateway by air. Malmo is an easy boat connection with Denmark. The entire western edge of Sweden borders Norway.

Some 90 percent of the population lives in Southern Sweden. Stockholm with its 1.3 million people is the largest city and capital of the country, complete with King and royal palaces. Goteborg has close to 700,000 people; Malmo, 454,000. Half the land is forested and lake covered. Thousands of tiny islands line the coasts. Southern Sweden has a surprisingly mild climate. January temperatures average around twenty-six degrees in Stockholm, in the mid-sixties during July and August. In June the average day has nineteen hours of sunlight.

Sweden hosts a little over two million visitors each year who leave about $1 billion. Only about twenty thousand of the visitors are U.S. citizens. SAS, the Scandinavian airline, flies from the U.S. to Sweden via Copenhagen. British Air, Lufthansa, and Finnair also

FIGURE 5.18 *Tourist attractions.* One of the biggest in Sweden is the warship *Wasa.* Built in 1628, it sailed a total of three hundred meters. The ship foundered and sunk in Stockholm harbor the day it was launched. It was raised from the mud between 1959 and 1961 and is now a museum piece.

Source: Maritime Museum and the warship *Wasa.*

arrive after one stop in their own countries. The Swedes themseves are ardent travelers, both within Sweden and abroad. Ninety-two percent of all Swedes fifteen to sixty-five years take holidays and 1.9 million traveled outside the country in 1981.

The Swedes seem much impressed with their Wasa Museum, which centers on the warship *Wasa,* built in 1628, which then capsized the same year as it moved out from drydock into the Stockholm harbor. Raised in 1961, a building was constructed around the ship and museum buildings supporting the ship added. Many replicas of famous ships of the past have been built. The *Wasa* is the original. There are also fifty museums in Stockholm.

For food lovers, Stockholm has the Operakellarn, perhaps Europe's most ornate restaurant, a part of the Stockholm Opera House. If you don't like or can't afford it, try one of the other five hundred Stockholm restaurants.

The Swedes, like the Danes and Norwegians, love their smorgasbords: hot and cold dishes laid out in buffet fashion. Herring is omnipresent. It comes pickled, smoked, marinated in sour cream. Cold herring in tomato sauce for breakfast takes some getting used to. Cold meats may include ham, pork, reindeer, elk, mutton, and venison. And don't overlook the Swedish meatballs. There is one dish that makes you wonder about what turns on a Swede. It's called Jannson's Temptation, a casserole of potatoes, onions, and anchovies baked in a cream sauce. If you just crave an American hamburger, there are seven McDonalds' in Stockholm.

As for drink, the Swedes like it so much the government has passed perhaps the toughest of all drink and drive laws. The penalties for driving while drunk are so severe that when a group of Swedes go out to dinner one volunteers as the driver and does not drink at all. Akavit chased with a beer is the Swedish equivalent of the old American boilermaker. The carbon dioxide in the beer paralyzes the stomach muscles, forcing the alcohol of both drinks directly into the blood stream. The result is instant "blotto."

The Gota Canal, connecting Goteborg, on the west coast, with Stockholm, 347 miles away, is highly recommended as a leisurely way to enjoy Central Sweden. The narrow canal does not permit fast travel. Three passenger boats that ply the canal coast-to-coast permit passengers to get out and walk or to explore a town, then catch up by taxi. The canal, owned by the government, is open to boat traffic May 15 through mid-September. Boating the canal is a good way to get acquainted with the Swedes since a majority of the passengers are Swedish. Inboard cabin cruisers accommodating six people can also be rented for the trip and there are guest marinas along the way. It's a three-day journey.

NORWAY

Norway, long and narrow—eleven hundred miles long, in fact—lies alongside Sweden. The mountains and fjords of Norway leave little land to farm and until recently Norway was the poor relation in Scandinavia, relying heavily on fishing and maritime commerce for survival. The discovery of oil off its Atlantic coast changed that and those same mountains and fjords make the country the most scenic of the Scandinavian countries.

The fingers of water reaching into the Atlantic coastline of Norway are "must sees" for tourists. Cruising through the fjords, the visitor sees tiny patches of land where a few acres make up a farm. Water transportation is the only way of reaching them. Farming in Norway is government subsidized, necessarily so because of the small size of most of the farms and the short growing season.

Roads in Norway are good and so, too, is the train system. The ride between Bergen and Oslo is particularly scenic. And when Norwegians disembark from train, bus, plane, auto—they soon leave everyone else behind. They walk as though they are cross-country skiing, poles in hand, straight ahead, moving fast. Their personalities are about the same, straightforward, energetic, relatively uncomplicated. The plumed-hatted soldiers who stride around the royal palace in Oslo may symbolize the national ethic, self-respecting and self-assured, without a trace of the belligerence associated with the military.

FIGURE 5.19 *Famous church.* The famous stave church at the Norwegian Folk Museum in Oslo, Norway, was built at Gol in the Hallingdal valley around 1250, but was transferred to Oslo in 1885.

Source: Norwegian National Tourist Office.

Scandinavians do themselves proud in building city halls. Those in Copenhagen, Oslo and Stockholm are among the finest buildings in their countries—impressive in size and design. Scandinavians are generally art conscious.

Sitting on Oslo's waterfront are the City Hall and a medieval fort, part of which houses a Resistance Museum. The City Hall is much more than an administrative center; it is a major art museum as well. The royal palace is within walking distance, a plain building as palaces go, enlivened by the handsome palace guard with jaunty step.

Don't look for aristocratic palaces in Norway. The Norwegians could not afford them psychologically or materially. There is one baronial home on the outskirts of Oslo, leftover from the days of Danish domination. This manor house is a short bus ride from the city and open to the public. In modern times Norway had but one noble family other than the royal family.

Frogner Park, not far from downtown Oslo, has an unforgetable sculpture park, a park in itself worth the trip to Oslo. It came about as a result of a unique contract between sculpturer Vigeland and the city fathers of Oslo in 1921. Vigeland agreed that all he had sculpted and might sculpt in the future would belong to the city. In return the city would provide the setting, the working materials and the help he would need. Both probably got more than they bargained for.

FIGURE 5.20   *Fjords.* The geiranger fjord in Norway's Fjord Country, seen from the famous Flydal canyon. Fjords, deep-water inlets from the sea, penetrate Norway's coasts to provide spectacular scenery.

Source: Norwegian Tourist Office.

Vigeland got artisans he needed for stonecutting, plating workshops, even a smithy. Oslo got an eighty-acre sculpture garden the likes of which are not approached elsewhere.

It took the city nearly a year to quarry and move through the streets the single stone which was to become the centerpiece of the park, the "Monolith of Life." It stands six stories high and weighs 260 tons. It and Vigeland's other works tell the cycle of human life, from birth to death, its joys, anguish, love and struggle. Life as portrayed by Vigeland is far from fun and games. All the figures are of stocky, for most part serious, types. There is no lightness of spirit as seen in Milles' sculpture park in Stockholm. People age, wither, and die and new generations are born. Vigeland's explicit nudity shocked earlier generations but seems mild enough today.

The park leaves a lasting impression of astonishing vigor, so much accomplished within one lifetime. On the twenty steps around the Monolith alone are thirty-six granite groups. A three-hundred-foot bridge has fifty-eight bronze figure groups.

FIGURE 5.21 *Monolith.* The famous Vigeland Monolith in Oslo's Frogner Park is fifty-six feet high and includes 121 sculptured humans. It consists of a single slab of rock, and three men worked for thirteen years—from 1929 to 1942—to shape the sculptures.

Source: Norwegian National Tourist Office.

A short ferry ride from the Oslo city hall is the peninsula of Bygdoy where preserved Viking ships are on display. Even more interesting is the Vestfold Folk Museum, a village of yesteryear that explains something of the Norwegian character. With little arable land and long winters, Norwegians had compact farm homes, planned for survival. Being practical people, there was a special room for grandma in every house.

Bergen, home of Edward Grieg, on the Atlantic side of Norway, is a base for fjord excursions. Going northward into the mountains it is not uncommon to see a herd of reindeer moving across the tundra.

Norwegian restaurants are nothing to write home about partly because the status of chefs is not high. One of the more interesting and less expensive meats served in restaurants is whale flesh. Solid muscle, it looks a little like liver, but tastes something like beef. Reindeer steaks are also good. Breakfast buffets can be enormous, with five or six kinds of cold herring being served.

FINLAND

Finland is an overlooked destination by Americans, a land about the size of England and Scotland, but with only 4.5 million people. Most visitors to Finland come from its next-door neighbors, Sweden, Germany and, believe it or not, Russia. The Russians come for three- and four-day junkets, mostly rewards from their government for meeting or exceeding production quotas. In fact, Russia and Finland have very good relations, this in spite of the fact that the two countries were at war twice in this century.

Of the two million visitors to Finland in 1983 only 4 percent were Americans and they usually came as a part of a Scandinavian tour or were in transit to and from the USSR.

Like the rest of the Scandinavians the Finns maintain very high sanitary standards and accommodations. The country has 843 hotels, dozens of lakes, forests, and farmland. The climate resembles that of Minnesota. The Finnish language, unlike the rest of Scandinavia, is not Germanic. Rather it is related to the languages spoken in Hungary, Estonia, and Lapland.

The Scandinavian countries experience what are called the "light nights." Being so far north the sun stands at only fifty-seven and one-eighth degrees above the horizon in the summer; in the winter it stands ten degrees above the horizon. Being so low under the northern horizon creates the "light nights." Being so far north also is responsible for the fact that daylight varies from a minimum of seven hours in the winter to seventeen hours in the summer. The range is even greater in Northern Norway, Sweden, and Finland.

The northern parts of Norway, Sweden, Finland, and Russia are home for the Lapps. Mostly they live on reindeer, the only domestic animal which can feed itself on the meager vegetation beyond the Arctic Circle. About the only things the Lapp family needs from the outside world are coffee and salt. They number about eight thousand in Sweden, twenty-thousand in Norway, twenty-five hundred in Finland, and perhaps less than two thousand in the Soviet Union.

ICELAND

OFFICIAL NAME: REPUBLIC OF ICELAND

Iceland suffers from a bad press, a public relations ploy pulled centuries ago when a Viking chieftain who was intent on selling what is now Greenland as a place to settle called the ice-ridden island Greenland. Iceland, which around the edges has a moderate climate, he called Iceland. The Gulf Stream sees to it that Reykjavik, Iceland's capital and only city, has a temperature in January, its coolest month, that is higher than that of New York City or Vienna. A midsummer afternoon is between fifty to fifty-four degrees. Being so far north there is sunlight almost around the clock during June. At that time in Reykjavik sunset separates sunrise by only two hours. In Northern Iceland the sun hardly sets at all during June.

Most Americans never heard of Iceland until World War II, when the island was used as a military base by the Allies. That lack of recognition would probably have continued had it not been for the establishment of Icelandic Airlines and the fact that its management decided to operate outside the International Air Transport Association, IATA. By doing so Icelandic Air could and did offer for many years the only reduced fares from New York to Europe on a scheduled basis. With propeller driven planes it was necessary to stop for refueling at Reykjavik. Passengers might stop over in Iceland before proceeding to Luxembourg, the only European country that allowed Icelandic Air landing rights.

Visitors who choose to stop in Reykjavik find several surprises. Glaciers are among Iceland's scenic attractions. They cover an area nearly as large as all of the glaciers in the rest of Scandinavia and the Alps put together. Hothouses produce tropical fruits. Summer temperatures almost never go above seventy degrees. The word "geyser" is derived from the Great Geyser in the south of Iceland. Put a piece of soap in some of the geysers and up they leap.

Reykjavik is one of the cleanest, most unpolluted cities in the world. It is possible to see a huge smog cloud approaching the island from Europe but Reykjavik itself has none because heating comes from hot water tapped from thermal wells. Sitting as it does on the ocean with brightly painted buildings and eighty-five thousand inhabitants, Reykjavik has been called a mini-Copenhagen. In fact, it was part of Denmark for centuries.

Icelanders are among the most literate, highly read, and democratic groups anywhere. The economy is based almost completely on fishing and sheep farming.

To experience this very unusual island take the ring-route, Highway I, an eleven-hundred-mile roadway around the entire island. Travel is by Mercedes Benz and Scania buses. Passengers can get off and on at any stop with the full-circle passport. Modestly priced hotels and guesthouses are available. A few campgrounds are also set up. Fishing and viewing Europe's largest waterfalls are reasons for taking the trip. Birdwatchers take note! Some 250 species of birds visit the island regularly. There is an Icelandic pony, a beautiful little animal. Riders usually ride one and bring another along for relief of the other. Sad to say the ponies also appear on the Icelandic table as food. Akureyri, with a population of thirteen thousand, Iceland's second largest town, is on the ring road and has several hotels, guesthouses and restaurants.

Geologically, Iceland is young, its oldest rocks hardly more than sixteen million years of age. Parts of the island are still growing. Heimaey, the only inhabited place on the Westman Island south of Iceland, was enlarged as recently as 1963-1966 and again in 1973 by lava flows, when more than four hundred homes were burned or buried by lava and ashes.

IRELAND

The Republic of Ireland has long been a "good buy" for tourists, offering accommodations from "bed and breadfast" to luxury castles and mansions. The country is an independent nation, not a part of the United Kingdom as is Northern Ireland. Not all the "B & B's" are attractive, but some are served up in attractive farmhouses and Georgian homes left over from the days when the English built mansions with cheap Irish labor. Ashford Castle in Cong and Cashel Palace Hotel in Cashel, Dromoland Castle near Shannon and Killiney Castle Hotel in Killiney are bona fide castles or palaces converted into hotels.

The Irish decided to coerce visitors into helping the economic development around Shannon, on the west coast. Only passengers flying Aer Lingus, the Irish national airline, can fly directly to Dublin from the United States. Buses take thirty-five minutes to get into the center of Dublin. Other airlines must put down at Shannon, 138 miles southwest. Passengers change to a local Aer Lingus flight into Dublin or bus to Limerick and into Dublin by train, a two-hour ride. Many visitors stop overnight, shop and enjoy the castle entertainment and meals nearby.

FIGURE 5.22   *A touch of Ireland.* A "must" for most tourists to County Cork, Ireland, is the ritual of kissing the blarney stone at Blarney Castle. The stone is said to make those who kiss it skilled in flattery.

Source: Irish Tourist Board.

Shannon offers a free port, authentic thatched-roof cottages for rent and dinner at a choice of three medieval castles—Dun Guaire, Bunratty, or Knappogue. Costumed waitresses serve what is supposed to resemble medieval fare downed with mead, the alcoholic beverage made from honey.

Getting around Ireland is easy by rented car. There is very little traffic on the roads outside the few cities and towns. The Eurail Pass is also good in Ireland.

Dublin, a city of a million sitting on the Liffey River, is known for its Trinity College, its pubs and its Irishness. The Trinity College Library has the Book of Kells, judged by many to be the most beautiful book ever produced. The library itself is grand in the manner of the royal library in Vienna. Visitors are taken with the homey quality of the pubs and the easy conviviality. Only the natives can wax eloquent over Guiness stout, which is almost a national drink. The Gresham and Shelbourne hotels are hostelries that have acquired reputations over many years. Don't try to remember Dublin's official name, "Baile Atha Cliath."

Called the Emerald Isle for a reason, Ireland is kept moist (too moist many say) by southwesterly winds blowing off the North Atlantic Drift (that originated as the Gulf Stream in the Caribbean). Rain is common and can come down in torrents. The Atlantic Drift also keeps the climate mild. The temperature seldom drops below freezing nor rises above seventy-five degrees. Most northwesterly of the Eurasian land mass, Ireland is separated from Great Britain by the Irish Sea. Don't plan to swim off Irish coasts. The water is too cold. Although most of the central parts of the island are an undulating plain, most of the island is rimmed by coastal highlands.

There are two Irelands, Northern Ireland and Ireland. Ireland is the southern portion, referred to as the "Irish Republic." It occupies five-sixths of the island and has two-thirds of the population, a little over three million people. The northeast corner constituted six counties of Ireland until the early 1920s. Today it is part of the United Kingdom of Great Britain and Northern Ireland. Northern Ireland's capital is Belfast, population 360,000. Ireland's capital is Dublin, population 680,000.

Ireland is a land of small towns and villages connected by paved, mostly narrow roads. Drive on the left side, please. And no honking between 11:30 p.m. and 7 a.m. The Irish are known for their love of ale, sports, and song. All three can lead to driving while under the influence—and severe penalties if picked up by the police.

The island has a number of lakes called loughs. Most visitors head for the Ring of Kerry, a circular road on the Iveragh Peninsula with spectacular views of mountains and ocean. Close by is Blarney Castle, where visitors line up to kiss the Blarney Stone and thereby, it is said, increase their skills in flattery or blarney. The Connemara on the west coast is rocky and mountainous. Thirty miles offshore are the Aran Islands, almost barren, windy and lonely.

Remember Tipperary, in the song, "It's a long way to Tipperary"? It's in the southwest, surrounded by hills and mountains.

Identification of an Irish cuisine is difficult because the famed Irish imagination has not been applied to cooking. It is substantial fare: bacon, Irish stew, soda bread, cabbage, carrots, and corned beef are well-known. Irish potatoes did not originate in Ireland but saved many an Irishman from famine. When the potato crop failed many died and millions left the country. Luckily, tens of thousands immigrated to the United States. Irish salmon and Dublin Bay prawns (large shrimp) are the grander type of food on the Irish menu. So too are oysters when in season. Spring lamb is delicious. When the Irish are not drinking tea it is beer, stout, ale, and Irish whiskey. The tea comes strong, hot and sweet; the beer comes with a higher-than-normal alcoholic content which apparently lubricates the fiddling and singing in Irish pubs.

GREECE

OFFICIAL NAME: HELLENIC REPUBLIC

In the past Greece has attracted many visitors who were unwanted. It has been overrun and ruled at various times by the Persians, the Romans, and in modern times by the Turks. Today's visitors are welcomed by the tens of thousands, welcomed to Athens and to dozens of places that ring of history—Marathon, Thebes, Delphi and Sparta. Greece includes fourteen hundred volcanic islands, two hundred of which are inhabited and are searched out each summer by Northern Europeans and Americans for their climate, beauty, and particular lifestyle. In 1982, Greece had about six million visitors, not many compared to the thirty-nine million visitors to Spain in that year. Tourism receipts were $1.7 billion.

The United Kingdom, with the help of mass air charter companies, provides the largest number of visitors, followed by Germany and France. The United States, ranking fourth in number of visitors, is first in tourist spending even though Americans stay an average of about two weeks compared to a month spent by the average European visitor. About 20 percent of American visitors take a cruise on one of the twenty-five Greek ships sailing the islands. The American market is identified as the upper-middle-class family. California is the best geographical market.

FIGURE 5.23 *Map of Greece.*

The romantic notion of Greece pictures shepherds tending sheep and goats, and raising garden crops or fishing. Actually more than half of the population are urban dwellers. Athens, the capital, has 2.7 million people; Greater Athens has 30 percent of the total population of 9.2 million. Greater Thessaloniki, the major city in the north, has 650,000.

The famous cities of the Golden Age of Greece (400 B.C.)—Corinth, Sparta and Thebes—have only their classic ruins to recall the days of glory. Corinth is a town of about twenty thousand; Thebes has about fifteen thousand. Sparta is a small country town of eleven thousand people.

The Athens of today is only about 150 years old. The Athens of 1830 was little more than a village of two thousand people under the heel of the Turks. The Athens of today is a bustling city that stretches to link up with Greece's principal port, Piraeus. It is from Piraeus that most Americans board for cruises to the more popular of the some five hundred Aegean Islands. The cruises often visit Crete to the south, round the Peloponnesus and sail north to Corfu, the most lush of the Greek isles.

The heart of modern Athens is Sytagama (Constitution) Square. The parliament building, formerly the royal palace, is here and so are the erzones, the guards dressed in red berets, short white kilts and wearing pompons on their shoes. Some spectators expect them to break into a ballet dance at any moment.

The Parthenon sits on the Acropolis overlooking Athens and at times is overrun by tourists. It was built in the fifth century B.C. Sadly, its sculptures are in London. They were shipped there by Lord Elgin early in the nineteenth century. The Parthenon has sound and light shows presented nightly at nine, from April 1 to the end of October.

Near the Acropolis are the Theater of Dionysus, the Theseion Temple, the Agora or ancient meeting place, and the temple of Zeus. The Acropolis Museum is down a side street.

Plaka, the historical heart of Athens, is an area of tile-roofed houses, flowered balconies and patios. It is also home to the counter-culture youth, with hashish and heroin freely available.

Near Constitution Square is the well-known restaurant, Gerofinikas. Like all the better Greek restaurants there are elaborate hors d'oeuvres (mezes) available. Roast lamb on a spit, seafood, stuffed peppers are favorite menu items. Greek taverns are less formal and less expensive than restaurants. Athens has seventeen luxury hotels and dozens rated A and B class. Recently the Greek government divested itself of about thirty-three hotels it owned and operated as the Zenia chain. Twelve hotels were kept and every lower-income Greek resident is eligible to stay at these hotels, free of charge, for a one-week vacation, meals included.

The Greek diurnal schedule is out of step with the rest of Europe. As in Mexico, the Greeks take a late lunch, a siesta and late evening meals. Most stores in Athens open around 7 a.m. Don't expect to read anything unless you understand the Greek alphabet and style of lettering, a real hardship at times.

Athens is a good base for excursions. The Temple of Poseidon is a half-day excursion; Corinth and Delphi take a day. One-day excursions to the three Saronic islands, Hydra, Poros, and Agenia, are popular.

FIGURE 5.24 *The Acropolis.* Probably the best known "ruins" in the world, The Acropolis, overlooking modern Athens. Tourists walking over its grounds and the smog are hastening its deterioration.

Source: Greek National Tourist Office.

Boats leave daily from Piraeus, port city for Athens, to the dozens of Greek islands south and east.

Greek islands of the Aegean Sea are grouped into the Cyclades, the Sporades (there are two groups of Sporades, north and south) and the Dodecanese. Rhodes is the chief island of the Dodecanese group. Crete is unto itself, the largest of the Greek islands. Off the west coast of Greece are the Ionian islands, the most popular being Corfu, which lies just off Albania.

Mykonos is often called the St. Tropez of the Aegean, possibly because of nude bathing by large numbers of "liberated" visitors. Part of the Cyclades group, Mykonos is the "in" island, called the "jewel of the Aegean." It is indeed liberated, where visiting males marry males and some women marry women. The Greeks themselves are much more conservative, in some things ultra conservative. For example, the monastery on Mount Athos in northern Greece requires all vessels coasting around the shores of Mt. Athos to stay a distance of 500 meters if women are on board.

The large islands of Corfu and Rhodes sport golf courses. Crete has thirty-four hundred caves for avid cave explorers. Delos is rich in archeological ruins. Corfu has a distinctly Venetian character around its main plaza. Crete is the fabled island of King Minos. Rhodes is not far away, known for its fortresses, especially those of the Knights Templar who once held sway there.

Approaching Greece by ship from the west, the first landfall is the island of Corfu (Kerkira in Greek). A few dozen miles to the south is the island of Ithaca, the kingdom of Ulysses, who was one of the world's best known tourists, long ahead of his time. Corfu and the Ionian group, of which it is a part, have Italian overtones because of their proximity to Italy.

At the entrance to the Gulf of Corinth, yachtsmen decide whether to take a short cut through the Corinth Canal to Piraeus (the port for Athens) or go around the Peloponnese. Taking the Corinth Canal the traveler usually stops at the harbor of Itea, a short bus ride from the Delphi oracle.

Greece is a land of mountains, most of which give a grudging livelihood to the inhabitants in the form of olives, a little grain, sheep, goats, and grapes. Who has not heard of Mount Olympus, where at 9,570 feet the gods of ancient Greece frolicked and feuded just like their human counterparts? Looking at the villages clinging to the mountainsides the viewer wonders how any food is produced.

Except for the northern part, Greece has no major rivers but does have several micro-climates set up by the mountains, the sea, and the prevailing winds. Much of the land is dry and rocky and only 28 percent is arable. Summer temperatures can be quite hot, even at night, and dry. Winters are mild and wet. For such a small country it has a remarkable amount of coastline—ninety-three hundred miles of it.

What is the best time of year to visit Greece? According to Homer, Greece has but three seasons—that of growing and ripening, the drought, and the rains. When it rains there is nothing but rain. During the midsummer it is hot and dry. Early summer, the sky is a constant blue and the sun holds back its intensity. During January the average Athens temperature is about forty-seven degrees. In Corfu it is fifty-four degrees. Crete, being farther south, has a much milder winter climate than the rest of Greece. The winter water temperature is only slightly higher than the mean air temperature, too cold for enjoyable swimming.

Summers can be unbearably hot, especially in some of the narrow streets of Athens. At night the young bloods take delight in roaring up the streets on their Vespas, leaving a wake of vibrating shutters and awakened sleepers. After a few hot, noisy nights some visitors have been overheard soliciting funds for a bounty on the Vespa nightriders.

Some commentators say that you must "smell" Greece to appreciate it. The dominant odors of Greece vary with the season. In the spring the scent of roses, thyme, laurel and other blossoms is said to be unforgettable. For the rest of the year, away from the cities there is a plethora of other odors from the multitude of goats, sheep and donkeys or from the fishing boats.

Greek cookery has been influenced by its neighbors and especially by the Turks who dominated Greece for long periods. Typical ingredients include tomatoes, onions, eggplant, grapes and grape leaves, okra, artichokes, lemons, and seafood. Meat revolves around lamb and mutton and goat. Olive oil is the common fat used. To love Greek food one must at least like olive oil. The favorite cheese is from the goat's milk, "feta." "Kasseri" is a creamy, mild cheese, "Manouri," an unsalted, soft white cheese. Dinner comes late, about 10 p.m. and includes the Greek salad usually containing sardines, cheese, olives, and tomatoes. Baklava, the many-layered pastry heavy with honey and sprinkled with nuts, is the best known of Greek desserts. Retsina wine and ouzo, a very potent licorice-flavored wine, are favorite alcoholic drinks.

The Greek salad is well-known in New York City and elsewhere with large Greek communities. It comes with or without feta cheese. Added flavor comes from oregano, olive oil and lemon juice. "Fasolada" is a favorite bean soup. Not everyone is fond of grapevine leaves stuffed with meat, egg and lemon sauce, characteristic of Greece and of several Middle Eastern countries. Another favorite is "Mousaka," baked eggplant with cheese, tomato paste and ground lamb. Clams, octopus, shrimp, mullet, and squid are favorite seafoods.

Gyros pita, now becoming popular in some U.S. cities, is made from a leg of lamb turning on a barbecue spit, thinly sliced, served in pita bread.

To try a variety of cheap wines travel six miles west of Athens to Dapni. Here an annual wine festival lasts from mid-July to mid-September. The price of admission entitles visitors to all of the wine they want. The wine is rough and so are some of the crowd after they've sampled everything in sight.

Modern-day Greeks are a far different race than those of classical Greece. Neither are they Europeans, and certainly not Turks, for whom there is unalloyed aversion. The Turks subjugated the Greeks and ruled with an iron hand until 1826. Greeks still distrust Turks even though the Turkish influence remains in Greek cookery and otherwise. The Greeks are conscious of being Greek and proud of it. Nikos Kazantzakis, who wrote *Zorba the Greek,* is a modern-day Greek hero, expressing the Greek character so well. The epitaph on his grave in Crete says it well:

> I expect nothing...
> I fear nothing...
> I am free.

There was once a real-life Zorba and he did get drunk and express his feelings by dancing. He also broke a few plates in the process. Breaking dishes at a "bazouki bash" has emerged as a custom, one unappreciated by the professional entertainers who use the dance floors as their stage.

Greek entrepreneurs around the world, especially the Greek shipping magnates, expect and get quite a lot. Aristotle Onassis is probably also a hero. He owned his own island, a fleet of ships, an airline, and he married Jacqueline Kennedy.

MALTA

Consisting of three Mediterranean islands fifty-eight miles south of Sicily, Malta is only 121 square miles in all.

The history-minded traveler loves Malta for its castles and fortresses. Valletta, Malta's capital, sits on a narrow spot of land bordered by two harbors. The Knights of St. John, the famous crusader order, was headquartered there between 1530 and 1798. Malta's seat of government occupies what was the Grand Master's Palace. Old inns, once used by the knights, now house government agencies. The National Archeology Museum exhibits finds from temples built on Malta as long as twenty-five hundred years ago. Tourists, mostly British, come to Malta on holiday. Package tours from Britain are frequent and a number of British have elected to retire in Malta. Formerly British, Malta became an independent nation in 1964. It is one of the most densely populated countries in the world, about 2,555 people per square mile, as compared with fifty-five per square mile in the United States.

Mdina, a village of one thousand, six miles west of Valletta, is a walled town virtually unchanged for five hundred years. An ancient sanctuary and underground temple carved out of solid rock about 2400 B.C. is located three miles south of Valletta. It consists of an elaborate series of rooms on various levels. During World War II it saved many Maltese lives when used as a shelter to escape bombs dropped for hours on end by German planes.

Malta's northwest coast is the site of a series of resort towns where the ocean water is said to be about the cleanest in the Mediterranean. Gozo, reached by ferry, has the walled town of Victoria and is Malta's fruit and vegetable garden.

ENDNOTES

1. Source: World Tourism Organization.
2. *Moscow Circles,* J.R. Dorrell, Norton, N.Y.C., 1983.
3. Georgia I. Hesse, Travel Section, *Los Angeles Times,* Sept. 4, 1983.

6

EASTERN EUROPE AND THE USSR

Variously defined, Eastern Europe as the term is used here consists of seven states: Poland, the largest; Czechoslovakia and Hungary, both landlocked; Romania and Bulgaria, bordering the Black Sea; and Yugoslavia and Albania, political independents with borders on the Adriatic Sea (see Figure 6.1). Boundaries of these Eastern European countries have shifted over time as wars and treaties have reallocated them. The term Balkanization refers to this reputation for dividing the region into small, quarrelsome, ineffectual states. Today all except Yugoslavia and Albania are well within the Soviet bloc, each with more or less reluctance. Albania, communist like the others, prefers its own brand of communism, different from that of the Russians and Chinese. Albania is one of the very few countries in the world that does not want visitors. Yugoslavia, its next-door neighbor, has avidly sought visitors by building a series of large resort hotels.

Interestingly, the Soviet bloc countries want noncommunist visitors, those with hard currency not tied to the Eastern Europe bloc. Strict restrictions have been placed on exports of food and consumer goods to prevent "shopping raids" by their neighbors. Hungary placed a limit on the number of East German visitors.

POLAND

In the past, Poland has received up to ten million visitors a year, mostly from communist neighboring countries. Orbis, the official Polish Travel Agency, owns and operates the major hotels.

Americans usually fly to Poland and land at Warsaw, the capital, sometimes using LOT, the Polish Airline, out of New York City. In 1979 Americans totaling close to sixty thousand visited the country. Probably much of this travel was ethnic. Superhighways enter the country from East Germany on the west, Czechoslovakia on the south, the Soviet Union on the east. The Polish State Railway, P.K.P., offers first- and second-class accommodations. Bus routes complement the railroad. Car ferries run across the Baltic Sea, from Swinoujscie to Ystad, Sweden. Other ferries connect Gdansk with Stockholm, Sweden, and with Helsinki, Finland.

FIGURE 6.1 *Map of Eastern Europe.*

Poland has more bodies of water than any European country except Finland. Most are found east of the Baltic coast. Central Poland is the heartland farming area that also has the Vistula River. Warsaw, the capital (1.35 million), lies in this region and sits on the banks of the Wista River.

The Baltic coast has over three hundred miles of sandy beach offering resorts, health spas, and little fishing villages. Water temperature in the Baltic during the summer is surprisingly warm, about seventy-two degrees.

The two principal destinations for Americans are Warsaw and Cracow (populations 600,000). Cracow (Krakow in Polish) is steeped in Polish history and was Poland's capital between the eleventh and seventeenth centuries. Its university is the second oldest in Europe and the city is a center for the Catholic church. The Vistula River runs through the city. Stalin gave Warsaw its cultural palace, a thirty-seven-story building housing theaters, cinemas, restaurants and cafes, museums, exhibition galleries, a swimming pool, and a three-thousand-seat congress hall.

Poland, about the size of New Mexico, has uncrowded highways and gas stations are located about every twelve miles on the major roads. Touring areas include the Baltic Coast, Central Poland, the Lake District, Mountain Regions, and Silesia. Besides Warsaw, other major cities are Lodz, Wroclaw, and Poznan.

Polish food resembles that of the rest of Eastern Europe, with an emphasis on soups, a plentiful hand with sour cream, cabbage and beetroot, stewed fruit, fish from the Baltic Sea, a variety of pancakes and dumplings. Dill, marjoram, caraway seeds are favored herbs. Wild mushrooms are eaten in a number of ways. Like the Russians, the Poles drink vodka, plain or flavored (and often).

ROMANIA

Romania extends inland halfway across the Balkan Peninsula and covers a large elliptical area of 91,699 square miles. The country is somewhat smaller than New York and Pennsylvania combined. Romania's location gives it a continental climate, particularly east of the Carpathians and south of the Transylvania Alps, where temperatures can be as extreme as in Russia. A long and sometimes severe winter, a hot summer, and a prolonged autumn (August–November) are the principal seasons.

Romania's Black Sea resorts are the country's principal tourist attraction. In 1980 Romania reported 6.5 million visitors. Only 10 percent arrived from Western Europe; the rest mostly were from neighboring communist bloc countries.

Transylvania, a part of Romania, has several resorts. One of the popular tours of the area capitalizes on the fifteenth-century Romanian Price Vlad Dracul, better known in Hollywood circles as Count Dracula. In his home area he was known as "The Impaler."

Travel by car is an excellent way to see Romania and Bulgaria. There is little traffic on the roads. The Trans-European Highway or E 5 North (Yugoslavia–Bulgaria–Turkey), E 20 (Greece–Bulgaria–Romania), and E 27 (Yugoslavia–Bulgaria–Black Sea), all intersect in Bucharest. Gas stations are well-spaced throughout both countries. English is likely to be spoken by the children who study it in school.

For those who long for longevity, Bucharest offers its Institute of Geriatrics. Injections of sheep placenta are purported to revitalize the human organs. Pictures of the institute's founder suggest part of the revitalization may be psychological rather than physical.

Foreign travel to Romania is organized by the Romanian National Tourist Office. Tours to Romania can be booked through travel agents, accredited by the office. Balkantourist operates in a similar manner for Bulgaria.

BULGARIA

Bulgaria, which sits on the southern border of Romania, also has a goodly slice of the Black Sea coast, and that is where the tourist business is centered. Bulgaria is about the same size as New York State.

Balkantourist, Bulgaria's national tourist organization, has created three ultramodern beach resorts on the Black Sea: Druzba, Albena, and Zltne Pjasaci. Balkantourist has seen to it that Bulgaria's section of the Black Sea will never be overcrowded. Only 20 percent of the beaches will be developed; the rest is to be kept natural.

Partly due to its mountainous terrain, Bulgaria's population density is one of the lowest in Eastern Europe, about 206 persons per square mile. More than half of the people live in urban areas, with Sofia being by far the largest city. Other major cities are Plovdiv, site of a major annual international trade fair; the Black Sea cities of Varna and Burgas; and Ruse on the Danube River.

In Central Bulgaria, about an hour's drive from Plondiv in the Valley of the Roses, is an enormous natural garden where acres of roses provide the oil base for most of the world's perfume. During May and June the fragrance of roses fills the valleys as millions of rose blooms are harvested.

CZECHOSLOVAKIA

Czechoslovakia has been famous for its "watering spots" for the elite since long before the Czechs were forcibly introduced to communism. Spas have thrived there since medieval times. About one thousand distinct natural sources of hot mineral water exist in the country. Prague is known for its historical buildings and as a cultural center. Other major cities are Bratislava, Ostrava, and Brno.

FIGURE 6.2 *Castle hopping.* A major experience for tourists to Czechoslovakia is visiting one of the some five hundred castles that are open to visitors. Hradcany Castle in Prague is pictured above.

Source: Cedok-Czechoslovak Travel Bureau.

The western part of Czechoslovakia, a rolling area surrounded by low mountains to the north, west and south, is politically and economically the most important part of the country. The central region is hillier than the west and has important coal and steel industries in the north. The east has rugged mountains in the central and northern part and lowlands in the south that are important for agriculture.

The country has a temperate climate. Lush springs and pleasant autumns alternate with cold summers and generally gloomy winters. Total precipitation in Prague, the capital, is low—about twenty inches annually. About 2.2 million foreign visitors were reported for the year 1980, the vast majority from communist bloc neighbors. Cedok, the Czechoslovak State Travel Bureau, arranges much of the travel within Czechoslovakia.

HUNGARY

Hungary receives about ten million visitors a year, 85 percent from other socialist nations. The number of visitors about equals the number of residents. Lake Balaton is the favored resort area, with sandy beaches and with a summer temperature of seventy degrees or higher. Lake Hevez, a few miles away, is a thermal body of water with a water temperature of ninety-five degrees in summer, seventy-eight to eighty-four degrees in winter.

Budapest has been called "Paris on the Danube." Buda on the west bank, Pest on the east, linked by eight graceful bridges. Wantonly destroyed by retreating Nazis toward the end of World War II, all have been rebuilt. Looking down on the Danube at night, the bridges festooned with lights are one of the memorable views of Hungary. Another memorable view is from the Hilton Hotel, which sits on Castle Hill. The hotel incorporates the tower and other remains of a thirteenth century Dominican church. The area around the hotel is fascinating because of its history.

The Casino Budapest is situated in the Hilton Hotel. Only foreign currencies can be used, which cuts out the resident Hungarians. The casino is especially appreciated by Austrians who come to gamble incognito. In Austria citizens must register whenever they visit a casino. Those who come too often are targeted for investigation.

With a fifth of the country's population, Budapest is the cultural, political, and economic center of the nation. The countryside is mostly flat plains, famous in the past for its horses and vast landed estates.

Just twelve miles from Budapest, also on the Danube, is the medieval town of Szentendre. Cobblestone streets, baroque-style houses, a cathedral and several museums make the place worth a trip. The Hungarian answer to Versailles, the mammoth Esterhazy Palace should be a part of any Hungarian tour.

In the little town of Fertod, near the Austrian border, Haydn was court conductor to the great Esterhazy family from 1761 to 1790. Concerts are held here each summer. Built in the shape of a horseshoe, the palace has 126 rooms and is surrounded by splendid gardens. The house in which Haydn lived is restored and there is a Haydn Memorial Museum.

The Danube is Hungary's best known river. Running across Hungary from Austria, it proceeds into Yugoslavia. The Risza River is lined with vineyards. Bull's Blood (bikaver) wine and Tokay wines are Hungary's offering to the world's wine list. Hungarian food is distinctively prepared. Meat is widely used and is part of the famous goulashes (gulyas), meat soups spiced with paprika. Chicken paprika sauced with onions and sour cream is a favorite. Stuffed cabbage and stuffed green peppers, noodles, and potatoes are widely eaten. Strudels come with a variety of fillings such as apples, cherries, nuts, and poppyseeds.

Hungary is an amalgam of cultures. The Magyars arrived in the ninth century. The Turks came in the sixteenth century and ruled for 150 years. The Hapsburgs of Austria came and with them came the baroque homes, the churches, and ecclesiastical buildings.

The small city of Estergom is called Hungary's Vatican. Forty miles up the Danube from Budapest, it has Hungary's greatest cathedral. In spite of communism, the church is still a force in the lives of many people. Private enterprise is also a factor. About 30 percent of the food is produced in small private plots.

Miskolc, Hungary's second largest city, has Diosgyor Castle, used on summer evenings for open-air concerts. Hungarians enjoy the "good life," food, music, fashion, and beautiful women. They have made tremendous cultural contributions, particularly in music.

Unfortunately, as in most communist countries, there is little incentive for service personnel to provide service. The rule seems to be "do as little as possible." The crossing from Austria into Hungary by train dramatizes the vast difference between service motivation in a capitalistic nation and a communist one. When the border is crossed, uniforms of the service people change from smart to bedraggled, smiles change to indifference. The dining car menu changes from clean to spotted. The list of food on the Hungarian menu is long—but all is not available. Waiters in hotel restaurants are there in person but not in spirit. It is virtually impossible to get their attention. At times room clerks simply disappear. The Statler slogan, "The customer is always right" changes to "The customer is almost always wrong." And do not believe what the Hungarian tourist office says about plenty of people around who speak English.

IBUSZ is the Hungarian national tourist office and staffs IBUSZ desks at the major hotels.

USSR

OFFICIAL NAME: UNION OF SOVIET SOCIALIST REPUBLICS

Russia is really a nation of nations—The Union of Soviet Socialist Republics—with a variety of ethnic cultures under the Soviet banner. Actually there are some 185 different racial groups: Ukranians, Greater Russians, Uzbeks, Tartars, Khazaks, Armenians, Georgians, Jews, Lithuanians, Moldavians, Turkomans, Kirghiz, and many minority groups. There are even two villages of Russian Negroes in the Caucasus Mountains.

Is the Soviet Union in Europe or Asia? It's in both. The low Urals mark the traditional division between Europe and Asiatic Russia. We must be careful to note that today "Russia" is technically but one, the biggest one to be sure, of the fifteen republics that together make up the Union of Soviet Socialist Republics. Theoretically, the fifteen republics have equal standing in the Union. However, the Russian Republic, with half the entire population, the capital city, most of the other major cities and three-fourths of the territory, is the undisputed leader. The Russian language is taught in all of the republics.

The Russia of Moscow and Leningrad is quite different than that of Samarkand or Yalta. The Soviet Union has done well in accommodating a variety of racial groups, religions and cultures. Turks, Mongolians, Ukranians are integral parts of the USSR. The northwest includes Lithuania and Latvia, at one time independent nations. The south has Georgia, Armenia, Azerbaydzhan, Turkmen, Uzbek, Tadzhik, and Kirghiz, each with its own loyalties and history.

Images of the Soviet Union include the vast steppes, fields of ripening grain, mighty rivers, unlimited expanses of land, deep lakes, and Caspian and Black Seas. They also include a people burdened by centuries of autocracy and today oppressed by even more conformity and bureaucracy, massed marches of troops on Kremlin Square, a people almost paranoid, and with good reason, about another cataclysmic war that would make even World War II—with its thirty million Russian dead—pale into insignificance. The Russian people have a mystical attraction for the land, deep emotions but unexpressive faces and they are a people liberally sprinkled with scientific, mathematical, musical, and literary geniuses.

The Soviet Union (population 268 million) dominates Eastern Europe geographically and politically. In fact, the Soviet Union, which extends from Eastern Europe all the way across Northern and Central Asia to the Bering Straits, occupies one-sixth of the world's land surface and is the largest of all countries. It also has the second largest gross national product. It is three times the size of the United States. However, three-fourths of the country lies north of the 50th parallel, which helps to explain why Russia must import large amounts of food, much of it from the United States and Argentina. She is the number one producer of petroleum and has large deposits of gold and diamonds. A map of the Soviet Union moves through some 150 degrees of longitude, bordering Finland, the Baltic Sea, Poland, and Romania on the west, and at one point comes only three miles from a point of Alaska. Most of the country lies above the latitude of Winnipeg, Canada. The Russians do have a small subtropical zone south of the famous steppes (plains) along the shores of the Black and Caspian Seas. Vacation spots for the czars and the nobility before the Russian Revolution of 1907, these seasides are now occupied by dozens of hotels and sanitaria where workers vacation and the ill convalesce.

The Soviet Union covers so much longitude that at one extreme it is day while at the other it is still night. The differences in latitude are equally large. Kushka, bordering Afghanistan, is only eight hundred miles from the equator while Cape Chelyuskin in Siberia is a bare eight hundred miles from the North Pole. The distance is three thousand miles between the two, not much in terms of longitude, but tremendous in terms of seasons and climate. In South Turkmenia spring comes in January. At Cape Chelyuskin, even in midsummer, the wind piles up ridges of ice on the shore. Apple trees around Moscow do not blossom until late May and in northern Siberia the surface of the tundra is not free of ice until the end of June. Larch trees in Siberia take a century to reach the thickness of a man's middle finger. The extremes of climate make grain harvesting in the south possible while snow is still falling in Kamchatka.

The Soviets love their land and their rivers. The soil, the mountains, and nature have a special hold on the people. The Volga, the Don and the Dnieper are major rivers in European Russia. In terms of volume of water carried and hydro-electric capacity, they are small compared to the great Soviet rivers Ob, Lena, and Yenisei. These tumble out of the southern mountains and flow north into the Arctic.

In 1982 only about 38,000 Americans visited the Soviet Union, down from a peak of 57,000 in 1959. One reason: the American is viewed with unalloyed suspicion, watched, segregated from Russian citizens and restricted from much of the country. Travelers from other countries number about five million. Travel restrictions and lack of service do not make the Soviet Union a pleasure travel destination. Most American visitors summarize their visit to Russia by saying something like, "I'm glad I went but would not want to return. The trip was highly educational but not any fun." Some tours of Americans have been known to break into spontaneous applause when returning from Russia and upon crossing the Russo-Finnish border.

If this vast land with its diverse peoples and cultures were really opened to tourism, it could become one of the most fascinating and enjoyable destinations. Yugoslavia, a semi-communist country, has shown what can be done with tourism when encouraged by state policy. Little known Soviet cities such as Samrakand, Tbilisi, Tashkent, and Irkutsk still await the veteran traveler.

The Soviet Union can be reached by land, sea or air. Aeroflot, the Russian government-owned and -operated airline, flew from New York direct to Leningrad and Moscow, but since 1983 has not been permitted to do so. Finnair, Air France, KLM (Royal Dutch Airlines) offer connecting flights to Russia from New York City. Within the country, air service is provided only by Aeroflot, an airline noted for poor service and poorly maintained equipment. Group travelers receive superior service compared to that given individuals. Even so, a two-hour wait for a meal is frequently reported. A Russian quip explains: "They pretend to pay us a good wage so we pretend that we are working." Costs are not cheap. The foreign dollar is needed.

Compared to Europe the Soviet Union has few major highways. Cars can be rented and driven around those parts of the country prescribed by Intourist. Travel by rental car is not recommended for those who do not speak Russian or for anyone except the adventurous.

Russia's rail system is extensive and modern. The Trans-Siberian Railway is said to be the greatest single travel experience a tourist can have (if you like to travel five days non-stop by train for 5,778 miles). Australians traveling to or from Europe as an adventure constitute a large group of foreign passengers. If you go, buy the "soft" class. "Hard" class passengers hire their own bedding. Russians using the train dress informally and it is not unusual to see a Russian official step off the train in pajamas adorned with his medals.

One popular tour of the Soviet Union moves up the Volga River by ship starting at Rostov-on-Don, gate to the Caucasus and a transportation center (a canal links the lower Volga with the lower Don River). Stops along the river include Volgograd (formerly Stalingrad), Zhilguli, Ulyanovsk, and Kazan.

Nearly all visitors to the Soviet Union go to Moscow (Moskva), the heart of the government and a city with about the same population as New York City. Moscow is the mecca of Russia, a mecca that is officially atheistic. Ironically the number one attraction, tourist or otherwise, in all of the Soviet Union, is the mummified remains of that mortal Lenin who was defied by his followers. The endless line of worshippers and the merely curious stretches for blocks. Moscow's Red Square is the largest city square in the world. The Kremlin with its onion dome towers identifies Moscow, a trademark similar to Paris's Eiffel Tower.

Visitors to Moscow are unanimous in their praise of the Moscow subway, the Metro, probably the cleanest and most decorated of any. It is also among the cheapest, costing about seven cents. It closes nightly from 1:00 a.m. to 6:00 a.m. for cleaning.

All travel within Russia is arranged and controlled by the Soviet tourist agency Intourist. This includes hotel accommodations as well. Groups are always shepherded in and around Russia by Intourist guides, who must be very careful to hold to the Party line in the interpretation of history and politics. Moscow has the world's largest hotel, the Russya, with something like six thousand rooms. The Russya is really a group of hotels which occupy an entire city block.

Class divisions in a "classless society" become immediately apparent. Ranking bureaucrats, research scientists, and military are eligible for the best of everything—dachas (country vacation homes), vacations, travel, clothing, and food. The average citizen gets much less.

Besides Moscow, the other "must" city is Leningrad, with a population close to four million. Sitting on the Baltic Sea, Leningrad was built under orders of Peter the Great as a "door to the West." Leningrad's great Hermitage Museum has some three million exhibits, including many by da Vinci, Rembrandt, Titian, and Michelangelo.

Almost all of the great architecture in Russia dates from the Imperial days before World War I. The Hermitage, perhaps the most impressive of all art museums, occupies five baroque buildings of the Czar's Winter Palace in Leningrad. The city itself is by far the most attractive in the USSR. It was built by Peter the Great in the early 1700s after Russia had taken the marshy land at the mouth of the Neva River that empties into the Gulf of Finland. Peter thought big and built according to the plans of leading European architects. There are cathedrals, parks, palaces, and statues.

Petrodvorets, twenty miles west of Leningrad, is Peter's version of Versailles. The palace has twenty-five hundred acres of formal gardens running down to the Gulf of Finland. It is a fairyland of gilded fountains, statues, pools, and canals. What the visitor sees has been reconstructed following its abuse as a Nazi barracks when the Germans encircled Leningrad for nine hundred days during World War II.

Russia's playground is the Black Sea Coast. Yalta and Odessa are full of resorts and health centers. Another resort center is Tbilisi, backed by snowcapped mountains. It sits on the boundary between Europe and Asia.

Kiev, a city of 1.6 million, represents the Ukraine. Rebuilt after World War II, it has wide streets and well kept churches (novel for many Russian cities). The Dnieper River is especially beautiful as it flows through the city. The Ukranians are said to be more individualistic than the Great Russians.

Do not expect to see people smiling in the Soviet Union, or in most of Asia for that matter. That is not to say they lack a sense of humor. The transition from stoic visage to laughter is swift. In the Soviet South, the temperament is more open, more gay and lighthearted.

Siberia is little known by the outside world; an area that holds great wealth in the form of water power, oil and natural gas, gold, coal, and iron ore, it has fifty-three thousand rivers and perhaps a million lakes. Altogether it totals about six million square miles, one-third of the Soviet Union's land mass.

By plane Siberia presents a bleak, hostile appearance: flat, with little form or color. Siberia has been known to the outside world as a place of exile and imprisonment. It is much changed. The largest city, Novosibirsk, is an industrial area with a population of more than a million. The city has six theaters, including an opera house, and a permanent circus. It is also the home of the Soviet Union's third most important ballet company after Moscow's Bolshoi and Leningrad's Kirov. The usual Memorial Plaza of all big Soviet cities commerates those who died in World War II. A number of top Soviet scientists have been enticed to Akademgorodok near Novosibirsk with high pay where they engage in top-level research. Akademgorodok is a satellite center of the Academy of Sciences and boasts a five-million-volume library. Some idea of the immensity of Siberia is gotten from the circulation area of the leading newspaper in the city, more than 100,000 square miles including twelve hundred towns and villages.

Irkutsk is the most visited of Siberia's cities, a major center for the Trans-Siberian Railway. About one-fifth of the city's workers are employed by the railway. Lake Baikal is nearby. A popular Russian song sings of it as, "Majestic ocean, holy Baikal." It is four hundred miles long, eighteen to fifty miles wide and about 5,712 feet deep, the deepest in the world. It is also the oldest lake in the world. It sits at 1,650 feet above sea level and is surrounded by mountains that tower up to nine thousand feet. Fed by 336 rivers, the lake has but one outlet. Because it contains seals and saltwater fish, fishermen say there is an underground tunnel linking the lake with the Arctic Ocean. Don't count on jumping in for a swim. The water temperature is never above fifty-two degrees.

Five thousand miles of the Soviet Union fronts on the Pacific, more than that of the United States including Alaska. Vladivostok (500,000 people) is the Pacific terminal of the Trans-Siberian Railway. Unfortunately for the Soviets, there is no warm ocean current to moderate the climate.

YUGOSLAVIA

Of the socialist countries of Europe, Yugoslavia is the most interesting for the tourist, partly because the government has gone all out to build its tourist business. In 1981, 6.6 million foreign tourists traveled in the country. About a third of them were German; 10 percent were from Italy, and 9 percent from Austria. Relatively few Americans make the trip, about 2 percent of the total. Belgrade is the capital. The country has been called a "cacophony of ethnic groups: Croats, Macedonians, Montenegrins, Serbs, Slovenes, Muslims, Albanians, Hungarians, Turks, Slovaks, Romanies, Bulgarians, Romanians, Ruthenians, Czechs, Italians, Ukranians, Germans and other." The Adriatic coast is ruggedly scenic.

The Adriatic coast attracts the most visitors and has a series of resort communities. The major tourist attraction is the museum town of Dubrovnik, once an important trade center. The climate there is hot in summer, mild and rainy in winter. Yugoslavia is about two-thirds the size of California. The Danube River, the most important water route from Central and Western Europe to the Black Sea, flows through most of Eastern Yugoslavia.

FIGURE 6.3   *Map of Yugoslavia.*

One of the natural attractions is the Plitvice Lakes region, opened as a national park in 1949. The 47,300 acre park is midway between Zagreb and Zadar in the rural interior of the Yugoslavian Republic of Croatia and is reachable by auto or tour bus. The appeal of the area is sixteen lakes connected to each other by waterfalls surrounded by forest.

Most visitors to the country head for the Adriatic coast, 3,823 miles of it, or some of the one thousand offshore islands. One of the more interesting Yugoslavian resorts is the restored village of Sveti Stefan, originally a fortified island, later a fishing village. Today it is connected by causeway to the mainland. Bathing beaches are along the fringes of the causeway. North of Sveti Stefan is Milocer, formerly the summer palace of the royal family, now a hotel. Dubrovnik is the all-out tourist favorite. Private enterprise is much alive in the tourist business with crowds of people waiting at transit points to offer rooms in their homes and in many cases, half or full board as well.

A problem with hotel service comes from the fact that management is a group enterprise; all employees participate. Managers and management committees are selected by the workers so that guest satisfaction takes second place to staff satisfaction. Hotels are graded L (luxury), A (first class), B (second class), C (third class), and D (fourth class).

Yugoslavian food reflects the various nationalities within the country, people who have been strongly influenced by neighboring cultures—Austrian, Turkish, Slavic, Hungarian, Italian and Greek. Much local wine is produced, none with an international reputation. "Turska kava," Turkish coffee, made of finely ground beans, rapidly boiled and very sweet, is not for your average visitor. Plum brandy, "sljivovica," is very popular, and taken with Turkish coffee.

7

THE CARIBBEAN REGION

After Europe, the Caribbean region attracts the most Americans as visitors. The Bahamas, the U.S. Virgin Islands, and Puerto Rico attract the most stay-over visitors, followed by Bermuda, Jamaica, Barbados and the Dominican Republic. (The Dominican Republic is a newcomer on the big-attraction list.) Geographically, Bermuda is too far north to be part of the Caribbean region. Historically and culturally it has much in common with the Caribbean and is included here.

The U.S. Virgin Islands, the Bahamas, Martinique, and the Dominican Republic have been most selected for cruise stops. Figure 7.2 gives the stay-over and cruise arrival numbers for Caribbean visitors for 1981.

In 1981, the Caribbean region attracted 7.2 million visitors, half of whom were Americans. On some islands 85 percent of the visitors are American.[1] The area has about five hundred hotels, of which, says the Caribbean Tourism Association, two hundred thirty have fewer than fifty rooms. The largest chain in the area has grown by default. The Jamaican government has taken over fourteen hotels that were in financial difficulty. The government cannot afford to permit the hotels to close. To fail to do so would force up the number of unemployed. Neither can the government afford to operate them. Under government operation the hotels lost millions of dollars. Employee theft extends to cutting out the carpets underneath the beds. Inefficiencies were rampant. So, where possible, the hotels are leased to chain operators from abroad.

CARIBBEAN TRAVEL MODES

Travel to and within the Caribbean Basin is relatively easy by air. Major airlines fly widebodied aircraft from Miami and other Eastern cities nonstop to San Juan's international airport. The large Puerto Rican population of New York City supports high density traffic between that city and San Juan. The result: air fares are among the lowest per mile anywhere. Numerous other direct flights come into the Basin from Europe. Smaller planes provide service between islands.

Flight schedules change seasonally, heaviest traffic being scheduled for the high winter season when Eastern can quickly flip-flop the weather by flying southward. A New Yorker

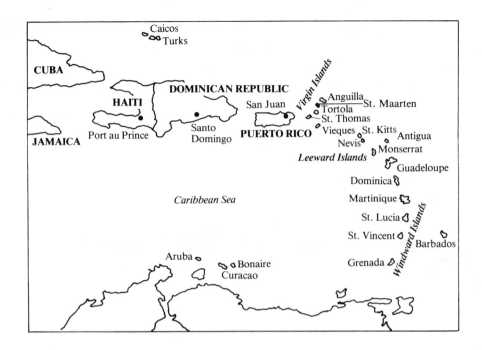

FIGURE 7.1   Map of the Caribbean region.

FIGURE 7.2   Caribbean stay-over tourist arrivals and cruise visitors, by country.

	Stay-Over Arrivals		Cruise Arrivals	
	1981	Percent Change 1980–81	1981	Percent Change 1980–81
Anguilla	11,726	43.5	—	—
Antigua and Barbuda	84,724	−2.2	113,157	−5.8
Aruba	221,325	17.1	54,971	−25.2
Bahamas	874,430[2]	−12.1	509,980	6.2
Barbados	352,591	−4.7	135,782	−13.2
Bermuda	429,802	−12.6	104,721	11.2
Cayman Islands	124,598	3.6	78,019	28.2
Curacao	158,154[1]	1.1	128,416	−7.6
Dominica	14,299	−0.2		
Dominican Republic	339,936	12.9	162,438	−11.3
Grenada	25,072	−14.8	77,596	−46.8
Guadeloupe	n.a.	n.a.	25,156	−49.4
Jamaica	406,355	2.8	129,672	4.2
Martinique	90,098	−18.0	202, 519	−0.5
Monserrat	9,408[3]	−13.9	—	—
Puerto Rico	699,617[1]	−2.4	—	—
Turks and Caicos Islands	12,558	5,6	—	—
St. Kitts/Nevis	30,625	8.0[4]	10,193[1]	76.3
St. Maarten/St. Martin	228,021	2.9	—	—
St. Vincent and the Grenadines	44,732	−11.2	33,451	−20.9
U.S.V.I.	782,691	−3.9	695,434	0.9

[1] January–November
[2] January–October
[3] January–August
[4] Provisional

Source: Caribbean Tourism Research and Development Center

or Bostonian leaves his city in zero weather and walks off the aircraft in San Juan or Barbados into the sun at eighty degrees.

Bermuda is comparatively close to the Eastern Seaboard, about an hour-and-a-half flight from New York City. The Bahamas, at about eleven hundred miles from New York City, can be reached in a little over two hours. Flying time to Puerto Rico and Jamaica at sixteen hundred miles is a little over three hours. Such flight times made the tropical weather of the Caribbean most appealing, especially during the winter.

Another way to experience the Caribbean is by cruise ship—the Caribbean being the most popular cruising waters in the world.

Most cruises begin in Miami or Port Everglades. Typically a cruise moves first to Nassau in the Bahamas where the passengers visit the straw market which sits near the docks, have their names embroidered on a straw basket or hat and walk around the small downtown section of town. They may take in a review of the police band that marches during the changing of the guard at Government House. Paradise Island, where there is a covey of hotels and casinos, is reached by bridge from Nassau.

San Juan is one of the layover ports. Old San Juan has two gigantic forts, El Morro and San Cristobel, that are well preserved. Both are national monuments. St. Thomas is another favorite cruise stop. Charlotte Amalie is mostly a giant shopping arcade featuring cameras, jewelry, watches, linens, and liquor.

Kingston, Jamaica, Curacao, and Aruba may be on the itinerary. On shipboard the passenger enjoys a cocoon-like existence, clustered around a small pool, playing games that elsewhere would be considered juvenile, gambling, drinking, and eating. Eating is a preoccupation. Breakfasts, luncheons, buffets, teas, dinners, and midnight soirees are almost continuous. Women usually out-number men, sometimes two to one. The longer the cruise, the older the passenger group.

Ships officers are likely to be Norwegian or British. The crew are multinational, Bajan (from Barbados), Italian, Spanish, Filipino, Greek and others. A rule of thumb: the ship's complement of crew usually number about one-half the number of passengers. If the ship sails with eight hundred passengers, the crew would total about four hundred.

Many yachts are available for rent in St. Thomas and Grenada. By renting, the owner can write off costs as a business expense. The larger yachts come with a crew. Smaller boats can be rented "bare-boat," stocked only with food and liquor and sailed by the people renting the boat.

Grenada and its string of neighboring islands, the Grenadines, is one of the finest of boating centers. Sailors are always within sight of another small island. The same is true for the Virgin Islands.

HISTORICAL IMPACT ON THE CARIBBEAN

Geographically and climatically, the Caribbean ties together; politically, culturally and economically, the Caribbean is more collage than community. The area is most notably divided between the British Commonwealth states and territories and those which are historically Hispanic, French, or Dutch. In much of the area, the Black/White syndrome, with its roots in slavery, permeates and complicates the differences. Three-fourths of the Caribbean people are at least partially descended from African slaves. The other quarter includes direct descendents of European colonists and East Indians and Chinese who came as indentured laborers after slavery was abolished in the nineteenth century. Economics, historical and current, serve to further differentiate cultures within the area. In 1961, there were only three independent Caribbean countries—Cuba, Haiti, and the Dominican Republic. Together they contained three-fourths of the Caribbean population. In 1980, ten were independent.

The Caribbean is thought of as a tropical sea with typical flora, mood, and sea breezes. The tradewind blows constantly over most of the area. Sugar, coconuts, bananas, political instability, languor, passion, and poverty create the image.

FIGURE 7.3 Major transit cities in Canada, United States, Mexico, and the Caribbean region.

FIGURE 7.4 *Codes for cities bordering on the Caribbean and Gulf of Mexico.*

ANU	Antigua, West Indies
BDA	Bermuda
CCS	Caracas, Venezuela
FDF	Fort de France, Martinique
GUA	Guatemala City, Guatemala
IAH	Houston, Texas USA
KIN	Kingston, Jamaica
MBJ	Montego Bay, Jamaica
MEX	Mexico City, Mexico
MGA	Managua, Nicaragua
MIA	Miami, Florida, USA
MID	Merida, Mexico
MSY	New Orleans, Louisiana, USA
NAS	Nassau, Bahamas
PAP	Port-au-Prince, Haiti
POS	Port of Spain, Trinidad
PTP	Pointe-a-Pitre, Guadeloupe
PTY	Panama City, Panama
SAL	San Salvador, El Salvador
SAP	San Pedro Sula, Honduras
SDQ	Santo Domingo, Dominican Republic
SJO	San Jose, Costa Rica
SJU	San Juan, Puerto Rico
STT	St. Thomas, Virgin Islands
STX	St. Croix, Virgin Islands
TIJ	Tijuana, Mexico
TPA	Tampa, Florida, USA

As a tourist attraction, the area is seen as all of a piece, a view which is only partly valid. White sandy beaches, warm ocean water, the opportunity to swim and sail are major appeals. For North Americans, the Caribbean projects palm trees waving in balmy breezes, the limbo dance, straw markets, and new hotels set in scenic beauty. More recently, the Caribbean has become a tropical sea cruised by sleek vessels manned with foreign crews, providing groaning tables and continuous entertainment with a series of one- or two-day stopovers at exotic islands with freeport prices.

EFFECTS OF GEOGRAPHY AND TOPOGRAPHY

Climate and topography favor tourism in most of the Caribbean. A general pattern of sunshine, easterly breezes, and puffy cumulus clouds prevails. Rainy seasons and the hurricane season in the fall mar the otherwise equable climate of most of the Caribbean Basin. December through April brings sunny weather; June, July, and August are usually quite pleasant, while May, September, October, and November more often are wet and humid. Temperatures rarely fall below seventy degrees or rise above ninety degrees in most of the sea level areas. Humidity rises during the rainy season, as would be expected. Tradewinds blowing from the east vary from about five to twenty knots, slowing noticeably during the rainy season.

Because of the constant wind direction, most islands have a windward and a leeward side, the windward side more likely to be lush while the leeward side is drier, especially if mountains are present to force the air up and cool it, precipitating rain. Almost all of the tourist destinations within the Caribbean are associated with beach front; the few "mountain resorts" are small and experience low occupancy. Old fortresses, left over from the days when European nations fought over the islands, are tourist attractions. The best known is El Morro, which guards the entrance to Havana. The mountains in the Caribbean mean rain, and on a mountainous island like Dominica where there is a plethora of rain and absence of white sandy beaches, the outlook for tourism on a large scale is bleak.

Flat, small islands in the Caribbean like Curacao, Bonaire, and Aruba experience a scarcity of water. Annual average precipitation is only twenty-two inches or less. One of the problems in establishing Caneel Bay Plantation on the relatively small island of St. John in the U.S. Virgin Islands was the scarcity of water. Water has to be barged in from Puerto Rico, a considerable distance, both to Caneel Bay Plantation on St. John and to the Rock resort Little Dix Bay on Virgin Gorda in the British Virgin Islands. Solar distillation has as yet not been economically practical.

The availability of relatively large amounts of water for guest use is a major consideration on the smaller islands, as the owners of resorts on their own private islands of Petite St. Vincent and Mustique in the Grenadines have found. On the larger islands, or the smaller ones with mountains, rainfall may vary sharply from point to point. Mount Diablotin on Dominica, for example, receives about three hundred inches of rain a year, one of the highest rates in the world.

The origin of an island largely explains its rainfall: those volcanic islands with high peaks have rainfall. The larger islands also have rainfall, while the small ones, which are exposed reefs formed on the submarine shelf or from reef-capped lateral lava flows, have little rainfall. Where water is at a premium, the roofs of houses are often used as catch basins, draining into cisterns below the house. In St. Thomas, U.S. Virgin Islands, large expanses of mountainside are surfaced and used for the same purpose. Sea water distillation plants are in use in St. Thomas and Curacao. As technology is improved and the cost reduced, sea water distillation can be a boon to tourism in places with minimal water.

Technically, the Caribbean is a sea arm of the Atlantic Ocean bounded on the north and east by the West Indies, on the south by South America, and on the west by Central America. The Gulf of Mexico merges with it and lies to the north. Because the Bahamas are so similar in culture and climate they are included in what is called the Caribbean Region.

The West Indies mark the eastern border of the Caribbean and form an arc of islands stretching south from Cuba (but also include the Bahamas).

Named for the fierce Carib Indians who dominated the region until the coming of the Spaniards, the Caribbean once generated sugar fortunes based on slavery. Today sugar farming is not competitive on the hilly islands but is still produced in Cuba, Barbados, Jamaica, the Dominican Republic, and a few other islands. Tourism is the big business.

THE BAHAMAS

The Bahamas receives 70 percent of its income from tourism and gets more visitors than any of the Caribbean Islands. There are few economic choices. The soil supports few crops except those like tomatoes or cucumbers. Most of the islands have limited fresh water. What the Bahamas has is some of the most beautiful sand beaches anywhere, a mostly benign climate, proximity to Florida and good air connections to the major cities of East Coast America.

Though there are said to be some seven hundred islands in the Bahamas, only a few are inhabited. Nassau, the country's capital, has a majority of the population. It and its sister, Paradise Island (accessible by bridge), have most of the hotels and are shopping centers for cruise passengers. Eleuthera and Grand Bahamas are the other islands with substantial populations. A big appeal for visitors are the casinos on Paradise Island, Nassau, and Grand Bahama.

In Nassau the only interesting buildings are those left from the days when it was a British colony. The Queen's Staircase, sixty-five steps leading to Fort Fencastle, was hand-carved by slaves in the eighteenth century. Fort Charlotte is one of the many rock fortresses throughout the Caribbean Region. Its dungeons recall the horrors of slavery and of the ever-present fear of raiders and of military attacks from rival European powers. Political tides shifted regularly, nations becoming enemies overnight and ever seeking to expand their colonial possessions.

Viewing the islands of the Exuma chain by plane from one thousand feet presents a glorious view of multicolored waters surrounding a chain of small desert islands.

The Bimini Islands are close enough to Florida to be reached by power boat. Each of the Bahamas has its own charm, though the lure is somewhat dimmed by heat and humidity in summer and cold snaps in winter.

Located just north of Cuba and Haiti, some of the Bahama Islands have problems with illegal immigrants from those two countries.

The Turks and the Caicos, located at the southern end of the Bahama chain, did not choose to join the Bahamas as a separate nation and remain dependencies of Britain. Air transportation from Fort Lauderdale has meant development of vacation homes and a few hotels on these remote, treeless islands.

An authentic Bahamian meal would include conch (pronounced conk), the large mollusk found on the sea floor, peas 'n rice, and possibly, grouper. The adductor muscle of the conch is a major source of protein for the islands, its export forbidden by law. It can be eaten raw, after being marinated in lime juice, or as "cracked conch," beaten with a cleaver to tenderize it and deep-fried.

The Bahamians, mostly descended from slaves, avoid menial work if possible. The agricultural work of producing the little sweet pineapples, tomatoes, and the few other crops that can be grown commercially is done by Haitians who are in the country illegally.

There is some resentment of "whitey" vacationers and some crime. Law enforcement is spotty. The Chief Justice of the Supreme Court of the Bahamas was mugged and robbed just outside his apartment. To be on the safe side he employed a personal bodyguard.

Some of the cays are known transit points for drugs, especially cocaine produced in Bolivia, processed in Columbia and smuggled into the U.S. At least one, Norman Cay, was at one time an armed camp with machine-gun armed guards employed by the smugglers.

The island of Eleuthera typifies the Family Islands. Flying over Eleuthera at ten thousand feet it is seen as a long, skinny strip of land hooked at both ends and so narrow at the upper end that the oceans come together and pass under a bridge. Translucent waters that change colors with the light provide the charm. Populated since 1648, initially by a group calling themselves The Eleutheran Adventurers, from Bermuda, it has been a base for ship-wreckers, pirates and for a brief time, cotton plantation owners. Today the base is tourism, small farming, fishing and the collecting of spiny lobsters, called crawfish.

Accommodations range from small motel-cottage colonies to what were private clubs of the elite and homes of the ultrawealthy. The Cotton Bay Club was one of the deluxe private clubs. It is now open to the public. Much of the development of South Eleuthera was the brain child of the aluminum tycoon, Arthur Vining Davis, who, it is said, helicoptered over the area pointing to sites he wanted to buy and develop. Two of his grand homes can be enjoyed at relatively modest rates. Rock Sound Club, near Rock Sound airport, was his principal island residence. Winding Bay Beach was his deluxe beach cottage; there the dining room, a place of quiet luxury, overlooks a private cove.

The Cape Eleuthera Resort at the south end of the island occupies six thousand acres and has accommodations for three hundred persons. With its own airstrip, visitors are chartered in from as far away as Colorado and Seattle. Many of the guests are members of travel clubs like the Atlanta Skylarks and the Jet Set of Seattle. With Club Med farther north, Cape Eleuthera is the largest of the Eleutheran resorts. Sailing off to a nearby cay, the guest can spear and barbecue fish that circle the cays in abundance. The divemaster supplies the resort with all of its fish. Diving is a major sport with one hundred scuba tanks and four dive boats on hand to take the daring off to spots which drop off to depths of twelve hundred feet. Attesting to the problems encountered in developing such a resort is the fact that 288 wells were drilled to meet the water demand.

Eleutherans seem uniformly friendly to visitors, waving to each passing car and ready to converse when approached.

Three little Bahamian islands are of special ethnographic interest: Spanish Wells, Man O War Cay, and Elbow Cay. They contain all-white communities left over from the time of the American Revolution, when their Tory forebears left the United States and settled in the Bahamas.

Spanish Wells, once the watering spot for Spanish galleons, is like something out of science fiction, a community of thirteen hundred people living apart from the rest of the Bahamas in a Lilliputian world of their own just off North Eleuthera. About half the town is old New England, the other half, South Florida masonry. The old part of town could be lifted from Martha's Vineyard, of an architecture style probably brought by loyalists who migrated to the Island from New England during the Revolutionary War, still supporting George III. Spanish Wellians have developed a culture unto themselves: churchgoing, law abiding, hard working, and distinctly ethnic white. Their per capita income from lobstering is the highest per capita income of any Caribbean island.

No locks on homes or resort guest rooms. The only crime is perhaps excessive boisterousness from having "one too many." The two Bahamian policemen stationed on the island must come to the scene of need either on motor scooter or on foot since one of the police scooters is broken down. Bicycling and scootering are "in" and the visitor can cover the island on a rented bike or scooter in an hour or so. Adjacent Russell Island is attached by a bridge.

Education on the island usually ends with the ninth grade, the residents seeing life and livelihood as revolving around the sea, with little need for higher education. The men begin fishing and spearing the spiny lobsters at about age fourteen. The boys can make from fif-

FIGURE 7.5 Spanish Wells, the Bahamas. Loyalists from New England settled here during the American Revolution. Their descendents, all whites, live here prosperously because of their fishing and lobstering. Two motels receive guests, who can bicycle around the island and use it as a base for sailing and snorkeling.

FIGURE 7.6   *Airline routes in the Bahamas.*

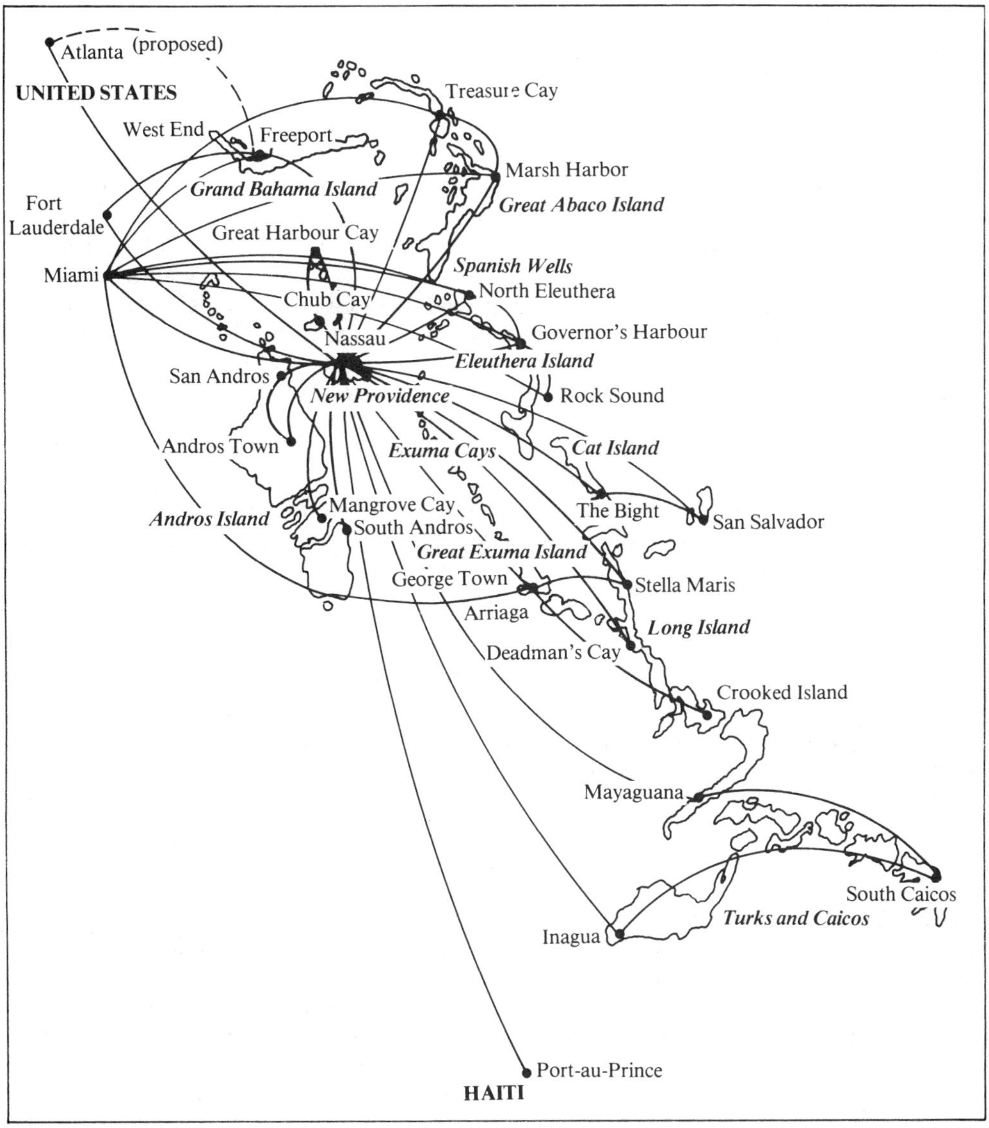

ty to one hundred dollars a day free-diving for lobsters, which they do until about the age of forty when the younger men take over. Free divers go as deep as ninety feet—the record catch of crawfish is twelve on one breath. (Scuba diving for crawfish is prohibited by law.) Diving is strenuous indeed. Men lose as much as ten to fifteen pounds during the three-week fishing trips. Almost to a man they are slender and often blond and blue eyed to an extreme.

No women's lib for Spanish Wells. Girls marry at sixteen or seventeen and are ardent homebodies. Cleanliness takes on a touch of obsession as wives do complete housecleaning with the departure of their fishermen husbands. All windows and screens are cleaned and even pots and pans are taken out and scrubbed. Yards are manicured. Tiny gardens and orchards flourish without the trace of a weed or an uncut blade of grass.

Spanish Wells is not completely white since about one hundred Haitians live on adjacent Russell Island and do much of the menial work. Residents from across the channel at Bluff on Eleuthera are also employed.

Visitors to Spanish Wells can enjoy snorkeling and scuba diving along the twenty- to twenty-five-mile-long reef accessible by speed boat. Swimming off the island is good only at high tide but makes for safety since the water depth is only a few feet for hundreds of yards off shore. As with several other Eleutheran beaches, the sand takes on a pinkish cast.

Harbour Island, reached by speed boat from the island of Eleuthera, is one large winter resort which in the summer closes as though a shopkeeper pulled down the shades of his windows. Only Valentine's Yacht and Beach Club remains open, a resort where the warmth and friendliness of the Valentine family overcome much of the lack of activity. The Valentine stamp is seen in the restaurant, where girls of fifteen or sixteen change uniforms for each meal, and dining alfresco around the pool is a principal attraction. Mr. Valentine, one of the few American expatriates to own and operate a Bahamian resort, has rejuvenated what was once a defunct yacht club. Aside from the excellent table, diving and fishing and swimming are options offered guests. The pink beach on the other side of the island, the result of bits of pinkish coral mixed with sand, is of interest.

Andros, the largest of Bahama's islands, is actually a number of smaller islands separated by a series of channels, dotted with lakes and creeks. Off the coast west of Andros is the third largest barrier reef in the world, paralleling the island for 120 miles. While most of the Bahamian islands periodically experience fresh water shortages, Andros has plenty. Water is barged to Nassau to supplement the local supply and that made by desalinating sea water.

PUERTO RICO

Puerto Rico, just east of Hispaniola, is a major Caribbean destination and the international airport in San Juan, the capital, is an air transit point for the Caribbean. Miles of beautiful beaches, comfortable swimming temperatures and easterly tradewinds make Puerto Rico a desirable winter vacation spot. Sometimes surly service by guest-contact employees and ambivalence toward tourists and tourism on the part of a large number of residents make Puerto Rico less attractive. This probably accounts for the fact that the number of tourists to Puerto Rico is less than 800,000. The Puerto Rican Tourism Company puts the numbers of visitors at two million, which undoubtedly includes Puerto Ricans returning for home visits and the cruise ship day-trippers.

San Juan, a city of 435,000, has first-class hotels and stores. It is reminiscent of Las Vegas with its revues and casinos. The Caribe Hilton sits on the site of an old fortress. Near San Juan is El Yunque, a tropical rain forest. Most visitors stay in the Isla Verde section, near the international airport, and the Condado Beach area, near downtown San Juan. The interior is hilly with a mountain range, the Cordella Central, running the length of the island. The highest point is 4,389 feet. Total population of Puerto Rico is about 3.2 million.

Although Puerto Rico is among the wealthiest of the Caribbean islands, its per capita income is about half that of the poorest state in the United States. Unemployment is at least 20 percent; half the population is eligible for food stamps. Sugar cane, once its main source of income, is now subsidized by the government and operates at a net loss, an outmoded public employment program. Puerto Rico has an ambiguous status, a so-called Commonwealth, not a full-fledged state of the United States. Puerto Ricans, however, are U.S. citizens.

"El Morro" in San Juan is one of the two massive forts built in the Caribbean. The other "El Morro" guards Havana harbor. These ponderous fortresses are unmatched among the dozens of forts in the Caribbean region. The only others that come close are La Citadelle in Haiti built by the mad ruler Henri Cristophe, and the British-built Brimstone Hill on the island of St. Kitts. Puerto Rico's El Morro sits on a cliff (morro) on an island

FIGURE 7.7 *El Morro Fortress.* A principal attraction of Puerto Rico is the El Morro Fortress, which guards the entrance of San Juan harbor. The massive fort, begun in 1539 and completed over a period of two-and-a-half centuries, was one of the principal bastions of the Spanish empire in the New World. A number of similar forts were built throughout the Caribbean as Britain, Spain, France, and the Netherlands vied for control of the area.

Source: Puerto Rico Tourism Development Co.

that forms part of San Juan Harbor. The fort was built over a two-hundred-year period. The governor's residence, also on the island, La Forteleza, lays claim to being the oldest such official residence in continuous use in the Caribbean. The Castillo de San Juan del Morro, official name of El Morro, is separated from Old San Juan by a nine-hole golf course and is maintained by the U.S. National Park Service. Visitors are welcome for a nominal charge. The governor's residence is often the scene of parties for visiting groups such as travel agents and dignitaries.

Old San Juan, which backs up to El Morro and La Forteleza, has its own fort, Fort San Cristobal. A central square, Plaza de Colon, and close to 250 buildings which have been restored, shops and restaurants, galleries and crafts centers, night clubs and residences make Old San Juan by far the most interesting tourist area in Puerto Rico.[2]

The government has tried valiantly to spread tourism to other parts of the one-hundred-by-thirty-five-mile island with moderate success. Small "paradors," inns, operated by families in various places around the island, are government protected. Culebra, a dependent island, is also being promoted. An hour and forty-five minutes by ferry from the village of Fajardo in Puerto Rico, Culebra is visited by snorkelers, scuba divers, and sailors.

The Dorado Beach Hotel and the Cerromar Hotel are luxury properties built by Laurance Rockefeller and now managed by the Regency Hotels, a Hong Kong based management company. The Caribe Hilton, built under the aegis of Operation Bootstrap in

1948, was the first of the modern-day high rise resorts in the Caribbean. It was built by the Puerto Rican government. Conrad Hilton received the contract to operate it and to get one-third of the profits. With a gambling casino, the hotel for many years produced $3 million a year in profits and stimulated resort development throughout much of the Caribbean. Puerto Rico today has about ten thousand guest rooms. The major market for the island is New York City.

Visitors to Puerto Rico usually eat in hotel dining rooms and many do not relish the native cuisine. Rice and beans, "habichuelas," are basic. Arroz con pollo, rice and chicken, is a typical dinner item. Paella, a transplant from Spain, has its own Puerto Rican character. Plantanos (a banana relative) are usually fried. "Lechon asado," roast suckling pig, is a festive dish. Restaurant dinner hours are generally 8 p.m. to 10 p.m.

VIRGIN ISLANDS

The U.S. Virgin Islands, about fifty altogether, are east of Puerto Rico, one thousand miles southeast of Miami. The major islands are St. Thomas, St. Croix, and St. John. All are mountainous with many beaches and bays with great appeal for beach lovers and for boaters. Charlotte Amalie on St. Thomas (population about 100,000) is the capital. St. Thomas is a vibrant, relatively prosperous island. The former Dutch proprietorship is still evident in the architecture. The town is always busy, known for night life, inexpensive drinks and higher-priced food. St. Thomas, along with the other U.S. Virgin Islands, receives about 790,000 stay-over visitors and about 700,000 cruise arrivals. It is the most frequent cruise ship stop-over, a place where passengers crowd in for a day's shopping, then back to the ship for the night.

A boat trip away from Charlotte Amalie is the magnificent little island of St. John, location for one of the most beautiful low-key resorts in the world, a Rock resort, Caneel Bay Plantation. About half of the island is the Virgin Islands National Park, donated to the U.S. government by Laurance Rockefeller. Included in the park are breathtaking underwater acres, considered by many the region's best snorkeling and scuba grounds. Cinnamon Bay, highly regarded campground in the national park, has concrete cabins, tents, and tent sites.

OTHER CARIBBEAN ISLANDS

Not far away are the British Virgin Islands with Roadtown, the capital, on Tortola Island. Of the thirty-six islands only sixteen are inhabited; they comprise a long chain of mountain coral and volcanic islands. Total population is only 10,500, most of whom are of African descent. Robert Louis Stevenson took the name of one of the islands, Treasure Island, for his own in his classic novel. Virgin Gorda has a Rock resort, beautiful and luxurious Little Dix Bay. The island is also known for The Baths, mammoth boulder formations at the edge of the sea creating caves and grottos, pools and coves.

Stringing southeast in an arc from the Virgin Islands are the islands of St. Kitts, Nevis, Antigua, and Montserrat. All are connected with the British government and receive aid from Britain. All depend on agriculture and tourism and are populated mostly by blacks, the descendents of slaves. St. Kitts is the larger member of the two-island confederation with Nevis. Basseterre, the capital, is a quiet English-style town. Nevis is the birthplace of Alexander Hamilton. Antigua has a wet and a dry side, the dry side being on the leeward side. It is known for its beautiful little Nelson's harbor, headquarters for Lord Nelson when he commanded the fleet in that part of the world. There is an exquisite coastline and several first class resorts. Tourism is its major source of income—about eighty thousand visitors each year. Barbuda, a separate island which rings a lagoon, is politically a part of Antigua. It was once a breeding center for slaves. Antigua gained independence in 1981 though it has only seventy-six thousand people. Montserrat is at a disadvantage touristically because of its rugged mountains and lack of white sand beaches.

The largest of the French-related islands in the Caribbean are Guadeloupe and Martinique. The people, mostly black, are French citizens. The capital of Guadeloupe is Basse Terre. Shaped like a butterfly in flight, Guadeloupe is made up of two islands, Grand Terre and Basse Terre. The first is a flat land with a few rolling hills, while Basse Terre is mountainous with volcanos rising to a height of 4,812 feet. Around the island are beautiful sandy beaches, three of which are set aside for nude bathing. Administratively, it is a full-fledged department of France and French in language, cuisine, currency, and customs. Martinique is the home of Napoleon's Josephine, and the dance the beguine originated here. In the last decade some luxury hotels have sprung up with casinos and night life. Cruise passengers are more than double the stay-over arrivals to this large, lush island with rain forests, beaches and Mont Pelee, the volcano that wiped out St. Pierre eighty years ago.

North of Guadeloupe are St. Maarten/St. Martin and St. Barthelemy. The island of St. Maarten is spelled two ways for a reason. About half is Dutch controlled; the other half is a dependent of Guadeloupe and is French speaking. Philipsburg, the Dutch capital, is a shopper's haven with international goods at duty free prices. The French capital, Marigot, is smaller and quainter. The southern portion, "Dutch Sint Maarten," offers a selection of full-service resorts with casinos, night life, and good beaches. It is livelier than French St. Martin.

A charming little island, St. Barthelemy is reachable from St. Martin by plane. The plane lands in a sheep pasture with only feet to spare before the runway gives way to the ocean. The harbor of its tiny town is picture-postcard beautiful where the visitor may tire of eating clawless lobsters because they are so abundant.

Not far away and reachable by a little plane is a five-square-mile island, Saba. The near vertical landscape offers lots of scenery and no beaches. It is a Dutch island where the language is English. Activities offered are horseback, burro-back, and hiking tours. The island is dominated by a three-thousand-foot extinct volcano. Almost completely populated by women, children, and old men, the young men must go abroad to earn a living.

Continuing south in the arc of the West Indian islands we come to the islands of St. Lucia and St. Vincent. St. Lucia is a mountainous island, and Soufriere, called the world's only drive-in volcano, has sulphuric fumes bubbling in the crater. Three of its peaks are attractions: the two Pitons, twenty-four hundred and twenty-six hundred respectively, are landmarks for sailors and afford mountain-climbing to the visitor. St. Vincent is the arrowroot capital of the world, the starchy root having made a comeback in world trade, now used in making computer paper. In the capital, Kingstown, arcaded buildings line the streets, where local crafts are sold. The Botanical Gardens are the oldest in the hemisphere and contain the famous breadfruit tree brought there from the South Pacific by Captain Bligh. (Remember Captain Bligh and "Mutiny on the Bounty"?) When faced with mutinous troops, he put in here with a load of breadfruit from Tahiti. Other sights are the ruins of Fort Charlotte overlooking the harbor, the fertile Marriaque Valley and sixty-foot Baleine Falls. About forty-five thousand stay-over visitors come to St. Vincent and its associated islands, the Grenadines.

Swinging west again, Grenada (pronounced Gre-nay-da) and the Grenadines continue the West Indian arc of islands. Stretched within sight of each other, the Grenadines form a beautiful chain of low-lying islands, perfect for the yachtsman to move from one to the other. St. George, capital of Grenada, is a major yachting center for the Caribbean. The land grows cloves, nutmeg, mace, and cinnamon. Grenada is one of the loveliest of the Windwards: Grand Anse Beach is two miles of pristine sand, inland are dense forests and steep mountains. In the crater of an extinct volcano is a thirteen-acre lake.

Barbados is quite British. It sits about two hundred miles north and to the east of Trinidad. Its population of 300,000 crowds the 166 square-mile island, which depends upon sugar and tourism for its livelihood. Mostly flat, the Caribbean side has some beautiful, calm beaches, Sandy Lane being the most lovely. There is an eighteen-hole golf course at Sandy Lane and such spectator sports as cricket, polo, auto and horse races, and horse shows. The harbor of Bridgetown, the country's capital, is a postcard scene of the harbor police dressed in eighteenth century sailor costumes. A botanical note: Barbados is home for the Barbados Cherry, several times as rich in vitamin C as the orange. Tourism produces about $270 million; sugar accounts for $35 million. All is not as tranquil as advertised. Theft is up. Some beach boys do more for women visitors than provide towels and sun lotion.

Sixteen miles north of Venezuela, Trinidad and Tobago complete the West Indian arc of islands. The two islands are separated by a twenty-one mile channel. Tobago is "sleepy" if compared to "lively" Trinidad. Tobago is for bird lovers and those who want tropical beaches without people. Trinidad, too, is for birdwatchers and its bird sanctuary in the Saroni Swamp is well-known. Trinidad is prosperous from oil and industry as well as tourism. Pitch Lake in Trinidad is made of tar, which has been used for roads in all parts of the world. Port-of-Spain, with 200,000 polyglot population, is the noisy, bustling capital of Trinidad. It is one of the Caribbean countries with a sizable East Indian population, about one-third of the one million people on the two islands.

The Netherland Antilles are an odd assortment of little Caribbean islands, two groups of three islands each. The two groups are 550 miles apart. Commercially they are concerned either with tourism or oil refining or both. One group—Aruba, Bonaire and Curacao—lies off the northwest coast of Venezuela. The other three—Sint Maarten, Sint Eustatius and Saba—are about 220 miles east of Puerto Rico. All have a maritime tropical climate blessed with constant northeast tradewinds. None of the islands is of agricultural value and so were largely spared the horrors of slavery.

Aruba is a dry, sandy strip of golden beaches, more desert-like than tropical. There is the duty-free capital of Oranjestad, and two strips of modern resorts offering night life, many amenities, and gambling. All hotels are government-owned. Its eleven first-class hotels with more than six thousand rooms run an occupancy exceeding 80 percent, thanks to a number of major airlines stopping there. Aruba and Curacao have large oil refineries because of a wish by some major oil companies to refine Venezuelan oil away from Venezuela. Oil tankers sail in single file, like a fleet on review. Total population of the Netherlands Antilles is about 250,000. Ethnically, 85 percent of the people are of mixed Negro stock. The sixty thousand residents on Aruba live well from the proceeds of tourism, oil refining, and aid from the Netherlands government.

Curacao is the largest of the Netherlands Antilles, a desert-like island with limited swimming beaches. Its capital, Willemstad, is very "Dutch." Royal Dutch Shell has been in business there since 1915.

Bonaire is a bird island, home to 145 species. The salt beds at the southern tip of the island, with one of the world's largest flamingo colonies, are a major tourist attraction. There are several resorts as well as rich scuba and snorkeling reefs. Part of its income is derived from Holland.

Cuba is the largest island. It contains more land than all of the other Caribbean islands combined. Only ninety miles from Florida, it was the destination for the first "overseas" commercial flights from the United States. Before Castro, Havana, the capital of Cuba, was the big Caribbean tourist destination. After Fidel Castro took over the egregiously corrupt government, most of the managerial and wealthy class left for the United States. The ten million who stayed seem satisfied with their communist government, especially since they receive millions in aid from Russia and a guaranteed market for their sugar. As of 1984 Cuba was off-limits to U.S. residents.

The Veradero Beach, about thirty miles from Havana, is the premier beach for visitors. Havana has a handful of first-class hotels and an impressive nightclub. A major tourist attraction is a visit to the rum distillery.

About eighty-five miles south of Cuba is Jamaica, with two million people, mostly Blacks, a sovereign nation, a part of the British Commonwealth. Kingston is the capital, hot and humid, with a population of 570,000. Most of the island is a mountainous plateau. The Blue Mountains rise to a height of seventy-four hundred feet (and produce some distinctive coffee). Roads up these mountains and elsewhere are narrow and winding. Tourist centers with a number of first-class hotels are at Montego Bay (with its own international airport), Ocho Rios, and Port Antonio. Stay-over arrivals total a little over 400,000 a year.

FIGURE 7.8 *Oldest cathedral.* Santo Domingo, Dominican Republic's Cathedral Santa Maria Le Menor, the oldest cathedral in the Western world. According to government authorities, it is the burial site of Christopher Columbus.

Source: Dominican Tourist Information Center.

147

In the 1970s, Jamaican tourism collapsed as a black-power movement and a pro-Cuban, anti-American government gained control. By 1984 the government had become pro-American and tourism was again growing.

The Cayman Islands, a British Crown Colony of 17,000 people, lying 470 miles south of Miami, offers one of the best models for tourist development found worldwide. (Together the total area is less than the borough of Brooklyn, New York.) The three islands that make up the Colony have several historical and geographical advantages. Beautiful beaches, one seven miles long, quiet bays and year-around water temperatures of between eighty and eighty-five degrees have helped keep annual room occupancy close to 85 percent. Like so many of the Caribbean islands that are not of volcanic origin, the Caymans barely stick their heads above water. A large part of the accommodations are in the form of condominiums that have proved excellent investments by the Americans who own them. (Avoid visiting in the summer unless you do not mind high humidity.)

The islands were never bedeviled by slavery because most early arrivals were shipwrecked English, Irish and Scotsmen, deserters from Cromwell's army in Jamaica or buccaneers hiding from the Royal Navy. Today about 40 percent of the residents are black. Subsistence farming, fishing and catching turtles were the principal occupations until after 1960, when tourism and tax-haven banking came along. Well over 400 banks have located in Georgetown and, emulating the Swiss, arrange for secret bank accounts to avoid and evade national taxes.

Tourism growth has been measured, construction of high-rise hotels banned and immigration controlled. The people's friendliness, the proximity of the islands to the United States and sensible government policy have made the Caymans the most prosperous of Caribbean islands. The big attractions are the climate and the surrounding waters, where the bottom can be seen two hundred feet in depth. Low-rise hotels served up with a British accent are places to rest between sunning, snorkeling and scuba diving. Forty percent of the visitors are scuba divers. Most are between the ages of 25 and 36. Of the 125,000 visitors to the islands each year, 75 percent are Americans. Grand Cayman, the major island, also has a unique tourist attraction, a ten-acre turtle farm where ten thousand turtles are raised at a time. It is said that when the turtles believe they are to be slaughtered, they cry with tears dropping from their eyes.

Hispaniola, to the east and slightly south of Cuba, contains Haiti, which occupies the western third of the island, and the Dominican Republic, which takes up the rest. Border disputes are not uncommon. Both have been dictatorships or militarily run for most of their national lives.

Haiti has about five million people; the Dominican Republic 4.5 million. Haiti's capital is Port-au-Prince and the language is French. The capital of the Dominican Republic is Santo Domingo and the national language is Spanish. Haiti's people are almost all blacks; the Dominican Republic's are 73 percent mulatto, with white and black minorities. Haiti is mountainous, dominated by three mountain ranges; the Dominican Republic has Pico Duarte, 10,407 feet, highest in the Caribbean. One of the highlights of a trip to Haiti is to trek to where the tyrant, Henri Christophe, built a huge castle and palace, gave his generals English peerages, and when they turned against him, shot himself with a silver bullet. Independent since 1804, Haiti was the Caribbean's first independent black nation. Its culture is a mix of African and French. It has voodoo, an ancient African folk religion, lush landscape, and a people who have inspired the Haitian school of primitive painting. Port-au-Prince is crowded with those who have come from the country in the hopes of a better life. People disturbed by viewing gross poverty are upset when visiting Haiti. It is the poorest nation in the Caribbean and one of the poorest in the world. Tourist arrivals are estimated at about 100,000 a year.

BERMUDA

Bermuda is a special travel destination for several reasons. It is a series of seven main interconnected islands of remarkable natural beauty with Caribbean characteristics but is located 650 miles east of North Carolina. The land area is small; greater New York City is fifteen times larger. New York City is 774 miles northwest; London more than three thousand miles northeast.

Because of its easy reach by air from Northeastern United States, it is highly popular with vacationers and receives close to a half million of them annually. Tourism is the principal and practically only business in Bermuda. A self-governing colony of about sixty thousand people with a governor appointed by the Queen of England, Bermuda seeks the affluent visitors: those with an income over $50,000 a year. The tourist office says, "We are not interested in the Coca-Cola and hamburger market." The islands have attracted a number of permanent residents from Britain partly because of being a tax haven.

Unlike the Caribbean region, Bermuda has little or no evidence of poverty. There are no shanty towns. Blacks constitute about two-thirds of the population and there is some racial tension which erupts from time to time in riots and strikes.

The tourist authority has cleverly promoted springtime in Bermuda in the form of a series of college weeks. Consequently, spring weekends are jammed with college students from the Eastern Seaboard of the United States. College weeks are scheduled anywhere from mid-March to the end of April, depending upon the date of Easter weekend.

Other promotional events are a Goodwill Golf Tournament and activities related to fishing, tennis, dog shows, bridge, amateur radio competitions, and yachting.

Familiarization trips for travel agents were begun in 1973. Agents are placed in groups of thirty and stay at different hotels, moving to a different hotel every four days.

Hamilton, Paget, and St. Georges are the only villages, all quaintly English. St. Georges is particularly attractive as a museum village. One of the hotels is operated as a hotel training school—it takes in guests and has a popular restaurant. More than one hundred resorts offer a variety of accommodation: large and small hotels, cottage colonies, housekeeping apartments, and guest houses. Most hotels offer the American plan—three meals a day included in the room rate, but there is also the Bermuda Plan, similar to the Bed and Breakfast. Breakfast is more comprehensive than the Continental plan of juice, roll or croissant and coffee. Hotel rates are comparatively high.

The way to get around is by boat, rented car or the fun way, rental scooter, motor bike or moped. There are about 150 miles of roadways and a government-operated ferry service.

Cruise ships have long made Bermuda a favorite port of call. The tourist board, however, limits the number of cruise ships in port at any one time to assure that the island tourist facilities are not overwhelmed.

Bermuda weather is not exactly as portrayed in the promotion brochures. Winter temperatures are likely to be in the fifties; summers can be unpleasantly hot and muggy. High winds are common from December through April.

The Caribbean Region will probably continue its growth in tourism and for a long time to come will continue its ambivalence towards tourism and tourists. The physical ingredients for tourism—sun, surf, and sin—are in place. As the attitudes and skills of the residents change, the Caribbean will become even more attractive.

ENDNOTES

1. Leventhol and Horwath.
2. *The Caribbean Heritage,* Virginia Radcliff, Walker and Company, N.Y. 1976.

SUGGESTED READINGS

Caribbean Hideaways, Ian Keowin, Harmony Books. Explores twenty-four islands and more than one hundred selected resorts. Contains a supplement on charter yachts.
Fielding's Caribbean, Margaret Zellers, William Morrow & Co. Among the best of the major travel guides. Should appeal to first-time visitors wishing luxury or simplicity.

Fodor's Caribbean and the Bahamas, Stephen Birnbaum, Houghton Mifflin.

The Caribbean, Bermuda and the Bahamas, Stephen Birnbaum, Houghton Mifflin.

Frommer's Dollarwise Guide to the Caribbean, Darwin Porter. Information leans toward the inexpensive but comfortable accommodations.

Travel Section, New York *Times,* Nov. 22, 1981.

8

SOUTH AND CENTRAL AMERICA

Pleasure travel to Central and South America has always been minimal and has not kept pace with most of the rest of the world. The total number of travelers from the U.S. to South America in 1981 was 486,052—only about a fourth of the 2.2 million U.S. visitors to Hawaii. Travel to the U.S. from South America, however, continues to rise as the well-to-do shop in Miami, gamble in Las Vegas and visit other American cities. Visitors from Venezuela, Colombia and Brazil are almost double the number of Americans who went to all of South America. Some of those from Colombia—the drug dealers—the U.S. could do without.

Travel between the Argentine and Uruguay is high as Argentinians vacation at Punta Del Este, Uruguay's holiday coast, not far from Montevideo, the capital. Chile receives a comparatively large number of skiers during the June-September period.

Western Argentina offers up the Andes for skiing during our summer periods. Bariloche, the best known of the ski resorts, is about one thousand miles west of Buenos Aires. It overlooks lakes and is surrounded by evergreen forests.

Figure 8.1 shows the major gateway cities of South America, which also happen to include nearly all of the major capitals. Nonstop routes are scheduled between the cities shown and the cities in North America. Caracas is the capital and gateway to Venezuela. Bogota is high in the mountains and is Colombia's capital and major city. Quito is Ecuador's capital; Guayaquil, its major port. Lima is the center of power and capital of Peru. La Paz, at twelve thousand feet, is the highest of capital cities of any importance, seat of government of Bolivia.

Santiago is Chile's capital. Buenos Aires (good airs) is the center of the cultural and political life of Argentina. Brasilia is an anomaly. The capital of Brazil, it is not nearly as important industrially or culturally as Rio or Sao Paulo. Belem is only a gateway because of its location at the mouth of the Amazon region.

Most of the continent's capital cities are also cultural, educational, and commercial centers. With the exception of Brazil and the Guianas in the northeast, the capital cities were all laid out by the Spanish conquerors around a central square or plaza dominated by a church or cathedral and flanked by imposing government buildings. The Plaza originally formed the hub and focus of the city.

FIGURE 8.1 *Major gateways to South America.*

South America might more appropriately be called Southeast America because most of the continent lies southeast of North America. Lima, the capital of Peru, on the west coast, is farther east than Miami, Fla. And the world map shows that the east coast of South America lies much closer to Africa and even to Southern Europe than does the mid-Atlantic coast of North America. The distance between South America and Asia is almost double the distance between the United States and Asia.

Physically, South America is dominated by the Andean Mountains in the west and the Amazon Basin in the north central region. The rest of the continent is mostly a plateau. From Antarctica come the cold waters of the Humboldt current that moderate the climate of Chile and Peru.

Regional contrasts are great, with few unifying institutions. However, the Catholic church provides one unifying element and all of the continent speaks Spanish, except Brazil where Portuguese is spoken, and little Guyana where English is spoken.

Urbanization is increasing rapidly. In 1925, about one in three South Americans lived in cities and towns. In 1980, the figure was two in three. One result has been high unemployment and the growth of "barrios" around the cities. Barrios are shack towns marked by poverty, illiteracy and health problems.

Development in South America has been slow because of the distances and natural barriers that separate countries and make some almost inaccessible. In this vast land are many illiterate, poverty-stricken Indians and people of mixed blood who have a separate culture. One observer described the country as "beggers sitting on golden footstools." The land has great untapped mineral wealth. Venezuela is rich in oil, Colombia has emeralds and diamonds, Ecuador is the greatest producer of bananas, Peru has vast fishery resources offshore, Chile has copper, Argentina is a producer of wheat and cattle, and Brazil is the world's largest coffee producer and second largest producer of soybeans.

Each South American country has its own character shaped by the land, its history and its people. Dictatorship is the rule. The strong man with charisma sits in the driver's seat, backed or soon to be ousted by the military. In Paraguay the dictator always carries his hat in his hand. Under his hat, he carries a gun. Few governments last very long.

Persistent political unrest has characterized nearly every South American country since the Spanish lost control in the first quarter of the nineteenth century. Bolivia, the most unstable politically of all the nations, has suffered 190 coups in 156 years. The majority of presidents are "elected" by the military via a coup. The democratically elected presidents are ousted to save the country "from the communists." An established oligarchy usually manages to maintain power and wealth.

FIGURE 8.2 *Some facts about countries in South America.*

Country	Population (millions)	Area (square miles)	Capital
Argentina	28.1	1,068,296	Buenos Aires
Bolivia	5.2	424,162	La Paz
Brazil	124.8	3,286,470	Brasilia
Chile	11.2	292,256	Santiago
Colombia	25.2	439,735	Bogota
Ecuador	7.8	109,483	Quito
French Guiana	0.6	37,740	Cayenne
Guyana	0.8	83,000	Georgetown
Paraguay	3.1	157,047	Asuncion
Peru	18.1	496,222	Lima
Suriname	0.4	63,037	Paramaribo
Uruguay	2.9	68,037	Montevideo
Venezuela	17.9	352,143	Caracas

Extremes of wealth and poverty are present in much of South America. The "machismo" tradition, a heritage from the Spanish, prevails and encourages men to be overly aggressive and courageous to demonstrate their masculinity.

With a few exceptions, much of the population suffers from malnutrition and poverty. A large part of the continent's people live on the fringes of a money economy. Brazil, with the world's tenth largest economy and some heavily industrialized areas, also encompasses large pockets of poverty. This has led some Brazilian economists to refer to their country as "a Belgium inside an India."

Until after World War II the whole of Latin America had only a few first-class hotels. In an effort to be a good neighbor and to stimulate investment and commerce in South America, President Truman set about encouraging hotel construction in the capital cities of South America. Only Juan Trippe, president of Pan American Airways, took up the challenge. Intercontinental Hotels was organized as a wholly-owned subsidiary of Pan Am. Hotels were built or management contracts were arranged in Caracas, Belem, Montevideo, Santiago, Bogota, Mexico City, and Havana. (At the time the only first-class hotel in Caracas was Avila, built by the Rockefellers.) Where possible, joint ventures with local investors were arranged. It was the beginning of a chain that by 1982 had hotels in leading cities of more than sixty countries. The Intercontinental Hotels, sold by Pan Am in 1982 to a British company, now number more than 90.

Most South American hotels today—with a few exceptions like those on Copacabana Beach in Rio de Janeiro—cater to the business traveler. Pleasure travelers into the continent are likely to travel as part of a package tour.

In broad terms South America for the tourist can be divided into the mountain world of the Andes, the flat, dry plains of much of the south of South America, and the jungles and water-laden lands of the Amazon and its tributaries.

The mountain world of South America is formed by the Andes, part of the chain of mountains that run the length of the Western Hemisphere, from Alaska in the north to Cape Horn in southernmost Chile. The Andes themselves rise in Colombia and extend southward for more than four thousand miles. Strings of mountains, "cordilleras," the Andes occasionally protect fertile valleys, but more often are separated by high, cold table lands. Higher and even more spectacular than the Canadian Rockies, the Andes are second only to the Himalayas in height. The Andean world includes parts of Colombia, Ecuador, Peru, Bolivia, Chile, and Western Argentina.

In several South American countries it is almost possible to dial-a-season, or more precisely, drive-a-season. Bogota, Colombia, for example, has a temperate zone climate similar to early fall year-round. To move to spring, merely drive down the mountain an hour where the climate affords permanent spring. Farther down are the tropics, a hot summer's day.

Traveling in these high mountains requires some physical adaptation. Visitors get splitting headaches and find themselves gasping for breath. Lying between Peru and Bolivia, Lake Titicaca, at 12,500 feet, is the world's highest lake navigable by steamship and South America's second largest. La Paz, capital of Bolivia, sits at twelve thousand feet; Cuzco, at eleven thousand; Quito, capital of Ecuador, at nine thousand feet. The native Indians live at altitudes up to seventeen thousand feet and are able to do so because their lungs and hearts are bigger than normal. The air sacs in their lungs are permanently dilated to provide maximum surface for oxygen transfer and they have an extra two quarts of blood needed for the extra red corpuscles to carry the oxygen.

The Andean Indian of the mountain plains and the Indian of the jungles live in different worlds from the Spanish and Mestizo of Lima or Santiago. The Indian lives a marginal, agricultural existence.

PERU

Visitors to the Andean countries of Bolivia, Chile, Ecuador, and Peru favor Lima, capital of Peru, and Cuzco, capital of the once mighty Inca Empire. The visitor to Peru usually lands at Lima and spends a day or so walking the downtown area, especially the two best known plazas, the Plaza de Armas and the Plaza de San Martin. They are joined by a five-block shopping complex where textiles, ceramics, and silver objects are excellent buys. For those who like churches, Lima has three colonial ones, San Pedro, Santo Domingo, and Santa Roda, all within easy walking distance of each other.

Purse snatchers and pickpockets are aggressive and adept. Watch your watch.

Mario Vargas Llosa, a celebrated Peruvian novelist, says that all of Peruvian literature might be divided into two camps: those who sanctify Lima and those who despise her. The weather is unusual, to say the least. From May to November the city is enveloped in a gauzy fog. An invisible drizzle, the "garua," makes everything damp.

Not far off are Pacific beaches with cold water and huge waves. Millions of poverty-stricken emigrants from the sierra have moved in to swell the population to close to six million. City utilities and transportation are no match for the masses of people. Since 1958, Lima's population has quintupled, from one million to 5.5 million, almost one-third of the country's population.

Limeans are sophisticated and ardent fans of soccer and bullfights. The major bullring, "Acho," is one of the finest to be found.

Peru is divided longitudinally into three regions, a fourteen hundred-mile coast, mostly desert; the Andes, and a part of the Amazonian jungle. Each is culturally as well as geographically different.

Cuzco is the other tourist city of Peru, capital of the Incas until looted in 1532 by Pizarro and his conquistadores. Some call them thugs. The Inca empire grew out from Cuzco and within 150 years expanded to cover what is now Peru, Bolivia, Ecuador and parts of Chile, Colombia, and Argentina. The conquerors built their own buildings on top of the Indian ones, which gives Cuzco an interesting Indian/Spanish architecture. The blocks of stone cut out of the mountains were chiseled with stone tools, transported and maneuvered into place with nothing more complex than a lever. The blocks were fitted together so snugly that not even a knife blade can be slipped between them. Since Cuzco sits at 11,400 feet, visitors need plenty of rest, and should eat and drink sparingly.

Seventy miles away from Cuzco by narrow-gauge train is the last of the Inca strongholds, Machu Picchu. The train stops one thousand feet below the ruins, which sit at nine thousand feet.

Machu Picchu is awesome. Built by the last Inca ruler as an impregnable refuge two thousand feet above the Urubamba Valley, Machu Picchu was only discovered in 1911 after centuries of somnolescence, unknown to Europeans. The Incas put together the largest and most cohesive empire in aboriginal America. Its population probably exceeded eight million. Like the Romans, the Incas were builders of roads, parts of which are still usable. A highland road ran from Quito, present-day capital of Ecuador, to Cuczo and down into Chile, a distance of three thousand miles.

What is incredible is how a force of Spaniards in 1532 under the direction of the Pizarro brothers and totaling only 180 men with twenty-seven horses was able to topple the Inca and change the course of life for millions of people thereafter.

BRAZIL

OFFICIAL NAME: FEDERATIVE REPUBLIC OF BRAZIL

Brazil is another land of contrasts. Rio and Sao Paulo are modern cities, bustling and with relatively high standards of living. The Amazon has been barely touched by civilization. The Northeast is poverty ridden and almost feudal in social structure. The gulf between rich and poor, the powerful and the weak, is great. The minimum wage of about $100 a month changes little except to reflect the huge inflation rate. The military has long played an active role in politics and periodically takes over the government or exercises behind-the-scenes control.

A national debt of ninety plus billion dollars brought on by the sharp increase in oil prices, giant public spending projects and subsidized industrial development places a staggering burden on the country.

Rio de Janeiro (the River of January), with ten million people, is to North Americans the most glamorous of South American cities. The exploring Portuguese came upon what they thought was a river. It was in January. Hence, the name Rio de Janeiro. By any standards the setting of Rio is spectacular. Rio is a Brazilian Miami Beach—hot and humid in the summer (our winter), pleasantly mild during the months of June through September.

Ranking with Mardi Gras in New Orleans and Fasching in Munich, Rio's Carnival begins on the Friday night before Ash Wednesday and continues, virtually nonstop, for four days. The Rio people—the Cariolas—go wild, fed by drinks, dope, and dancing.

Travel films of Rio always show the Copacabana beach with its hotels and its tiled beach walk, tiles of several colors. Actually Rio has sixteen beaches and some of the shapeliest women in the world are certain to make sure you notice. It also has magnificent views from Sugar Loaf Mountain and from the top of Corcovado, on which stands the huge statue, Christ the Redeemer.

Sao Paulo has Ibirapuera Park, largest of its kind. The park covers two million square meters and contains ten exhibition halls. The Zoological Park is also the largest in the world. Sao Paulo is Brazil's Chicago and Detroit put together. One of the world's largest cities, it continues to grow as peasants move in from around the country hoping for a better life.

It comes as a surprise to most that Brazil occupies half the land mass of South America and contains half the continent's population. It is the fifth largest country in land size in the world. Brazil is the eighth largest industrial power in the world. Its Itaipu hydroelectric project, shared with Paraguay, on the Parana River will produce 12.6 million kilowatts of electricity, the largest hydroelectric facility in the world. Another similar project, Tucurui, has a projected generating capacity of 8.4 million kilowatts.

One of the most awesome, and in some ways, frightening, of exotics is a trip on the Amazon, mightiest of rivers, almost the longest. With its ten thousand tributaries it holds 20 to 25 percent of the world's fresh water and dumps eleven times the output of the Mississippi into the Atlantic Ocean. The Amazon also refers to a region, one larger than Western Europe, one that extends from Belem on the Atlantic, two thousand miles across Brazil and includes a corner of Peru and a section of Colombia. It covers almost half of Brazil. An island, Marajo, is the size of Denmark. Belem is a large city. Iquitos in Peru and Santarem in Brazil have populations of about 150,000. Belem will soon have a Hilton Hotel. Iquitos has a Holiday Inn.

Manaus, 1000 miles up the Amazon from the Atlantic, is an anomaly, a thriving industrial city of close to 200,000 people in the middle of Amazonia. The reason: it is Brazil's only free port and the Japanese have moved in to set up assembly plants. The city has direct air links with major South American cities and with the United States. The Tropical Hotel is one of Brazil's finest resorts. Santarem, halfway down the Amazon from Manaus, has around 100,000 residents, some the descendants of Confederate diehards who migrated there after the U.S. Civil War.

Even with its immensity, the determined traveler can fly direct from Miami to either Belem, at the mouth of the Amazon River, or to Manaus, the unofficial capital of the region, about half way up the river. Santarem, about a fourth of the way up the river, and Iquitos, Peru, are also served by air. At the headwaters of the Amazon, Brazil shares the river with Peru and Colombia. Leticia, Colombia, is one of Colombia's drug centers, drugs that end up in Europe and the United States.

To "experience" the Amazon means travel by river boat. Enasa, the navigation line owned by the Brazilian government, runs a regular but infrequent schedule between Belem and Iquitos (eight days upriver, four down watching the world's biggest jungle glide by). Along with insect repellent and medicine in case of food poisoning, the traveler should take a mosquito net.

The climate can scarcely be more monotonous—hot, humid and daily rains—with more rain during the rainy season, January to June. The temperature difference from hot to cool months is only about three degrees.

Why visit the Amazon? Some like the climate as it is. Bird watchers are delighted. There are birds that moan, others screech, some break into fits of laughter (humor unknown). Of course there is another reason: how many people can tell about their trip on a two-decker boat and the opulent opera house in Manaus with its forty thousand blue, green, and gold ceramic tiles imported from Alsace? In the Amazon forest, trees reach three-hundred-foot heights. In an area about four square miles there can be as many as seven hundred fifty different kinds of trees, four hundred kinds of birds and one hundred twenty-five species of mammals.

The soil, however, is not rich. Less than 10 percent is good for agriculture and even tree farming has yet to prove profitable.

Ethnologists, or the simply curious, can meet a few of the Amazon Indians via a package tour. Want to take a blowgun lesson from a Yagua Indian or dance with bark-clothed Boras Indians? All quite possible, flying from Miami to Iquitos, then by boat. Bring T-shirts, marbles, and lipstick for trading purposes. (Blue jeans are not yet in fashion.)

Brazil and Argentina share the Iguassu Falls, a series of 275 falls that many viewers swear out-perform Niagara Falls, between the U.S. and Canada, and Victoria Falls, shared by Zambia and Zimbabwe in Africa.

Aerolinas Argentina flies daily to the Argentine side of the falls; Varig Brazilian Airlines does the same to the Brazilian side. Nearby is Itaipu Dam which stands sixty-two stories high and stretches more than ninety city blocks, the largest producer of electricity of any dam. The roar of the water can be heard five miles away.

A million and a half people live in Brazil's remote capital, Brasilia. The site was deliberately selected because it was thought that Brazil would never attain its fated greatness unless it ventured away from the comforts of the coast, particularly Rio de Janeiro. The high plain of the area, the planalto, presents a flat landscape with agreeable weather year-round. The city was built in three years and dedicated in 1960, a planned capital in almost every detail.

Government buildings are spaced far from each other and the city is tracked by highways. The highways are laid out with as few intersections as possible to permit a continuous traffic flow. It is not a place for walking for there are few sidewalks.

The city is remote from other Brazilian cities; it is 450 miles from Belo Horizonte, and Rio de Janeiro is nineteen hours away by bus.

Feijoada is the Brazilian feast dish, originally a dish made up of leftovers given to the slaves by their masters. A kind of stew, it contains pig's feet, tongue, ears, tripe and tail, plus the vegetable kale, with rice and plenty of black beans. Eat it and take a nap. Churraco gaucho is a Rio specialty: cowboy steak and sausages, barbecued and served on a short sword or skewer, with peppers, onions, and manioc meal. The "cafezinhos," half coffee, half sugar, is the jump start favored in the outdoor cafes of Rio.

Brazil is a country with immense—but largely undeveloped—natural resources. Cynics say, "Brazil is a nation with a great future, and always will be."

Visitors to a country may have little interest in an indepth study of a culture. Nevertheless, they probably want to know what behavior is acceptable, what would be resented by the residents. The Language and Intercultural Research Center, Brigham Young University, has published "Culturgrams" mainly for use by Mormon missionaries. The information collected is valuable to any visitor to a country.

For example, proper public conduct in Argentina, where etiquette is taken seriously, includes:

- Addressing people by a title (Mr. or Mrs.), and when shaking hands, inclining the head to show respect.
- When eating, hands should always be above the table.

- When approaching an official such as a policeman or customs official, greet him before asking a question.
- Using a toothpick is bad manners.
- When eating with others and it is necessary to blow one's nose or clear the throat, excuse oneself and do it out of the hearing of others.
- For women to cross their legs in public is considered unladylike.
- Hands should never be placed on the hips.
- Waiters are called by raising a hand with the index finger extended.

Improper conduct includes:

- When greeting from a distance, never call out. Raising a hand or smiling are appropriate.
- Women do not talk to strangers without an introduction.
- Affection between a man and woman is not shown in public.

VENEZUELA

Venezuela is visited mainly by business travelers. In 1980, some sixty-five thousand visitors to the country were from the United States. Caracas, the capital, is the cultural, political, and population center. Fortunately it sits at an altitude that produces a pleasantly mild climate year-round. An autopista (superhighway) links the city to the coast and to the international airport.

The government owns a series of first-class hotels throughout the country. In Caracas the Hilton and the Intercontinental Hotels are the most prominent. On the coast, near Caracas, the government converted a lavish officer's club into the country's leading resort. The Island of Santa Margarita in the Caribbean is part of Venezuela and is popular with Venezuelans as a holiday spot.

COLOMBIA

Visitors to Colombia usually go to Bogota, the capital, which sits at 8,630 feet, where the weather is never warm, often cool and overcast. Bogota has South America's largest hotel, the Tequendama, with 1,040 rooms. It is relatively safe from revolution, being owned by the military's pension fund. Major tourist attractions in the country include the Bogota Gold Museum, the National Archeological Park at San Augustin, and the Caribbean resort of Cartegena, with its massive seventeenth century fortifications.

Flights to Bogota, Barranquila (Colombia's major seaport), Cali, and Medellin are easily arranged from the United States. Cali and Medellin are leading industrial centers. Colombia, with twenty-seven million people, is the third most populous nation in South America, after Brazil and Argentina. Bolivia and Colombia are known to be the origin of major cocaine smuggling into the United States.

ECUADOR

Air departures from the United States to Ecuador totaled only 40,527 in 1981. Still, the country is worth reviewing for students of travel because of the beauty of the capital city, Quito, and because of the natural history packaged in the Galapagos Islands (owned by Ecuador). Quito, at 9,250 feet, takes some altitude adaptation for the arriving traveler. Though a globe-topped monument marking the equator is only fifteen miles north of Quito, the altitude gives the city springlike days and crisp, cool nights. Quito is easily accessible by air from New York City, Miami, and Los Angeles.

Ecuador's port city and largest town, Guayaquil, lies on the Pacific, undistinguished except for being the world's biggest shipper of bananas.

Visitors to Quito never forget the rugged beauty of the surrounding mountains. The white-walled, green-domed cathedral, La Compania, is a church famous for its glittering interior coated with gold leaf. The archeological Museum of Banco Central is reported as having one of the finest archeological collections in the Americas. Nearly all tourists take trips to market towns a few hours by car where surprisingly beautiful woolen goods including woven tapestries, clothing, and rugs can be had at incredibly low prices. (Bartering is expected.)

For the naturalist, the dream trip is to the Galapagos Islands, 656 miles off Ecuador's coast. The flora and fauna of the islands have fascinated scientists ever since Charles Darwin arrived in 1835 and substantially documented his theory of evolution by observing the numerous species of animals that had developed unique characteristics, isolated from the rest of the world. Biologists report that 37 percent of the shore fish and 96 percent of the reptiles are found nowhere else. Forty-seven percent of the plants are unique to the Galapagos. The islands are easily reached by air via either Quito or Guayaquil. Island cruises are also available including an eleven-day round trip on the Ecuadorian Navy's passenger-supply ship that takes civilians as paying passengers.

For the intrepid, there are the trips down from the mountains into the Amazon region. The Jivaro Indians have an unusual tourist trinket for sale—shrunken heads. The guidebooks tell us that most are imitation, made from goat hides, and can be purchased for about $3. To the chagrin of the shrunken head connoisseur, visitors are no longer used as raw material for the heads.

As in most Latin American countries, don't drink the tap water. Ecuadoran beer has a formidable reputation as in a number of other South American countries where the Germans long ago set up breweries. For the fruit juice lover there is "naranjilla," a flavor cross between peach and citrus. The local aguardiente, sugar cane alcohol, is used in "paico," made of two parts fresh lemon, one part aguardiente. "Llapengachos" is a mashed potato/cheese specialty. The squeamish may not go for the national delicacy, baked guinea pig.

At this time so few North Americans are traveling to the other South American countries that they will not be discussed.

CENTRAL AMERICA

Central America is usually considered as comprising those countries south of Mexico and north of South America: Honduras, Guatemala, El Salvador, Nicaragua, Belize (formerly British Honduras), Costa Rica, and Panama. The population there continues to explode, having doubled between 1960 and 1984. About half of the people are age fifteen or younger. The mountainous sections have a pleasant, springlike climate; the lower sections are tropical in character. Parts of the area are scenic and some places are historically interesting.

The violence going on in Nicaragua, El Salvador and Guatemala has cast a pall over the entire Central American region. Even though Costa Rica and Panama are not directly involved, the number of North Americans going there has dropped since 1980. In 1981 U.S. citizens' air departures for Panama were about thirty thousand. In that year Costa Rica received about forty-eight thousand arrivals by air from the United States. Guatemala had 41,233 arriving by air from the United States; Honduras had 31,275.

Costa Rica, Honduras, and Guatemala have the best tourist potential. Access by air to the region from the United States is easy, with frequent flights by the national airlines. Mexico City and Panama City are connecting points for the region. The Pan American Highway runs from the U.S. border through Mexico on into Panama. Parts of the highway are still incomplete or in poor condition.

FIGURE 8.3   *Map of Central America.*

Running north from Colombia into Panama is a long, thin mountain chain. The mountains slope down to the coasts, which are covered with rain forests. Panama City is the capital of Panama with 406,000 people; total population of Panama is about 1.5 million. The Panama Canal is the country's major source of income and employment as well as being a tourist attraction on a grand scale. The Canal is about fifty miles long and ships are lifted or lowered eighty-five feet in the course of the trip across the Isthmus. Ships are normally in Canal waters between fourteen and sixteen hours. The trip can be costly for the ship's owners. Tolls are based on displaced tonnage. Richard Halliburton was charged thirty-six cents when he swam the Canal in 1926. The toll for the QE 2 on one of its transits was $68,499.46.

Panama has more than eight hundred off-shore islands, some of which could be developed touristically. A major tourist attraction is the San Blas islands, hundreds of tiny palm-fringed islands, where the Indians who inhabit them welcome day-trippers who observe the village life and buy their unique appliqued cloth, handwoven by the women.

Heading north from Panama, the mountains rise and become part of Costa Rica. Poas and Irazu are active volcanic mountains. Irazu showers San Jose, capital of Costa Rica, with volcanic ash from time to time.

Costa Rica ("rich coast") is one of the loveliest of all Latin American countries, as several thousand North American retirees who live there attest. The country is also for bird lovers; the 850 species of birds found there outnumber those of the United States and Canada. There are 700 species of butterflies and 320 amphiban and reptile species. Eight percent of the land has been set aside for conservancy.

The country is mostly Spanish in background, without the large Indian population of most of the rest of Latin America. The wide gulf between haves and have-nots does not exist and the government is by far the most democratic of Latin countries. The nation of 2.4 million prides itself on having no army, only guards and police who are political appointees. North Americans are well liked. San Jose sits at thirty-eight hundred feet and most of the population live on the central plateau at similar altitudes. Unfortunately the country is deeply in debt and dependent largely upon the sale of coffee and bananas for its foreign exchange.

Nicaragua borders Costa Rica on the north, and like Costa Rica and Panama, is bounded on the west by the Pacific Ocean and on the east by the Caribbean. Managua, the capital, has 450,000 people. The coastal plains are partly swampland on the east. The interior is wooded mountains. Lake Nicaragua is one of the world's largest lakes; it contains alligators and fresh water sharks. Dominated for decades by the Somoza family, which was overthrown by a revolution, the country in 1984 was in political turmoil. The total population of Nicaragua is about 2.2 million. The best road through the country is the Pan American Highway, which runs south from Mexico through Central America to Panama.

Honduras is best known to the tourist for its ruins of the great Mayan civilization, Copan, first discovered by an American in 1837. The capital, Tegucigalpa, population 267,000, is fairly comfortable weather-wise because of its altitude. The people of the Bay Islands, offshore in the Caribbean, speak English as a first language and Spanish, the Honduran national language, second. The islands once served as sanctuaries for English buccaneers who left their descendents and their language. The Bay Islands have the distinction of sitting on the second largest barrier reef in the world (after that of Queensland, Australia). Barrier reefs offer good snorkeling and scuba diving. Adventuresome Canadians, Americans, and Englishmen operate small Bay Island resorts catering to divers and yachtsmen. A problem for the visitor is getting there. Several plane transfers are usually necessary to get to Riordan, the departure point for the islands.

Honduras is mountainous, with volcanic peaks reaching as high as eighty-two hundred feet. If the term Banana Republic applies to any country, it is Honduras. The United Fruit Company developed banana plantations before the turn of the century and bananas have been the primary source of income ever since. The government changes presidents frequently as one military man removes another and steps in to acquire wealth and move on. Ninety percent of the 3.5 million residents are mestizos (European-Indian). The country has a small coast on the Pacific as well as its coastline on the Caribbean.

El Salvador, the smallest country in Central America, borders Honduras on the east and south, Guatemala on the north. It has a narrow coastal strip on the Pacific. A central plateau runs between mountains, including active volcanoes. Four million people crowd into this tiny country, creating the greatest population density on the American mainland. San Salvador, the capital, alone has a population of almost one million. Coffee plantations run almost up to the rims of many of the country's twenty-two volcanoes. Political unrest has resulted from the fact that a few families have controlled the country and most of the wealth for many years.

Guatemala borders Mexico and Belize is to the east. Guatemala's 7.5 million population, about half of whom are pure Amerindian, make it the most populous of the Central American nations. Guatemala City, the capital, has 750,000 people and because of its altitude and latitude has a pleasant year-round temperature. Chichicastenango has probably the best known native market in South America. A well-known colonial town, "Chichi" is one of those prizes every visitor must take home in the form of snapshots.

Belize, just below Mexico's Yucatan Peninsula, also has a spectacular off-shore reef and some cays. Hot and humid, one-third of Belize's 145,000 people live on the coast. Fifty miles inland is Belmopan, the capital, built there to avoid hurricanes experienced in Belize. From the coast the land gradually rises to the Mana Mountains of the interior.

Because of violence in some of the Central American countries and the region's general reputation for violence, it will be some time before it will come into its own as a place attractive to the pleasure traveler.

9

THE PACIFIC BASIN

Growth and travel within and to the Pacific Basin area rose three-and-a-half times in the 1969–1979 decade, well ahead of the world average. The Boeing company forecasts that Trans-Pacific traffic will grow at an annual rate of 12 percent between 1980 and 1987. Intra-Orient traffic will increase, says Boeing, at 15 percent per annum.

A Pacific Area Travel Association study in 1980 showed Australia and Japan to hold the most appeal for potential travelers, followed by Hong Kong, Tahiti, New Zealand, and Mainland China. Some fifty different travel experiences have been defined in the Basin, from butterfly searching in Papua New Guinea, to bargain shopping in the Ginza of Tokyo. A variety of cultures can be observed first hand.[1] New Zealand is decidedly traditional British in a setting of remarkable natural beauty. The South Pacific could absorb a lifetime of study in observing the hundreds of islands and their peoples. Most North Americans are only vaguely aware of and have little interest in the East Asian nations of Malaysia, Indonesia, Taiwan, Thailand, and Korea. Much of the lack of interest stems from unfamiliarity with the region. Potential travelers to the Pacific Basin were asked which of a number of possible sources of information they would consider using in planning a trip to the Pacific. The reliable sources in their minds were travel agents, friends, acquaintances, or relatives who had visited the Pacific areas.

Travel to and within the Pacific area has the ring of romance. The very words South Pacific, Far East, Cathay invoke images of faraway places, mystery, and the unknown. And they have been far away for North Americans. In the days of steamship travel it took as long as twenty-three days to cross the Pacific. Even today with six hundred mph jet travel, the hours roll on when en route from the United States across the Pacific. The immensity of the Pacific is overwhelming, extending from the Arctic Circle to the Antarctic regions, and from Western North America and Western South America to East Asia and Australia—an area encompassing almost seventy million square miles.

Consider French Polynesia. It covers an area as big as Europe without Russia, about 1.5 million square miles. French Polynesia is only a small part of the South Pacific. Its seat of government is Tahiti, land of beaches, tropical breezes, plenty of rain, and mostly Polynesians.

Dotting the South Pacific are hundreds of islands, many of them in clusters hundreds of miles distant from other clusters. Fiji and New Caledonia are such clusters. So is Tonga, ruled over by a king and thirty-three nobles. So is Western Samoa, ruled by four paramount chiefs. So is American Samoa. Halfway between Hawaii and New Zealand and halfway between Fiji and Tahiti are the Cook Islands. Only twenty thousand people populate the fifteen Cook Islands.

Few people have heard of Kiribati. Until 1976 it was the Gilbert and Ellice Islands, a British Colony. It is now a nation of forty thousand Micronesians with one twenty-six-room hotel, one twenty-four-room hotel and some rest houses. It is also a country where if you should see a woman without a nose, you can be pretty sure she strayed from the marital bed. With tradition to support him, her husband bit off her nose.

The South Pacific has other island clusters, several of them little known to North America. The Solomon Islands are another independent country of about 200,000 persons, mostly Melanesian. New Caledonia is a French Overseas Territory with plenty of nickel for mining.

And we must not overlook Nauru, a nation of seven thousand people built on dung. Bird dung, that is. The island's chief and almost only source of income is from phosphate built up over the centuries in the form of bird droppings. Thanks to the birds the standard of living is one of the highest in the entire Pacific. There is even a Nauru airline. When the dung which is made into fertilizer runs out, the nation will move to another island.

The Far East is called East Asia by the Pacific Area Travel Association and comprises China, The Republic of China (Taiwan), Hong Kong, Macau, Japan, and Korea. The same association treats Bangladesh, India, Nepal, Pakistan and Sri Lanka (formerly Ceylon) as South Asia. Southeast Asia as defined by PATA comprises Indonesia, Malaysia, the Philippines, Singapore, and Thailand.

Japan, as a leading industrial nation, is the number one generator of travelers in the entire Pacific. Quite naturally the Japanese frequent the countries close to home: The Republic of China, Korea, and Hong Kong. Japanese men are fond of group tours that involve girls as entertainment. Korea tried banning prostitution, mostly patronized by the Japanese; tourism fell drastically, and the ban was removed.

Hong Kong, a world trade center in the Far East, is on lease from Mainland China, countenanced by China for its own convenience. Only 404 square miles, this British Crown Colony—really a city-state—contains more than five million people, mostly Chinese. It sports some of the world's finest hotels built on some of the world's most expensive land.

One reason that travel within and to the Pacific Basin countries is growing more rapidly than world travel in general is that about 65 percent of the world's population lives in the countries bordering the Basin. Mainland China alone has a billion people and is vigorously building new hotels and seeking more foreign exchange brought by visitors. In just a few years tourism has become one of the country's largest sources of foreign exchange. Tokyo, Hong Kong, and Singapore are world financial centers. Japan, third largest industrial nation, after the U.S. and Russia, has a middle class eager for travel. New Zealanders and Australians have the money and urge for travel. Korea and Taiwan are rapidly industrializing and Mainland China is opening up to the outside world. For every one U.S. tourist visiting Asia, two Asian tourists visit the United States.

HAWAII

After Canada and Mexico, the number one choice of U.S. overseas travelers is Hawaii, the "Aloha State." Aloha is a good tourist word. It can mean hello, I love you, and goodbye. In a 1983 Roper poll, 43 percent of the respondents picked Hawaii as the overseas destination they would most like to visit. While travel to Hawaii is not "international" it is so treated here because of the islands' distance from mainland U.S.A.

In that state tourism has edged out agriculture—mainly sugar and pineapple production—and military spending as its biggest source of income. In 1982, 30 percent of the state's

FIGURE 9.1 *Major transit cities in the Pacific basin.*

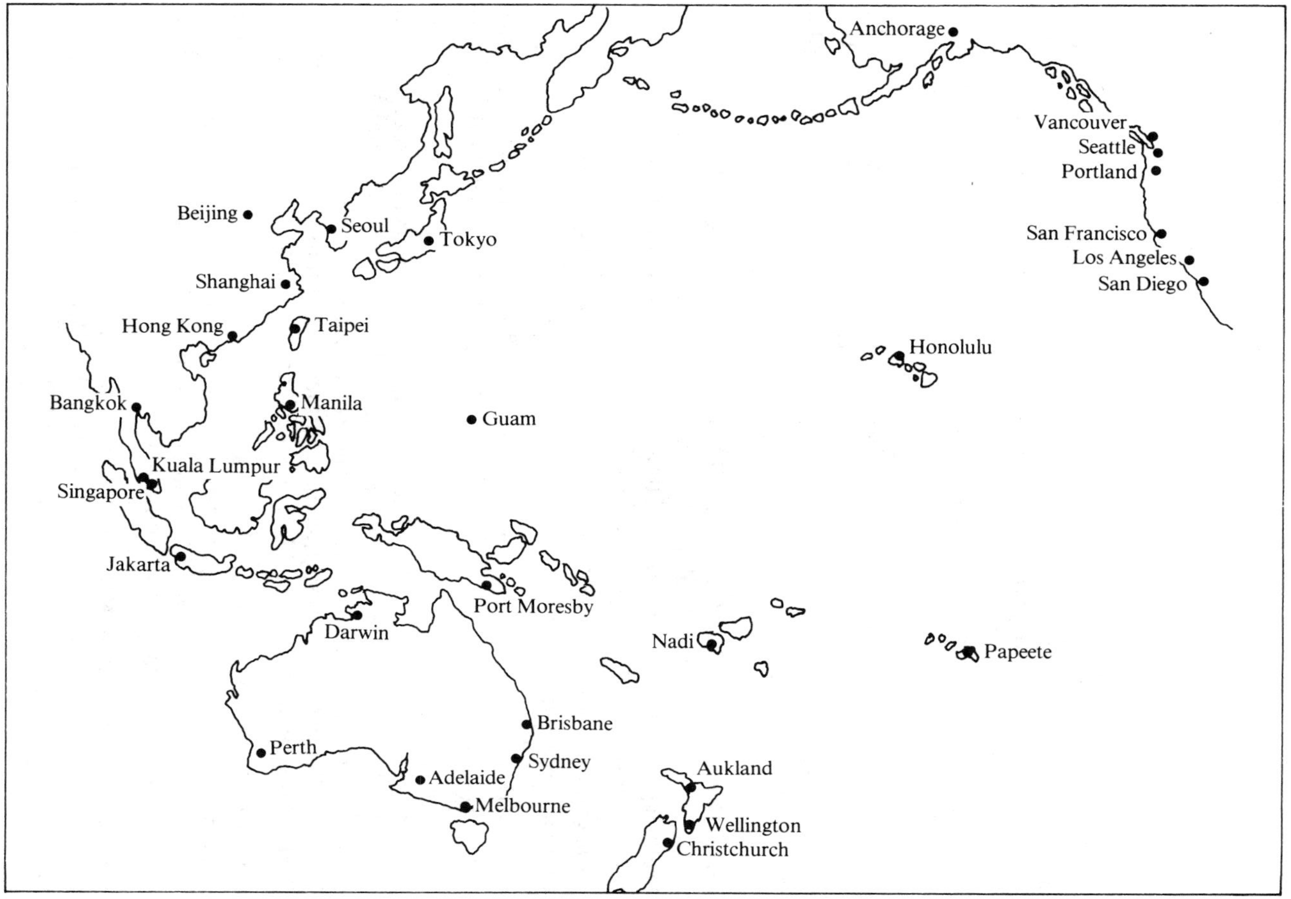

gross personal income, $3.55 billion, was from visitor expenditures. More than four million visitors—four times the resident population and about the same number of Americans who visit all of Europe—come to enjoy what is undoubtedly the world's best tropical vacation destination. Only a dozen major nations receive more visitors than Hawaii. The Japanese, 690,000 strong, arrived in 1981, a large percentage of whom came as part of a group and could be seen following a tour guide around Oahu taking dozens of pictures and buying luxury goods like steaks and Scotch. Indeed, Hawaii, in about twenty years, has become a "wunderkind" of tropical tourism.

Cheap airfares and a plethora of hotel rooms and condominium rentals have brought the cost of the Hawaiian vacation down to reach the mass middle-class market. The Hawaiian Visitor's Bureau would like more of the "quality market," the big spenders. McDonald's and Burger King would not be so crowded and the $150-a-day luxury resorts would benefit. On an expenditure-per-day basis the Japanese visitor to Hawaii should be welcomed with fanfare. One study found the average Japanese tourist to Hawaii spent $180 a day, compared to Europeans who spent $75 and Americans, $71. Canadian visitors spent $65 per day.

The Hawaiian Visitors Bureau provides these capsule descriptions of the Hawaiian Islands:

MAUI: (Population 52,900) The Valley Isle produces sugar, pineapple, cattle, horses. The 10,023-foot Haleakala is the largest dormant volcano crater in the world. Lahaina was Hawaii's capital before 1845, and still has some of the atmosphere of an old whaling town. Nearby is the Kaanapali resort area and golf course. Heavenly Hana and Iao Valley draw many visitors.

MOLOKAI: (Population 6,400) The "Friendly Isle" has pineapple plantations, ranching, and some spectacular cliffs along its northern Pali Coast. On a 13-square-mile peninsula below high cliffs is Kalaupapa, the Hansen's Disease settlement, officially called Kalawao County, with a population of 173 in 1978.

LANAI: (Population 2,100) Contains 140 square miles. Almost the entire island is a Dole Company pineapple plantation.

KAHOOLAWE: (Population 0) Uninhabited. Used as a target by U.S. Navy and Air Force. Littered with unexploded shells. No one is allowed to go ashore without permission.

HAWAII: (Population 80,900) The Big Island has spectacular contrasts...the mighty volcanoes Mauna Loa (13,677 feet) and Kilauea, lofty snow clad Mauna Kea (13,796 feet), the Ka'u Desert, gorgeous waterfalls, the Puna Fern Forest, the colorful orchids of Hilo. The island grows sugar, coffee, cattle and macadamia nuts. Hawaii Volcanoes National Park; Kealakekua Bay; Kailua-Kona; Kawaihae; Parker Ranch; Waipio Valley.

OAHU: (Population 719,600) The "Gathering Place," Honolulu is the Capital City, the principal port, the major airport, the business and financial center, and the educational heart of the State, and Oahu is the Military Command Center of the Pacific. Waikiki is the visitor center. Nuuanu Pali; Diamond Head; Pearl Harbor.

KAUAI: (Population 34,400) The "Garden Island" offers magnificent scenery and lush vegetation, beautiful waterfalls, the spectacular Waimea Canyon, the great "hidden" valley of Kalalau, colorful tropical plants and flowers, Hanalei Bay, Wailua River, Nawiliwili Bay, Poipu Beach.

NIIHAU: (Population 266) Privately owned island, with livestock raising as its principal industry. Legend says it was original home of the Goddess Pele.

For many years a radio program from the Islands was aptly named, "Hawaii Calls." It calls in a number of ways. Of all tropical vacation areas it is one of the safest and most beautiful while offering a variety of entertainment. An abundance of fine hotels back the beaches. It has a fascinating native culture accompanied by its own unique music. Altogether there are fifty-one thousand guest rooms.

Our fiftieth state, Hawaii, consists of eight major southerly islands in a chain and 124 minor islands. The land mass totals 6,450 square miles, of which 98 percent forms the six major islands. Their coastline runs for 750 miles.

Flying time is five to six hours from the west coast of the U.S. to Honolulu. First to come to view by air is the big island of Hawaii, off to the left of the plane. Two huge mountains, Mauna Kea and Mauna Loa, dominate the island. The southern tip of the island turns out to be the southernmost point of the entire United States. Mauna Kea is the state's highest peak, 13,796 feet.

Next in view is the island of Maui with its one huge mountain, Haleakala. Then comes Molokai. The plane passes over Diamond Head and Waikiki Beach, then lands at Honolulu International Airport on the Island of Oahu. From the air the islands seem to float in the water. Actually all are the tops of volcanoes originating deep in the ocean.

The capital city of Honolulu, on Oahu, is 1,367 miles from Kure Atoll (the westernmost end of the state), and 2,397 miles from San Francisco.

The Punchbowl, another crater from an extinct volcano, and a military cemetery, along with the Sea Life Park and the Polynesian Cultural Center, are principal attractions on Oahu. Honolulu also has Iolani, the only royal palace in the United States. It was occupied until the 1890s by the last two Hawaiian monarchs.

To many visitors Honolulu and the island it sits on, Oahu, *is* Hawaii. The quip goes that "if one more visitor comes to Waikiki the whole island of Oahu will flip over." Waikiki Beach, once the province of a few cottages kept for the king's favorites, is now a solid row of highrise hotels and condos. The view from the beach looking toward Diamond Head, an extinct volcano, is still something special. Pearl Harbor is another big tourist attraction as well as being the biggest naval base outside the continental United States and scene of the Japanese attack on December 7, 1941.

Maui has two airports, the larger one being about a forty minute drive from the major tourist areas, Kaanapali Beach and Kihea Beach. The "Valley Island" Maui developed rapidly; it was once known primarily for its little village of Lahaina, a whaling center when whales were pursued for their fat to be boiled into oil. Lahaina is still picturesque, its old hotel a landmark, where a sign placed by its Chinese owner told the "salts" of yesterday what they could and could not do. Included was "you pea in bed, out you go."

Maui and Molokai are well within visual range of each other, each adding to the beauty of the other. Kaanapali Beach on Maui is the first of the Hawaiian master-planned resort developments. Its three-mile swimming beach is backed by a series of hotels, a golf course and condominiums. After Oahu, Maui is the largest resort concentration in the entire Pacific Basin.

You get no argument from residents of Hana, Maui that the road that gets there from the populated part of Maui is the worst in all the United States. The residents want to keep it that way. They say, "As long as the road is rough as Hell, the life in Hana will remain like Heaven." They want only a limited number of visitors. The road is full of "pukas," potholes. The scenery along the narrow winding road, one lane at times, is beautiful. The combination of bad roads and good scenery means about fifteen miles per hour over the fifty-five-mile road.

The Hana Hotel in Hana is low key, first-class and provides its guests with bountiful buffets and access to their beach, a cove described by James Michener as "the most beautiful in the Pacific."

A little farther down the road is the grave of Charles Lindbergh, who loved Hana and wished to remain there forever.

The big island of Hawaii is the one place in the United States that provides a big, bubbly, burning volcano that erupts every year or so. Only thirty-five minutes from Hilo, the state's second largest city, Kilauea Volcano comes with the Volcano House Hotel located on the rim of a huge crater in Volcanoes National Park. Sulphuric smoke rises from hundreds of tiny fissures and makes the thousands of visitors who walk directly into the crater wonder if it is all that safe. The locals say that their island is the most rapidly growing of all the islands. When Kilauea erupts it often sends lava down the slopes and hissing into the ocean, gradually adding acres to the island's geography.

The first church built in Hawaii, in 1823, Mokuaihaua Church, sits in Kona. Drawings within the church show Kona as it was soon after King Kamehameha died nearby in 1819. In the drawings the church sits majestically amidst a village of small grass huts. Also near-by is the summer palace of King Kalakaua, more like the home of a middle-class business-man than a palace.

King Kamehameha's residence was adjacent to what is now the King Kamehameha Beach Hotel. The king, about six feet eight inches tall, was not only respected but feared. One story that survives relates how commoners who fell within his shadow were executed on the spot.

Kona, which now has its own very pleasant little airport a few miles from town, is known worldwide for its Hawaiian International Billfish's Tournament. More than a dozen Pacific blue marlin weighing over one thousand pounds each are boated within an hour's run of the Kona pier.

The Moana Kea Hotel, built by Laurance Rockefeller, is a half-hour's drive north along the coast and through extensive lava beds. Now operated by Westin Hotels, it has one of the few good beaches on the big island. Close by and closer to the airport are the Sheraton Waikoloa and Mauna Lani Bay Hotels, both with gorgeous golf courses and tennis courts hacked out of lava beds. The Mauna Lani Bay, Japanese owned, and the Mona Kea are the island's two luxury hotels, quite properly located on the leeward side of the island where the rainfall is something under ten inches a year.

Hilo has a population of about forty-five thousand. Described as a daylight city, the place largely closes down at sunset. It is also the U.S. orchid and macadamia nut capital. United Airlines offers direct flights to Hilo International Airport from the Mainland.

Molokai, "The Friendly Isle," fifth largest of the Hawaiian islands, along with the even smaller island of Lanai, is the most laid-back. Only forty-eight miles from Honolulu, it is a great deal farther away in lifestyle. Maui and Lanai can both be seen from Molokai on clear days. Thirty-seven percent of its six thousand residents claims native Hawaiian descent. The island is described as the most bucolic, poorest and funkiest. Its principal town, Kaunakakai (try saying that one), is hardly a town at all. Three hotels and several condo rentals complete the roster of room rentals. The "friendly" natives have a lingering resent-ment towards the Haoles (the Caucasians) that sometimes erupts into open hostility.

Molokai is known for its leper colony at Kalaupapa, still occupied by over a hundred persons whose disease is now arrested. One of the heroes of our age, Father Daimien, a Belgian priest, served the lepers and died himself horribly mutilated by the disease. No roads lead to the leper colony but it is reachable by mule. The trip lasts all day and involves fifteen switchbacks. The mule ride down the Grand Canyon in Arizona is somewhat similar.

For those who want total tranquility, there is Lanai, the little "Pineapple Island." It has one hotel and gentle rolling hills. Lanai is the place for those who want the lovely sandy beach all to themselves.

Hawaii is the one state in the Union where Caucasians, the Haoles, are a minority. Nearly two-thirds of the population of about one million are of Asian, Polynesian, or Pacific descent.

The population is young, 50 percent under 28.3 years of age in 1977, and racially diver-sified, with 29 percent of the total being the product of mixed marriages. Everyone in Hawaii is a member of a minority. Hawaii's ethnic groups are: Caucasian—26.2 percent; Japanese—25.2 percent; Filipino—9.7 percent; Hawaiian and part-Hawaiian—19.7 per-cent; Chinese—4.2 percent; Korean—1.1 percent; Negro—1.1 percent; Samoan—0.9 per-cent; Puerto Ricans—0.6 percent; mixed (except part-Hawaiian)—10.2 percent; and other groups—1.0 percent.

Hawaii's balmy climate is close to ideal for those who like the tropics. Variations in temperature and rainfall depend more on location than season. Mountain tops and the windward sides of islands are wet, the leeward sides comparatively dry.

The extreme temperature range reported in downtown Honolulu is from fifty-seven degrees to eighty-eight degrees. Average precipitation ranges from 5.7 inches near Kawaihae on the Big Island to 486.1 inches atop Waialeale on Kauai. The summit of Waialeale is the wettest spot in the United States. The longest volcanic eruption in Hawaii's history lasted 867 days and the highest tsunami (tidal wave) reached fifty-six feet.

To get to Kauai, the "Garden Island" farther west, or to fly to Molokai, Maui or Hawaii means a smaller plane and another nineteen to forty minutes of flight.

Kauai, oldest of the Hawaiian islands, has deep green valleys and dazzling flowers. One main road moves around most of the island's periphery. The road will probably never completely circle the island because of the ruggedness of much of the coast. Kauai has a little Grand Canyon, Waimea. It also has the Wailua River, up which tourist boats move to the Fern Grotto. As the name implies, it is a grotto almost completely covered in ferns, ceiling included. Lihue is the only town of any size on Kauai, a few minutes from the airport.

Hawaii is known for its rum drink, the Mai Tai: three kinds of rum, tropical fruit juices, and lots of ice. Every hotel of any size has its weekly luau, the centerpiece of which is Kalua pig—a pig baked in an "imu," an earthen oven. The pig is covered with cloth, put in a hole lined with very hot rocks. It comes out tender, moist and tasty. Poi, the pounded root of the taro plant, was the basic carbohydrate in old Hawaii. Natives still enjoy it. Visitors liken its taste to starch glue.

Nearly all of the native Hawaiians have intermarried over the generations, but Hawaiiana lingers on to delight the visitor. The story goes that a Hawaiian who used to fish for squid always wore a malo, a loincloth. Tourists would pay $5 to take his picture. Soon, no need to fish for squid. He made so much money soon he sent his son to Harvard. The boy came home to the Islands. Take over his father's business. Only he charges $10 to pose. He got college degree.

Hula dancing is an essential ingredient of all Hawaiian entertainment. Visitors in the audience are nearly always invited—or dragooned—to dance along, much to the enjoyment of the onlookers. The hula as it was seen in old Hawaii was an accompaniment to chanting. The early missionaries added music to make it the art form it is today.

THE SOUTH PACIFIC

The South Pacific refers to that huge expanse of water more or less south of Hawaii stretching from New Guinea, Australia and New Zealand to South America. The South Seas generally include eight countries which added together cover only twenty-one thousand square miles of land, in all, one-third the size of Florida. The total population of the area is 1.3 million but it is scattered over distances hard to imagine. Tonga, spread over an area as large as England, has land a third the size of the Isle of Wight. Its population is 100,000. The fifteen Cook Islands are scattered over an area the size of Western Europe.

The jet plane made tourism as a principal industry possible for Tahiti and for the entire South Pacific. The number of air carriers to the islands and the fares charged determine to a large extent the number of visitors that arrive. A route change by a major carrier is instantly reflected in visitor arrivals. Prior to 1961, before the jets arrived, the South Pacific was exotica, only for the business traveler, the yacht people, and the cruise passenger. In 1965 Tahiti's principal visitor was the businessman. By 1975 it was the vacationer. The most pleasurable way to see the remote islands is by cruise ship or plane. Taking the inter-island ships can be torturous and dangerous. Traveling on a yacht is a great challenge but can also be hazardous.

FIGURE 9.2 *The South Pacific.*

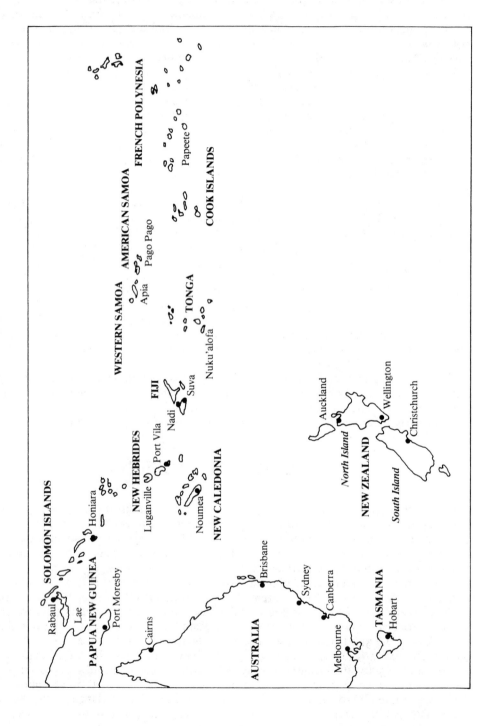

Getting to the South Pacific is easy. Getting around within the area is more complex. The kind of planes and the flight schedules are varied, to say the least. Be they ever so humble, each nation has its own subsidized airline. Vanuatu (until 1980, the New Hebrides) has Air Vanuatu, Western Samoa has Polynesian Airlines. For Papua New Guinea, it is Air Mugini. Tiwalu, formerly the Ellise Islands, has a plane or two. Solair is the national airline of the Solomon Islands. Fiji has Air Pacific. The airline of the Marshall Islands serves those islands, newly independent in 1982. The tiny island of Nauru has invested $35 million in Air Nauru and has its own shipping line.

The American tourist will probably never be interested in many of the Pacific Islands, some mere coral outcroppings where a few hundred people grow taro and yams, harvest coconuts, and fish.

For Americans the best known and most visited of the South Pacific is Tahiti, part of French Polynesia. Papeete (pa-pay-et-tay) is the capital and has the international airport for the region. Pago Pago (pang-o-pang-o) is the chief harbor and town of American Samoa. Apia has the international airport for Western Samoa, an independent nation. Nandi is the international airport for the numerous islands that make up Fiji. Fiji gets almost 200,000 visitors a year. Some 38 percent originate in Australia and 19 percent in New Zealand.

Some islands are really for those who are serious about getting away from it all. Wallis and Futuna is an overseas territory of France, two small groups of islands between Fiji and Samoa. Total population is nine thousand. The place has a four-bungalow establishment for traders, and one public eating house described as "cheerful and clean."

The South Pacific is inhabited mostly by Polynesians, people with brown skins and straight hair. Off to the west is Melanesia, meaning black islands, a name derived from the darkness of island vegetation or the dark tones of the region's inhabitants. The inhabitants tend to have kinky hair. Micronesia, to the northwest, means small islands, aptly describing the tiny islands, several of which were the scene of bloody battles during World War II. The inhabitants are brown-skinned, with Malaysian and Polynesian traits. All are believed to have originally come from Asia by way of the Malay Peninsula.

Eighty percent of the visitors to the South Pacific come via North American travel agents. The area lends itself to Special Interest Travelers (SIT's) and Group Inclusive Travelers (GIT's). Package tours are a natural for the South Pacific as well as for the individually planned tours, the FIT's. Don't bother to take the inter-island freighters that ply the waters of French Polynesia, or of Tonga either. They frequently break down and concern over lifeboats is negligible, if they are available.

Only a few years ago accommodations in the smaller islands were few and modest. Today, places like Tahiti and Fiji have elegant hotels and the lesser known islands of Tonga and Western Samoa have a few first-class hotels.

Old-timers may not feel as comfortable in the new Tusitalia Hotel in Western Samoa, a government-owned property, as in Agie Grey's, a rambling assemblage of rooms with plenty of atmosphere and the only good hotel in Western Samoa for many years. If so inclined, today's visitor can experience the local culture by living in a native fale, an open hut, on one of the less developed islands in Western Samoa. The average tourist would find it fairly uncomfortable.

South Sea island-hoppers favor Tahiti, not too quiet, nor is it another frenetic Waikiki Beach. All of the guest rooms in Tahiti do not total those in the Sheraton Waikiki. The Maevo hotel with seven floors is the largest in the South Pacific. It broke the old rule that no hotel should be higher than a coconut tree. The Tahara is Papeete's upside down hotel, the guest enters the lobby at the top level, with ten levels of rooms terraced down the hillside beneath it. All hotel managers are not as enthusiastic about the island as many of the visitors. The laid-back lifestyle of the employees includes taking off a few days whenever the whim strikes.

Tahiti is for the romantic and for lovers of natural beauty, those who like Hawaii but want something less developed, yet are not inclined to try the even more remote underdeveloped South Sea islands. About 100,000 visitors appear in Tahiti each year, 45 percent of them from the United States. The average visitor to Tahiti is about fifty-one years old. Almost half of them travel with a spouse. Of the approximately 100,000 people residing in the 110 islands that compose French Polynesia, almost 60 percent live on the Island of Tahiti, the international gateway to French Polynesia. Thirty miles long and eighteen miles wide, volcanic in origin, its highest point is Mount Orahena, 7,321 feet. It is only one island in French Polynesia, which includes some 1,544 square miles of ocean and the Marquesas Islands. While most tourists to French Polynesia limit their visits to Tahiti or to Moorea, twelve miles to the northwest of Tahiti, a few also visit Raratea, 116 miles from Tahiti; Tahaa, two miles from Raratea; Bora Bora, thirty-five miles northwest of Tahaa; and Hualine, twenty miles east of Raratea.

One little island, Feteraroa, is owned by Marlon Brando. When he bought the island not one native lived there. Everything must be imported including personnel to operate his little group of fares, the open-air huts, characteristic homes of the islanders.

Barrier reefs that surround the principal islands form protected lagoons excellent for swimming, fishing, and snorkeling.

The average temperature of seventy-eight degrees and the offshore-onshore breezes make for a humid, balmy climate. During the night or early morning hours, air cooled by the mountains flows downward to the coastal areas. By mid-morning the mountain slopes, heated by the sun, cause the air to rise, drawing in moist air from the surrounding seas. Unfortunately there are periods of heavy rain and, from time to time, typhoons that cause havoc in the low-lying islands.

As a French Overseas Territory, French Polynesia has a governor appointed from Paris and a sizeable contingent of French troops stationed on the islands.

FIJI

Flying 2,775 miles southwest from Hawaii, the traveler can land at Nandi, the international airport for the South Sea nation of Fiji. It has been a nation since 1970 when it became an official part of the British Commonwealth. As recently as 1854, the natives, a mixture of Polynesian and Melanesian, were busy warring against each other, the losers (and some stray Europeans) appearing on the day's menu of the victors. As a matter of curiosity, one of the souvenirs of Fiji is a so-called cannibal fork made of wood. The standard reply made by the salespersons when asked if the forks were really used is, "Certainly, we weren't savages, you know."

A story is told about the late Sir Edward Cakobau, Oxford-educated former commander of Fijian militia, who supposedly was traveling by ship to England a number of years ago. Sir Edward was seated for dinner with a group of British when he instructed the waiter by loudly calling out, "Never mind the menu, bring me the passenger list."

Fijians are known for their joviality and good humor. Not so humorous is their relationship with the other half of the population, some 300,000 Indians whose ancestors were brought in by the English to work the coconut and sugar plantations. Land ownership is very difficult for them. Eighty-four percent of the land is communally owned by the native Fijians and by law cannot be sold, only leased. This proviso safeguards the natives from being dispossessed, as largely happened in Hawaii as the chiefs sold or gave away most of Hawaii to non-Hawaiians.

The island of Viti Levu is the center of population even though some one hundred of the more than three hundred islands are populated. Suva, a city of 120,000, retains a colonial British atmosphere. Hereditary chiefs still hold much of the political power throughout Fiji. An unwritten rule holds the heights of hotels to "no higher than a coconut palm." As in most South Pacific islands, the climate is tropical maritime, which means warm and humid.

Visitors have a choice of a number of modern hotels but also can stay in the native "bures," the one-room huts made of reeds and thatch. Several resorts occupy all of the small islands. The visitor can weave a mat, catch shrimp, plant taro, and learn how to ward off evil spirits. At night there is dancing, and dancing, and dancing, sometimes all night long.

The ceremonial drink is made from pounded pepper tree root, called yagona. (It is called kava in other South Pacific island groups.) The imbiber gets a mild glow from the drink. Kokoda is a popular dish made of raw fish marinated in lime juice and served in coconut milk.

Nandi is located on the dry side of Viti Levu. Suva, on the wet (or leeward side), receives more than enough rain.

Fiji is an example of how dependent some destinations are on air transportation. Several airlines once used the Nandi airport enroute to and from Australia, New Zealand, North and South America and some Pacific Islands. Fiji's tourist business grew rapidly and with it the number of hotel rooms. Tour packages could easily be assembled with Fiji as a few-days stopover, or as part of the package tour of the South Pacific. The airlines scheduling Fiji as a stopover also promoted the little country. Prices were comparatively cheap. Some 200,000 visitors came in 1981, 60 percent from Australia and New Zealand, three or four air hours away. With the 1982 recession, several of the flights were cancelled by the airlines and tourism declined.

Australians and New Zealanders are major markets for Fiji. Fiji is seventeen hundred miles northeast of Sydney, eleven hundred miles north of Auckland, New Zealand.

The *National Geographic* magazine traces the peopling of the Pacific as originating in China, Taiwan, and the Philippines and also from Borneo and Java, dating between 3000 B.C. and A.D. 300. The more recent Polynesian voyages are dated between A.D. 300 and A.D. 1000. These later migrations, over thousands of miles of open ocean, are believed to have started from the Marquesas Islands. Probably because of over-population and war, various chiefs led their followers north to Hawaii, south to Easter Island and southwest to Tahiti and New Zealand. The migrations continue today as South Sea islanders emigrate to New Zealand, Australia, Hawaii, and mainland United States.

The Polynesian Triangle is formed with Hawaii as one point, New Zealand another and Easter Island as the third. Easter Island is a curiosity because of the gigantic figures sitting erect around the island, carved without metal and moved without wheels. The island was a microcosm of people's suspicions of each other who are slightly different. At one time two groups of Polynesians occupied the island. One group had long ears, the other short. The short-eared ate the long-eared.

The unity of the Polynesian Triangle is borne out by the appearance of the people and the commonality of culture. The word for house or residence is similar throughout the islands. In Hawaii it is "hale," in Fiji it is "vale." Home in Tahiti is "fare." In Tonga and the Samoas the word for dwelling is "fale." In far off New Zealand where the Maoris settled the word has changed to "whare."

Fiji is regarded as a South Pacific crossroads where the Melanesian dark-skinned people mingled with the browner-skinned Polynesians. About half the population of Fiji's 500,000 people are today descendents of laborers brought to Fiji from India almost a century ago. The melding of races continues.

SOUTH SEA ISLAND MYTHS

Some myths about the South Sea islands hang on. People sitting in their New York offices can fantasize about eluding the pressure cooker of city life and escaping to the South Seas. Gauguin did it, why not me? Beautiful, available girls, balmy breezes, gorgeous ocean views and little need for work. Captain Cook's crew and Captain Cook himself partook of these idyllic treasures until one day the dark side of the scene rose up and Cook was murdered on one of those lovely beaches. Fletcher Christian led the seamen who mutineed on the Bounty and sailed away to eventually settle, with the mutineers and a group of Polynesians, on Pitcairn Island. Before Christian died nearly all of the men had murdered each other. Despite the realities of the South Seas the myths hang on—never mind the heat, the humidity, and the lethal typhoons.

Ironically a large portion of the Polynesians living in the Polynesian Triangle—Hawaii, Easter Island, New Zealand—want out. The young people living on Pukapuka Island in the Cook Islands, for example, want desperately to go to Rarotonga, seven hundred miles away, capital of the twenty-thousand-strong nation. Those in Rarotonga would like to live in Auckland, New Zealand. So do a lot of other people in the constellation of islands that span three thousand miles. Many of them have joined the Polynesians native to New Zealand, the Maori, to give Auckland the largest of all Polynesian populations.

It is reasonably certain, says John Dyon in his fine book, *The South Seas Dream*[2], that two distinct racial types sailed into the South Pacific from Southeast Asia. One racial group, the black, frizzy-haired Melanesians, settled on New Caledonia, the New Hebrides and most of Fiji. The Polynesians of Tonga, Samoa, Tahiti, Hawaii, and New Zealand are a second racial group, brown-skinned with straight hair. The Polynesians sailed by the islands already occupied by Melanesians and settled in the Marquesas and Society Islands (now part of French Polynesia). Later groups under their chiefs loaded up huge canoes with people, coconuts, bananas, breadfruit, yams, taro. Animals were included—pigs, dogs and fowl—and sailed out into ocean spaces as large as Africa. Navigation was done by locating themselves within patterns of stars.

Their social structure was feudal. Lesser chiefs reported to paramount chiefs, as is done today in the Samoas. The land was owned by the king or the alii, the nobility. In Tonga today all land is owned by the king and thirty-three nobles who theoretically apportion it to every male on arriving at age sixteen. The 8¼ acreas the boy is given could produce 250 coconut palms and room enough to grow a variety of fruit and vegetables. Only there is not enough land to go around.

Tongan men tend to be large and have more than enough macho. In the old days they prided themselves on stealing women from Samoa and boats from the Fijians. Their aggressiveness is seen today when playing rugby. It has been described as a terminal game—bodies all over the field.

In contrast, the Tongans are very religious and are shocked at seeing public displays of affection, unchaperoned dating and working on Sunday.

The native kava party is different from a beer bust. No one gets drunk even though kava is made from the roots of the kava plant and is mildly intoxicating. Women prepare it, men drink it. Visitors are not overly impressed with the drink since it looks like old dishwater and is slightly astringent. Custom decrees that no one at a kava party gets drunk or displays anger.

Tongans living abroad have had their share of adjustments to make. A large number have settled in Salt Lake City. *The Wall Street Journal* reported that a Tongan saved up to buy a Shetland pony advertised for sale. The owner asked what he intended to do with the animal. "For my son's birthday," replied the man. And the deal was closed.

The buyer picked up a two-by-four, clubbed the pony to death, dumped the carcass in his pickup truck and drove off. Police later found the pony trussed and roasting in a luau pit. Tongans learned to eat horsemeat from the early European missionaries.

The level of culture varied widely within the South Pacific, and still does. In Vanuatu, a new nation, formerly the New Hebrides, observers wonder just how bright some of the natives are who are trying to lift something they are standing on. Or why they start moving a pile of bricks by picking those out of the center first. Until the nineteenth century most of the islanders were engaged in more or less constant war with one another. To the victor belonged the spoils, which in many parts of the South Seas included a meal made by roasting or stewing the victims. In New Zealand North Island's Maoris almost depopulated the South Island. Behind every battlefront the fires were kept going for the feast. In Fiji, the old were strangled, the sick buried alive.

The tribal system is much alive on many of the islands. In Fiji today the "kere-kere" system of everyone sharing everything acts as a disincentive. Once anyone gets something he automatically shares it with relatives. Responsibility for anything, maintaining an outboard motor, chain saw, or automobile, belongs to everyone, hence no one.

Evidence that paradise is not likely to be found on a South Sea island comes from the Samoas—American Samoa, an unincorporated territory of the United States, and Western Samoa, an independent nation since 1962. The thirty-two thousand people who live on the seven small islands that make up American Samoa are subsidized annually at $20 million through U.S. Department of the Interior. Western Samoa has a huge deficit in imports versus exports.

Though there is an abundance of fish, taro, coconuts, mangos, and breadfruit, the residents have come to prefer canned fish, corned beef, rice and margarine. Beer is the favorite drink. Chiefs (and about one in ten persons is a chief) can usually be identified by their beer bellies. On Western Samoa the suicide rate among young people between ages fifteen and twenty-four is said to be the highest in the world.

To experience the way of life of Samoa a visitor can visit a village and live in a "fale," the native thatched hut with roll-up sides. There will be electricity, an outdoor toilet, radio, movies, and lots of churchgoing. Villagers are fined by the chiefs for not attending the frequent services. Apia, the capital of Western Samoa, has a beautiful, modern hotel, the Tusitala, air-conditioned rooms and an open-air dining room. A government-operated craft store sells an array of tapa cloths, each with its own stamped design, finely crafted bowls and mats. The attractive clerks will even provide a taste of kava. As in most tropical settings in less developed countries, be careful in eating and drinking to avoid food poisoning.

Pago Pago, capital of American Samoa, has one first-class hotel, one that changes hands frequently for lack of profitability.

The myth about sexual freedom in the South Seas needs serious qualification. Margaret Mead, the anthropologist, helped spread the idea that at least in the Samoan Islands life was free and easy, sex included. True, when Captain Cook was ranging the South Seas, the price of sex was one nail (an iron nail to someone who had no iron was a prize). If what Margaret Mead said was true in Western Samoa, it is not so today. The society has long been tightly structured with life severely constricted by taboos and a highly stratified social system. Mead's book *Coming of Age In Samoa,* some critics say, was highly colored, and the country was never the paradise she depicted.

The male visitor to the islands who expects beautiful, nubile maidens to run to his embrace will be disappointed.

As in the Caribbean and elsewhere, the South Sea islands have been strongly influenced by the occupying powers, British, French, or American. Micronesians have picked up the beer-guzzling habits of GI's stationed on several of the islands during World War II. Canned corned beef is widely popular where the British were an influence.

Wherever the Frenchman goes, the baguette is sure to follow. On the French-controlled islands of the Pacific the natives pick up the long slender loaves of bread once a day. The bakery is often operated by a Chinese. The French themselves must have their pates and wines. Noumea, capital of New Caledonia, is called "the Paris of the Pacific," with good French restaurants and Paris-style boutiques.

AUSTRALIA AND NEW ZEALAND

Australia and New Zealand, though one thousand miles apart, are close in spirit and culture. Both were originally settled by people from England and Ireland, Wales and Scotland. Both are sparsely settled even today. They are each other's largest trading and travel-exchange partners, and avid competitors in sports. Affectionately they refer collectively to themselves as Anzacs, but are not above poking fun at each other. New Zealanders call Australians POHMs, "Prisoners of His Majesty," an acronym referring to the first settlers in Australia, who were mostly convicts shipped out from Britain. New Zealanders call themselves KIWIs after the nocturnal bird found nowhere else but in New Zealand.

Close to a million people visit Australia each year, about 100,000 of them from the United States. About a third of the visitors come from New Zealand. New Zealand receives about a half million tourists a year, almost 17 percent of them from the United States. Half of New Zealand's visitors come from Australia. These numbers are growing as a result of reduced air fares and as the two countries become better known worldwide. "Aussies" are big international travelers. About 10 percent of the population aged over thirteen goes abroad each year.

One reason for the large percentage of foreign travel is the cost of internal travel. It has been cheaper for Australians to fly to Fiji, Singapore, or Bali than to fly between Perth and Sydney.

NEW ZEALAND

New Zealand is first and foremost a pastoral country. Some seventy million sheep are committed unconditionally to keeping the grasses cropped and to helping make the sheep farms look almost as manicured as the Swiss Alpine villages. About twenty million lambs slaughtered annually, frozen and exported, are the major source of income. The sheep also produce sheepskins and wool; even their bones are pulverized for fertilizer.

Orchards are also prominent in various parts of the north and south islands, the fruits coming on so as to meet winter markets throughout Europe and North America.

FIGURE 9.3 *Natural beauty.* Milford Sound in New Zealand is one of many scenic extravaganzas in New Zealand. The country offers a range of natural beauty and climate.

Source: New Zealand Government Tourist Office.

New Zealand resembles California in several ways. It is about the same length and its climate is generally benign except for the mountain areas. No place in New Zealand is far from the oceans or mountains. There is a serious earthquake hazard. The soil is productive, especially when fertilized.

New Zealand incorporates the natural beauty of several countries. The southern Alps in the South Island resemble the European Alps, but most of the New Zealand mountains are neither as precipitous nor as high as the European Alps. Rather the New Zealand mountains form high gradual valleys. Sheep can be raised at the higher levels and as they age are moved to the plains where their productive life is extended a year or so.

The three most "touristic" areas in New Zealand are The Bay of Islands at the northeastern end of North Island, Marlborough Sound lying at the northern end of the South Island, and The Queenstown area in the south central area, the point of departure for sightseeing and hiking in the southern Alps and viewing Milford Sound. The whole area is reminiscent of Norwegian fjords.

For the tourist, New Zealand offers a composite of Polynesian images (it has the Maoris and the North Island, the waving palms and sandy beaches). It also has mountain scenery, gorgeous lakes, glaciers, fjords, and modern cities. North Island is subtropical. The south of South Island is temperate. Snow is usually confined to the mountains and high country. When discovered by Abel Tasman, a Dutch navigator, in 1642, the native Maoris were living well on a diet of moa and other flightless birds, fish, and a type of sweet potato (and each other).

The country is said to be more British than Britain, though various Europeans have settled there and mixed with the native Maori. Altogether there are about three million people. The number one destination for New Zealanders is Australia, followed by Singapore and Fiji.

Geologically New Zealand is believed to be a separate rise of land, formed vocanically. Separated by one thousand miles of the Tasman Sea from Australia, it was probably never a part of Antarctica as was Australia. The two major islands, North Island and South Island, that form most of New Zealand are separated by straits that the traveler crosses by government ferry, a three hour and twenty minute trip, or by plane. Climate throughout New Zealand is largely determined by prevailing winds, the presence or absence of mountains and the ocean, which is never far away.

The North Island has a few mountains in its center; the South has its Southern Alps that account for the most spectacular scenery in the country. Microclimates are determined largely by mountains and water. Nelson in the South Island sits in a cove surrounded on three sides by mountains. Together the conditions create a small Shangri-La, providing more days of sunshine than anywhere else in New Zealand. Another microclimate is in the northeast of the North Island, around the little town of Kerikeri, a climate that makes citrus production possible.

Wellington, the capital city which lies at the southern tip of the North Island, is reminiscent of Chicago in the summer, because of its reputation for being windy.

Mount Cook in the South Island is the best known of the mountains and a great tourist attraction. The Franz Josef glacier is another natural attraction. Tourists reach it and land by ski plane. The New Zealand government operates twelve resort hotels located at most of the more glamourous natural-beauty spots. There are ten national parks.

Except for highways around Auckland and Wellington, New Zealand roads are country style—narrow and winding. Even the principal highway No. 1, running north and south, includes numerous one-lane bridges—slow and without recommendation.

A distinct concern for the motoring traveler is the lack of public toilets. Service stations do not provide them and while á number of small towns have one set of public toilets (usually very well kept), some towns have none. Numerous small snack shops offering "teas" also lack public facilities. In some sections the only public facilities are for ladies. Men shift for themselves, very likely ending up asking to use a toilet in a garage. The Automobile Association has offices in most of the larger towns. Directions and maps are offered but not restrooms.

The principal population centers are Auckland and Wellington on the North Island, Christchurch and Dunedin on the South Island. Auckland, with a population of almost 800,000, is more than double that of Wellington, the capital. It also has the largest Polynesian population in the world. (Polynesians comprise about 14 percent of the total population of New Zealand. The original Maori tribes have been supplemented by large numbers of immigrants from Tonga, the Cook Islands, Western Samoa, and other South Sea islands.)

The vast majority of New Zealanders are ethnic English, Welsh, Scottish, and Irish.

Like the early Hawaiians, the Maori are Polynesian, probably from the same ancestral home, perhaps in the Cook Islands or the Marquesas. New Zealand, like Hawaii, isolated by water, had no mammals. The moa, now extinct, was a flightless bird, some standing ten feet tall. They and other flightless birds were easy prey.

The Maori, like the Hawaiians, numbered about 250,000 in Captain Cook's time but had been decimated by disease to about 60,000 by 1860. Only about half of present-day Maoris live in rural communities.

The early Maoris were even more warlike than the Hawaiians, with feuds running through several generations. The vanquished were enslaved or eaten. Today they constitute about 10 percent of the population.

The Maoris and their culture are of major tourist interest. Their war dances are something to remember. In posture dancing the warriors keep the rhythm by stamping their feet. With war clubs in hand they respond to the leader's commands with gestures, feet stamping and sticking out their tongues and making facial contortions—the Maori version of macho.

Unfortunately for New Zealand many of its young people leave the country each year because of what they view as lack of opportunity at home. University graduates particularly feel stymied in their careers and go abroad. The Aussies joke about this exodus from New Zealand and quip, "The last one out, turn out the lights."

AUSTRALIA

Twelve million years ago, give or take a few hundred thousand years, a piece of Antarctica broke off, drifted northward and finally stopped to become Australia. Australia is both forbidding and delightful. Roughly three-quarters of it is composed of Pre-Cambrian rock, most of it worn down by wind, rain and time, to form a vast, low-lying plateau.

Even though it is the smallest of the continents, the country is one of the largest. It is almost the size of the United States, excluding Alaska and Hawaii, yet its population is only fifteen million. Papua New Guinea, once governed by Australia, and Indonesia are to the north. The Tasman Sea, an arm of the Pacific, forms the eastern border. The Indian Ocean is south and west.

The official name of Australia is the Commonwealth of Australia, and it is divided into six states and a Northern Territory. Tasmania, the island south of Australia, is a state with Hobart as the capital. The other states are Western Australia, South Australia, Victoria, New South Wales and Queensland.

Australia can be thought of as a huge country populated around its eastern and southern rims. Most of Australia's fifteen million people are urban dwellers. Only 15 percent of the population live in rural areas. Sydney, on the southeast coast, with a population of three million, is the oldest and largest city, and let no one forget, it has the much vaunted wing-shaped Opera House. Sydney bustles and is noisy like most cities, saved only by its location on the ocean with twenty-two surf beaches close at hand. Most pictures are taken from the harbor and include the opera house. Melbourne, farther down on the coast, is only slightly smaller with over two million. It claims to be more reserved, more intellectual, more cultural. It is the financial center of the nation. Brisbane, also on the coast, but north of Sydney, has a little over a million residents. It is much like the American midwest —fifty years ago. The people are relaxed and friendly. Adelaide, population 600,000, has

FIGURE 9.4 *International symbols.* The two international symbols of Sydney are the Opera House and Harbor Bridge.

Source: New South Wales Department of Tourism.

the best climate, Mediterranean—lots of sunshine, vineyards and orchards not far from the city center. Perth, on the soutwest coast with 500,000 population, also has a favored Mediterranean climate. Canberra, the capital, is the result of rivalry between the two largest cities, Melbourne and Sydney. Neither would permit the other to be named capital. Canberra is a planned capital, planted squarely in the country. Hobart is the urban center on Tasmania, the island constituency south of Australia. It is a seafaring town and tourist center.

The south coast climate is Mediterranean in character, relatively dry and temperate. Heavy rainfall characterizes the northeast coast and the north coast is semi-tropical.

The vast interior, 85 percent of the land, the "outback," is semi-desert, with sheep and cattle "stations" that cover thousands of acres. Until a few years ago one cattle station, The Victoria River Downs, covered an area the size of Belgium. The nearest neighbor of a station manager may live two hundred miles away; the front gate of a property can be thirty miles from the front door. The "outback" is Australia's frontier; it tests man's fortitude with droughts, floods, heat, and loneliness. Out in the desert is the largest rock in the world, Ayers Rock, sacred to the aborigines and still used as a ceremonial center. There are a few small towns. Alice is one of the best known, with a population of twenty thousand. One-third of Australia is desert; another third is fit only for grazing.

Because of its size, the topography and climate vary widely: dense jungles in the north; deserts in the center with temperatures up to 140 degrees; hundreds of miles of virtually flat land, yet mountains high enough for skiing. A long stretch of mountains, the great Dividing Range, runs the length of the east coast.

About one in every five Australians is foreign born. The largest number are British. Immigrants from Italy, Greece, the Netherlands, Germany are also present. The original inhabitants, the aborigines, constitute less than one percent of the population. A large percentage of Australian men are addicted to beer and sports.

Travel destinations in Australia are mostly to the large cities of Sydney and Melbourne. Travel trademarks include the Opera House, the Koala bear, the kangaroo, and Ayers

Rock. North of Sydney are the Gold Coast and the Sunshine Coast—Australia's number one resort area. The Gold Coast resembles Miami Beach—high rise hotels and communities that are even called Miami and Palm Beach. Offshore stretches the Great Barrier reef, running north and south off Queensland for more than two thousand km (twelve hundred miles), the longest coral reef in the world. Stretching a point, it is said to be the longest "living thing" in the world, more than one thousand varieties of coral. Coral is alive, tiny animals, coral polyps. Their stomachs secrete lime, which is deposited around the polyps forming a coral skeleton. It is a favorite place for snorkeling, scuba diving, and fishing. It is not unusual to take hundreds of fish in a few hours of fishing.

On fifteen of the six hundred islands are fifteen small resorts that cater to the water sportsman and naturalists interested in the nearly nine hundred species of fish. (Watch out for the poisonous ones.) The next largest coral reefs lie off the island of Andros in the Bahamas and off the coast of Honduras.

The south Australian waters have more than enough sharks, so many that helicopters are used to spot them near popular beaches and shark nets are installed at other beaches. The Great White Shark, most fearsome of the many species, and best actor in the movie *Jaws,* are also around, ready and willing to tear off a limb or two of a hapless human in the water. Now there is a movement to conserve the "Great White," which is said to be quite timid and seldom eats a person unless confused (or hungry?).

What does the visitor do in Australia besides being photographed holding a koala bear or petting a kangaroo? If driving long distances is fun, moving around Austalia will be an ecstatic experience. The distances are unbelievable. Super-highways there are not. Off the main thoroughfares the roads may be one lane wide. On-coming cars simply put two wheels off the roads to allow each other to pass, sometimes at speeds above sixty mph. Campers can be rented. There is no dearth of places to park for the night. Watch out for the kangaroos.

FIGURE 9.5 *Gold Coast.* Like Florida, Queensland, Australia, has its Gold Coast with dozens of hotels in a semi-tropical setting.

Source: Australian Tourist Commission.

While the interior thirsts for rain, the northeast and north coasts get more than enough rain, as much as two hundred inches a year.

Much of the wildlife of Australia is found nowhere else in the world—the platypus, the wombat, the koala, and the kangaroo. Speaking of the koala bear, the advertising symbol of Qantas Airlines since the mid-1950s, the bear has had some bad press. The minister for tourism called the cuddly "living toys" flea-ridden, rotten little things. "If picked up," he said, "it piddles on you; it stinks and it scratches." Koala bear defenders quickly leaped to their defense. A newspaper headline read, "Minister Mocks Marsupial," and pointed out that the little animal helps lure a million tourists to Australia each year. Another koala bear champion conceded that since koalas eat eucalyptus leaves exclusively they do tend to have bad breath. Their calm, sluggish nature may result from the oil of eucalyptus leaves, which breaks down during digestion into a muscle-relaxing-drug—in other words the koala is perpetually stoned.

Rail travel buffs can enjoy a twenty-five-hundred-mile ride between Sydney and Perth, a ride aboard a first-class train that is billed as one of the "great rail journeys of the world."

Typical Australians, usually of English or Irish stock, regard themselves as egalitarians and down to earth. They own property, think of themselves as middle-class and are politically conservative. The men emphasize masculinity, sports and somehow equate copius beer drinking with these traits. Male friendships tend to be stronger than friendships between the sexes. They are generally fun-loving, tolerant and have a strong sense of justice. They take the side of the underdog, even to the point of believing "authority is always wrong." Even so, the typical Australian is well aware of his or her social station but enjoys putting down the person who has climbed too high.

The language is English, the pronunciation Australian or "strine." A "bonzer blok" is a nice chap. To yabber is to chatter. A "chappie" is slightly perjorative term for a male. "Fair dinkum" can mean "oh, really?", "honest" or "that's the truth."

Australia is well aware that in 1787 a fleet of eleven ships transporting 1473 convicts, men and women, and accompanied by two hundred marines, began a settlement at Botany Bay near Sydney. Altogether some six thousand prisoners were exiled to New South Wales. The beginnings may account for the Aussie's distrust of authority and a driving desire to be his own man.

If the Australian worships anything, it is sports and the out-of-doors. They have plenty of the latter, and revel in it.

In the past a generalization about Australian eating habits was, "They eat lots of meat, drink lots of beer and have little variety in their menu." This no longer holds because of the influx of Europeans—Italians, Greeks, French, German, Yugoslavians—as immigrants. The meat pie, minced meat with gravy in a pastry, comes as close as any food to being the national dish. Australia has fifteen principal wine-producing areas and some of the wines are outstanding.

Australians, like Italians, like to go on strike. The ostensible reasons usually deal with money, but observers report strikes are a way of getting a few additional days off.

Although the country advertises heavily to attract visitors, it does a few things to discourage them. A $20 departure fee at airports is one thing. Heavy landing fees for foreign planes is another. Cameras are not allowed to be passed manually around the X-ray machine unless the shutter is clicked, wasting a picture.

PAPUA NEW GUINEA

Geographers include Papua New Guinea as part of Australasia. The largest "island," after Greenland, Papua New Guinea is shared by the independent nation of Papua New Guinea and Irian, an Indonesian dependency. The place is huge. Many of the residents are stone-age in culture. They are said to be very friendly but when a group of tourists laughed at a group performance they were attacked with spears. Even so, Port Moresby, the capital, has a university and is setting up an extension program. It is a gateway town, population about sixty thousand.

Papua New Guinea is for the travel connoisseur, not your everyday vacationer. It is remote, primitive, and decidedly different. The highland country is primitive indeed. It was not until 1933 that the natives first saw a white man. Tribes of the interior still carry on spear fights with their neighbors. Those killed are smoked and set on a view site above their village so that they can continue to see what is going on with their people. Today in some villages guests are received, for a fee.

Parts of Papua New Guinea are incredibly isolated and primitive. Valleys are separated by rugged mountains, so difficult to traverse that some tribes believed they were alone on this earth. The campfires from the next valley were thought to be from the spirit world. Constant warfare between tribes was the norm, headhunting a preoccupation. Today at least one tribe is under contract to stage a headhunting show for tourists, re-enacting the hunt for the camera.

The airplane lifted the people directly out of the stone-age, but with some confusion. The natives quite naturally saw the planes as huge birds. One chief brought a basket of bananas to feed the first plane to land and inquired about its sex. The airplane was first used to search for and mine gold. Today it is still the only means of access for much of the country. The natives quickly accepted air transport and use it for personal travel and as a means of transporting coffee, their principal export crop.

Five hundred provinces offer a diverse scenery and people. The country's highest mountain is only 420 miles from the equator but often powdered with snow. The people live primarily on sweet potatoes, taro, bananas, and pigs. Pigs are the traditional item of the wealth.

The Sepik River is a mile wide at its mouth and navigable for almost all of its seven-hundred-mile length. The Fly River in the Western Province flows south from the center of New Guinea for 650 miles. When it reaches the sea it is fifty miles wide.

Though 717 languages have been recorded, official languages for the three million people of Papua New Guinea are pidgin, English, Melanesian, and police motu. "Bisnis bilong turis," pidgin for the "tourist business," is picking up as roads and landing fields are built and as the natives acquire a taste for the tourist dollar. Don't be in a big hurry in New Guinea. "Melanesian time" has a lot in common with the Latin American "manana."

ENDNOTES

1. Headquarters office of the Pacific Area Travel Association is at 228 Grant Avenue, San Francisco, CA 94108.
2. *The South Seas Dream, An Adventure in Paradise,* Little, Brown and Co., Boston, 1982.

10

SOUTHEAST ASIA AND THE MIDDLE EAST

Again, following the regional definitions stated by the PATA (Pacific Area Travel Association) Southeast Asia is made up of Indonesia, Malaysia, the Philippines, Singapore and Thailand. We shall deal only with Indonesia, Thailand, the Philippines, and Singapore, also including India, which is to the west of the region.

SINGAPORE

OFFICIAL NAME: REPUBLIC OF SINGAPORE

Singapore is the wonder child of the Orient. Like Japan, in less than twenty years it has moved front and center on the world financial stage and is now the major trading and money exchange for a large part of the Far East. Its port is the world's second busiest in tonnage handled. Its 2.4 million people enjoy a standard of living second only to Japan in the Far East. A city/state sitting on a 238 square-mile island, Singapore did not begin its present form as an independent nation until 1965, when it broke away from Malaysia. A crossroads of East Asia, Singapore sits on the southern end of the Malay Peninsula, accessible to the Indian Ocean, the South China Sea, and the Java Sea.

What is remarkable is that so much has been done with such a diversity of ethnic groups, 76 percent Chinese who speak about a dozen Chinese dialects, 15 percent Malaysians. A third tongue is Tamil, an Indian dialect. Also of note, all of this activity takes place in a hot, humid climate. As of 1984 the official language was Malay. Plans are underway to make English the official language.

More than three million visitors come each year to Singapore, more than the population of the country. In 1983 it had fourteen thousand hotel rooms, several of luxury class, and by 1985 it will have eleven thousand more.

Singapore has become a major tourist center for not only Asians but for Australians and people from around the world. Its appeal was neatly summed up by one commentator:

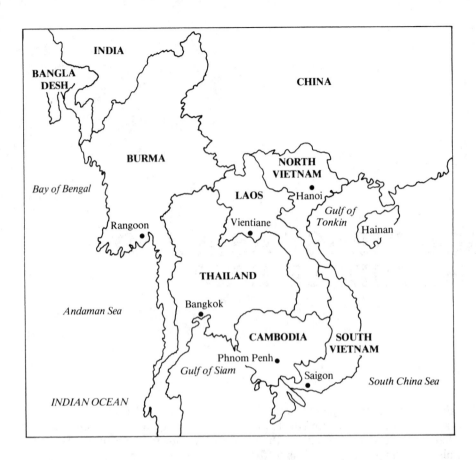

FIGURE 10.1   *Map of Southeast Asia.*

> Its eye scans the future...
> Its mind defines today...
> Its heart beats to the past[1]...

Visitors are struck by the pervasive cleanliness and courtesy. The government punishes lack of cleanliness and exhorts people to behave courteously. Littering is heavily fined. Youths with long hair have it forcibly cut. "Courtesy is our culture, don't lose it," is seen on public signs. "Care for the aged as they have cared for us," and near a factory, "Commitment to work and training bring family security." "Work as a team, live as a people."

The government rules with a firm hand. Young people caught with drugs are caned, a carryover practice from when the British ruled the island.

Despite the high heat and humidity, work proceeds at rapid rate. Bamboo scaffolding precedes the laying of brick walls or huge buildings. The bricks are laboriously carried up by hand as the walls rise.

In spite of being in the tropics, Singapore has a population density of ten thousand per square mile. About 70 percent of them live in wnat has been called the world's most successful public housing scheme, apartment blocks, ten and twenty stories high.

The Chinese, like the French, are said to eat anything that moves. The street market in Singapore includes almost everthing that flies or swims, including boa constrictors and bats. Change Alley, another open-air emporium, can provide the shopper with something more than valentines to inspire love. A variety of aphrodisiacs and love potions are on hand to give Cupid a helping hand.

Many Americans will be disappointed when eating in Chinese restaurants. There are no fortune cookies and no one can break one open and pretend to read, "Help, I'm being held captive in a fortune cookie factory."

Almost everyone who visits Singapore tells tales of its cuisine, a blend of Malay and Chinese. The two are married to form "nonya" food combining pork, coconut milk, shrimp paste, and a variety of spices, heavy on the chili. At the Raffles Hotel, probably the best known hotel in the East because of its literary heritage, a weekly buffet of nonya dishes is an experience. The Raffles figured in some of the Somerset Maugham stories and represents the old British raj way of life, pre-World War II. A number of new high rise, glamour hotels supercede the Raffles in modernity and efficiency.

Occidental visitors are taken aback at several of the foods displayed in the morning market in Chinatown. Cages of frogs, buckets of pale duck feet and century-old eggs are displayed. A python lies coiled, later to appear at someone's table as steaks.

With so many people in such a small space there are some problems.

Taxis are scarce during rush hours. Traffic on the causeway north that leads to Malaysia can be jammed. Customs delays are common. Movies are censored. TV programs are pallid and limited; nightclubs and cabarets expensive. Most social life centers around private clubs. In other words, say expatriates who live there, life is safe and sanitary but dull.

There is no question about Singapore's commitment to tourism. Mass air travel made Singapore in its present form possible. Singapore's dictatorial government brooks no opposition to tourism growth. There are no riots, no picket lines allowed, as the government has set about constructing a new airport that will be capable of handling thirty million air travelers a year.

The national Singapore Airline trains its "Singapore Girls" to be the most polite, service-oriented flight attendants in the air. The girls are selected for their beauty and the airline ads feature the real hostesses, not models. As a result, as airline unions and work rules have made courtesy a forgotten word on many airlines, Singapore Airlines business has grown rapidly.

THAILAND

Bangkok, like Tokyo, Hong Kong and Singapore, is a major transit point within the Far East. It is also a vacation destination for 2.25 million visitors, 150,000 of them from the United States. Americans visit Thailand as a stopover and Bangkok for its shopping and exotic culture. About thirty international airlines fly to Bangkok. Malaysians, Singaporeans, Japanese, and Germans come in the largest numbers. Americans choose to stay in the luxury hotels of Bangkok and remain about 5.5 days sightseeing and shopping for silks and gems and sex.

Little known to American visitors to Thailand is Khao Yai National Park ("cow-ye"), two hundred miles northeast of Bangkok. It is so big that it spreads over parts of four provinces. This jungle park has butterflies galore, at least two hundred species of them, and also about two hundred elephants, not to mention fifty to one hundred tigers. Travel with a guide unless you feel like becoming cat food. The State Railway of Thailand arranges special tours from Bangkok's Hualampong Station.

Bangkok, with a population of five million, is hot, overcrowded, noisy, and polluted. Some of the hotels are outstanding for their luxury. The Oriental, about seventy-five years old, has an international reputation. The newest deluxe hotel, The Mandarin, is said to be even more luxurious. (At least the rates are higher.) It is owned by Cathay Pacific, the Hong Kong-based airline. Altogether Bangkok offers some fifteen thousand first-class hotel rooms.

Europeans tend also to visit Thailand's number two city, Chiang Mai, about four hundred miles north of Bangkok. It is much cooler, especially during the winter months, because of the altitude. The ladies are said to be the most beautiful in the country. The city has a number of interesting wats (temples) and not far away elephants can be seen at work moving logs.

Pattaya is a sea resort town to the south of Bangkok.

Tropical fruits, many unknown to the American visitor, can be ordered via room service in the better hotels. Mangosteens are available, a fruit that connoisseurs choose above all others. Jackfruits, custard apples, rose apples, and rambutans are others that should be tried.

Thai cuisine—seafood, rice, a variety of spices—has its aficionados. One writer characterizes Thai food as coming in three varieties, hot, hotter, and hottest. Coriander, garlic, pepper and chili peppers are widely used. Lemon grass adds a distinctive flavor to seafood soups. Like the Chinese, the Thais spend considerable effort in presenting their foods.

The Thai Tourist Authority states that Thailand has five hundred tourist attractions, many of them Buddhist shrines and temples. The Thai people are notably friendly. One of a kind is the bridge over the River Kwai, where during the last week of November a Light and Sound Show is presented. World War II veterans and others come to remember how the bridge was built at the cost of hundreds of lives of Allied prisoners of the Japanese.

Boxing in Thailand is a paradox. Maythai (pronounced moo-eee-tie) boxing is vicious. The Thais, steeped in Buddhist gentleness, love their special kind of boxing, which combines kicking with traditional fisticuffs to inflict serious injury. Elbows, knees or any part of the body, except the head, are used to inflict serious damage. One person is killed in the ring about every three months. Many more are badly injured. Rabbit-punching and kicking the kidneys are an approved part of the contest. Kicking is so strenuous the fighter's feet are anesthetized between rounds to block out the pain.

THE PHILIPPINES

The Philippines are a blend of Occident and Orient, primitive and modern, Christian and Muslim. The Philippines are the only predominantly Christian nation in the Orient, made so when the Spanish colonized the islands. Even though Spanish and several dialects are spoken, the Philippines are the third largest English-speaking nation in the world.

The Philippines attract a heavy ethnic market and the business traveler. Close to nine million people visit the islands each year. Twenty-three percent are from Japan, 17 percent from the United States, 10 percent from Hong Kong and 7 percent from Australia. Pleasure travelers are likely to stop a while in Manila, the capital, where, thanks to President Marcos' wife, some twelve thousand rooms in first-class hotels were built. The climate is not the most pleasant except for those who enjoy tropical heat and humidity. A hot, dry season occurs in March and May. Heavy rains come from June to November. November through February is the best visiting time; the weather is relatively cool and dry.

Residents escape the heat by retreating to the "summer capital," Baguio, 155 miles away. At forty-six hundred feet the climate is cooler but equally wet. Terraced rice paddies characterize the surrounding mountains.

INDIA

To describe India in a page or two is of course absurd. It's somewhat like the book in the Dag Hammarskjold Library at the United Nations, called *India at a Glance*.

It contains 1,896 pages.

No country contains greater cultural diversity: politically, in religion, in language, and in other ways. Centuries of class consciousness crystalized into the caste system, stratifications based on ancestry, family ties and occupations. It is a wonder that India holds together at all. In the late nineteenth century there were over 550 sovereign territories or "native states." Today India is the world's most populous federal state, consisting of twenty-two states and eight union territories. Continuous tension exists between the majority Hindus and the minority Moslems. The caste system is also a cause of major social tension. The fact that there are fourteen official languages and many dialects does not make for social harmony. Hindi is spoken by nearly one-third of all Indians and is one of fourteen languages given national status by the Indian constitution. English is the lingua franca.

India lies at the heart of the world's largest population cluster. Two river systems, the Ganges-Brahmaputra and the Indus, are crucial lifelines for hundreds of millions of people. Generally speaking there are three regions: the northern mountains, the southern peninsula plateau and between these two, a belt of river lowlands.

The best known of India's rivers is the Ganges, sacred to the Hindus. It flows southeast from the Himalayas in northern India, 1550 miles into the Bay of Bengal.

The climate varies from tropical in the south to temperate in the north. In large parts of India the climate is hot and muggy.

Parts of India are very wet, up to four hundred inches annually in the northeast, the Assam Hills. Rains come in the southwest, November to January. Parts of the northwest are desert. The monsoon rains elsewhere that come June to October can inundate a region.

India is big, twice the size of Alaska, with a population of perhaps 800 million. Only China has more people. The Indian people are backward and poor. Over 60 percent of the population are illiterate. The vast majority of people have a marginal existence. The British tried hard to change India, to get rid of its caste system that bound millions in semi-servitude. They tried to eradicate illiteracy and disease. Today's government is still trying, but not very hard. India is suspicious of change. Of all institutions that are supposed to enlighten and lead the way to a better life, the university is supposed to be number one. If numbers of students were a criterion of excellence, India would be paramount. The University of Calcutta has 200,000 students at its Calcutta campus and the 257 other colleges stretched over three states. What do the students major in? Courses mostly unrelated to the needs of India, courses for which there are no jobs following graduation.

India's cities are not attractive as cities, too big, too poor. If the traveler is not very careful he ends up with "Delhi Belly," traveler's diarrhea. New Delhi/Delhi is the capital, population four million. Calcutta is seven million, Bombay six million, Madras 3.2 million.

One reason more foreigners are not attracted to India is its extreme poverty. The squalor of the slums of Calcutta, with dead bodies being picked up on the streets, is something never to be forgotten, and preferably missed. The State of Kashmir, by contrast, is a fertile green valley at the foot of the Himalayas, a place with a magic ring to it. The climate is cool and the place is known for its lakes and gardens. About one thousand houseboats, many of them lavish, are for rent on Dal Lake or Nal Lake. Fully furnished, these boats, many of them left over from the British raj, come equipped with staff including a chef who operates from an attached cook boat. Prices are cheap. To keep occupied, visitors trek into the nearby mountains, shop for Kashmir rugs, ski in the winter or fish the several streams and rivers in the area.

About 850,000 foreigners visit India a year. Though the number is relatively small, the average stay is long, almost twenty-five days.

Amongst tourism specialists, much ado is made over the percentage of money left by a tourist in a country that remains in the country. Only 6 percent of the tourist dollar leaves India. This is a very low figure for a developing country. In some countries such as Fiji as much as 75 percent of tourism income goes out of the country almost immediately in the form of purchases from abroad, profits sent out and so on.

Domestic tourism involves millions of travelers. As many as twelve million people visit the Ganges River to purify themselves in its waters.

It is difficult for a Westerner to realize the desperate poverty of the average Indian. Per capita income averages about $190 a year. (The U.S. figure is over $11,000.) Seventy percent of India's vast population lives and works in some 421,000 villages not connected by good roads. According to one study, 60 percent of rural transport of goods and passengers depends solely on bullock carts. The people are too poor to improve the carts with such items as ball bearings, brakes, or shock absorbers.

When the British governed India they wisely took to the hills during the periods of extreme heat, and the hill stations are still favorite destinations for Indians and visitors alike. Trekking and climbing are favorite hill and mountain country experiences. Some say that there is no quarter of the globe that can compete in beauty with the ''Roof-of-the-World'' quality of places like Kashmir and Ladakh, which lie alongside Tibet and China in the north. A fourteen-thousand-foot-high pass must be crossed to reach the more hospitable valleys.

Wild animal hunting by camera is another reason for visiting parts of India. The Kaziranga Wild Life Sanctuary has its buffalo, elephants, and tigers. It also has the one-horned rhino, which is rapidly disappearing because the horn is believed to be a powerful aphrodisiac. About the only way it is seen is from an elephant's back; the sixteen-foot-tall elephant grass makes other locomotion virtually impossible. Also the rhinos have a reputation for their tempers. In Northern Uttar Pradesh, the Lake District of the Krimaon Hills, is Corbett National Park. It extends over some 125 square miles and is home for a variety of wild animals including elephants, tigers, leopards, and black bear. The Ganges has its origin in this high region. Fish are quite tame here because they are regarded as sacred.

India is said to be a paradise for the railway enthusiast. The British started an extensive rail system which has some sixty-three thousand miles of track. Unfortunately there are four separate railway gauges which necessitate trans-shipments and different sets of equipment. The major cities are linked by ''mail'' trains, normally faster than the others. There are special expresses. The one from Bombay to Delhi covers the distance in five hours.

Travelers to India have long been able to ride elephants, hunt tigers with a camera and live in former maharajah palaces. Now for about $100 a day they can ride a princely train, the Palace on Wheels. Every carriage was built for a maharajah and has been polished and painted white. The train runs from New Delhi carrying thirty-two attendants—turbaned cooks, waiters, porters, assistant porters—and an engine crew. A dozen armed guards ride in the carriages at either end.

Marigold garlands worn around the passengers' necks are changed several times a day. A sixty-eight-seat bus is ready for sightseeing at selected stops. The Palace chugs along about twenty-four mph and reaches Agra, where passengers can view India's foremost architectural beauty and major tourist attraction, the Taj Mahal. About two million tourists visit the Taj Mahal each year. Shah Jehan built it as a remembrance for his wife. His fate was not kind. His son not only imprisoned him but set about to drive the old man mad. When Jehan caught two of his concubines mocking his virility it was too much. He took an overdose of aphrodisiacs and died.

The train moves on into Rajasthan, where the weather can be beastly hot. When the maharajahs traveled in such circumstances their carriages were draped with grass curtains and hosed down with rose water. The Palace on Wheels merely stops running.

The train makes three-night and seven-night journeys. Only one train is given precedence over the Palace on Wheels, The Parliament Express, that carries civil servants to work, a commentary on the vicissitudes of power.

Nepal, that remote little kingdom, surrounded by India on three sides and China on the other, is for travel connoisseurs. It is a long way from the Western world, difficult to get to and good for a travel namedropper at a cocktail party. It is for trekking, for taking pictures and for birdwatching. It is also a base for the mountain climber. It has eight of the ten highest mountains plus forests of rhododendron that reach up sixty feet in height. It has six thousand streams, many of them wild-running, that could be harnessed for hydroelectric power.

Nepal is uncomfortably dependent upon India and shows its desire for independence by keeping its clocks ten minutes ahead of its big neighbor. The population of eighteen million is outstripping agricultural production. A per capita annual income of $110 a year makes Nepal one of the poorest of countries. Life expectancy is only forty-six years and the literacy rate is 23 percent.

PAKISTAN

Once a part of India, Pakistan broke away after World War II amidst great bloodshed and suffering. The official name, Islamic Republic of Pakistan, provides a clue to the turmoil. Most of the people in the Pakistani area are Moslems, where the majority religion in the rest of India is Hindu. Not unusual, genocide was committed in the name of religion and the resulting countries carry on under an uneasy truce. Karachi (3.5 million) was the first capital. Karachi sits on the Arabian Sea: hot, dusty and with little to appeal to visitors. The present capital, Islamabad (population 250,000), sits in the far north. The entire country is about the size of California but has a population in excess of eighty-two million. Lahore (2.1 million) is the second largest city and lies near the Indian border in the east. The official language is Urdu but it is only spoken by 9 percent of the people. English is the lingua franca if there is one.

Northwestern Pakistan appeals to those seeking mountain beauty. The little kingdom of Hunza is celebrated throughout the world for its happy, long-lived citizens. Situated in a high valley, the people are said to be the healthiest in the world, partly, according to one study, because of their diet. The Hunzas east primarily fruit, seeds and a little meat. Tea is the universal beverage. The kingdom comprises 150 villages laid in a ninety-mile long valley with altitudes ranging from 5,300 to 8,250 feet. Another tiny kingdom lies in the Swat Valley, described as "a country of stirring beauty." The visitor to these northern areas stays in rest houses provided by the government or in the few modest hotels. The rest of Pakistan is of little tourist interest. Literacy is only 24 percent, the life expectancy fifty-one years.

INDONESIA

OFFICIAL NAME: REPUBLIC OF INDONESIA

It may come as a surprise that the world's fifth largest country in population is Indonesia (148 million). Java, one of three thousand inhabited islands that make up Indonesia, has ninety million people living in an area the size of New York State. The total area is slightly smaller than Alaska and California combined. Also strange is the fact that some peaks in Borneo are continuously capped with snow.

Most of Indonesia is not your favorite tourist destination. Jakarta (5.5 million) is hot, humid and lackluster. Because of the climate, two changes of clothing a day are frequently required. The island of Bali with its bare-breasted damsels and religious dancing is favored. The two monsoon seasons, December through February and June through August, are times to avoid in Indonesia.

Bali was described by India's famous prime minister Nehru as "The Morning of the World." It is also known as "The Island of the Thousand Temples." Much of the everyday life in Bali revolves around religious ceremonies, which have become major tourist attractions. The Balinese capital of Denpasar has direct flights from Singapore and Sydney and a number of domestic flights. Big hotels are expensive but seaside bungalows and guest houses are reasonable. Bali has many temples, the oldest and most sacred being Pura Besakih, built on the slopes of a volcanic mountain known as "the navel of the world."

Surabaya is the capital of East Java and second largest city of Indonesia. Like the British in India, the Dutch who controlled Indonesia before its independence built hill stations for rest and recreation, away from the stifling tropical heat. Tretes (pronounced tray-tess) is about an hour's drive from Surabaya. Mount Bromo, seven thousand feet high, has a smoking crater which erupted as recently as 1948.

Borobudur, on the island of Java, is the world's largest Buddhist monument. This "temple on the hill" is a stepped pyramid of stone built over an eighty-year period in around A.D. 800. It rises eight tiers, each sitting a little smaller than the one below. Total height is 105 feet. Covered with 460 carved panels depicting the World of Desire, the panels are illustrated texts from Buddhist books and folktales. Seventy-two stupas (bell-shaped Buddhist shrines) enclose figures of Buddha. Indonesia and UNESCO together are restoring this great ruin so that admirers from around the world can climb the ruin and feel the yearning for the eternal expressed in stone.

Sumatra, one of the largest of Indonesia's islands, has Lake Toba, pleasant climatically because it sits at a 3000-foot altitude. The lake, over 400 square miles in size, is twice the size of Lake Geneva. There are good swimming, waterskiing, fishing and boating. The food can be delicious, especially some of the lesser known tropical fruits. One such fruit, the durian, is thought by some to be the superlative of fruits. Even so it hides behind a horrible smell. It has been likened by Anthony Burgess, a British writer, to "eating strawberry blanc-mange in an unspeakably foul public lavatory."

The natives of the area, the Bataks, are known for their unique architecture, homes in which as many as 12 families live, with distinctive, saddle-backed, twin-peaked roofs. There are no windows and the home is entered by a ladder through a trapdoor in the raised floor. Today the Bataks welcome visitors. Their reputation around the turn of the century was not so good because cannibalism was then a ritualized practice in the Batak culture. Only outsiders, however, consenting old people, and certain criminals were placed on the menu. If a Batak from another village was convicted of a capital offense, the raja of his area acknowledged the sentence as just by sending two items: a cloth to cover the face of the condemned and a plate of salt and lemons for garnish. (How thoughtful can you get?)

Indonesia has one of the most vexing of population problems. More than 75 percent of the people live on the island of Java, where as many as fifty thousand people live in an area of a square kilometer. Such population density is not a problem in advanced industrialized nations but can be calamitous in a nation that is essentially agricultural.

The sovereign nation of Brunei in northwest Borneo is not high on the list of most-want-to-visit places. Its interest to international travelers is that in 1984 it became the 169th sovereign nation, another of those countries that reluctantly left the protecting arms of Great Britain. About as big as Delaware, the country's population of 205,000 could squeeze into about two stadiums the size of the Rose Bowl in Pasadena.

The country is remarkable for two things: it is oil- and gas-rich and it is ruled absolutely by a benevolent sultan who lives in a 2,200 room palace that cost $300 million. The people, all Muslims, are not complaining. Each one gets a free pilgrimage to Mecca and the right to a good living by doing little if any hard work. Some 25,000 foreign workers keep the economy going.

THE MIDDLE EAST

The Middle East is variously defined. Egypt and Israel are sometimes included, sometimes not. In this book Egypt has been treated as part of Africa. *The Random House Dictionary* includes these countries as part of the Middle East Region: the United Arab Republic, Sudan, Israel, Jordan, Lebanon, Syria, Turkey, Iraq, Iran, and the countries of the Arabian Peninsula.

Much of the region is desolate desert, semi-desert, or mountainous. Summer heat can be debilitating. Temperatures in parts of the Arabian Peninsula reach 130 degrees. In Kuwait summer temperatures reach 140 degrees and rainfall averages less than four inches annually. Most of Saudi Arabia is desert, including Rub al-Khali, the vast empty quarter. The country has no permanent rivers or lakes.

Pleasure travel to the area has been sharply limited in the last several years because of wars in the area. Travel for business and religious reasons to Saudi Arabia and Israel continues high. About 2.2 million Muslin pilgrims visit Mecca in Saudi Arabia each year.

Since money is a small consideration in Saudi Arabia it is spent with abandon. The new airport in Riyadh, capital of the country, is one of the world's largest. Occupying an area roughly 7.5 by 12 miles, it is designed to serve some fifteen million passengers by the year 2000. In the center of the passenger terminal complex is a mosque that can accommodate 5,000 worshipers inside plus 3,000 more on the plaza outside.

Pilgrimages are still much in vogue and constitute a large travel segment. During one week planes landed at Jeddah airport every two minutes to empty a load of pilgrims. In one week two million Muslims can circle the Ka'aba in the central courtyard of the Grand Mosque in Mecca. For the pilgrims the "hajj" is an opportunity to wash away all sins and take on a new name. One prayer said in the Grand Mosque is worth 100,000 said elsewhere. The "hajj" is responsible for a number of blacks living in Saudi Arabia today. Nigerians and Sudanese would sell their children in Mecca to help pay for their journey home. (Slavery was not abolished in Saudi Arabia until 1962.)

Saudi Arabia is not for the pleasure traveler, too expensive, no tourist attractions to speak of, too many restrictions. The average cost of a meal in one of the better restaurants is $100 for two people. This is without liquor, banned throughout the nation. Americans living in the country can hardly wait to take their extended travel vacations or return home. A little over a million visitors go to Israel annually.

Much of the Middle East is in rapid transition, being jerked by the power of oil money from a feudal society into the modern world. Construction of hotels, office buildings, schools, and hospitals proceeds at a furious rate, the work being done by non-residents who arrive by plane, stay a few months or years and return home with their earnings. In some of the oil emirates foreigners outnumber the nationals.

Slavery may still exist in part of the Middle East. The Old Sultan of Oman, who ruled until 1970, fought modernization of his country. He allowed himself an automobile but would not buy gas. Slaves pushed his car. No schools were built during his reign, because, he said, Britain's mistake in India was in educating the people. Neither were hospitals built, because, he said, they kept too many people alive.

The oil kingdoms bordering the Persian Gulf (Bahrain, Qatar, Oman, and the Emirate sheikdoms) in the 1950s were destitute, having lost their importance as trade centers and no longer able to pursue the slave trade. The people lived largely on fish and dates. The value of pearls that had made many families rich was no longer profitable. Cultured pearls from Japan had reduced the value of those found in the sea by 90 percent.

FIGURE 10.2   *Some facts about countries in the Middle East.*

Country	Population (millions)	Area (square miles)	Capital
Israel	3.8	8,019	Jerusalem
Jordan	3.2	37,737	Amman
Lebanon	2.9	4,015	Beirut
Syria	8.5	71,498	Damascus
Saudi Arabia	9.3	829,995	Riyadh
Iraq	13.6	167,924	Baghdad
Iran	40.0	636,293	Teheran
South Yemen	1.9	128,559	Aden
Yemen	5.1	75,290	Sanaa
Oman	0.9	82,030	Muscat
Kuwait	1.3	6,880	Kuwait
United Arab Emirates	0.9	32,278	Abu Dhabi
Turkey	46.7	301,380	Ankara
Afghanistan	15.1	249,999	Kabul

When the value of oil multiplied, the greatest transfer of wealth in history began. It continues today. Literally millions of dollars a day pour into these tiny countries. Nonetheless the oppressive heat and humidity make visiting this part of the world attractive only to the business person and the adventurous.

Lebanon, once called the Paris of the Middle East, is now a violence-ridden shambles. Iran and Iraq are at war. Afghanistan, never much of a tourist destination, is occupied by the Russians. The Arabian Peninsula countries, Syria and Jordan have never attracted the pleasure traveler in number.

As a matter of information, Figure 10.2 lists some basic statistics on Middle Eastern countries.

Saudi Arabia is the largest country in area—its size being somewhat less than one-third that of the United States. Turkey, with 46.7 million people, is the most populous.

Women traveling alone in Southern Europe, North Africa and especially in the Mid-East should be aware that the men feel that all American women are available. In some cases the wolf whistles, cat calls, and out-right propositioning is, in the eyes of the male, a form of flattery. Any kind of response on the woman's part may be taken as a come-on. The best advice: ignore the would-be Romeos; be rude if necessary. In real emergencies call for help. Avoid riding alone in train compartments, especially at night. Wear a bra; avoid halter tops and shorts.

ISRAEL

OFFICIAL NAME: STATE OF ISRAEL

Little Israel gathers peoples from around the world who come to worship, to relive history, to see firsthand villages and towns about which they have heard most of their lives. There are few holiday tourists as such. For the Israeli government, tourism has become a major source of foreign exchange. (America sends an additional $3 billion in aid.) Some twenty-eight thousand hotel rooms exist and more are being built. Of American visitors to Israel about 70 percent are Jewish. Christian pilgrims are also there and nearly every Christian pastor feels it necessary to have visited Christ's tomb and the places represented by such names as Bethany, Bethlehem, Hebron, Nazareth, the Sea of Galilee and, above all, Jerusalem—holy names to Christian and Jew alike.

Jerusalem has three holy days every week: Friday for the Moslems, Saturday the Sabbath for Jews, and Sunday for Christians. As one of the most polygot cities in the world, nationality means little as compared to one's religion. A person is either Christian, Moslem, or Jew. Religion overrides race and nationality. Remember that bus and train service ceases from Friday night to Saturday after sundown in honor of the Jewish Sabbath.

Major cities in Israel are the capital, Jerusalem (population 392,000), Greater Tel Aviv (population 1.2 million), and Haifa (population 534,000).

Israel, about the same size as New Jersey, lies with the Mediterranean Sea to the west and Egypt, Jordan, Syria, and Lebanon to the south, east and north. It has four topographical regions: the coastal plain, the central mountains, the Jordan Rift Valley, and the Negev Desert. The Negev, located in the south, comprises half of the country's total area.

Elevations range from Galilee's Mt. Meron at 3,930 feet above sea level, to the Dead Sea, which, at 1,300 feet below sea level, is the lowest point on earth.

Jerusalem sits at 2,600 feet and sweaters may be needed in the evenings even in summer. The winters are similar to those in California, mild with a short rainy season. The Dead Sea is like the Great Salt Lake, too salty to drown in (but don't drink the water). Remove jewelry before going in to prevent corrosion by the salts.

Nearby is the flat-topped mountain, Masada, where the Jewish zealots held out for several years against Roman armies. Besides being a famous tourist attration, Masada is used as the site for swearing in members of the Israeli army. Take the cable car up 1,400 feet to the top unless you want a thirty-minute climb by footpath. It can be very hot. So too can Elath, Israel's major beach resort. It sits at the head of the Gulf of Aqaba, where temperatures reach above one hundred degrees.

For those so inclined there are the kibbutzes, collective farms, that offer hotel-like guest houses and a variety of sports and allow guests to take part in picking fruits or vegetables or working in the fields. Lest you think most Israelis live in kibbutzes, the fact is that they contain less than 4 percent of the population.

Israeli tour guides have their own union, the Israel Tourist Guide Association. Guides must complete a two-year course including history, first aid, geology, and the Bible.

The Jewish menu in Israel resembles that offered in New York City. Hotel buffet breakfasts are an invitation to overeat, with thirty or more choices of cheese, fish, eggs, fruit, vegetables, even salads. Israelis tend towards being vegetarians. The most popular food item is "felafel"—fried, mashed chickpeas served in pita bread. Some restaurants are kosher, meaning that meat and dairy products are never served at the same meal.

ENDNOTE

1. "Singapore," Robin Tucker, Home Section, Los Angeles *Times,* March 13, 1983.

11

EAST ASIA

Following the regional definitions of the Pacific Area Travel Association East Asia comprises The People's Republic of China, The Republic of China (Taiwan), Hong Kong, Macau, Japan, and Korea. Japan is the dynamic force of the region. Hong Kong exists as a trade center and gateway to huge China. Macau, a Portuguese possession, is an hour's ride by jet-foil from Hong Kong, a scruffy Las Vegas of the Orient. Korea is forcing its way into the industrial world and actively pursues the tourist. Tokyo services by far the most air traffic. South Korea has Seoul, China has Beijing (Peking) and Shanghai. Taipei is the major airport for Taiwan (Republic of China). Manila is the gateway to the Philippines. Hong Kong is often used as the gateway to People's Republic of China. Bangkok, Thailand; Delhi, India; Colombo, Sri Lanka (formerly Ceylon); Djakarta, Indonesia are the capitals of their respective countries and major air gateways. The island nation of Singapore is a leading tourist city for Southeast Asia.

American tourist visits to Asia are growing more rapidly as a percentage than to any other region. Japan is visited most often of the Asian nations, followed by Hong Kong, the Philippines, South Korea, India, Taiwan, and Singapore. Air departures for Asian countries by U.S. citizens in 1981 totaled a little over a million.

Air departures for Asian countries by U.S. residents during 1981 were as follows:

Mainland China	8,950
Taiwan	41,468
Hong Kong	112,220
India	46,727
Japan	373,447
South Korea	82,423
Philippines	100,958
Singapore	22,587
Thailand	5,963

JAPAN

Japan, the third largest industrial nation after the U.S. and Russia, is the number one generator of travelers in the entire Pacific and in some years provides the most visitors to the U.S. after Canada and Mexico.

The Japanese are the big per-capita travelers of Asia. Slightly over four million went abroad in 1981 and their expenditures reached $4.6 billion. Receipts from foreign visitors were $735 million, leaving the country with a travel deficit of over 3.8 billion, the largest of any for 1981 except West Germany.

The Japanese National Railways (JNR) maintains the world's tightest scheduled train service and claims to offer the most comfortable and efficient service in the world. An extra charge is made for travel on green cars (former first-class), and for the express trains, berths and reserved seats. A Japan Rail Pass can be bought at Japan Air Lines offices in the United States and from authorized travel agencies. Passes cannot be bought in Japan.

Travel within the largest cities—Tokyo, Osaka, Kyoto, Nagoya, Yokohama, and Sapporo—is fastest via subway. Rental cars are available but not recommended because of the language barrier. Tokyo and Kyoto, the two places most visited by Americans, have bus tours with English-speaking guides available. Quite naturally the Japanese frequent the countries close to home: The Republic of China, Korea, and Hong Kong.

One of the most crowded countries in the world, Japan has some 119 million people, who live on a chain of mountainous islands in a two-thousand-mile arc off the east coast of Asia. Most of the population is centered on four main islands: Hokkaido, Honshu, Shikoku, and Kyushu. The flat plain between Tokyo and Osaka is one vast connurbation, the Japanese population center. Honshu, the main island, has the major tourist sights and the major cities. There are numerous first-class hotels but for the visitor who wants to sample Japanese home life there are about five thousand family inns and over eighty thousand Ryokan (Japanese inns). Rates include supper and breakfast and for the adventuresome, the communal bath.

Tokyo and Osaka are the major gateways for air and ship travel to and from Japan. Tokyo is by far the largest and the major gateway to Asia from the United States. The American visitor is likely to leave from San Francisco or Los Angeles and travel a great circle route via Alaska, a distance of about fifty-two hundred miles. Honolulu to Tokyo is thirty-nine-hundred miles, and a stopover in Honolulu is a pleasant way of breaking the journey from the continental United States. Because the international dateline is crossed during the trip, the time difference between the U.S. West Coast and Japan is seventeen hours. When it is 9:00 a.m. Pacific Standard Time on a Monday in San Francisco, it is 2:00 a.m. the next day, Tuesday, in Tokyo.

Travel growth, in and out of Japan, between 1965 and 1981 has been phenomenal, possibly the greatest in any large nation. Several years the increase exceeded 40 percent. In 1965, 366,649 visitors came to Japan. The figure was 1,583,043 in 1981. Japanese traveling out of the country rose from 158,827 in 1965 to over four million by 1979. U.S. residents contributed the largest number of visitors to Japan, about 27 percent of the total, followed by Taiwan and the rest of Asia. Male visitors outnumbered females two to one, because so many of the trips were for business purposes.

Spring and autumn provide the best climate for visiting the country. June is rainy; September, the typhoon season. The summer is hot and humid. Winters can be cold and overcast. Mean temperatures in Tokyo and Kyoto range from about thirty-nine degrees in winter to seventy-seven degrees during the summer. Japan's rivers are short and quick-flowing after rains. Lakes and hot springs contribute to the scenic beauty. Unfortunately Japan experiences earthquakes, typhoons and volcanic eruptions.

The pleasure visitor usually begins his trip in Tokyo, then goes on to Kyoto and Osaka. Travel information and reservation assistance can be had in the Tourist Information Center (TIC) at Yuroku-cho in Tokyo. Tourists using the center are full of praise for the

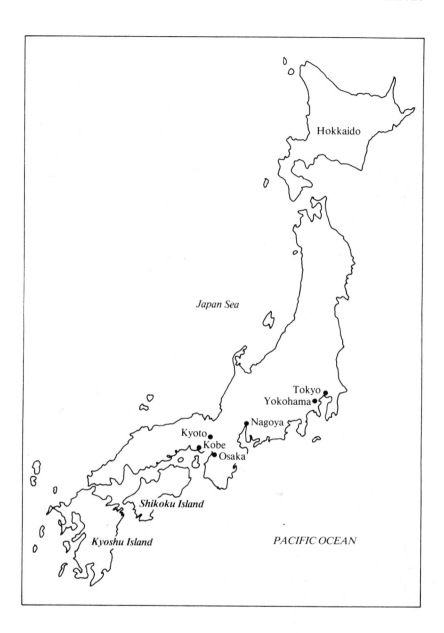

FIGURE 11.1 *Map of Japan.*

cordiality and services offered. A Tele Tourist Service, a taped information service, gives tourist information including the events of the week. In Kyoto a TIC office is located to the left of Kyoto railroad station. A weekly English-language newspaper distributed in Tokyo hotels provides entertainment and shopping suggestions as well as other practical information such as how to use a Japanese-style toilet (a hole in the floor designed to work only when the user faces the wall. Negotiating one any other way makes for an unpleasant surprise.)

Since about 1970 the Japanese have become major world travelers. Cameras at the ready, they are likely to appear in groups, taking advantage of package tours. The island of Guam is known as a honeymoon island for the Japanese. Several of the major hotels in Hawaii are Japanese owned and the Japanese comprise a large percentage of Hawaiian visitors. Australia and New Zealand are also favorite pleasure-travel destinations.

In Tokyo the big tourist sights are the Imperial Palace and the Meijii Shrine. The modern pulse of Tokyo is felt in the Ginza, Tokyo's major shopping center and number one nightspot. Though only an eighth of a mile square, it has more than eleven hundred bars and five hundred restaurants. The modern hotels of the city are the same high rises found in Occidental cities, with equally high tariffs.

Tokyo has several very large hotels. The highest is the Klio Plaza, forty-five stories. The New Otani has 2,057 rooms, the Klio Plaza, fifteen hundred. The Shinjuki has thirteen hundred. The Imperial Hotel, which replaced the original Imperial designed by Frank Lloyd Wright, has 1,130 rooms. In 1984 the Japanese Hotel association (JHA) had 338 members.

Eating in Tokyo can be very expensive. The expense-account restaurants in the first-class hotels are nearly all for those persons who are not budget conscious or who are dining at company expense. The business executives in Japan have unlimited expense accounts and the hotel restaurants and fancier restaurants cater to them. There are numerous other choices. Tokyo has close to ninety thousand, mostly small, restaurants. On weekdays the restaurants in office buildings are open to the public and are reasonably priced. So too are the multitude of restaurants on the side streets, along the Ginza and in the subway arcades.

It is easy to get lost in Tokyo and elsewhere in Japan. To help visitors a "Travel Phone" system provides assistance in the city and out in the countryside. The calls are free and the assistance is given in English. To get connected a ten-yen coin is needed. Outside of Tokyo or Kyoto find a blue or yellow phone and when an operator comes on say, "Collect call for TIC."

For those who want to experience more Japanese culture, Kyoto is the place. Surrounded by an arc of hills open to the South, Kyoto has hundreds of temples and shrines in and around the city and many art treasures, ancient and modern.

Osaka is known for its numerous restaurants, some thirty-five thousand in this city of 2.8 million people. Vending machines abound in Osaka streets, dispensing such foods as noodles, rice crackers, soda, and dried seaweed.

Visitors are amazed at how well the Japanese do with their limited space. Thanks to surrounding waters most of the needed protein comes from fish and seafood.

For those who want to mingle with the resident Japanese and save money at the same time, the family inns, "minshuku," are highly recommended. They are the Japanese version of bed and breakfasts. Rates are moderate. The inns are usually operated by a family. The overnight charge includes two meals served family style. Guests sleep on mattresses laid out on the tatami mats on the floor. House rules call for guests to take up their bedding in the morning and store it in a closet.

Every visitor to Japan should ride the Shinkansen (bullet) train to Kyoto, with its several many-tiered castles, former residences of the war lords. Japanese castles, quite unlike those in Europe, are architectural beauties as well as having been defensive structures. During rush hours Japanese trains are packed, literally packed in by rail employees, who push and shove people into the cars to achieve maximum load. So packed are the trains that at the end of the day an array of personal garments are collected, including garter belts, shoes, and bras lost in the melee. Station stops are only 45 seconds. If not close to an exit, the traveler goes on to the next station.

Unlike most of the rest of the world, in Japan about one-fourth of the railway system is privately owned. The "bullet" trains are computer controlled and cover the distance between the two commercial hubs of Japan—Tokyo and Osaka—in three hours and ten minutes. The average speed is 120 mph.

As in Britain, driving in Japan is on the left. Speed limits are much lower than in the United States. Like our American Automobile Association (AAA) the Japanese Automobile Federation (JAF) provides maps and road service for auto drivers. International road signs are easily read by the visitor. It is inadvisable for visitors to drive in the cities.

Within this small country, air service requires relatively short times. Osaka is fifty-five minutes from Tokyo by plane. Tokyo to Okinawa takes two hours and forty minutes.

The traveler should attend a Sumo wrestling match. The contenders, behemoths in breechcloths, charge each other like rutting bulls. The appeal to the Japanese perhaps is the sharp contrast in size and behavior of the contenders to the average Japanese male, who is usually slightly built, constrained in behavior and carefully schooled in courtesy. Judo, kendo (bamboo sword fighting), karate and aikido can be observed, or even learned.

FIGURE 11.2 *Symbols.* What better symbols of touristic Japan than Mt. Fuji and the Shinkansen, the bullet train, speeding below the mountain. The Japanese railway system is generally considered the most advanced in the world.

Source: Japan National Tourist Organization.

In contrast to these violent activities are Japanese flower arranging and the tea ceremonials, both subtle and highly refined.

The mountains to the Japanese are things of beauty and poetry. Mt. Fuji figures in the folklore and painting of the nation. Every year during July and the first three weeks of August thousands of people, young and old, climb the heights of this famous volcano. The climbers have a choice of six paths to the top of Mt. Fuji. Ten stations have been provided for rest and refreshment. The climb takes between seven and nine hours and can be broken up by an overnight stop in a stone hut at the seventh and eighth stages. Transportation is available to the fourth or fifth stations. Some idea of the rigor of the climb is gained from the old saying in Japan that, "He who climbs Mt. Fuji once is a wise man, but he who climbs it twice is a fool."

Japan has taken up skiing with a vengeance. The majority of the best ski resorts are in the Japan Alps. Avoid weekends when the mob makes the mountain look like solid skiers. Travel time by train from Tokyo to the Japan Alps region is between two and eight hours. The Ishiuchi ski resort claims to be the largest. Mt. Koya is one of several "religious" mountains with temples, monasteries, schools, and graves. Overnight guests are welcome but must be prepared for a vegetarian diet.

Stay in a Japanese-style hotel. Sleep on a "futon," a mattress with a quilt laid on the floor and take a Japanese-style bath. Don't worry about tipping in Kyoto or anywhere else in Japan; it's not good form. A 10 percent service charge is made for rooms, food and beverages in all hotels. Eat the Kyoto specialty, tofu (bean-curd cake), which is served with all meals, or try zen food, vegetarian food originally concocted for zen monks. Yakitori, a kind of chicken shish-kebob, is good and so are the less expensive noodle dishes.

Japan's country inns, the Ryokan, are an experience in courtesy and a different lifestyle. There are some eighty thousand of these Ryokan. Most of the better ones belong to the Japan Ryokan Association (JRA). The owners greet you and on departure wish you well. Part of the experience is the hot bath. Wash first; then soak in the hot tub. Don't wash in the tub! Japanese visitors to hotels in this country sometimes do the same, much to the discomfiture of the management, especially when the water from the ablutions runs down through the floor to the guest rooms below.

Ryokan etiquette is precise. Remove your shoes before entering. Wear the slippers provided. When walking over areas covered with tatami mats, remove the slippers. Japan also has about five thousand family inns.

One of the most homogeneous of societies, Japan is also one of the most industrious and productive despite a shortage of basic raw materials. Industrial growth since 1960 has been nothing less than astounding. During the period 1964 to 1984, Japan became the number one producer of ships, watches, cameras, radios, televisions, and automobiles. Loyalty to the family is carried to the extent of reverence for ancestors. The same loyalty overlaps to the workplace and includes a deep emotional attachment to the company or other organization for which one works. The Japanese have been called a nation of workaholics. Certainly they have one of the most orderly and disciplined of societies.

Buddhism is a leading religion, one that foregoes the worship of a god. Shintoism, the other prominent religion, includes ancestor worship.

The typical Japanese is extremely polite in formal situations, highly sensitive in interpersonal relations and much concerned about how others perceive him. Success or failure is seen reflecting on the family to a larger extent than in most societies.

Japanese food is probably the most refined in the world, if by refined is meant small portions, delicately prepared and displayed. One writer characterizes Japanese food as "modular," a gastronomic experience. It requires highly trained food preparers, razor-sharp knives to prepare the small bits of foods, rolled, wrapped, and garnished. Color and harmony of foods are as important as flavor.

Some of what the Japanese consider delicacies do not enrapture the Westerner. A breakfast of raw tuna belly, live tiger shrimp and abalone rectums is not the same as bacon and eggs.

HONG KONG

Hong Kong, long a rest and recreation area for British overseas soldiers and merchants, now attracts over two million visitors a year. They fly in to enjoy a taste of the Orient in first-class hotels, to shop, to move north into Mainland China. The Suzie Wong industry, prostitution, has been a big draw. Hong Kong has been China's principal access to the outside world and is one of the Orient's major financial and trade centers.

Called the "Pearl of the Orient" Hong Kong has also been described as "a borrowed place and a borrowed time." The "borrowed time" refers to the lease arrangement by which Britain controls the city. This lease between China and Britain on the largest part of Hong Kong is due to expire in 1997. That area includes the Kai Tak International Airport, the Kwai Chung container terminal and huge new town developments.

The principal problem with Hong Kong, unless you love crowds, is that the city has 5.2 million people in a space where 100,000 would comfortably live. Everyone seems to be on the move. Buses and subways are jammed. A big travel bargain and an experience is the famous Star Ferry that travels between Hong Kong Island and Kowloon. The fare is ten cents.

The Peninsula Hotel has been a fixture of Hong Kong since 1928. Its lobby is in the grand tradition of hotel lobbies seen in only a handful of hotels the world over. Where else can shark's fin and crabmeat soup be ordered any of twenty-four hours a day by room service? Suites and the more expensive rooms command harbor views from enormous windows. Next door, the YMCA offers cream of leek soup, grilled veal with vegetables, apple pie, and coffee. The same view of Hong Kong Harbor can be had at about one-seventh the cost.

The YMCA guest probably arrives via shanks mare; the Peninsula's guests routinely arrive in the hotel's chauffeur-driven Rolls-Royces. Escorted to their rooms, they find an array of tea, flowers, fruits, and chocolates. The YMCA guest can read in the library, run in the gym, take a dip in the pool, or attend chapel. If bored he can read one of Hong Kong's most popular books, "The World of Suzie Wong." Or if he wants to live dangerously he can meet one of the ten thousand Suzie Wongs, Hong Kong's ladies of the evening.

To get away from the solid-people atmosphere of Hong Kong Island, an hour's ferryboat ride takes the traveler to the craggy island of Lan Tao. Buddhist and Christian monasteries along with only thirty thousand people occupy this quiet island. The Po Lin monastery takes guests if reservations are made in advance. It serves vegetarian meals only. Views of the South China Sea are said to be magnificent.

Hong Kong is known for its eclectic cuisine, bringing together East and West. Like other oriental areas, Hong Kong features some menu items over which Westerners may become squeamish. Puppy dogs, monkeys and snakes are examples. Snake soup has its fanciers. It is said that snake soup strengthens the ankles, cures malaria and prevents diseases that result from exposure to cold winds. How, ask the Cantonese, can you be certain that Adam and Eve were not Chinese? Easy; they ate the apple, not the snake.

THE PEOPLE'S REPUBLIC OF CHINA

The People's Republic of China has become an "in place" to visit. Even the *Love Boat* made the trip in 1983. China is hurrying to build the facilities needed to attract more tourists. In 1981, 670,000 tourists other than Chinese from Hong Kong made the trip. Japan supplies the largest number of visitors to China, followed by the United States, France, and Germany. The number of Americans who arrived in 1981 was estimated at seventy thousand. More than seven million ethnic Chinese from abroad visited in 1982.

Most visitors enter China via eighty-nine miles of track linking the Hong Kong border with Canton's Kwangchow stations. Train passengers transfer at Lo Wu and walk across a covered bridge to board the Canton train at Samchun.

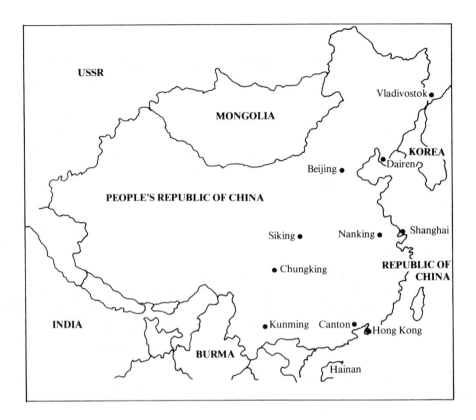

FIGURE 11.3   *Map of China.*

From Canton an express train runs north to Shanghai. The trip takes eight hours. As with Russian rail service, two types of train accommodations can be had, hard and soft. "Hard" means berths without bedding and no carpets on the floor. "Soft" gets the traveler made-up beds in compartments. Another train from Lo Wu heads north on a thirty-six hour trip to Beijing (Peking).

The Shanghai Express, a train with a history, runs between Shanghai and Beijing. The nine-hundred-mile trip takes twenty-two-and-a-half hours. China's Luxingshe is the official state tourist organization for looking after foreign visitors.

Visitors to China, like those to Russia, are much impressed by the trip but do not find it entertaining or particularly comfortable. In the summer parts of China get very hot and air conditioning is scarce. Air conditioning in some of the airplanes consists of the traveler being handed a popsicle and a fan.

In China, rent a car and you also get a driver. No driver, no car. Car use fits the chauffeur's schedule, 8:00 a.m. to noon, two hours for lunch, then 2:00 p.m. to 6:00 p.m. Schedule changes, however, can be arranged.

Steam locomotives are still around. In fact, a factory in Mainland China continues to make them.

The overwhelming impression of China by outsiders is that of tens of millions of people —people everywhere, people walking, people riding bicycles, part of the total population of one billion.

China has four major tourist attractions: the Forbidden City, the Great Wall, the hundreds of clay soldiers at Xian and the Grand Canal, the ancient one-thousand-mile water route connecting Beijing with Hangzhow near Shanghai. The Canal was built by hand twelve hundred years ago. It is said that some 300,000 men worked ten years to construct the Great Wall. The restored part of the wall is customarily visited at Ba Da Ling, about forty miles from Beijing. Xian is home to six thousand warrior statues standing in a 3.5 acre area, each different, each there to guard the builder of the Great Wall.

Beijing, China's capital city, is laid out in three rectangles. The innermost is the Forbidden City, principal tourist attraction of China, once home to the Ming and Qin emperors, now a museum and public park. Beijing has five thousand hotel rooms and is rushing to build more. Throughout China some fifty new Western-style hotels are scheduled to be built before 1985. The new hotels are major tourist attractions for the Chinese and would be overrun by locals if guards did not keep them out. At the new White Swan Hotel in Canton, house rules allow anyone who arrives by taxi to enter the hotel. Some Chinese hire a cab just around the corner to be able to get in for a look. Foreign visitors report that service is excellent and that tips may be considered an insult.

The Forbidden City, palace of the Chinese emperors until 1911, is enclosed with thirty-five-foot-high walls, itself enclosed in the Imperial City and that again enclosed within the walls of Beijing itself. The Forbidden City occupies about 250 acres and contains six Imperial palaces, one behind the other on a north-south axis. Five to six thousand cooks were needed to cater to the thousands who lived off the court. The emperors thought of their residence as the cosmic center of the world.

The Chinese spoken varies with the region. The language used in Beijing is so different from that of Canton the Cantonese cannot understand the news broadcast from the capital. The Chinese guides are not only learning English, they are learning to speak Japanese and German. The Japanese provide the largest number of tourists, the Germans the third largest number, after English speakers.

As in Russia special stores are set aside for foreign buyers. In China their Friendship Stores sell silks, rugs, jewelry, embroidery and the like. The clerks speak English.

As one travel student pointed out, telephoning in China is difficult because of the lack of phones. Also there are so many "Wings" and "Wongs" in China people keep winging the wong numbers.

The Chinese have difficulty pronouncing the letter "l." It usually comes out as an "r." A visiting congressman was somewhat nonplussed when he was toasted at a dinner party and the smiling host said:

"Rots of ruck for your next erection."

Traditionally, the Chinese do not make eye contact as they speak. This is a sign of respect for the other party, not necessarily disinterest, nervousness or lack of confidence.

The major ethnic group, known as the Han people, comprises 94 percent of the population. The remaining 6 percent, or about sixty million, are divided into fifty-five "national minorities." The better known of these are the Mongols and Tibetans.

The Chinese work an eight-hour day, six days a week; a two- to three-hour lunch break is commonplace. Yet per capita income per year is *less* than $300.

Suggesting the importance of food to the Chinese is the traditional greeting not of "How are you?" but "Have you eaten?" It also suggests that in the past food has not always been easy to come by.

Good table manners in China include slurping your soup, raising the rice bowl to the mouth to avoid spilling rice, putting the bones from soup on the table and belching softly after a meal to show how much the meal was enjoyed. In Chinese restaurants never tap on a glass, plate or teacup to get a waiter's attention. That is incredibly bad manners. It is polite to tip back your teapot lid to signal the waiter that you liked the tea and could use some more.

In China, the mother of Oriental cooking, four methods of food preparation are used: deep-frying, stir-frying, steaming, and cooking in liquid (fuel was too scarce for oven-roasting to gain a foothold). The visitor finds that the cuisine varies regionally: Cantonese in the south, Beijing-style in the north, and Szechwanese to the southwest. The Cantonese style is most familiar to Americans since it was the Cantonese who most often emigrated to the U.S. and set up Chinese restaurants. Cantonese dishes are described as robust and colorful, many prepared by stir-frying. Characteristic foods are pork, chicken, tomatoes, and snow peas. Dim sum, originating in Canton, is a meal of numerous, bite-size foods, usually accompanied with tea. Beijing-style cooking features Peking and Mandarin Duck and Mu Shu Pork. Szechwanese cooking is hot and spicy.

In China food is seldom wasted. Blue mako shark's fins, chicken feet, tripe, and pig skin become delicacies.

At Chinese parties or celebrations, be prepared to feast and eat as much as humanly possible. It is polite, however, to leave a bit of food on each dish. Bones are tossed on the floor. The more succulent the food, the richer the sounds of eating. It is even okay to spit on the floor.

The pinnacle of culinary pleasure for the Chinese is Peking Duck. Force-fed ducks, kept closely penned to reduce exercise, become the piece-de-resistance via a complicated preparation process. Compressed air is injected between the skin and flesh to permit the fat to drip out while cooking. The birds are scalded and coated with a syrup, then hung to dry before roasting.

Diners get the complete duck. Besides duck soup, webs, tongues, hearts and wings are served. The best part for some is the crisp, savory skin and flesh wrapped in a soft wheat pancake with shredded green onion and a sweet bean or plum sauce. In Beijing the local malty beer is said to be the best accompaniment.

SOUTH KOREA

Korea calls itself "The Land of Morning Calm." Scenic beauty abounds. Depending upon location, winters can be very cold and summers hot and humid. The climate is varied. While U.S. service personnel are being raked by cryogenic blasts at Panmunjun on the border with North Korea, the island Cheju, where the principal crops are tangerines and pineapples, is experiencing a subtropical climate. Cheju sits on about the same latitude as San Diego and El Paso.

A direct flight from Los Angeles to Seoul, Korea's primate city of eight million, takes twelve hours. Tokyo to Seoul is a two-and-a-half hour flight. Korea has three international gateway cities—Seoul, Pusan, and Cheju Island. Regular connections are available between Seoul and Japan, Hong Kong, Taiwan, and Thailand. A flight to Korea can be part of an Asian junket, breaking up the long flight to Seoul by stopping in Tokyo, then on to Seoul, Hong Kong and back via Taipei and Honolulu. An interesting trip back from Korea can be done via the Pusan Ferry that takes seven hours and runs between Pusan on Korea's east coast and Shimonoseki, Japan.

Getting around Korea is easy. "Super-express" trains operate between the major cities. The run between Seoul and Pusan, Korea's second city in importance, takes five hours and forty minutes. Bus service is frequent.

Shopping in Korea means ceramics, lacquerware, silk, dolls, brassware, tailored clothing and, yes, good old ginseng and wigs. Myongdong, Korea, is Korea's answer to Tokyo's shopping and entertainment center, the Ginza. The amount of ginseng taken out of the country is limited. Travelers can take out a maximum of five ladies' wigs, three gentlemen's wigs, not more than twenty cuttlefish or two hundred pairs of false eyelashes. Pity the poor tourist who needs a lifetime supply of eyelashes and is just crazy about cuttlefish.

South Korea has twenty-five thousand hotel rooms, about ten thousand of them in the country's capital, Seoul. Hotels are rated, five stars being the top award. Fourteen hotels have the five-star rank, among them the Hotel Lotte and the Hyatt Regency. The Japanese are Korea's biggest visitor group, many of them males come to enjoy the Korean women. A total of about 1.1 million visitors arrive in Korea each year.

Korea is one of the few countries where travel agents and hotel managers must pass an examination to be licensed. The same is true for tour guides, interpreters, and overseas escorters.

Japan has its Ryokan; Korea its yokwans, the country inns. Unlike the Ryokans which can be very expensive, the yokwans are cheap. Guests sleep on the floor on a mattress. The

FIGURE 11.4 *Map of East Asia.*

pillow or headrest is often filled with buckwheat husks. The heating system may be the "ondol," or hot floor, the heat applied from below the floor. The Ryokan offers elaborate meals. In the yokwan food must be ordered from outside and eaten in the room.

Hotels in Korea are classified into Deluxe (A), First Class (B), Second Class (C) and Third Class (D). Rate ranges are government mandated. Thirteen hotels are rated in the deluxe category. Visitors report that the service is unexcelled.

A spiny backbone of mountains runs down the middle of Korea so that only about one-fifth of the land can be cultivated. The coastal plains of the west and south produce most of Korea's rice, the Orient's equivalent of bread. Sweet potatoes, cabbage, turnips, cucumbers are common vegetables.

Visitors to Korea's restaurants can try a number of foods, some common to other Oriental countries, others unique. (Puppy dogs and snakes have been ordered off the menus of restaurants for fear of offending tourists.) Dinner might begin with Kujolpan, an hors d'oeuvre tray with a difference. Cooked meat and vegetables are arranged on a large platter in a circle of contrasting color. A mound of paper-thin pancakes is piled in the center. The pancakes are picked up with chopsticks, meat and vegetables placed on them, the pancake rolled up and popped into the mouth.

A main course could be Sinsollo, a mixture of meat, fish, vegetables, and bean curd over which beef broth has been poured. This cooks in a brass bowl which encloses a brazier filled with red-hot charcoal. Pulgogi, marinated beef sliced paper thin and grilled over charcoal, is the best known meat dish in Korea.

Soups containing seaweed, meat or fish are always served. Seasoning includes red and black pepper, garlic, seasame seed oil and soy sauce.

Kimchi is a highly seasoned and fermented pickle of cabbage, turnip or cucumber, Korea's staff of life, usually eaten three times a day. Pungent smelling, kimchi is not to every visitor's taste. Some eat it out of self-defense. Stored in large pots, it comes in "summer" and "winter" forms. Red peppers add fire to the cabbage to make a dish that westerners may find "too much." Kimchi provides vitamins B_1, B_2, B_{12}, and C, plus iron, calcium, and other minerals.

For those who need to be jump-started, ginseng is said to be the answer. Korean ginseng is said to be the best. Its vaunted aphrodisiacal power may be due only to the fact that the heart is stimulated.

Beer halls where patrons are expected to at least buy a dish of snacks—peanuts, dried fish or raw vegetables—are fun places. Wine houses called subjip are the working man's bars. Makkolli is a milky-white brew made from rice. Soju is particularly potent. Accompaniments include green onions, garlic, and sesame leaves. Pachon, fried leeks with small shelled clams in an egg batter, and todorimook (wild acorn gluten) are there for the adventurous.

There are also tabans, tearooms ("ta" means tea; "bang" means room). During the summer, strawberry, watermelon, peach, or apple juice may be served. Barley tea is always available.

TAIWAN

Taiwan is presented to the world as a democracy—which it is not. The Taiwanese, who constitute 85 percent of the eighteen million residents, have only 10 percent of the representation in national legislative bodies. Martial law has been in effect for more than a third of a century, ever since Chiang Kai-shek fled from Mainland China in 1949. Under the military rule established, the island has prospered. Its per capita income of $2,350 is the third highest in Asia.

When being forced out of Mainland China, Chiang Kai-shek and his troups thoughtfully removed a goodly share of China's art treasures. Today many of them, in fact ten thousand pieces, are on display at the National Palace Museum in the mountain suburbs of Taipei. Moreover, upwards of 200,000 Chinese treasures are stored in air-conditioned caves located behind the museum. English-language tours of the palace are conducted daily at 10:00 a.m. and 3:00 p.m.

New Park, one block from the Presidential Building in the center of Taipei, contains the Taiwan Provincial Museum, which houses a collection of life-size statues of Taiwan's several aboriginal tribespeople.

Taipei's coffee shops usually have an English menu.

Taiwan offers a range of accommodation, from youth hostel to luxury hotel. Tatami rooms, where floor mats are used as beds, are a novelty for the western visitor, and are inexpensively priced.

About 1.4 million people visit Taiwan each year and leave approximately $1 billion while there. One-half of the visitors come from Japan. Hong Kong supplies 16 percent. Ninety percent of American visitors go for business reasons.

12

AFRICA

Americans travel to Africa in relatively small numbers. Egypt's antiquities hold the greatest appeal. Some 155,000 Americans went there in 1981. In that year about sixty-three thousand Americans visited Morocco, mostly by ferry, crossing over from Spain. Tangiers, Morocco, which sits facing Gibralter, fills with tourists, mostly over for the day from Spain. A few thousand Americans went to Tunisia. South Africa and Kenya, with their magnificent game parks, are the other African countries that attract North Americans in significant numbers. Three nations that offer the Mediterranean climate—Tunisia, Egypt and Morocco—attract more than a million total visitors annually. The French are particularly fond of Morocco. Figure 12.1 is expressed in thousands of visitor arrivals and in millions of dollars received from tourists.

FIGURE 12.1   *African international tourism, 1980.*

	Arrivals	Receipts
Algeria	291	$ 48
Cameroon	86	n.a.
Egypt	1,300	890
Ethiopia	39	11
Gambia	22	18
Ivory Coast	194	60
Kenya	372	198
Malawi	46	n.a.
Morocco	1,097	397
Nigeria	n.a.	55
Senegal	186	68
Tanzania	n.a.	21
Togo	83	13
Tunisia	1,602	604
Zimbabwe	268	24
South Africa	702	600

Source: World Tourism Organization

New York City to Casablanca is only a six-and-a-half-hour flight. Ferry boats from Malaga and Algeciras, Spain, link Europe with Tangiers, Morocco. Visitors to Morocco can glimpse the royal touch by staying in one of the several palaces that have been converted to hotels. Hotels are categorized from one to five stars.

The two showcase hotels in Morocco are the Mamounia in Marrakesh and the Palais Jamai in Fez. Both are owned by the King of Morocco, who has employed the top management of the Paris luxury Hotel Crillon to supervise the operations. The Palais Jamai is, as the name implies, an old palace, townhouse for a 19th century minister of culture. The French influence on Morocco is strong because it was for a long period controlled by France. French is the second language, after Arabic.

Couscous is a favorite dish, made from rolled semolina wheat to which meat has been added. Bastilla is a grand banquet item made of paper-thin pastry leaves stuffed with pigeon and almonds. Never mind the antelope horns.

The Rif and Atlas mountains that run roughly north and south in the interior provide skiing in the winter months while temperatures are in the seventies in Agadir and other Atlantic coastal towns.

Tunisia has been around as a culture for thirty centuries. Berbers, Phoenicians, Romans, Vandals, Byzantines, Arabs, Turks, and most recently the French, all left something of themselves. Carthaginians and Romans left their monuments and archaeological treasures. El Jem has the remains of a colisseum that seated thirty-five thousand, one of the largest in the Roman world. Carthage, famed antagonist of Rome, occupies what today is a suburb of Tunis, Tunisia's capital city.

Visitors to Tunis come in tours. Package tours arrive from Germany, France, England, and Italy. Over a million a year come mostly for the sun and the Mediterranean and reasonable prices. Jerba Island has Africa's largest hotel, the 2,450-bed Dar Jeteba. Besides fronting on the Mediterranean, Tunis stretches south into the Sahara desert, where nomadic tribesmen are being encouraged to settle down. The indigenous people, the Berbers, live on the mountain ridges that divide the southern coastal plain from the harsh desert. French and Arabic are the languages, Islam the religion. Total population is six million, with one million concentrated in Tunis.

Transportation to Africa varies widely in availability and quality. Some parts of Africa are still virtually inaccessible. Air travel to parts of Africa are circuitous. A number of flights originate in Paris and serve West Africa because France was a colonial power in West Africa. Rome is a major terminal for flights into East Africa. Madrid connects with Las Palmas in the Canary Islands off Africa's west coast since the Canary Islands are a part of Spain. The Canaries are a major vacation spot for visitors from northern Europe seeking the winter sun. Johannesburg and Capetown, South Africa, are well served by direct flights from the United States, Europe, and Rio de Janeiro. Nairobi, Kenya, is an active air transit point and serves tourists visiting the some six million acres of national parks and game preserves.

Transportation within Africa is dicey, often difficult or nonexistent. Africa spans seven time zones and to fly from Nairobi, Kenya, in East Africa to Dakar, Senegal, in West Africa, takes longer than to fly from New York to London. Traveling within Black Africa, those forty-six countries south of a line drawn from Morocco to Egypt, is particularly difficult, with the one exception of travel within the nation of South Africa. Black Africa has twenty-eight national carriers that routinely bump passengers, fly irregular schedules and lose money. Only the Gambian Airways makes a profit and it has no airplanes. The profit is made by running an office that sells tickets on other airlines. The quickest way to get to East from West Africa is usually via Europe. Travel to the Republic of South Africa via the national airline, however, is efficient and well done.

Customs and immigration officials can be corrupt. "Dash," petty bribery, is commonplace in Africa. A Zaire customs official told a visitor that his health certificate had expired and he would have to pay so much for a new one. The visitor pointed out that the date on his certificate was still valid. The official: "I say it has expired and the health officer will say the same thing." Any Zairian money a traveler has left when leaving the country is confiscated by the customs people.

Scenically Africa offers spectacular beauty, grand mountains, awe-inspiring waterfalls, vast savannahs, deserts and great forests and rivers. For naturalists and wild life enthusiasts Africa is it! Historically and archeologically North Africa and Egypt have great interest. Tunis was the seat of the Carthaginian empire; the ruins of Carthage are on the coast northeast of modern Tunis. Egypt is a major factor in Middle East politics, home of the oldest civilization of which we have a continuous record, one that goes back to 4000

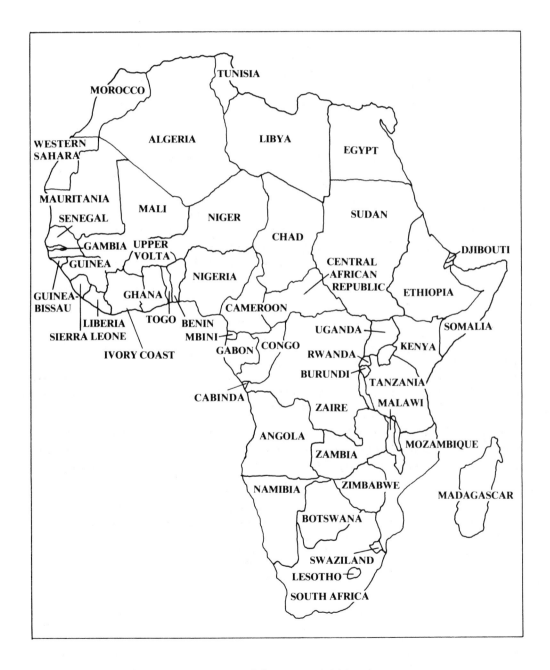

FIGURE 12.2   *Map of Africa.*

Source: Wall Street Journal, Sept. 16, 1982.

B.C. Nigeria is important for business travel because of its oil. West Africa produces peanuts, palm oil, and cocoa. Copper comes from Central Africa. South Africa is a major source of gold, diamonds, and other minerals and is the strongest of African nations militarily.

The "Statistical Profile" taken from the excellent book, *The Africans,* by David Lamb,[1] details the various African nations, their populations, per capita income, major dollar earners, and people per square mile. It is quickly seen that, with the exception of Libya with its huge oil income, the average African is desperately poor. In 1982 per capita income was $365 a year. Nigeria takes in the most oil income but also has the largest population so that per capita income is low.

South African whites are another exception and it should be quickly pointed out that wealthy elites exist in almost every African state. All of the countries could benefit financially from tourism and nearly all of the governments encourage tourism growth.

EGYPT

Egypt is Africa's number one attraction with about 1.3 million visitors each year. U.S. visitors number about 150,000 annually. Tourism is nothing new for Egypt; it was a destination for the ancient Romans. Egypt with its Nile River trips and its ancient tombs and temples is fascinating for those who enjoy a sense of ancient history. To the visitor much of Egypt is a living museum. The Nile, lifestream of Egypt, provides a ribbon of oasis in Egypt the desert. Without the Nile, Egypt as it is and has been would be impossible. Rising in Ethiopia and Uganda and flowing north, the Nile provides the water and the new soil needed to sustain agriculture. Like Egyptians have done for several years, the modern-day tourist can ride the current in a boat north on the Nile and then on the return trip go with the wind in the opposite direction.

Boat trips on the Nile have been popular at least since the time Cleopatra took Anthony for a "trip." Thomas Cook, the first recognized travel agent, scheduled regular Nile excursions before the turn of the century. Perhaps the most pleasant way to see Egypt even today is to travel the twisting Nile via a luxury yacht or a steamer. Passengers are detached from the heat and the crowds yet can visit all of Egypt's wondrous ruins at will.

For the Nile the old warning "don't go near the water" takes on particular potency. In fact don't even put your fingers in the Nile, or shake hands with someone who has Nile water on his hands. Schistosomiasis, snail fever, is a serious disease picked up from the larvae of worms that infest the Nile and many other fresh-water rivers and lakes in Africa and South America.

Egypt, officially the Arab Republic of Egypt, is located in the northeastern corner of the African continent. With forty-four million people it is the largest Arab nation and Africa's most populous country after Nigeria. It is bounded by the Mediterranean Sea, Libya, Sudan, the Red Sea, the Gulf of Suez, and the State of Israel. The total area is slightly larger than California, Nevada, and Arizona combined. Only the land along the Nile and a few isolated oases, about 3 percent of the total land, can be cultivated. Because of the scarcity of water the population crowds into the Nile valley and delta, giving it a density of 3,900 people per square mile, one of the highest in the world. Bread is almost given away, less than a penny a loaf, subsidized by the government. The United States has provided much of the aid to Egypt largely to try to stabilize the Mid-East. Cairo, the capital, is bursting at the seams with more than eight million people, a metropolitan area population of fourteen million. If it continues to grow at the present rate, it will overtake Mexico City and Tokyo in population within a relatively short time. Alexandria, founded by Alexander the Great in the fourth century B.C., is the second largest city, with 2.5 million people.

Egypt's train system between Cairo and other cities along the Nile is efficient and on time. Only the first-class cars, however, are air-conditioned. All tickets should be reserved. The trains are usually crowded and dusty.

Luckily for us moderns, the ancient Egyptians looked upon this life as only an antecedent to eternity. Great pains and colossal effort were taken to prepare the powerful for a

FIGURE 12.3 *A statistical profile of the countries of Africa.*

Country	Capital	Last Colonial Power	Independence	Population (in millions)	Annual Per Capita Income	$$$ Earner	People per Sq. Mile
Algeria	Algiers	France	1962	18.0	$1,260	oil	20
Angola	Luanda	Portugal	1975	7.0	300	oil	14
Benin	Cotonou	France	1960	3.3	230	cotton	78
Botswana	Gaborone	Britain	1966	0.75	620	diamonds	3
Burundi	Bujumbura	Belgium	1962	4.3	140	coffee	372
Cameroon	Yaounde	France, Britain	1960	8.0	460	cocoa	44
Cape Verde	Praia	Portugal	1975	0.35	160	sugar cane	199
Central African Republic	Bangui	France	1960	2.0	250	diamonds	11
Chad	N'Djamena	France	1960	4.3	140	livestock	9
Comoros	Moroni	France	1975	0.4	180	copra	577
Congo	Brazzaville	France	1960	1.5	780	oil	11
Djibouti	Djibouti	France	1977	0.32	430	foreign aid	12
Egypt	Cairo	Britain	1922	43.5	400	cotton	109
Equatorial Guinea	Malabo	Spain	1968	0.35	100	cocoa	32
Ethiopia	Addis Ababa	—	—	31.0	120	coffee	65
Gabon	Libreville	France	1960	0.6	3,600	oil	5
Gambia, The	Banjul	Britain	1965	0.6	230	groundnuts	142
Ghana	Accra	Britain	1957	11.0	400	cocoa	119
Guinea	Conakry	France	1958	5.2	210	bauxite	50
Guinea-Bissau	Bissau	Portugal	1974	0.8	200	groundnuts	39
Ivory Coast	Abidjan	France	1960	8.0	1,000	cocoa	61
Kenya	Nairobi	Britain	1963	16.0	320	coffee	66
Lesotho	Maseru	Britain	1966	1.3	280	exported labor	109
Liberia	Monrovia	—	1847	1.8	460	rubber	40
Libya	Tripoli	Italy	1951	2.8	7,000	oil	4
Madagascar	Tananarive	France	1960	9.0	250	coffee	37
Malawi	Lilongwe	Britain	1964	6.0	180	tobacco	124
Mali	Bamako	France	1960	6.5	120	livestock	14
Mauritania	Nouakchott	France	1960	1.6	270	livestock	4
Mauritius	Port Louis	Britain	1968	1.0	830	sugar cane	1,169
Morocco	Rabat	France	1956	19.0	670	phosphate	110
Mozambique	Maputo	Portugal	1975	10.0	140	cashew nuts	33
Namibia	Windhoek	South Africa	—	0.95	1,080	diamonds	3
Niger	Niamey	France	1960	5.0	220	groundnuts	10
Nigeria	Lagos	Britain	1960	80.0	560	oil	202
Rwanda	Kigali	Belgium	1962	4.5	180	coffee	444
Sao Tome and Principe	Sao Tome	Portugal	1975	0.09	490	cocoa	215
Senegal	Dakar	France	1960	5.4	340	peanuts	71
Seychelles	Victoria	Britain	1976	0.06	1,060	tourism	351
Sierra Leone	Freetown	Britain	1961	3.3	210	diamonds	118
Somalia	Mogadishu	Italy, Britain	1960	4.0	130	livestock	14
South Africa	Pretoria	—	1910	28.5	1,480	gold	59
Sudan	Khartoum	Britain-Egypt	1956	18.0	320	cotton	18
Swaziland	Mbabane	Britain	1968	0.55	590	sugar cane	81
Tanzania	Dar es Salaam	Britain	1961	17.0	230	coffee	46
Togo	Lome	France	1960	2.5	320	phosphate	110
Tunisia	Tunis	France	1956	6.0	950	oil	96
Uganda	Kampala	Britain	1962	13.0	200	coffee	140
Upper Volta	Ouagadougou	France	1960	5.5	160	exported labor	62
Western Sahara	El Aaiun	Spain	—	0.075	200	phosphate	0.7
Zaire	Kinshasa	Belgium	1960	26.0	210	copper	31
Zambia	Lusaka	Britain	1964	5.3	480	copper	19
Zimbabwe	Harare	Britain	1980	7.0	480	chrome	46

Source: The Africans. David Lamb, Random House, N.Y. 1982.

continuation of life after death. Whatever was useful and beautiful was buried along with the mummified remains of the rulers. The tombs contained frescoed walls, furniture, golden sandals, pharano statues, and piles of jewelry along with food and transport to the next world (neatly packaged for eternity). The Valley of Kings, a huge burial site on the west bank of the Upper Nile, leaves the visitors spellbound.

Where the spirits have gone is unknown; the artifacts and the mummies are on display in Cairo, a tourist attraction and a grim reminder of mortality. Closer to home, the New York Museum of Art also contains forty thousand such objects.

Visitors to Egypt are left spellbound by the massive pyramids. The biggest, standing near Giza, seven miles from the heart of Cairo, was built by the Pharoah Cheops forty centuries ago. It reaches up forty stories high, awesome, mysterious. Covering about 13 acres, it is the largest stone structure in the world. Was it a tomb for Cheops, a quest for immortality or merely a monument to one man's vanity? This monolith of perfect geometry was once gleaming white and smooth on the outside. Inside are passages, the purposes of which are still not completely clear even today. It is estimated that 100,000 workers toiled for over thirty years in building the massive pile of rock. Close by is the five-star Mena House Oberoi, a desert resort hotel for pyramid visitors.

As Mexico City, London, and Paris dominate their countries, so Cairo is Egypt's primate city. Alexandria, on the shores of the Mediterranean, is 135 miles north of Cairo. Luxor, location of the Valley of the Kings, is 422 miles south. No fewer than 64 Pharoah tombs have been found there. The Aswan Dam and its nearby tombs and temples are 534 miles south, located near the Nile's first cataract. Aswan is a winter resort. Summer temperatures can reach 115 degrees, but with a dry heat like our Palm Springs. It is so hot that even the pitchmen normally around retreat to the shade. Abu Simbel, with its great temple dedicated to the Sun God, Ra, and its Smaller Temple, dedicated to the goddess Hathor, is about 170 miles south of Aswan. Both are more than three thousand years old.

The Hilton, Concorde, Sheraton, and Marriott hotels all operate Nile steamers, small cruise ships that take tourists from Cairo to Luxor and Aswan in five days.

Business travelers to Cairo are advised to stay in a downtown hotel to be able to walk to most government or private offices. Hiring a car is cheaper than taking a taxi. Taxi drivers automatically double their rates when they see a western face. Do not drive yourself. It is virtually impossible to find your way around or to locate a parking space.

Driving in Egypt can be adventuresome to say the least. "The Mobile Motoring Guide to Egypt" includes this advice:

"The danger of uncleared land mines (some twenty thousand World War II mines remain in the north coast, Oattara area; and 1973 mines remain along the Red Sea Coast) is very real.

"In case of injury or death of persons or domestic animals, remember that you cannot protect yourself from the crowd."

People who like a hot, dry climate can revel in Egypt's climate, except for the season of the "khamsin" when for about fifty days in the spring dust becomes the curse of Cairo. Here is a description of "khamsin" from the *Los Angeles Times*[2]:

"The western sky suddenly turns fiery red. The breeze dies. The waters of the Nile seem to stand still. Then wind stirs, the horizon darkens and great expanses of Egypt fall temporarily lifeless under the attack of powder-fine desert sand.

"Visibility is no more than a few feet, and throngs of Cairo pedestrians, their eyes squinting and their noses full of dust, bounce off one another like windup toy men. The International Airport and the Suez Canal close and cars inch along, even at mid-day their headlights glinting dully."[3]

The cause comes from winds blowing in from the desert to fill a low-pressure area: hot, dry, dusty winds come from the south and humid heavy winds from the north. After the winds come the terrible heat of the summer. There is no scarcity of sand in Egypt. Ninety-five percent of the country is desert.

The most pleasant time to visit Egypt is between October and May, when the weather is surprisingly cool. During the summer temperatures in Cairo hover between ninety and one hundred degrees. In upper Egypt, in Luxor and Aswan, temperatures are usually between 105 and 110 degrees in the shade (about the same as in Las Vegas).

A word of caution about being too eager to see everything. Unless exceptionally eager and fit, admire the Pyramids at Giza from the outside. To reach the burial chamber inside can be an ordeal. The passageway leading to the chamber is two to three feet wide, steep, and lacks headroom to walk upright. It is extremely hot and has little air. Traffic jams of people occur and when the burial chamber is reached, there is nothing there. Grave robbers took the trip centuries ago.

Egypt has about thirty-eight thousand hotel rooms, by far the largest number of any nation in the Middle East or in Africa. Egypt has 31 government-backed hotels plus 214 privately owned ones. The Cairo Marriott is the largest hotel in the Middle East. Tourism income is expected to total about $1 billion a year, much needed in view of the fact that per capita income is less than $600 a year.

SUB-SAHARA AFRICA

The average American has never heard of Upper Volta, Mali, or Guinea-Bissau and probably is not interested. The peoples of Sub-Sahara Africa are mostly black but are anything but a homogeneous race. The Pygmy, the Zulu, the Masai, the Falani, and the Ibo are strangers or actively hostile to each other. At least two thousand languages or dialects are spoken but the language of government is that left by the last colonizing station—Britain, France, Spain, Portugal, or Italy. Tribal rivalries make political accord almost impossible within even small countries.

A major reason for the poverty is political. Governments are notoriously inept, corrupt and in many instances, cruel. Since independence, Black Africa has suffered eleven wars, more than fifty coups and the assassination of at least twelve heads of state. Might makes right. Military men rule twenty African countries and civilian rulers dare not leave their countries for fear of being deposed while absent.

Though lacking the industrial capacity to support cities, the peasants overflow urban areas, where 25 percent of the total population already lives. African leaders have held down crop prices to satisfy city dwellers, which only forces more peasants to leave the land.

Like South America, Africa has tremendous undeveloped resources but half of its 455 million people are no older than fifteen years. The population is growing at an alarming rate. Thirty countries have growth rates of over 2 percent a year; ten others have more than 3 percent. Only Gabon has achieved population stability and this is largely because 30 percent of the women have venereal disease.

According to one expert on Africa, Black Africa lives on the international dole. If the East and West were to cut off their flow of guns, money and technology to Black Africa, says this expert, almost every government would collapse in a matter of months.[4]

Americans and Europeans enjoy "going on safari" in relative comfort and security, a far cry from the days of going to Africa to bag a lion or elephant trophy. Game parks in East Africa and South Africa are well policed and provided with comfortable accommodations. A few lodges overlook watering spots, favored by a variety of animals. Guests can look down at them while there is momentary truce as they drink.

Kenya (pronounced Keen-ya by the British, Ken-ya by the natives) is best known for game parks with a great concentration of elephant, giraffe, antelope, and zebra. Surprisingly one of the large animal parks is adjacent to the capital city, Nairobi. Not far away by rented limousine or day-tour live the Masai, whose men are never seen without their spears and whose test of manhood is to use the spear in killing a lion.

In all about 7.5 percent of Kenya is given over to National Parks and Animal Reserves. There are eleven national parks and twenty-two national reserves, nearly all of which have game lodges within their boundaries. Really small hotels, most game lodges have terraces

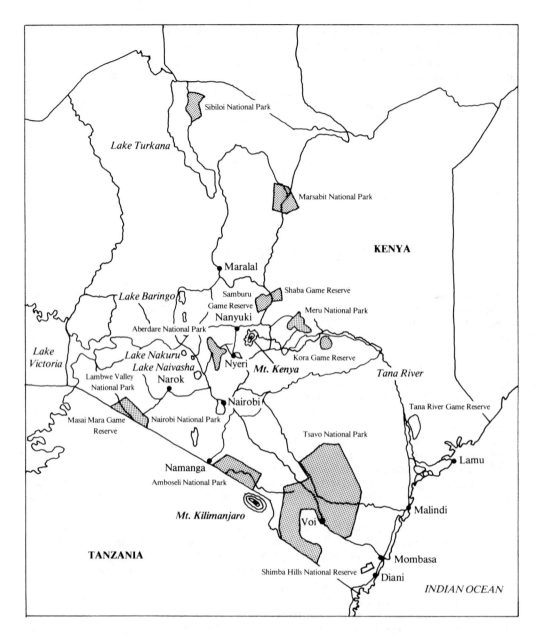

FIGURE 12.4   Map of Kenya.

Source: Kenya Tourism Guide, Ministry of Tourism, Nairobi, 1982.

from which game can be viewed. Parks are under central government authority; reserves are controlled by a local authority. The five most popular parks are the Masai Mara, the Nairobi National Park (just outside of Nairobi, the capital of Kenya and its only city), Meru National Park (home of the white rhino), Amboseli (which sits at the foot of Mount Kilimanjaro, Africa's highest mountain), and Tsavo (where the largest elephant herds live).

Kenya is also for bird lovers. More than twelve hundred species have been listed. Lakes Bogoria and Nakuru see a million or more flamingos so crowded together that they form a shimmering pink mass.

Nairobi is one of the few modern cities in Black Africa. Within eighty years it has grown from a village to a city of more than 800,000. It is the most popular safari base in Black Africa and the major air transit point for East Africa. The months of July and August—Kenya's winter—are the coolest and driest.

Tourism to Kenya's coast has grown rapidly since 1970. In 1980, 650,000 visitors left $120 million, more money than from any other export. Sadly the country of Kenya is being overwhelmed by population, too many to be supported by the agricultural lands and methods available. Kenya's birthrate is one of the highest, perhaps the highest in the world. Corruption in high places is common.

Zambia and Zimbabwe share Victoria Falls, a falls twice as big as Niagara Falls. The force of the falling water raises a cloud of spray that can be seen twenty miles away. Zambia also has a large wildlife park.

Visitors to Tanzania think first of the Ngorongoro Conservation area, highlands with peaks, collapsed volcanoes and rift walls. The Ngorongoro Crater has walls of two thousand feet and a crater which varies from ten to twelve miles that is covered with some twenty-five to thirty thousand animals. About two-thirds of the crater floor contains short grass, and the crater also has permanent fresh water. Mt. Kilimanjaro is 130 miles away. The Serengeti Plains are not far away, a prime area for animal-watching safaris.

West Africa is a string of little countries, most bordering the Atlantic. None of them was a nation until after World War II. That can be said of most of the African nations. Strangely, each has a vote in the United Nations, no matter how poor, small or otherwise insignificant. Many had only a handful of university graduates as citizens when becoming a nation.

West Africa occupies the big bulge of land in the west which includes Senegal, the Gambia, Guinea-Bissau, Guinea and Sierra Leone. Farther south along the Atlantic are Liberia, the Ivory Coast, and Ghana.

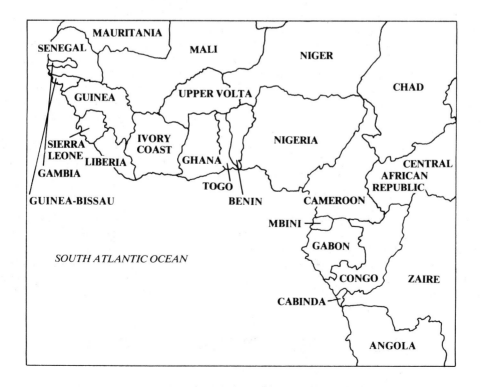

FIGURE 12.5 *Map of Western Africa.*

Not many Americans visit West Africa. One reason is that malaria is endemic. Ninety percent of the people have it. There are some good beaches but the distance from the United States and travel costs are so high and health hazards so great that other options take precedence. Dakar, capital of Senegal, is a big transit point for West Africa.

Sierra Leone and Liberia have interesting origins. About 600,000 persons in Sierra Leone are called Creoles, descendents of black settlers from Great Britain or North America. In Liberia about 45,000 are descendents of emancipated slaves from the United States. Ironically they now constitute the elite of the nation and have until recently controlled the government and much of the wealth.

Nigeria is an important country not because of its accomplishments but because of its physical size, population of eighty million (the largest in Africa), and production of large amounts of oil.

Bordering Nigeria on the north is Niger, a desperately poor and hot country.

South of Nigeria on the coast is Cameroon. Referred to as the "hinge" of Africa, it is the western port of the continent on the Gulf of Guinea (an arm of the Atlantic), about midway between Senegal and the Republic of South Africa. Equatorial Guinea is the next country south, followed by Gabon. Gabon, it may be remembered, was where Dr. Albert Schweitzer, world famous humanitarian physician/musician/philosopher, had his hospital.

The Ivory Coast represents the best of West African countries. It has had no coups, no mass rioting, no tribal wars. Moreover it has the highest standard of living in Black Africa and its $1,060 per capita income is one of the continent's highest. It is Africa's largest coffee producer and ranks first in world cacao production. Independence from France was gained in 1960 and French wines, cheeses, and canned goods are plentiful in French supermarkets. In Abidjan, the capital, the Hotel Ivoire has an ice-skating rink. There is also a Club Med nearby.

Having said this, here are some other statistics. Literacy is 25 percent, life expectancy forty-six years. More than half of all Ivoireans believe deeply in animism, a cosmos where the boundaries between man and spirit blur, dream and reality blend and meld. Panthermen of the W'e tribe spend seven months living in the bush as wild animals. At the Abidji tribe's Dipri festival, an hour's drive from Abidjan, pandemonium reigns. A man plunges a knife into his abdomen, pulls out a portion of his intestines, pushes them back in, then makes the wound heal by rubbing it with egg, herbs and kaolin. The elephants, whose tusks the country is named for, are being poached out of existence. Twenty-five years ago dense forests covered a third of the country. Less than 10 percent of the country is now wooded. The Club Med places malaria-prevention pills on the dining tables along with the salt and pepper shakers.

Unless travelers want to live dangerously they should avoid Central African countries like the Central African Republic, the Congo, and Zaire. They present not only a variety of health hazards but unpredictable transportation, poor accommodations and possibly personal danger. In Zaire mobs have been seen pulling a driver from a car that has struck a pedestrian and beating him to death on the spot.

The visitor to several Black African countries can be infested by such exotic maladies as green monkey disease, a viral infection. Victims develop a high fever and start bleeding from the mouth and rectum. Death usually follows within a week. The tsetse fly, carrying sleeping sickness, is still around in some countries. In Upper Volta tiny black flies known as Buffalo gnats, burrow into their victims, penetrate the eye and cause partial or complete blindness. The elastic layer of skin can be destroyed, causing itching so constant and painful that suicide is common.

THE REPUBLIC OF SOUTH AFRICA

The richest of the African nations, South Africa also has one of the most attractive climates and an abundance of natural attractions. Generally moderate, the climate pro-

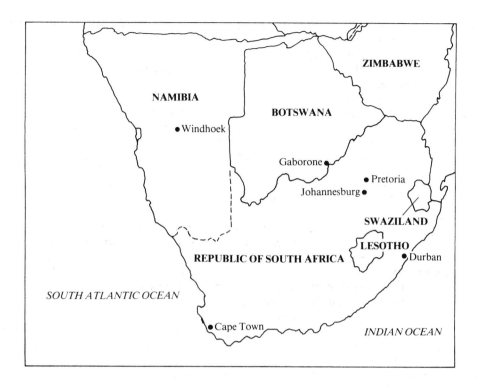

FIGURE 12.6 *Map of Republic of South Africa.*

vides sunny days and cool nights. The average mean temperature is remarkably uniform, the most southerly point having a mean average temperature of about sixty-two degrees while Johannesburg, one thousand miles north, has a mean temperature only one degree lower. The reason: Johannesburg sits on a fifty-seven-hundred-foot plateau. The interior plateau ranges from three thousand to six thousand feet above sea level. A twenty-seven-hundred-mile coastline has some excellent swimming and surfing beaches. Visitors to the country exclaim over the abundance of natural beauty, the land itself, the coastlines, the range of flowers, birds, and wild animals.

The United Kingdom is the source of most visitors; the United States is in a distant second place, followed by Germany and France. Tourism brings in about $600 million a year. The South African Tourism Board has one of the largest national tourist office budgets, close to $20 million a year.

Johannesburg is the business center of the country with a population of 1.4 million. Cape Town, in the south, is slightly smaller, 1.1 million. The country maintains three capitals: Pretoria for administration, Cape Town for legislation and Bloemfontein for judicial functions. Durban, on the Indian Ocean, is the most popular vacation destination.

South Africa has the most and probably the best of wildlife parks. They come under different names. The really big ones, the National Parks, are run by the government. The provinces operate their own game reserves and there are also nature sanctuaries run by local authorities or organizations. There is a variety of private game parks, shooting ranches and wildlife farms.

Kruger Park is the biggest, best and best known. Land for the park was set aside in 1898 by the great Boer leader, Paul Kruger. It lies in rather flat, bushveld country against the border with Mozambique. Comfortable rondavels, adaptations of the traditional African beehive hut, with hot and cold water, are available for the visitor en route from Johannesburg. There is even freshly cut well-dried firewood stacked for the traveler's convenience.

Adjoining Kruger Park is the Sabie-Sand Game Reserve (150,000) acres), one of many such private reserves.

Namibia, formerly Southwest Africa, is a ward of South Africa, funded and controlled by South Africa. Wildlife enthusiasts revel in Namibia's Etosha National Park. Described as the world's largest corral, it covers 8,598 square miles and stretches 175 miles from east to west. Some eighty thousand mammals, including five hundred lions and twenty-five hundred elephants, live there under natural conditions. The Park is like a mammoth zoo in that there are five hundred miles of fences and the animal population is controlled. If, for example, zebra multiply excessively, they are sold to South African farmers, who then sell hunters the right to stalk and shoot the animals.

About fifty thousand tourists visit Etosha each year. Because of the soil and climate conditions the lions and elephants are thought to be the largest in Africa. The lions are certainly big, big enough to have eaten a few tourists who were foolish enough to leave their vehicles.

Sun City, a Las Vegas-like enclave in Bophuthatswana, is about two hours by car from Johannesburg, a place where color prejudice disappears in the bedroom, with casino gambling and Vegas-like entertainment.

In the whole of Black Africa the country of South Africa is an oasis of order and prosperity. The nation of South Africa is the most varied, lovely and safe in which to travel. It is also one of the most anomalous. Wrote Sir Francis Drake after rounding the Cape of Good Hope in 1580, "This Cape is the most stately thing and the fairest Cape we saw in the whole circumference of the earth." Blacks constitute 67 percent of the 28.5 million people. It is the only industrialized country in Africa, the world's richest in terms of white per capita, non-petroleum wealth. Fewer than 4.5 million whites control a country with twenty million blacks, three million "coloureds" and one million Asians. Only one Black African nation, Malawi, has diplomatic relations with South Africa. Many African nations will not put through phone calls to South Africa. Virtually no Black African nation admits to doing business with South Africa. Even so, many do.

South Africa has superior air service but the flight times from the United States total about seventeen hours. Almost every country in Africa denies South Africa landing rights. Long-haul flights from Houston, New York City, and London must stop to refuel on the island of Ilha do Sal, one of the Cape Verde Islands off the west coast of Africa. The islands, a sovereign nation, have only the skimpiest of travel facilities.

South Africa's Blue Trains, running between Pretoria and Cape Town, are said to be the ne plus ultra of train travel. Others are not sure. The train travels about 50 mph, on an average a bit slow—good, say the enthusiasts, for viewing the scenery. The trains are all compartments and all but the least expensive come with their own toilets or toilets plus showers. The most expensive compartment includes a tub and its own liquor cabinet. Full, the trains carry only 106 passengers.

Even before the train departs, white-jacketed stewarts deliver sparkling wine to the passengers. Food aboard the train is the same as is served in the parliament building in Cape Town. A British breakfast with kippers, or poached fish, broiled tomatoes or chicken livers starts the day. Seven-course lunches and dinners are elegantly served and there are excellent South African wines. Meals are included as part of the fare. Passengers can ring at any time for snacks and drinks to be served in their compartments.

The trip takes a little over twenty-four hours versus two hours by air. South Africans view the Blue Trains somewhat as the French once looked upon the *S.S. France,* a symbol of national prestige. The *S.S. France* is now the *S.S. Norway* and cruises in the Caribbean Region. Let's hope the Blue Trains continue to offer rail elegance.

Two reasons stand out why relatively few North Americans visit South Africa: distance and its corollary, cost. Another reason relates to insecurity derived from the kind of image of South Africa projected by the news media. The nation, with whites as a minority, is controlled by the whites through the use of considerable repression. Present policy is to move toward granting some political power to the coloureds and Indians, but not to the blacks. With this political arrangement many would-be visitors to South Africa are simply afraid to go there.

This policy of Apartheid, meaning "apartness" or "separateness," a system that segregates whites from blacks, Indians and coloureds, also keeps a distance between South Africa and the rest of the world. As part of the apartheid policy "homelands" were set aside by the government, each a state for a particular tribe. Each is supposed to be independent; each has a president, a parliament and some political autonomy. As of 1982 there were four such states: Transkei, Bophuthatswana, Venda, and Askai. Because of their dependence upon South Africa, no government other than South Africa extends them diplomatic recognition.

South Africa has immense mineral wealth. It has only 6 percent of the total population of Africa while its production output is equal to one-quarter of that of the whole continent. It is the world's largest producer of gold each year and a large producer of diamonds. The country is the world's largest producer of platinum and electrolytic copper, ferro-chrome and ferro-manganese. There are antimony, chrome, lithium, manganese, uranium, nickel, and vanadium. Coal is also abundant.

The South African National Tourist Board is very active and the national airline has reduced round-trip fares from Houston and New York to Johannesburg. The Tourist Board is also active in the Durban Hotel School. The Board is in charge of rating South African hotels. The ratings range from one to five stars; fifteen hotels hold the coveted five-star rank. More Americans are likely to visit the country once it becomes better known and as visitors report back on their experiences.

Is there a distinctive South African cuisine? The Afrikaner kitchen comes closest to being original, a combination of Dutch, German and native foods and cooking skills. Boerewors, a well-spiced sausage in six-foot lengths cooked on the hot wood coals of a campfire, along with cornmeal mush cooked very firm and almost dry, is said to be an experience. The melktert (milk tart) is said to be enjoyed even by those who neither like milk nor tarts. Among the array of seafood dishes, pickled fish is a favorite. The fish is curried in a piquant sauce with onion rings. If it is really good the eater perspires copiously and perhaps screams a little. Smoked snoek is similar to smoked salmon, but cheaper.

South Africans are outdoors people and favor the barbecue with plenty of meat. South Africans are delighted to have guests. If you are a keen meateater, you will be delighted too. As one writer puts it "If you are a vegetarian, you had better hide in a darkened room with a handful of nuts."[5]

ENDNOTES

1. *The Africans,* David Lamb, Random House, N.Y. 1982.
2. *Los Angeles Times,* May 16, 1982.
3. *Ibid.*
4. David Lamb, *op. cit.*
5. *South Africa,* Dennis Kiley, B.T. Batsford Ltd. London, 1976.

This book started with a quotation from Art Buchwald. We end it with one of his tourist prayers, this one for women traveling with their husbands:

> "Oh God, let not our husbands make fools of themselves in foreign bars, cafes, and night clubs. Let them not look longingly at the native women, and compare them with us. Above all, Oh God, do not forgive their transgressions, for they know exactly what they do."

APPENDIX

FOREIGN TRAVEL & TOURISM

INFORMATION SOURCES

Afghanistan
Visa Regulations: U.S. Citizens—valid passport required (valid for minimum 6 mos.); visa required; visa valid for 30 days; 3 photos; cost $10.00; guarantee of sufficient funds; ticket to leave; Exit Permit. Inoculations required for typhoid, cholera, smallpox.

Canadian Citizens—same as above.

Consulate: New York, NY 10001, 122-126 W. 30th St., 212/736-8150

Information: Afghan Tourist Organization
New York, NY 10017, 535 Fifth Ave., 212/697-3660

Algeria
Visa Regulations: U.S. Citizens—valid passport required (valid for minimum 6 mos.); visa required; visa valid for 3 mos.; 4 photos; cost $5.25; guarantee of sufficient funds; ticket to leave; **business travelers must have letter of guarantee from employer.** Inoculations required if coming from infected area for yellow fever, smallpox.

Canadian Citizens—same as above.

Embassy: Washington, D.C. 20008, 2118 Kalorama Rd., NW, 202/328-5300

Angola
Visa Regulations: U.S. Citizens: valid passport required; visa required. Make application to Corpo de Policia de Angola Divisao de Estiangeiros e Fronterirs Luanda Angola. Inoculations required for smallpox; if coming from infected area, yellow fever and cholera.

Canadian Citizens—same as above.

Consulate: New York, NY 10017, 747 Third Ave., 18th Floor, 212/752-4612

Source: Hotel & Motel Redbook, 96th Annual Edition. For the latest visa and other requirements, check with the relevant consulate.

Antigua
Visa Regulations: U.S. Citizens—passport not required; visa not required; guarantee of sufficient funds; ticket to leave. Inoculations required if coming from infected area for smallpox, yellow fever.
Canadian Citizens—same as above.
Consulate: New York, NY 10022, 845 Third Ave., 212/752-8400
Information: Antigua Dept. of Tourism & Trade
New York, NY 10020, 610 Fifth Ave., Ste. 311, 212/541-4117

Argentina
Visa Regulations: U.S. Citizens—valid passport required; visa required; visa valid for 4 yrs.; no charge. No inoculations required.
Canadian Citizens—visa not required for stays of less than 3 mos.
Consulate: New York, NY 10019, 12 W. 56th St., 212/397-1400
Information: Argentina Consulate Tourist Dept.
Washington, D.C. 20009, 1600 N. Hampshire Ave., 202/322-7100

Aruba
Visa Regulations: U.S. Citizens—proof of citizenship required; visa not required; ticket to leave.
Canadian Citizens—same as above.
Consulate: New York, NY 10020, One Rockefeller Plaza, 11th Fl., 212/246-1429.
Information: Aruba Tourist Bureau
New York, NY 10020, 1270 Avenue of the Americas, 212/246-3030

Australia
Visa Regulations: U.S. Citizens—valid passport required (valid for minimum 6 mos.); visa required; visa valid for 4 yrs., 1 photo; no charge; guarantee of sufficient funds; ticket to leave; **business travelers must have letter of guarantee from employer.** Inoculations required if coming from infected area for smallpox, cholera, yellow fever.
Canadian Citizens—same as above.
Consulate: New York, NY 10111, 636 Fifth Ave., 212/254-4000.
Information: Australian Tourist Commission Office
New York, NY 10020, 1270 Avenue of the Americas, 212/489-7550
Los Angeles, CA 90010, 3550 Wilshire Blvd., 213/380-6060

Austria
Visa Regulations: U.S. Citizens—valid passport required; visa not required. Inoculations not required unless coming from an infected area.
Canadian Citizens—same as above.
Consulate: New York, NY 10021, 31 E. 69th St., 212/737-6400
Information: Austrian National Tourist Office
New York, NY 10017, 545 Fifth Ave., 212/679-0651
Chicago, IL 60601, 200 E. Randolph Dr., 312/861-0103
Vancouver, B.C. V6Z 1J2, 736 Granville St., 604/683-5808

Bahamas
Visa Regulations: U.S. Citizens—proof of citizenship required; inoculations required if coming from infected area.
Canadian Citizens—same as above except **business travelers require passport.**
Consulate: Miami, FL 33131, 25 S.E. Second Ave., Ste. 104, Ingraham Bldg., 305/373-6295

Information: Bahamas Tourist Office
New York, NY 10020, 30 Rockefeller Plaza, 212/757-1611
Chicago, IL 60601, 875 N. Michigan Ave., 312/787-8203

Bangladesh
Visa Regulations: U.S. Citizens—valid passport required; visa required; visa valid 3 mos.; 2 photos; no charge; Exit Permit; **business travelers require letter of financial guarantee from employer.** Inoculations required if coming from infected area for cholera, smallpox, yellow fever.
Canadian Citizens—visa not required for stays up to 3 mos.
Embassy: Washington, DC 20007, 3421 Massachusetts Ave., NW, 202/337-6644

Barbados
Visa Regulations: U.S. Citizens—proof of citizenship required; valid passport required if entering from country other than U.S.; visa not required for stays up to 6 mos.; ticket to leave. Inoculations required if coming from infected area for smallpox, yellow fever.
Canadian Citizens—same as above. Passport required only if entering from country other than Canada.
Consulate: New York, NY 10017, 800 Second Ave., 17th Fl., 212/867-5770
Information: Barbados Board of Tourism
New York, NY 10017, 800 Second Ave., 17th Fl., 212/986-6516

Belgium
Visa Regulations: U.S. Citizens—valid passport required; visa not required; sufficient funds and/or ticket to leave; documents for onward journey.
Canadian Citizens—same as above.
Consulate: New York, NY 10020, 50 Rockefeller Plaza, Rm. 1104, 212/586-5110
Information: Belgium National Tourist Office
New York, NY 10020, 745 Fifth Ave., 212/758-8130

Bermuda
Visa Regulations: U.S. Citizens—passport not required; proof of citizenship required; valid for stay of 21 days or less; visa not required. Inoculations required for smallpox if coming from infected area.
Canadian Citizens—same as above.
Consulate: New York, NY 10022, 845 Third Ave., 212/752-8400
Information: Bermuda Dept. of Tourism
New York, NY 10111, 630 Fifth Ave., 212/397-7700
Chicago, IL 60610, 300 N. State St., Marina Towers Bldg., 312/329-0777

Bolivia
Visa Regulations: U.S. Citizens—valid passport required; visa required for **business travelers;** 1 photo; cost $20.00. Inoculation required for smallpox.
Canadian Citizens—same as above.
Consulate: Washington, DC 20008, 3014 Massachusetts Ave., NW, 202/232-4828

Brazil
Visa Regulations: U.S. Citizens—valid passport required; visa required; visa processed regionally and valid for 90 days; 1 photo; no charge. **Business visa valid for 6 mos.** Brazilian health certificate, police clearance letter, notarized letters of support from business firm required. Inoculations required for yellow fever if coming from infected area and polio vaccination for children age 3 mos. to 6 yrs.

Canadian Citizens—no visa required for tourists.

Consulate: New York, NY 10020, 630 Fifth Ave., Rm. 2720, 212/757-3080

Information: Brazilian Government Trade Bureau
New York, NY 10017, 551 Fifth Ave., 212/682-1055

British Virgin Islands

Visa Regulations: U.S. Citizens—passport not required for visits of 6 mos. or less; proof of citizenship required; visa not required; guarantee of sufficient funds; ticket to leave. Inoculations not required unless coming from infected area.

Canadian Citizens—same as above.

Consulate: New York, NY 10022, 845 Third Ave., 212/752-8400.

Information: British Virgin Islands Information Bureau
New York, NY 10022, 575 Madison Ave., 212/371-6759

Bulgaria

Visa Regulations: U.S. Citizens—valid passport required; visa required; visa valid for 6 mos.; cost (transit) $9.00, (tourist & visitors) $14.00. Business visa requires letter of guarantee from employer. Inoculations not required unless coming from infected area.

Canadian Citizens—same as above except fees.

Embassy: Washington, DC 20009, 2100 16th St. NW, 202/387-7969

Information: Bulgarian Tourist Office
New York, NY 10017, 50 E. 42nd St., Ste. 1508, 212/661-5733

Burma

Visa Regulations: U.S. Citizens—valid passport required; visa required; visa valid 3 mos.; 3 photos; cost $4.80. Exit Permit and tax clearance or exemption certificate required. Inoculations required for cholera, smallpox, yellow fever.

Canadian Citizens—same as above except fees.

Consulate: New York, NY 10021, 10 E. 77th St., 212/535-1310

Canada

(Alberta / British Columbia / Manitoba / New Brunswick / Newfoundland & Labrador / Northwest Territories / Nova Scotia / Ontario / Prince Edward Island / Quebec / Saskatchewan / Yukon Territory)

Visa Regulations: U.S. Citizens—passport not required for tourists; proof of residency and identity required. **Visa required for certain business travelers.** Inoculations for smallpox required if coming from infected area.

Consulate: New York, NY 10020, 1251 Avenue of the Americas, 212/586-2400

Embassy: Washington, DC 20036, 1746 Massachusetts Ave., NW, 202/785-1400

Information: Canadian Government Office of Tourism
New York, NY 10020, 1251 Avenue of the Americas, Rm. 1030, 212/757-3583
Chicago, IL 60604, 332 S. Michigan Ave., Ste. 1710, 312/782-3760
Dallas, TX 75201, 2001 Bryan Tower, Ste. 1600, 214/742-8031
Los Angeles, CA 90014, 510 W. Sixth St., 213/622-1029

Cayman Islands

Visa Regulations: U.S. Citizens—proof of citizenship required; visa not required; ticket to leave required. Inoculation for smallpox required if arriving from infected area.

Canadian Citizens—same as above.

Consulate: New York, NY 10022, 845 Third Ave., 212/752-8400

Information: Cayman Islands Dept. of Tourism
New York, NY 10170, 420 Lexington Ave., Ste. 2312, 212/682-5582
Chicago, IL 60601, 333 N. Michigan Ave., Ste. 1521, 312/782-5832

Chile
Visa Regulations: U.S. Citizens—valid passport required; visa required by travelers who will receive any remuneration in Chile and for students; tourist card required; tourist card valid 90 days. No inoculations required.
Canadian Citizens—same as above.
Consulate: New York, NY 10017, 866 Second Ave., Ste. 501, 212/688-8807
Information: Chilean National Trourist Board
New York, NY 10020, 630 Fifth Ave., 8th Fl., 212/582-3250
Chicago IL 60601, 333 N. Michigan Ave., Ste. 305, 312/322-5885

China, People's Republic of
Visa Regulations: U.S. Citizens—valid passport required; visa required; 2 photos; cost $7.00. Exit Permit required. Inoculations required if coming from infected area for cholera, smallpox, yellow fever.
Canadian Citizens—same as above except 1 photo and fee of $8.00 required.
Embassy: Washington, DC 20008, 2300 Connecticut Ave., 202/797-9000

Colombia
Visa Regulations: U.S. Citizens—valid passport required; visa required for performers or entertainers; **visa or tourist card required for business travelers;** tourist card for tourists; tourist card valid 60 days; 2 photos; no charge. No inoculations required.
Canadian Citizens—same as above.
Consulate: New York, NY 10017, 10 East 46th St., 212/661-4680
Information: Colombian Government Tourist Office
New York, NY 10022, 140 E. 57th St., 212/688-0151

Congo, People's Republic of Brazzaville
Visa Regulations: U.S. Citizens—valid passport required; visa required; 3 photos, cost $10.00; transit visa valid 72 hrs.; ticket to leave and documents for onward travel; Exit Permit (if traveling to Angola). Inoculations required for smallpox, and yellow fever if traveling from infected area.
Canadian Citizens—same as above.
NOTE: Contact French Consulate to obtain visa.
Embassy: Washington, DC 20008, 2535 Belmont Rd., 202/234-0990

Costa Rica
Visa Regulations: U.S. Citizens—valid passport required unless hold Tourist Card and proof of citizenship; visa required; visa valid for 30 days; tourist card accepted in place of visa for stays of less than 6 mos.; visa requires passport; **business travelers require letter of guarantee from employer;** ticket to leave required; documents for onward travel required; Exit Permit for stays over 30 days. Inoculations required for smallpox if entering from Ethiopia and Somalia (directly or indirectly).
Canadian Citizens—same as above except passport required; visa and Exit Permit not required.
Consulate: New York, NY 10017, 211 E. 43rd St., Rm. 606, 212/867-3922

Cuba
Visa Regulations: U.S. Citizens—valid passport required; visa required. Alien Registration Card or Re-entry permit required. Guarantee of funds and ticket to leave required. Inoculations required if traveling from infected area, Africa or South America for yellow fever.
Canadian Citizens—same as above.
Cuban Interests Section: Washington, DC 20009, 2630 & 2639 16th St. NW, 202/797-8609

Cyprus
Visa Regulations: U.S. Citizens—valid passport required (valid for minimum of 6 mos.); visa not required; guarantee of sufficient funds; ticket to leave. Inoculations not required unless coming from infected area. NOTE: travelers entering via ports or airports of Er-can/Famagusta/Kyrenia or Karavostassi will be refused entry into zone controlled by Cyprus.
Canadian Citizens—same as above except ticket to leave not required.
Consulate: New York, NY 10016, 13 E. 40th St., 212/686-6016
Information: Cyprus Trade Center
New York, NY 10016, 13 E. 40th St., 212/686-6016

Czechoslovakia
Visa Regulations: U.S. Citizens—valid passport required; visa required; transit visa valid for 24 hrs.; 2 photos, cost $9.00; entry visa valid for 30 days; 2 photos, cost $9.00; copy of Cedok Service voucher required. Inoculations not required unless coming from infected area.
Canadian Citizens—same as above except fee.
Embassy: Washington, DC 20008, 3900 Linnean Ave. NW, 202/363-6308
Information: Cedok Czechoslovakian Travel Bureau
New York, NY 10016, 10 E. 40th St., Ste. 1902, 212/689-9720

Denmark
Visa Regulations: U.S. Citizens—valid passport required; visa not required; guarantee of sufficient funds; ticket to leave; necessary documents for onward travel. Inoculations not required unless coming from infected area.
Canadian Citizens—same as above.
Consulate: New York, NY 10017, 280 Park Ave., 212/697-5101
Information: Danish Tourist Board
New York, NY 10019, 75 Rockefeller Plaza, 212/582-2802

Dominican Republic
Visa Regulations: U.S. Citizens—passport not required; proof of citizenship required; visa not required for tourists; tourist card required, valid up to 15 days, cost $5.00. **Business visa valid 2 yrs.; 2 photos, passport, notarized letter of guarantee from company, cost $25.00;** ticket to leave required. Inoculation required for smallpox if coming from infected area.
Canadian Citizens—same as above.
Consulate: New York, NY 10020, 1270 Avenue of the Americas, Ste. 300, 212/265-0630
Information: Dominican Tourist Info Center
New York, NY 10022, 485 Madison Ave., 212/826-0750

Ecuador
Visa Regulations: U.S. Citizens—valid passport required; visa required for stays of less than 3 mos.; ticket to leave required; guarantee of sufficient funds required. No inoculations required.
Canadian Citizens—same as above.
Consulate: New York, NY 10020, 1270 Avenue of the Americas, Rm. 2411, 212/245-5380

Egypt
Visa Regulations: U.S. Citizens—valid passport required (valid for minimum of 3 mos. beyond period of stay); visa required; transit visa valid 7 days; entry visa valid 30 days; 1 photo, all applicants must contribute $3.00 to Abu Simbel Fund; persons visiting Egypt for a short time must register at Office of Foreigners and Nationality within 7 days of ar-

rival. Inoculation required for yellow fever if coming from infected area or a designated area (contact consulate for detailed list of designated areas).

Canadian Citizens—same as above except ticket to leave and documentation not required.

Consulate: New York, NY 10022, 1110 Second Ave., 2nd Fl., 212/759-7120

Information: Egyptian Government Tourist Office
New York, NY 10020, 630 Fifth Ave., 212/246-6960
San Francisco, CA 94102, 323 Geary St., 415/433-7562

El Salvador
Visa Regulations: U.S. Citizens—valid passport required for **business travelers;** proof of citizenship required by tourists; **visa may be required for business travelers;** 1 photo, cost $3.00; letter of guarantee from employer required. Inoculations not required unless coming from infected area.

Canadian Citizens—same as above.

Consulate: New York, NY 10016, 46 Park Ave., 212/889-3608

Ethiopia
Visa Regulations: U.S. Citizens—valid passport required; visa required; visa valid up to 3 mos.; 3 photos, cost $4.85. **Business visas require prior permission from Foreign Ministry, cost $7.25.** Ticket to leave required; Exit Permit for stays over 30 days. Inoculations required for cholera, smallpox, yellow fever.

Canadian Citizens—same as above.

Consulate: New York, NY 10017, 866 United Nations Plaza, Rm. 560, 212/421-1830

Finland
Visa Regulations: U.S. Citizens—valid passport required; visa not required; ticket to leave; guarantee of sufficient funds; necessary documents for onward travel required. Inoculations not required unless coming from infected area.

Canadian Citizens—same as above.

Consulate: New York, NY 10022, 540 Madison Ave., 212/832-6550

Information: Finland National Tourist Office
New York, NY 10019, 75 Rockefeller Plaza, 212/582-2802

France
Visa Regulations: U.S. Citizens—valid passport required; visa not required. Inoculations not required unless coming from infected area.

Canadian Citizens—same as above.

Embassy: Washington, DC 20008, 2535 Belmont Rd., 202/234-0990

Information: French Government Tourist Office
New York, NY 10020, 610 Fifth Ave., 212/757-1125

Gambia
Visa Regulations: U.S. Citizens—valid passport required; visa required; transit visa cost $2.50; entry visa cost $5.00; visitor pass valid 1 mo., no charge; ticket to leave required. Inoculations for smallpox and yellow fever if coming from infected area.

Canadian Citizens—same as above except visa not required for stays of less than 90 days.

Consulate: Stanfordville, NY 12581, P.O. Box F, Deuell Rd., 914/868-7411

German Democratic Republic (East)
Visa Regulations: U.S. Citizens—valid passport required; visa required (issued at border); visas require presentation of visa entitlement certificate or voucher; Exit Permit required. Inoculations required for smallpox if coming from infected area or Ethiopia.

Embassy: Washington, DC 20036, 1717 Massachusetts Ave. NW, 202/232-3134

Germany, Federal Republic of (West)
Visa Regulations: U.S. Citizens—valid passport required; visa not required for stay of 3 mos. or less; guarantee of funds and/or ticket to leave. Inoculations not required unless coming from infected areas.
Canadian Citizens—same as above.
Consulate: New York, NY 10022, 460 Park Ave., 212/940-9200
Embassy: Washington, DC 20007, 4645 Reservoir Rd. NW, 202/298-4000
Information: German National Tourist Office
New York, NY 10020, 630 Fifth Ave., Ste. 1418, 212/757-8570

Ghana
Visa Regulations: U.S. Citizens—valid passport required (must have 6 mos. remaining validity); visa required; tourist visa required; valid 4 days, 3 photos; Cedi voucher, cost $4.35; ticket to leave. Inoculations required for cholera, yellow fever.
Canadian Citizens—same as above except visa valid 5 days, cost $2.00.
Consulate: New York, NY 10017, 19 E. 47th St., 212/823-1300
Information: Ghana Tourist Office
New York, NY 10022, 445 Park Ave., Ste. 903, 212/688-8350

Great Britain
(Northern Ireland, Scotland & Wales)
Visa Regulations: U.S. Citizens—valid passport required; visa not required. Inoculations not required unless coming from infected area.
Canadian Citizens—same as above.
Consulate: New York, NY 10022, 845 Third Ave., 212/752-8400
Embassy: Washington, DC 20008, 3100 Massachusetts Ave. NW, 202/462-1340
Information: British Tourist Authority
New York, NY 10019, 680 Fifth Ave., 212/581-4700
Chicago, IL 60611, 875 N. Michigan Ave., Ste. 3320, 312/787-0490

Greece
Visa Regulations: U.S. Citizens—valid passport required; visa not required for stay of 3 mos. or less; guarantee of sufficient funds required; ticket to leave required. No inoculations required unless coming from infected area.
Canadian Citizens—same as above.
Consulate: New York, NY 10021, 69 E. 79th St., 212/988-5500
Information: Greek National Tourist Office
New York, NY 10022, 645 Fifth Ave., Olympic Tower, 212/421-5777

Guatemala
Visa Regulations: U.S. Citizens—**valid passport required for business travelers;** proof of citizenship with photo required by others; **visa required for business travelers;** tourist card required by others, valid for 6 mos., cost $1.00. **Business travelers require letter of character recommendation.** No inoculations required.
Canadian Citizens—same as above except visa valid 30 days.
Consulate: New York, NY 10020, 1270 Avenue of the Americas, Rockefeller Center, 212/246-5877
Information: Maya Information Service
New York, NY 10017, 501 Fifth Ave., Ste. 1611, 212/490-0766

Haiti
Visa Regulations: U.S. Citizens—passport not required; proof of citizenship required; visa

not required for stay of 30 days or less; tourist card issued aboard carrier, valid 30 days, cost $2.00; ticket to leave required. Inoculations required for smallpox, unless coming directly from a 14 day or more stay in the U.S., and for yellow fever if coming from infected area.

Consulate: New York, NY 10017, 60 E. 42nd St., 212/697-9767
Information: Haiti Tourist Bureau
New York, NY 10020, 30 Rockefeller Plaza, 212/757-3517

Hong Kong
Visa Regulations: U.S. Citizens—valid passport required; visa required for stay over 30 days; cost $8.00; guarantee of funds; ticket to leave. Inoculations required for smallpox if coming from infected area.
Canadian Citizens—same as above except visa not required for stay of 90 days or less.
Consulate: (Great Britain) New York, NY 10022, 845 Third Ave., 212/752-8400
Information: Hong Kong Tourist Association
New York, NY 10036, 548 Fifth Ave., 212/947-5008
Chicago, IL 60601, 333 N. Michigan Ave., 312/782-3872
Los Angeles, CA 90014, 510 W. Sixth St., Ste. 1217, 213/627-3253

Hungary
Visa Regulations: U.S. Citizens—valid passport required (6 mos. remaining validity); visa required; transit visa, 2 photos, cost $6.00; entry visa valid 6 mos., 2 photos, cost $6.00. Visa obtained at Hungarian Embassy, Consulate, upon arrival at the border (if not by train), and at airport; 2 photos. No inoculations required unless coming from infected area.
Canadian Citizens—same as above except fees.
Consulate: New York, NY 10021, 8 E. 75th St., 212/879-4127
Information: Ibusz Hungarian Travel Bureau
New York, NY 10020, 630 Fifth Ave., Room 520, 212/582-7412

India
Visa Regulations: U.S. Citizens—valid passport required (6 mos. remaining validity); **visa required by business travelers;** visa required for tourists stays over 30 days. Entry Visa valid 3 mos., 1 photo, cost $2.00; ticket to leave required; documents for onward travel. Inoculations recommended for cholera, smallpox; required for smallpox if coming from United Kingdom or infected area; for yellow fever if coming from infected area, Africa, Central America or South America.
Canadian Citizens—same as above except visa required only by missionaries.
Consulate: New York, NY 10021, 3 E. 64th St., 212/879-7800
Information: Government of India Tourist Office
New York, NY 10020, 30 Rockefeller Plaza, N. Mezzanine, Ste. 15, 212/586-4901

Indonesia
Visa Regulations: U.S. Citizens—valid passport required (minimum validity 6 mos. from date of visa); visa required, 2 photos, cost $3.00 (tourist), $5.50 (business). **Business travelers require letter of guarantee from employer;** guarantee of sufficient funds; ticket to leave. Inoculations required if coming from infected area for cholera, smallpox, yellow fever.
Canadian Citizens—same as above.
Consulate: New York, NY 10021, 5 E. 68th St., 212/879-0600
Information: Indonesian Tourist Office
San Francisco, CA 94102, 323 Geary St., Ste. 305, 415/981-3584

Iraq

NOTE: Persons holding passports containing Israeli Validity stamps, visas even though expired, or any stamp or document indicating passenger has been in Israel are prohibited from entry or transit on the same aircraft.

Visa Regulations: U.S. Citizens—valid passport required; visa required; **business visas require cable of permission from Ministry of Industry & Miners, Baghdad, Iraq;** 4 photos, letter of purpose from employer. **Exit Permit required for business stays over 15 days.** Inoculations required for smallpox; if coming from infected area, for cholera, yellow fever.

Canadian Citizens—same as above.

Iraqi Interest Section: Washington, DC 20036, 1801 P St. NW, 202/483-7500

Ireland

Visa Regulations: U.S. Citizens—valid passport required; visa not required; guarantee of sufficient funds or ticket to leave required. No inoculations required unless coming from an infected area.

Canadian Citizens—same as above.

Consulate: New York, NY 10036, 580 Fifth Ave., 212/245-1010

Embassy: Washington, DC 20008, 2234 Massachusetts Ave. NW, 202/462-3939

Information: Irish Tourist Office
New York, NY 10036, 590 Fifth Ave., 212/246-7400
Chicago, IL 60601, 230 N. Michigan Ave., Ste. 1312, 312/726-9356

Israel

NOTE: Passengers intending to visit both Israel and Arab League countries must make sure passports do not contain Israeli visa or stamp.

Visa Regulations: U.S. Citizens—valid passport required; visa not required for stay of 3 mos. or less. Inoculations required for smallpox if coming from infected area.

Canadian Citizens—same as above.

Consulate: New York, NY 10017, 800 Second Ave., 212/697-5500

Information: Israel Government Tourist Office
New York, NY 10018, Empire State Bldg., 350 Fifth Ave., 212/560-0650
Chicago, IL 60603, 5 S. Wabash Ave., Rm. 1402, 312/782-4306

Italy

Visa Regulations: U.S. Citizens—valid passport required; visa not required for stay of 3 mos. or less. No inoculations required unless coming from infected area.

Canadian Citizens—same as above.

Consulate: New York, NY 10021, 690 Park Ave., 212/737-9100

Embassy: Washington, DC 20009, 1601 Fuller St. NW, 202/234-1935

Information: Italian Government Travel Office
New York, NY 10020, 630 Fifth Ave., 212/245-4822
Chicago, IL 60611, 500 N. Michigan Ave., Ste. 314, 312/644-0990

Jamaica

Visa Regulations: U.S. Citizens—valid passport required by students, **business travelers,** those seeking employment in Jamaica, tourists entering from all points other than U.S., Puerto Rico, U.S. Virgin Islands; proof of citizenship required for travelers staying 6 mos. or less, whose trip started and will end in U.S., Puerto Rico or U.S. Virgin Islands; guarantee of sufficient funds; ticket to leave; documents for onward travel. Inoculations required if coming from infected area for smallpox, yellow fever.

Canadian Citizens—same as above except proof of citizenship accepted in place of passport if coming from Canada or via U.S. and staying 6 mos. or less.

Consulate: New York, NY 10017, 866 Second Ave., 212/935-9000

Information: Jamaica Tourist Board
New York, NY 10017, 866 Second Ave., 212/688-7650

Japan
Visa Regulations: U.S. Citizens—valid passport required; visa required; tourist visa valid 48 mos.; no charge; **business visa requires 2 photos, detailed letters from employer;** ticket to leave. Inoculation required for smallpox if coming from Ethiopia or Bangladesh.
Canadian Citizens—same as above except visa not required for tourists staying less than 3 mos.
Consulate: New York, NY 10017, 280 Park Ave., 212/986-1600
Embassy: Washington, DC 20008, 2520 Massachusetts Ave. NW, 202/234-2266
Information: Japan National Tourist Organization
New York, NY 10020, 45 Rockefeller Plaza, 212/757-5640
Chicago, IL 60601, 333 N. Michigan Ave., 312/322-3975
Los Angeles, CA 90017, 624 S. Grand Ave., 213/623-1952

Jordan
NOTE: All persons holding passports containing valid or expired Israeli visas are prohibited from entering Jordan. If transiting Jordan, they must proceed by same or first connecting flight within 24 hrs. and may not leave airport.
Visa Regulations: U.S. Citizens—valid passport required (must have minimum 1 year remaining validity); visa required; visa valid 1 year; 1 photo; **business travelers require letter of purpose, arrival data, length of stay, and list of appointments from employer.** No inoculations required unless coming from infected area.
Canadian Citizens—same as above.
Consulate: New York, NY 10017, 866 United National Plaza, 212/759-1950
Information: Jordan Information Bureau
Washington, DC 20006, 1701 K St. NW, 202/659-3322

Kenya
Visa Regulations: U.S. Citizens—valid passport required; visa required; visa valid 3 mos. to 6 mos.; cost $3.35; ticket to leave; **business travelers require letter of recommendation.** No inoculations required unless coming from infected area.
Canadian Citizens—same as above except visa not required for stays of less than 3 mos.
Consulate: New York, NY 10022, 60 E. 56th St., 212/486-1300
Information: Kenya Tourist Office
New York, NY 10011, 60 E. 56th St., 212/486-1300

Korea, Republic of (South)
Visa Regulations: U.S. Citizens—valid passport required; visa required; tourist visa valid for 4 yrs.; no charge; **business travelers require 1 photo, letter of purpose with length of stay and guarantee of financial responsibility from employer.** No inoculations required.
Canadian Citizens—same as above except fee.
Consulate: New York, NY 10022, 460 Park Ave., 212/752-1700
Information: Korean National Tourism Corp.
New York, NY 10022, 460 Park Ave., Rm. 628, 212/688-7543

Kuwait
Visa Regulations: U.S. Citizens—valid passport required (must have at least 3 mos. remaining validity); visa required, valid for 3 mos., 1 photo, $1.00–$4.00. Ticket to leave required; **business travelers require letter stating purpose of visit and guarantee of financial support.** Inoculations required for smallpox; yellow fever if arriving from infected area. Inoculations required for cholera if arriving from infected area, Iran, Jordan, Lebanon,

Pakistan, Saudi Arabia, Singapore, or Syria.
Canadian Citizens—same as above.
Consulate: New York, NY 10017, 801 Second Ave., 212/661-1580

Lebanon
NOTE: Holders of passports containing a visa for Israel, either valid or expired, used or unused, are refused entry.
Visa Regulations: U.S. Citizens—valid passport required (must have 6 mos. remaining validity); visa required; 2 photos, cost $10.00. **Business visa requires 2 photos and letter from company with guarantee of financial support.** Inoculations required for yellow fever if coming from an infected area.
Canadian Citizens—same as above except fees.
Consulate: New York, NY 10021, 9 East 76th St., 212/744-7905
Information: Lebanon Tourist Office
New York, NY 10022, 405 Park Ave., 212/421-2201

Liberia
Visa Regulations: U.S. Citizens—valid passport required; visa required, valid 3 mos.; 3 photos, cost $2.00. Physician's certificate of freedom from communicable diseases and statement of good health required. Greater than 7 day stay must be reported to Immigration Office within 48 hrs. of arrival; 2 photos. Inoculations required for cholera, smallpox and yellow fever.
Canadian Citizens—same as above except fees.
Consulate: New York, NY 10017, 820 Second Ave., 212/687-1025

Luxembourg
Visa Regulations: U.S. Citizens—valid passport required; visa not required for stay of 90 days or less. Guarantee of sufficient funds and ticket to leave required. No inoculations required unless coming from infected area.
Canadian Citizens—same as above.
Consulate: New York, NY 10017, One Dag Hammarskjold Plaza, 212/751-9650
Information: Contact Consulate.

Malaysia
NOTE: Government may refuse entry to those who do not comply with general appearance and clothing standards.
Visa Regulations: U.S. Citizens—valid passport required; visa not required for stay up to 3 mos. (tourist) or 14 days **(business).** Guarantee of funds or ticket to leave and necessary documents for onward travel required. No inoculations required.
Canadian Citizens—same as above.
Consulate: San Francisco, CA 94111, 26th Fl., Two Embarcadero Center, 415/421-4627
Information: Malaysian Tourist Centre
San Francisco, CA 94111, 600 Montgomery St., 36th Fl., 415/788-3344

Malta
Visa Regulations: U.S. Citizens—valid passport required; visa not required. Inoculations required for cholera and yellow fever if arriving from an infected area, and for smallpox if arriving from an infected area of countries in Africa, Asia and America (excluding Canada and United States).
Canadian Citizens—same as above.
Consulate: New York, NY 10016, 249 E. 35th St., 212/725-2345

Martinique
Visa Regulations: U.S. Citizens—passport not required for stay of 21 days or less; proof of identity required; visa not required; ticket to leave required. Inoculations required for smallpox if arriving from an infected area.
Canadian Citizens—same as above.
Embassy: Washington, DC 20008, 2535 Belmont Rd., 202/234-0990
Information: French West Indies Tourist Board
New York, NY 10020, 610 Fifth Ave., 212/757-1125

Mexico
Visa Regulations: U.S. Citizens—passport not required for stay of 3 mos. or less; proof of citizenship in form of valid passport, birth certificate, naturalization certificate or Voter's Registration Certificate required; **visa required for business travelers;** tourist card required for others. Inoculations required for yellow fever if arriving from infected area.
Canadian Citizens—same as above except Voter's Registration Certificate not accepted as proof of citizenship; passport or visa required for stay over 3 mos.
Consulate: New York, NY 10017, 8 E. 41st St., 212/689-0456
Embassy: Washington, DC 20009, 2829 16th St. NW, 202/234-6000
Information: Mexican National Tourist Council
New York, NY 10022, 405 Park Ave., Ste. 1002, 212/755-7212
Chicago, IL 60611, John Hancock Center, Ste. 3612, 312/649-0090

Monaco
Visa Regulations: U.S. Citizens—valid passport required; visa not required. Inoculations required for smallpox unless coming from United States, Canada, Europe or Oceania, and for cholera and yellow fever if coming from infected area.
Canadian Citizens—same as above.
Consulate: New York, NY 10017, 20 E. 49th St., 212/759-5227
Information: Contact Consulate.

Morocco (including Tangier)
Visa Regulations: U.S. Citizens—valid passport required; visa not required for stay of 3 mos. or less. Inoculations required for cholera if coming from an infected area.
Canadian Citizens—same as above.
Consulate: New York, NY 10017, 597 Fifth Ave., 212/758-2625
Information: Moroccan National Tourist Office
New York, NY 10017, 521 Fifth Ave., Ste. 2800, 212/421-5771
Chicago, IL 60603, 6 S. Michigan Ave., 312/782-3413

Mozambique
Visa Regulations: U.S. Citizens—valid passport required; visa required, **issued to business persons only,** 2 photos, cost $9.00. Visitors must change the equivalent of ESM 1000 into local currency upon arrival. Inoculations required for smallpox, and for cholera and yellow fever if arriving from infected area.
Canadian Citizens—same as above.
Consulate: (Permanent Mission to the UN)
New York, NY 10017, 866 United Nations Plaza, Rm. 523, 212/753-4620

Netherlands
Visa Regulations: U.S. Citizens—valid passport required (must have validity at least 30 days after intended stay); visa not required for stay of 3 mos. or less; ticket to leave; documents for onward travel. No inoculations required unless coming from infected area.

Canadian Citizens—same as above.

Consulate: New York, NY 10020, One Rockefeller Plaza, 11th Fl., 212/246-1429

Information: Netherlands Tourist Office
New York, NY 10036, 576 Fifth Ave., 212/245-5320

New Zealand

Visa Regulations: U.S. Citizens—valid passport required; visa not required for stay of 30 days or less; ticket to leave; guarantee of sufficient funds. Inoculation required for smallpox if coming from infected area.

Canadian Citizens—same as above except visa not required for stay of 6 mos. or less.

Consulate: New York, NY 10020, 630 Fifth Ave., Ste. 530, 212/586-0060

Information: New Zealand Tourist Office
New York, NY 10020, 630 Fifth Ave., Ste. 530, 212/586-0060
San Francisco, CA 94111, 1 Maritime Plaza, Ste. 970, 415/788-7404

Nigeria

Visa Regulations: U.S. Citizens—valid passport required (6 mos. remaining validity); visa required; short visit visa valid 3 mos., 1 photo, cost $2.55; must have ticket to leave; residence visa required for stays more than 3 mos.; **business travelers must have letter of recommendation or invitation to Nigeria.** Inoculations required for cholera, yellow fever.

Canadian Citizens—same as above except fees.

Consulate: San Francisco, CA 94108, 360 Post St., Quantas Bldg., 5th Fl., 415/433-6500.

Norway

Visa Regulations: U.S. Citizens—valid passport required; visa not required for stays of 3 mos. or less (period begins on entry into any Scandinavian country); guarantee of sufficient funds or ticket to leave; necessary documents for onward travel. No inoculations required unless coming from infected area.

Consulate: New York, NY 10022, 825 Third Ave., 212/421-7333

Information: Norwegian/Swedish National Tourist Office
New York, NY 10019, 75 Rockefeller Plaza, 212/582-2802

Pakistan

Visa Regulations: U.S. Citizens—valid passport required; visa required by business travelers; visa not required by tourists for stays of 30 days or less; **business travelers require letter of purpose and statement of financial support from employer.** Inoculations recommended for cholera, smallpox; required for cholera, smallpox, yellow fever if coming from infected area.

Canadian Citizens—same as above.

Consulate: New York, NY 10021, Pakistan House, 12 E. 65th St., 212/879-5800

Information: Pakistan Mission to the UN
New York, NY 10021, 8 E. 65th St., 212/879-8600

Panama

Visa Regulations: U.S. Citizens—valid passport required; visa required for stays over 30 days and **for business travelers;** visa valid 48 mos., no charge; tourist card valid 30 days, cost $3.00; ticket to leave; documents for onward travel. Inoculation required for smallpox if coming from infected area; for cholera if coming from infected area or Ethiopia.

Canadian Citizens—same as above.

Consulate: New York, NY 10020, 1270 Ave. of the Americas, Ste. 2417, 212/246-3773

Information: Panama Tourist Bureau
New York, NY 10020, 630 Fifth Ave., Rm. 1414, 212/246-5841

Paraguay
Visa Regulations: U.S. Citizens—valid passport required; visa not required for stays up to 90 days; tourist card required, valid 90 days, cost $1.00. Inoculations required for small-pox and yellow fever if coming from infected area.
Canadian Citizens—same as above.
Consulate: New York, NY 10048, 1 World Trade Center, Ste. 1609, 212/432-0733

Peru
Visa Regulations: U.S. Citizens—valid passport required; visa not required for tourist stays up to 90 days; Cedula "C" required; ticket to leave; documents for onward travel. Exit Permit required for travelers who do not enter Peru on a Cedula. **Business travelers must report to immigration within 15 days of arrival.** Inoculation required for smallpox; for yellow fever if coming from an infected area.
Canadian Citizens—same as above.
Consulate: New York, NY 10020, 10 Rockefeller Plaza, Rm. 729, 212/265-2480
Information: Peru Tourist Office
Van Nuys, CA 91406, C/O TCI, 7833 Haskell, 213/902-0726

Philippines
NOTE: Children under 15 yrs. are not permitted entry unless accompanied by parents, joining their parents in the Philippines or holding waiver of exclusion from Commissioner of Immigration, Manila.
Visa Regulations: U.S. Citizens—valid passport required; **visa required by business travelers** and tourists staying over 21 days; 1 photo, no charge. **Business travelers require letter of guarantee from employer.** No inoculations required.
Canadian Citizens—visa required; visa valid 3 mos., 1 photo
Consulate: New York, NY 10036, 556 Fifth Ave., 212/764-1330
Information: Philippine Ministry of Tourism
New York, NY 10036, 556 Fifth Ave., 212/575-7915

Poland
Visa Regulations: U.S. Citizens—valid passport required (must have 6 mos. validity beyond intended stay); visa required (issued to tourists and those visiting relatives); visa valid up to 90 days, must be used within 6 mos., 2 photos, cost $10.00; ORBIS coupons or vouchers must accompany application (ORBIS coupons or vouchers available through ORBIS or its agents); regular visa issued to **business travelers,** those traveling on educational or scientific purposes; invitation from Poland required; **business travelers may apply for supporting letter from Polish Commercial Consular Office to expedite processing;** transit visa valid 48 hrs. No inoculation required unless coming from infected area.
Canadian Citizens—same as above except fees.
Consulate: New York, NY 10016, 233 Madison Ave., 212/889-8360
Information: Polish National Tourist Office
New York, NY 10036, 500 Fifth Ave., 212/354-1487
Chicago, IL 60601, 333 N. Michigan Ave., Rm. 224, 312/236-9013

Portugal
Visa Regulations: U.S. Citizens—valid passport required; visa not required for stay of 2 mos. or less. No inoculations required unless coming from infected area.
Canadian Citizens—same as above.
Consulate: New York, NY 10020, 630 Fifth Ave., Rm. 655, 212/246-4580

Information: Portuguese National Tourist Office
New York, NY 10036, 548 Fifth Ave., 212/354-4403
Montreal, PQ H3A 2N4, 1801 McGill College Ave., Ste. 1150, 514/282-1264

Puerto Rico
Visa Regulations: U.S. Citizens—passport not required; proof of citizenship recommended to facilitate reentry in the U.S.; proof of citizenship required by those traveling to Puerto Rico with stopover in foreign country; visa not required. Inoculation required for smallpox if coming from infected area.
Canadian Citizens—same as above except proof of Canadian residence required.
Information: Puerto Rico Tourism Co.
New York, NY 10019, 1290 Avenue of the Americas, 212/541-6630
Chicago, IL 60603, 11 E. Adams, Ste. 902, 321/922-9701

St. Kitts
Visa Regulations: U.S. Citizens—passport not required; proof of citizenship required; visa not required; sufficient funds; ticket to leave. Inoculation required for smallpox if coming from infected area.
Canadian Citizens—same as above.
Consulate: (Great Britain) New York, NY 10022, 845 Third Ave., 212/752-8400
Information: Caribbean Tourism Association
New York, NY 10017, 20 E. 46th St., 212/682-0435

Samoa (Western)
Visa Regulations: U.S. Citizens—valid passport required; visa not required for stay of 30 days or less; ticket to leave. No inoculations required unless coming from infected area.
Canadian Citizens—same as above.
Consulate: Los Angeles, CA 90039, 3422 Madera Ave., Box 39818, 213/666-2154

Saudi Arabia
NOTE: Holders of a passport with Israeli visa (valid or expired) and/or any indications that traveler has been in Israel and Jewish passengers whose Jewish religion is mentioned in passport are prohibited from entering or transiting Saudi Arabia.
Visa Regulations: U.S. Citizens—valid passport required (minimum 6 mos. remaining valid); visa required; visa valid 1–2 mos.; 1 photo, cost $6.00. Visa issued only to persons making a pilgrimage, persons visiting relatives, and business. **For business visa,** two letters of purpose, guarantee of support from employer and invitation from Saudi firm required with application; ticket to leave. Inoculations required for cholera, smallpox; for yellow fever if coming from infected area.
Consulate: New York, NY 10017, 866 United Nations Plaza, Rm. 480, 212/752-2740

Scotland
(See Great Britain)

Singapore
Visa Regulations: U.S. Citizens—valid passport required (passport must be valid before entry into Singapore and remain valid for reentry to country of origin; visa not required for stays of 90 days or less; ticket to leave or sufficient funds. Inoculation required for yellow fever if coming from infected area; recommended for cholera.
Canadian Citizens—same as above except visa not required for stay of less than 14 days.
Embassy: Washington, DC 20009, 1824 R St. NW, 202/667-7555
Information: Singapore Tourist Promotion Board
New York, NY 10017, 342 Madison Ave., Ste. 1008, 10th Fl., 212/687-0385

South Africa, Republic Of

Visa Regulations: U.S. Citizens—valid passport required (passport valid at least 1 yr.); visa required; visa valid 1 yr., no charge; ticket to leave; guarantee of sufficient funds. Inoculation required for yellow fever if coming from infected area.

Canadian Citizens—same as above except duration of stay determines validity of visa.

Consulate: New York, NY 10022, 425 Park Ave., 212/838-1700

Information: South African Tourist Corp.
New York, NY 10020, Rockefeller Center, 610 Fifth Ave., 212/245-3720

Spain

Visa Regulations: U.S. Citizens—valid passport required; visa not required for stays of 6 mos. or less; Exit Permit required for stays over 6 mos. No inoculations required unless coming from infected area.

Canadian Citizens—same as above except visa not required for stays of 3 mos. or less (can be extended locally for 3 mos.)

Consulate: New York, NY 10022, 150 E. 58th St., 212/355-4080

Embassy: Washington, DC 20009, 2700 15th St., 202/265-0190

Information: Spanish Tourist Office
New York, NY 10022, 665 Fifth Ave., 212/759-8822
Chicago, IL 60611, 845 N. Michigan Ave., 312/944-0215

Sri Lanka

Visa Regulations: U.S. Citizens—valid passport required; **visa required by business travelers;** visa not required for tourist stays up to 30 days; visa valid 3 mos., 1 photo; ticket to leave; sufficient funds. **Business travelers require letter of purpose and copy of invitation from individual or organization defining purpose of visit.** Inoculations required if coming from infected area for cholera, smallpox, yellow fever.

Canadian Citizens—same as above except visa not required for tourist stays up to 3 mos.

Consulate: Chicago, IL 60603, 11 S. LaSalle St., 312/641-3535

Information: Ceylon (Sri Lanka) Tourist Board
New York, NY 10017, 609 Fifth Ave., Ste. 308, 212/935-0369

Sudan

Visa Regulations: U.S. Citizens—valid passport required (must be valid for 6 mos. from date of entry); visa required; entry visa valid 3 mos.; **business visa requires letter** (in duplicate) **from employer;** visitors staying in Sudan longer than 3 days must report to police; ticket to leave; **business travelers must hold business visa before doing business.** Inoculations required for cholera and yellow fever.

Canadian Citizens—same as above except fees.

Embassy: Washington, DC 20037, 600 N. Hampshire Ave. NW, Ste. 400, 202/338-8565

Sweden

Visa Regulations: U.S. Citizens—valid passport required; visa not required for stays up to 3 mos. NOTE: period begins when entering any Scandinavian country; ticket to leave; sufficient funds; documents for onward travel. No inoculations required unless coming from infected area.

Canadian Citizens—same as above.

Consulate: New York, NY 10022, 825 Third Ave., 212/751-5900
Chicago, IL 60601, 333 N. Michigan Ave., Ste. 2301, 312/726-9868
Los Angeles, CA 90024, 10960 Wilshire Blvd., Ste. 304, 213/473-0901

Information: Swedish/Norwegian National Tourist Office
New York, NY 10019, 75 Rockefeller Plaza, 212/582-2802

Switzerland

Visa Regulations: U.S. Citizens—valid passport required; visa not required for stays up to 3 mos. No inoculations required unless coming from infected area.

Canadian Citizens—same as above.

Consulate: New York, NY 10022, 444 Madison Ave., 212/758-2560
Chicago, IL 60601, 307 N. Michigan Ave., Ste. 705, 312/782-4346

Information: Swiss National Tourist Office
New York, NY 10020, 608 Fifth Ave., 212/757-5944
Chicago, IL 60603, 104 S. Michigan Ave., Rm. 200, 312/641-0050

Syria

NOTE: All travelers working with communications media must check with Embassy for special visa instructions.

Visa Regulations: U.S. Citizens—valid passport required; visa required; transit visa valid 72 hrs., 3 photos, cost $2.50; Entry visa valid up to 6 mos., 3 photos, cost $8.20. NOTE: 3 days required to process visa. **Business travelers require letter of purpose from employer.** Visitors staying longer than two wks. must report to Immigration Department. Inoculations required for cholera; required for yellow fever if coming from infected area.

Canadian Citizens—same as above except visa no charge.

Embassy: Washington, DC 20008, 2215 Wyoming Ave., 202/232-6313

Tahiti

Visa Regulations: U.S. Citizens—valid passport required; visa required for stays over 30 days; tourist visa requires 4 photos, cost $3.25; ticket to leave or guarantee of sufficient funds. No inoculations required unless coming from infected area.

Canadian Citizens—same as above.

Embassy: (France) Washington, DC 20008, 2535 Belmont Rd., 202/234-0990

Information: Tahiti Tourist Board
New York, NY, 10017, 230 Park Ave., Ste. 453, 212/972-9444

Thailand

NOTE: Entry may be refused to travelers not complying with Thai requirements regarding general appearance and clothing.

Visa Regulations: U.S. Citizens—valid passport required; visa required by those **on business** and tourists staying longer than 15 days; tourist visa valid 60 days; must be used within 90 days of issuance, 3 photos, cost $5.00 (tourist), **$15.00 (business);** ticket to leave. No inoculations required unless coming from infected area.

Canadian Citizens—same as above except fees.

Consulate: New York, NY 10007, 53 Park Pl., 505, 212/732-8166

Information: Tourism Authority of Thailand
New York, NY 10048, 5 World Trade Center, Ste. 2449, 212/432-0433

Trinidad & Tobago

Visa Regulations: U.S. Citizens—valid passport required; visa not required of tourists for stays of 2 mos. or less; **visa required by business travelers;** ticket to return to U.S. (tourists); **ticket to leave (business and tourists staying over 6 mos.)** Inoculations required for smallpox if coming from infected area.

Canadian Citizens—same as above except visa not required for stays of 3 mos. or less.

Consulate: New York, NY 10017, 420 Lexington Ave., 331 Graybar Bldg., 212/682-7272

Information: Trinidad & Tobago Tourist Board
New York, NY 10017, 400 Madison Ave., Rms. 712–714, 212/838-7750

Tunisia
Visa Regulations: U.S. Citizens—valid passport required; visa not required for stays of 4 mos. or less; ticket to leave; sufficient funds; Exit Permit required for stays over 4 mos. Inoculations required for smallpox if coming from infected area or any country except Algeria, Canada, Europe, Morocco, U.S.A.; required for yellow fever if coming from infected area.

Canadian Citizens—same as above except visa not required for stays of 3 mos. or less.

Consulate: San Francisco, CA 94118, 3760 Washington St., 415/922-9222

Information: Tunisian National Tourist Office
New York, NY 10020, 630 Fifth Ave., Ste. 863, 212/582-3670

Turkey
Visa Regulations: U.S. Citizens—valid passport required; visa not required for stays of less than 90 days; visa required for stays over 3 mos., cost $17.50. Inoculation required for smallpox if coming from Africa (except Morocco), Asia, and infected area.

Canadian Citizens—same as above.

Consulate: New York, NY 10017, 821 United Nations Plaza, 212/247-5308

Information: Turkisk Tourism Office
New York, NY 10017, 821 United Nations Plaza, 212/687-2194

Union of Soviet Socialist Republics
NOTE: Travelers visiting relatives must register with local police upon arrival and have registration entered in visa.

Visa Regulations: U.S. Citizens—valid passport required; visa required; visa valid for exact dates for which Intourist hotel accommodations are purchased in advance; letter from Intourist agent showing confirmation number must accompany visa application. **Business travelers require letter of invitation from U.S.S.R. and letter of purpose with financial guarantee from employer;** visa for visiting relatives arranged directly through Embassy or Consulate. Inoculation required for smallpox if coming from infected area or Ethiopia.

Canadian Citizens—same as above.

Consulate: San Francisco, CA 94123, 2790 Green St., 415/922-6642

Embassy: Washington, DC 20036, 1125 16th St. NW, 202/628-7551

Information: Intourist Information Office
New York, NY 10011, 630 Fifth Ave., Ste. 868, 212/757-3884

Uruguay
Visa Regulations: U.S. Citizens—valid passport required; visa not required for stays of 3 mos. or less; ticket to leave; documents for onward travel. Inoculation required for smallpox if coming from infected area; required for cholera if coming from Cairo, Casablanca, Dakar, Las Palmas, Monrovia, Nairobi, Rabat, Santa Cruz de Tenerife, Tangier, Tripoli or Tunis.

Canadian Citizens—same as above.

Consulate: New York, NY 10017, 301 E. 47th St. #19A, 212/753-8193

Venezuela
Visa Regulations: U.S. Citizens—valid passport required; **visa required by business travelers; business visa valid 60 days.** Tourists require tourist/landing card required; proof of citizenship required for tourist/landing card; valid 60 days, must be used within 6 mos. of issuance; sufficient funds; ticket to leave; documents for onward travel; **business travelers require Exit Permit.** Inoculation required for smallpox if coming from infected area; recommended for yellow fever.

Canadian Citizens—same as above.

Consulate: New York, NY 10022, 7 E. 51st St., 212/826-1660

Information: Venezuelan Government Tourist Bureau
New York, NY 10022, 450 Park Ave., 212/355-1101

Yugoslavia

Visa Regulations: U.S. Citizens—valid passport required (1 yr. remaining validity); visa required, valid 1 yr.; transit visa valid 7 days; entry visa valid 30 days. No inoculations required unless coming from infected area.

Canadian Citizens—same as above.

Consulate: New York, NY 10022, 488 Madison Ave., 19th Fl., 212/838-2300

Information: Yugoslav National Tourist Office
New York, NY 10020, 630 Fifth Ave., Ste. 210, 212/757-2801

Zaire (Republic of)

Visa Regulations: U.S. Citizens—valid passport required (must have 3 mos. remaining validity beyond entry into Zaire); visa required; transit visa valid for up to 8 days, 3 photos, cost $8.00; tourist visa valid 90 days for stays up to 3 mos., 3 photos, cost $20.00; proof of roundtrip transportation required for visas; travelers entering for extended stay must hold proof of return transportation and proof that they have spent minimum of ZAI 20 during visit. Inoculations required for cholera, smallpox, yellow fever.

Canadian Citizens—same as above except fees.

Embassy: Washington, DC 20009, 1800 N. Hampshire Ave. NW, 202/234-7690

WORLD TRAVEL GUIDES

Guide	Coverage	Frequency	Circulation	Cost	Listings	Advertising
A-Z Worldwide Hotel Guides	Hotels worldwide and their advertising	Semi-annually; five national editions in Germany, France, United Kingdom, N. America, Asia/Pacific	Distributed to travel agents, tour operators and corporate planners; 20,000 in N. America, 6,000 in Europe, 5,200 Asia/Pacific	Available only to travel agents and tour operators at a cost ($35 per year for N. America)	Free	Accepted
Hotel & Travel Index	Listings of 30,000 hotels, motels and resorts worldwide and 5,000 advertisements; 145 destinations include geographic locator maps	Quarterly in March, June, September and December	43,000 paid and audited subscriptions worldwide	$25 for a single copy; $50 for four issues for travel agents and NPTA members; $70 per year for others	Free	Accepted
HSMA Hotel Facilities Digest	Includes names of hotel/motel sales executives from around the world	Annually	25,000 worldwide	$5 per copy	Contact the office	Accepted
Meetings & Conventions Magazine's Annual International Directory	Hotels in North, South and Central America, Europe, Asia, Africa, Caribbean	Annually	75,242 subscribers	Free to qualified meeting planners	Free but limited to hotels containing meeting facilities	Accepted
OAG Travel Planner & Hotel/Motel Guide, European edition	9,000 hotel/motel listings in 34 countries	Quarterly	16,000 including 11,113 travel agents, 4,479 business and 431 airline	$25 for a single copy; $60 for an annual subscription	Free but limited	Accepted
Official Hotel & Resort Guide	30,000 hotels and resorts worldwide	Annually	22,000; issued in a set of three volumes for U.S., Europe and rest of the world	$215 for travel agents and others	Free	Accepted
Official Meeting Facilities Guide	Major meeting hotels worldwide	Semi-annually	15,400 meeting planners in U.S., Canada and Europe	$30 for a single copy; $60 for an annual subscription	At cost and limited to meetings facilities	Accepted
Travel '800'	All travel-related companies and hotels worldwide with access to an 800 toll-free number for booking reservations	Quarterly in February, May, August and November	15,000; including 13,500 travel agencies	$10 for a single copy; $25 for an annual subscription	Free for companies with toll-free number or access to it for reservations	Accepted

Source: Lodging Hospitality, August 1983.

243

MAJOR INTERNATIONAL AIRLINES

AER LINGUS
122 E. 42nd St.
New York, NY 10017
(212) 557-1090

AEROLINEAS ARGENTINAS
1 Biscayne Tower
Mezzanine Level
Miami, FL 33131
(305) 371-4800

AEROMEXICO
8390 NW 53rd St.
Miami, FL 33166
(305) 592-1300

AEROPERU
8181 NW 36th St., Ste. 5
Miami, FL 33166
(305) 591-9240

AIR CANADA
1 Place Ville Marie
Montreal, PQ, Canada H3B 3P7
(514) 874-4560

AIR INDIA
345 Park Ave.
New York, NY 10022
(212) 407-1300

AIR JAMAICA
100 N. Biscayne Blvd.
Miami, FL 33132
(305) 358-4038

AIR NEW ZEALAND
9841 Airport Blvd., Ste. 1020
Los Angeles, CA 90045
(213) 642-7200

AIR PANAMA INTERNATIONAL
7220 NW 36th St.
Miami, FL 33166
(305) 593-1927

ALITALIA AIRLINES
666 Fifth Ave.
New York, NY 10019
(212) 582-8900

ALM ANTILLEAN AIRLINES
1150 NW 72nd Ave.
Miami, FL 33166
(305) 592-4612

ALOHA AIRLINES, INC.
P.O. Box 30028
Honolulu, HI 96820
(808) 836-1111

AVIANCA
6 W. 49th St.
New York, NY 10020
(212) 399-0850

AVIATECA
P.O. Box 592496
Miami International Airport
Miami, FL 33159
(305) 526-6401

BAHAMASAIR
228 SE 1st St.
Miami, FL 33131
(305) 379-2843

BRITISH CALEDONIAN AIRWAYS
16630 Imperial Valley Dr.
Houston, TX 77060
(713) 445-3542

BWIA INTERNATIONAL
See Trinidad & Tobago Airways Listing

DOMINICANA AIRLINES
1444 Biscayne Blvd.
Miami, FL 33132
(305) 358-6470

ECUATORIANA
Miami International Airport
P.O. Box 522970
Miami, FL 33152
(305) 526-5864

EL AL ISRAEL AIRLINES
850 Third Ave.
New York, NY 10022
(212) 940-0708

Source: Hotel & Motel Red Book—96th Annual Edition, New York City.

FINNAIR
10 E. 40th St.
New York, NY 10016
(212) 689-9300

GULF AIR
489 Fifth Ave.
New York, NY 10017
(212) 599-0015

IBERIA AIR LINES
97-77 Queens Blvd.
Rego Park, NY 11374
(212) 793-5000

ICELANDAIR, INC.
630 Fifth Ave.
New York, NY 10020
(212) 975-1200

INTERNATIONAL AIR BAHAMA
Reservations handled through Icelandair.

JAPAN AIR LINES, LTD.
655 Fifth Ave.
New York, NY 10022
(212) 758-8850

K.L.M.—ROYAL DUTCH AIRLINES
437 Madison Ave.
New York, NY 10022
(212) 759-2400

KOREAN AIR LINES
1813 Wilshire Blvd.
Los Angeles, CA 90057
(213) 484-2550

KUWAIT AIR LINES
30 Rockefeller Plaza
New York, NY 10020
(212) 581-9760

LASCA
42 NW 27th Ave., Ste. 414
Miami, FL 33125
(305) 643-4221

LAN-CHILE AIRLINES
7855 NW 12th St.
Miami, FL 33126
(305) 591-3900

LANICA AIRLINES
321 SE Second St.
Miami, FL 33131
(305) 377-4777

LOT-POLISH AIRLINES
21 E. 51st St.
New York, NY 10022
(212) 371-1260

LUFTHANSA
1640 Hempstead Turnpike
East Meadow, NY 11554
(516) 794-2020

MEXICANA AIRLINES
5757 W. Century Blvd.
Los Angeles, CA 90045
(213) 646-0401

NIGERIA AIRWAYS
15 E. 51st St.
New York, NY 10022
(212) 935-2700

NORTHWEST ORIENT AIRLINES
Minneapolis-St. Paul
    International Airport
St. Paul, MN 55111
(612) 726-2111

OLYMPIC AIRWAYS
647 Fifth Ave.
New York, NY 10022
(212) 838-3600

PAN AMERICAN WORLD
AIRWAYS, INC.
Pan American Bldg.
200 Park Ave.
New York, NY 10017
(212) 880-1234

QANTAS AIRWAYS
360 Post St.
San Francisco, CA 94108
(415) 445-6539

SABENA-BELGIAN WORLD
AIRLINES
125 Community Dr.
Great Neck, NY 11021
(516) 466-6100

SAUDI ARABIAN AIRLINES
747 Third Ave.
New York, NY 10017
(212) 758-4727

SCANDINAVIAN AIRLINES SYSTEM
138-02 Queens Blvd.
Jamaica, NY 11435
(212) 520-5500

SINGAPORE AIRLINES
510 W. Sixth St., Ste. 506
Los Angeles, CA 90014
(213) 620-8900

SOUTH AFRICAN AIRWAYS
605 Fifth Ave.
New York, NY 10017
(212) 826-1245

SWISSAIR
608 Fifth Ave.
New York, NY 10020
(212) 262-2060

TAP AIR PORTUGAL
1140 Avenue of the Americas
New York, NY 10036
(212) 556-8400

TRANS WORLD AIRWAYS, INC.
605 Third Ave.
New York, NY 10158
(212) 557-3000

TRINIDAD & TOBAGO
(BWIA INTERNATIONAL)
AIRWAYS CORP.
202 S.E. First St.
Miami, FL 33131
(305) 371-2942

UTA FRENCH AIRLINES
9841 Airport Blvd., Ste. 1000
Los Angeles, CA 90045
(213) 649-1810

WORLD AIRWAYS, INC.
P.O. Box 2332
Oakland, CA 94614
(415) 577-2500

INDEX